SEATTLE

Sixth Edition © 2008 by **ACCESS**®PRESS. All rights reserved. No portion of this publication may be reproduced or transmitted in any form or manner by any means, including, but not limited to, graphic, electronic, and mechanical methods, photocopying, recording, taping, or any informational storage and retrieval systems without explicit permission from the publisher. **ACCESS**® is a registered trademark of HarperCollins Publishers Inc.

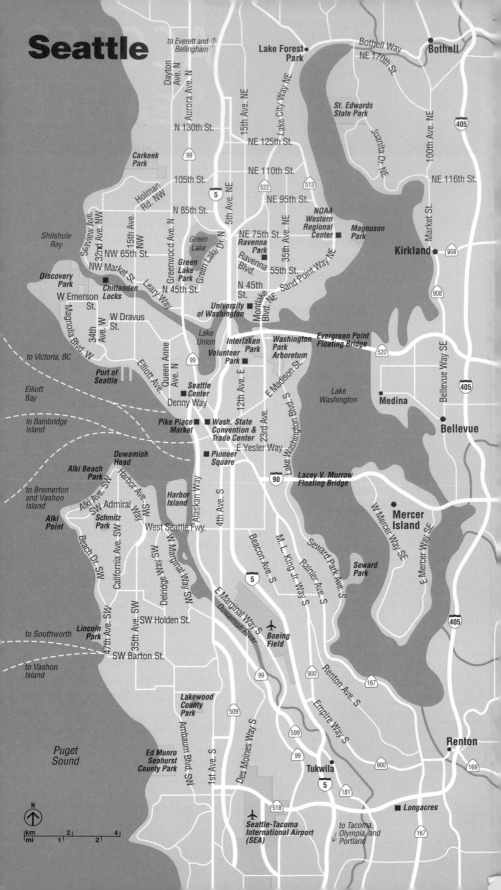

In November 1851, when city founder Arthur Denny and his party of 23 anchored their ship in a rainstorm off what is now **West Seattle**, they dubbed their new home New York-Alki, Chinook for "New York By-and-By." This bit of wishful thinking came to seem prophetic more than a century later when, in 1989, the city's skyline had grown so tall and dense that height-restrictive building codes had to be instituted. Fueled by both the tourism industry and the national media, who "discovered" the city during the 1980s, the area's population grew by 18% (twice the national average) during that decade. Attracted by low unemployment and exponential growth in the high-tech industries, its reputation for cleanliness and safety, and an innovative and enthusiastic arts community, people from as far away as Vietnam and as nearby as Los Angeles flocked to Seattle. The newcomers couldn't shut the entry gates behind them fast enough to safeguard what they'd found, but the influx could not be stemmed. Housing prices shot up, and residents started to fret that air pollution, not just fog or rain clouds, was obscuring the city's noble vistas.

And the panoramas are noble indeed, filled with breathtaking beauty. There are the sharp peaks of the **Cascade** and **Olympic Mountains** embracing the city from east and west, neighboring **Puget Sound** swimming with giant octopuses and sea lions, and sparkling modern downtown towers of glass and steel alongside the gleaming white terra-cotta structures of earlier days, all seen through the drizzle of winter... and spring... and fall... and sometimes summer. In *Another Roadside Attraction*, Washingtonian Tom Robbins describes the Puget Sound basin as having "a blurry beauty (as if the Creator started to erase it but had second thoughts)." And though Seattle hates to be called mellow, life among its 579,000 or so residents remains relatively calm; after all, it's mostly ferries—rather than more expeditious bridges—that carry commuters across the water to the city.

Visitors too should take their time enjoying the city—not the mythological Seattle of rain-washed skies and leaping salmon, but the real city, which is much more interesting. Without doubt, the city's most popular attraction is the lively 100-year-old **Pike Place Market**, where there's far more color than just that of the carrots, crabmeat, and chrysanthemums for sale by the more than 600 merchants. **Pioneer Square**, with cobblestone streets and 19th-century brick buildings built after the Great Fire of 1889, was the city's original downtown; today it's home to many art galleries and boutiques. North and west, through the **Business District's** high-rise office buildings, is the recently renovated **Seattle Center**, a futuristic remnant of the 1962 World's Fair, complete with the **Space Needle** and **Monorail**. Architecture buffs might want to wander the streets of **Capitol Hill** or **Queen Anne**, and bibliophiles may head for the **University District's** many bookstores and cafés. Hikers and cyclists can meander the city's many areas of green—there are 6,189 acres of parks spread from one end of Seattle to the other. The water sports enthusiast can also find lots of pleasant activities—from windsurfing on **Green Lake** to sailing from **Shilshole Marina** in **Ballard**. And, finally, back to West Seattle, where it all began, where the **High Point**, literally the highest point in the city, affords skyline views of the self-proclaimed Emerald City in its splendid setting of mountains and sea.

How to Read This Guide

ACCESS® SEATTLE is arranged by neighborhood so you can see at a glance where you are and what is around you. The numbers next to the entries in the following chapters correspond to the numbers on the maps. The text is color-coded according to the kind of place described:

Restaurants/Clubs: Red

Hotels: Purple | Shops: Orange

⚲ **Outdoors/Parks: Green** | **Sights/Culture: Blue**

♿ Wheelchair accessible

WHEELCHAIR ACCESSIBILITY

An establishment (except a restaurant) is considered wheelchair accessible when a person in a wheelchair can easily enter a building (i.e., no steps, a ramp, a wide-enough door) without assistance. Restaurants are deemed wheelchair accessible *only* if the above applies *and* if the rest rooms are on the same floor as the dining area and their entrances and stalls are wide enough to accommodate a wheelchair.

RATING THE RESTAURANTS AND HOTELS

The restaurant star ratings take into account the quality, service, atmosphere, and uniqueness of the restaurant. Going to an expensive restaurant doesn't necessarily ensure an enjoyable evening; a small, relatively unknown spot could have good food, professional service, and a lovely atmosphere. Therefore, on a purely subjective basis, stars are used to rank the overall dining value (see the star ratings at right). Keep in mind that chefs and owners often change, which affects the quality of a restaurant. The ratings in this guidebook are based on information available at press time.

The price ratings, as categorized at right, apply to restaurants and hotels. These figures describe general price-range relationships among other restaurants and hotel in the area. The restaurant price ratings are based on the average cost of an entrée for one person, excluding tax and tip. Hotel price ratings reflect the base price of a standard room for two people for one night during the peak season.

RESTAURANTS

★	Good
★★	Very Good
★★★	Excellent
★★★★	Extraordinary Experience
$	The Price Is Right (less than $15)
$$	Reasonable ($15–$25)
$$$	Expensive ($25–$35)
$$$$	Big Bucks ($35 and up)

HOTELS

$	The Price Is Right (less than $100)
$$	Reasonable ($100–$175)
$$$	Expensive ($175–$225)
$$$$	Big Bucks ($225 and up)

MAP KEY

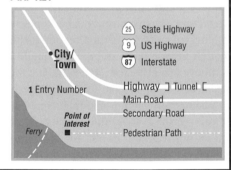

25	State Highway
9	US Highway
87	Interstate

• City/Town

1 Entry Number

Highway ⌐ Tunnel ⌐
Main Road
Secondary Road

Point of Interest ■

Ferry

Pedestrian Path

Area code 206 unless otherwise noted. This area code must be dialed as a prefix to every phone number.

Getting to Seattle

Seattle-Tacoma International Airport (SEA)

www.portseattle.org/seatac

This sprawling airport—also known as Sea-Tac—sits 11 miles south of Seattle. The layout is simple: a main terminal with four concourses, and two satellite terminals. An efficient subway connects the main terminal with the satellites; be sure to allow an extra 15 minutes to reach the outlying gates.

AIRPORT SERVICES

Airport Emergencies 911
Business Communications Center 242.6977

Currency Exchange 248.0401
Ground Transportation 431.5906
Information 431.4444
Lost and Found 433.5312
Parking 431.4444
Police 433.5400
Travelers' Aid 433.5288
US Customs 553.7979

AIRLINES

Aeroflot Russian 888/340.6400
Air Canada 888/247.2262;
www.aircanada.com
Air Tran Airways 800/247.8726;
www.airtran.com

Alaska Airlines 426.0333, 800/252.7522;
www.alaskaair.com
America West.. 800/235.9292;
www.americawest.com
American .... 800/433.7300; www.aa.com
Asiana .... 800/227.4262; www.usflyasiana.com
British Airways....................................... 800/247.9297;
www.britishairways.com
China Airlines.. 800/200.5118
Continental .... 800/525.0280; www.continental.com
Delta............................ 800/221.1212; www.delta.com
EVA Airways.........................242.8888, 800/645.1188
Frontier.. 800/432.1359;
www.frontierairlines.com
Hawaiian Airlines.................................. 800/367.5320;
www.hawaiianair.com
Horizon Air .... 800/547.9308; www.horizonair.com
Northwest Airlines ....800/225.2525; www.nwa.com
SAS ....800/221.2350; www.scandinavian.net
Southwest..............800/435.9792; www.southwest.com
United Airlines............. 800/241.6522; www.united.com
US Airways .... 800/428.4322; www.usairways.com

Getting to and from Seattle-Tacoma International Airport

BY BUS

The trip between the airport and downtown Seattle takes from 30 to 50 minutes by bus, depending on traffic conditions. **Gray Line Airport Express** (626.6088; www.graylineofseattle.com) buses leave between 5AM and 11PM and drop off passengers at eight downtown hotels. Return trips to the airport run daily between 5AM and 11PM; departure times depend on the stop. The trip takes about 30 minutes. One-way adult fare is $10.25; round-trip is $17. Children between ages 2 and 12, $7.25; round trip, $12. Reservations are not necessary.

Metro Transit (553.3000) has two separate airport buses: **Nos. 174** and **194**. Both run every 30 minutes during the day. **Route 174** has service from 6AM to 4AM; **Route 194**, from 4:30AM to 11PM. Schedules are posted outside baggage areas at the airport, and they are available at Metro stands and buses around the city.

BY CAR

The airport is about a half-hour drive from downtown, except during peak traffic periods (between 3 and 6PM on most days), when the trip can take up to an hour.

To get to downtown Seattle from SEA, take **Route 518** east and then **Interstate 5 (I-5)** north; to get to the **Eastside**, stay on Route 518 east, which becomes **Interstate 405 (I-405)**. There are well-marked exits all along the way.

To get to the airport from downtown, head south on I-5, or take I-405 south (becoming Route 518) if you are

coming from the Eastside. Long- and short-term parking lots are within easy walking distance of the main terminal.

RENTAL CARS

Most national and local car-rental agencies are located at and around SEA, and most major hotels have car rental counters. Weekly (a minimum of 5 days) or 3-day weekend rates are usually the best deals, but you should always shop around. Contact the following major companies for their current rates:

Ace Extra Car .... 248.3452; www.extracar.com
Advantage...........................824.0161, 800/777.5500;
www.advantagerentacar.com
Alamo.................................431.7588, 800/462.5266;
www.alamo.com
Avis 433.5231, 800/831.2847;
www.avis.com
Budget/Sears/Save More 800/527.0700;
www.budget.com
Century...............................246.5039, 888/288.6768;
www.centuryautorentals.com
Dollar..........433.6777, 800/800.4000; www.dollar.com
Enterprise 246.1953, 800/736.8222;
www.enterprise.com
Hertz............433.5275, 800/654.3131; www.hertz.com
National...............................433.5501, 800/227.7368;
www.nationalcar.com
Thrifty..........878.1234, 800/847.4389; www.thrifty.com

BY LIMOUSINE

Those who prefer private car service can make arrangements for limousine service from the airport through **STILA**, an organized cooperative of limousine vendors (431.5904). The cost to a downtown hotel is $30 for four people, with another $5 for each additional passenger. If you want to make out-of-town arrangements earlier, you may call **Washington Limousine** (523.8000, 800/422.5466; www.walimo.com) or **Ashton Limousine** (628.6461, 800/395.7317; www.ashtonlimo.com).

BY TAXI

There are usually taxis waiting at the airport for passengers; if not, pick up one of the "hot line" phones outside the baggage claim area. The fare to downtown Seattle is about $25, excluding tip.

Getting Around Seattle

BICYCLES

Most of Seattle and the suburbs are laced with bicycle routes, clearly marked with the universal two-wheel bike trail symbol. Cyclists have several scenic recreational options; chief among them are **Myrtle Edwards Park** (see page 78) and the **Burke-Gilman Trail** (see page 178). Bikes can be rented from **Gregg's Greenlake Cycle** (7007 Woodlawn Avenue NE, between Ravenna

Boulevard and 71st Street; 523.1822), which also offers information and maps of bicycle routes.

BUSES

Negotiating the streets of Seattle aboard Metro Transit buses is easy. Be sure to request a transfer while paying the fare to the driver. If you are traveling beyond downtown, you will need to show it as you leave the bus. Transfers are stamped with the current time, and they are good for approximately 2 hours on any bus in the same zone.

Service is free in the commercial core (bounded by I-5, **Sixth Avenue**, **Elliot Bay**, and **Jackson**, **Pine**, and **Battery Streets**) between 6AM and 7PM daily. But beyond that, a two-zone system charges $1.25 within the city ($1.50 at peak times, Monday through Friday, between 6 and 9AM and 3 and 6PM) and $1.25 if you travel beyond the city limits ($2 at peak times). Heading out of downtown, pay when you get off; going in, pay when you board. Drivers don't carry change, so have the correct amount in hand or overpay in dollar bills. On weekends and holidays only, an All-Day Pass (costing $2.50) permits an unlimited number of rides for 1 day.

Bus stops (identifiable by their yellow-and-white-signs) are usually posted with current timetables, but schedules are also available aboard the buses and at most public locations around town, including libraries and shopping malls. The buses are generally clean, comfortable, and on time. Most are wheelchair accessible, and some even sport exterior bicycle mounts (you'll see them on the fronts of buses). Drivers can be quite garrulous, launching into tour monologues as they pilot through the city.

An L-shaped bus tunnel, designed to shave a whopping 5 minutes off the time needed to travel through the congested downtown traffic, runs beneath the commercial core; there are five stations between the **Washington State Convention & Trade Center** and the **International District**. Call Metro Transit's help line (553.3000; www.transit.metrokc.gov) for trip-planning information 24 hours a day.

Greyhound (628.5508, 800/231.2222) handles long-distance bus service from Seattle; the terminal is at 811 Stewart Street (between Ninth and Eighth Avenues).

DRIVING

The vote was to pump money into more freeways rather than into mass transit. Today, even the most placid Seattleites have begun to honk their car horns downtown, as the cumulative swell of bicycle couriers, buses, cabs, and pedestrians forces motorists to run an obstacle course between red lights. Beware especially of the human crush at **Pike Place Market**, where pedestrians always enjoy the right-of-way. Even some outlying routes, such as **45th Street** between **Wallingford** and the University District, **Broadway** on Capitol Hill, and **Lake City Way** and **Bothell Way** rounding Lake Washington's upper reaches, crawl on weekday afternoons. And it's a wonder there haven't been riots in front of the **Fremont Bridge**, which opens to allow boats passage.

Freeway traffic snarls here cause the average commuter to take about 30 minutes to drive into downtown. The average speed during rush hours is 22 mph, and peak-period delays are only expected to worsen. The two floating bridges that cross Lake Washington are particularly congested. Express lanes relieve some of the pressure on I-5 and westbound on **Route 520**, **Aurora Avenue** (**Route 99**) remains a decent alternative to I-5. In general, however, you're better off avoiding freeways and highways altogether Monday through Friday between 6 and 9AM and 3 and 6PM.

FERRIES

The **Washington State Ferry System** is the nation's largest. The busiest run on weekdays is between **Bainbridge Island** and downtown, a 25-minute commuter chug. On weekends, and especially during the summer, the **Edmonds-Kingston Ferry** is shoehorned full of tourists, and it's not uncommon to wait 3 hours for car space on ferries at **Anacortes** (about 90 minutes north of Seattle) bound for **Victoria, British Columbia**.

Walk-ons stand a better chance than drivers of catching their boat of choice. Most passengers pay a round-trip fare up front, and costs vary according to distance. Food and beverages on the boats are mediocre at best, so you may want to pack something to snack on. Credit cards are not accepted, and travelers headed for Canada must have a passport or another official form of identification (such as a driver's license, birth certificate, or voter registration card). Schedules change from winter to summer; call 464.6400 or 800/843.3779 or see www.wsdot.wa.gov/ferries for current departure times and rates.

MONORAIL

Built for the 1962 World's Fair, the **Monorail** runs only a 90-second, 1.2-mile route from downtown's **Westlake Center** to the old World's Fair grounds, now the **Seattle Center**. It's great for children, who love the train's smooth and uninterrupted ride. Adults pay $1.75 one way ($3.50 round trip). Children/seniors one way is 75 cents ($1.50 round trip). Trains depart every 15 minutes between 7:30AM and 11PM Monday through Friday and between 9AM and 11PM on Saturday and Sunday. Call 441.6038 for more information.

TAXIS

There are about 2,300 cabs in King County, and they're a fairly cheap means of transport, but they're controlled by dispatchers and almost impossible to hail from the street. They usually can be picked up at the bigger downtown hotels (especially the **Fairmont Olympic Hotel** and the **Westin**), as well as at the **King Street** train station. Otherwise, call; one will arrive in 10 to 30 minutes. Companies include **Farwest Taxi** (622.1717), **Graytop Cab** (282.8222), **Orange Cab** (522.8800; offers a $22 flat rate), and **Yellow Cab** (282.8222). **STITA** (246.9999) is a cooperative cab enterprise offering transportation between downtown and the airport.

TRAINS

Long-distance train service is provided by **Amtrak** (382.4120, 800/872.7245); there are daily arrivals and departures from King Street Station (303 S Jackson Street; between Second Avenue Extension and Second Avenue).

TROLLEYS

Seattle's real trolleys were stripped from service decades ago, but Metro Transit (553.3000) has imported vintage machines from Australia to make the 15-minute trip along the waterfront from **Pier 70** through Pioneer Square to the International District. The fare is $1.25 Monday through Friday between 6 and 9AM and 3 and 6PM; it's $1 all other times; children younger than 5 ride free.

WALKING

Long city blocks, some daunting hills, and the polar separation of Seattle's two principal tourist meccas, Pioneer Square and Pike Place Market, make downtown an area best taken in small doses—take a bus from one point of interest to another, then walk around in that immediate area. There's an impressive diversity of architecture and street life in the city, but green spaces are mostly relegated to the neighborhoods, with little open space downtown; it's basically concrete canyons between **Cherry** and **Pike Streets**.

Neighborhoods offer better strolling opportunities, particularly along Broadway on Capitol Hill, along **Market Street** in Ballard, and down **University Way** in the University District. On the suburban Eastside, only downtown **Kirkland** boasts enough sites within a small area to be walkable.

An excellent program worth checking is the **See Seattle Walking Tours**. Group and individual tours are planned for all levels of walking. Call 425.226.7641 or see www.see-seattle.com

WATER TAXI

In the summer months, the **Elliot Bay Water Taxi** can take you from **Piers 54** and **66** on the Seattle waterfront to **Seacrest Park** in West Seattle, where it connects with the **773** free Metro shuttle. For information about the water taxi, call the hot line (553.3000).

FYI

ACCOMMODATIONS

In addition to the individual hotel and bed-and-breakfast listings in each chapter, there are general reservations services available that help match visitors' needs to available properties. The **Seattle Super Saver** SS (800/535.7071; www.seattlesupersaver.com) offers one-stop shopping for price and location of downtown hotels. **Pacific Reservation Service** (784.0539; www.seattlebedandbreakfast.com) lists over 200 bed-and-breakfasts, cottages, condos, and guest houses in Seattle and throughout the Pacific Northwest. Both services are free and operate between 9AM and 5PM Monday through Friday; Super Saver is also open 1 to 4PM Saturday and Sunday.

CLIMATE

The predictions of local meteorologists are often studies in equivocation, along the lines of "partial sunshine, followed by partial low cloudiness, and maybe turning to showers in the afternoon." Look out your window for an accurate assessment, but remember that the weather you see may be quite different from what's going on only 2 miles away.

Warm offshore currents, mountains, and cold fronts from the north conspire to give Seattle a changeable but fairly moderate climate. July and August are the warmest months of the year, with relative humidity of 50% and usually no more than an inch or so of rain. Winter is substantially wetter, with an average of 5 inches of rain each month, but the temperature is warm enough to make snow and ice infrequent; when they do hit, however, the city turns into a huge frozen sculpture and traffic stops dead in its tracks.

MONTHS	AVERAGE TEMPERATURE (°F)
December–February	46
March–May	58
June–August	73
September–November	53

FERRY TALES

The Washington State Ferry System—the largest in the country—calls itself the state's number-one tourist attraction, and its boast seems justified: It affords the ideal vantage point for taking in the sunlit waters and salt air of Puget Sound, the snowcapped Cascade Mountains, the stunning Seattle skyline, and wildlife. Each year, it carries more than 23 million people to 20 ports of call throughout Puget Sound, its inland waterways, and the **San Juan Islands**. The 25 vessels that make up the fleet range from small, sleek, passenger-only boats to massive car ferries. Many of their names, such as *Hyak, Elwa, Cathlamet,* and *Sealth,* come from local tribal languages. Some passengers use the ferries to commute to or from work; others ride them for purely recreational purposes.

The options are almost endless, from sightseeing trips that last only a few hours to longer trips to the beautiful San Juan Islands or the charming city of Victoria in British Columbia. If you want to avoid crowds, don't travel during peak commuter hours (7 to 10AM and 4 to 6PM, Monday through Friday) or on summer weekends.

No matter when you go, however, you may have to wait for a place on a boat, so bring something to keep yourself entertained. (By the way, the food sold on board is mediocre, so bring your own snacks if you think you'll want to eat.) The schedule varies by season; for information on departure times and ticket prices, call the Washington State Ferry System (464.6400, 800/843.3779; www.wsdot.wa.gov).

DRINKING

Washington's legal drinking age is 21. Bars usually stay open until 2AM, and wine and beer are available at most supermarkets and groceries. Hard liquor must be purchased at one of the many state-regulated liquor stores.

HOURS

Opening and closing times for shops, attractions, coffeehouses, and so on are listed only by day(s) if normal hours apply (opening between 8 and 11AM and closing between 4 and 7PM). In unusual cases, specific hours are given.

MONEY

Banks are generally open Monday through Friday between 9:30AM and 5PM, and some are also open on Saturday mornings. Most of the larger downtown institutions will exchange foreign currency and traveler's checks. Better rates may be available weekdays at **American Express** (600 Stewart Street, at Sixth Avenue; 441.8622). On weekends, **Check Mart** (1206 First Avenue, between Seneca and University Streets; 622.2274) exchanges money on Saturday between 9AM and 9PM and on Sunday between 11AM and 5PM.

PARKING

There are numerous covered garages and open-air lots throughout the city. Facilities like the **Safeco Field** and **Husky Stadium** have their own lots, as do most downtown hotels. Centrally located garages charge up to $20 per day; less expensive ones are located on the fringes of downtown—along **Alaskan Way** on the waterfront, in the International District, and near **First Avenue** and **Bell Street**. Free parking options in the city are relegated to the rim areas—at the southern end of the waterfront near Jackson Street, for instance, or on **Elliott Avenue West** near **Myrtle Edwards Park**. Closer to downtown, most meters offer only a half-hour's time, and many others (marked in yellow) are off-limits except to delivery vehicles. Beware of parking infractions: An overtime parking ticket costs about $20; for parking in a truck-loading zone, the fine is a little higher; and parking illegally in a handicapped-only spot results in a $50 ticket.

PERSONAL SAFETY

The Seattle police force patrols the streets by motorcycle, car, mountain bike, horse, and on foot, which is reassuring to everyone but jaywalkers (more than 3,500 jaywalking tickets are issued here annually). Pickpockets are rare, but they do turn up in such crowded areas as Pike Place Market, along Broadway on Capitol Hill, and in shopping malls. Panhandlers can be a problem too, although they are essentially harmless. Seattle isn't known for its violent crime (theft is the principal threat here), but as in any large city, be more careful at night, especially in Pioneer Square and the Business and International Districts.

PUBLICATIONS

The city's two daily newspapers—the Seattle Post-Intelligencer (also called the P-I) and the Seattle Times—have been in the velvet grip of a joint operating agreement since 1983, ending an often vituperative rivalry. They publish separate papers Monday through Saturday, but only one Sunday edition. The morning P-I is strong on news and sports but unimaginative in feature sections. The more successful afternoon Times is better known for its feature writing. The Eastside's principal paper is the daily Eastside Journal, which is loaded with upscale-neighborhood stories. The free Seattle Weekly, which you can pick up on Thursday, has shed its scrappy "alternative" image over the years, becoming successful and mainstream, but the tabloid continues to attract readers with its arts coverage, essays, and opinionated calendar of events. Slick bimonthly Seattle magazine

covers a scattershot of topics, from politics to gardening and history, whereas Pacific Northwest offers a nine-times-a-year editorial menu of travel, food, and pictures. The Rocket (biweekly) concentrates on the local pop-music scene, as does the Stranger (available on Thursday), an often outrageous weekly tabloid.

The Puget Sound Business Journal (weekly) and the Daily Journal of Commerce both keep track of local financial transactions, but the PSBJ is usually more readable. Seattle Skanner, the Medium, and the Facts all serve the African-American community on a weekly basis. The monthly Seattle's Child features a wealth of activities and health materials directed at families. Every Friday, Seattle Gay News reports on subjects of interest to the local gay and lesbian population. The Seattle Chinese Post, a Chinese weekly newspaper, publishes an English-language edition, Northwest Asian Weekly. The North American Post (published three times a week) is the Northwest's only Japanese-language paper, and Hispanic News is a weekly published in Spanish and English.

Up-to-date calendars of events can be found in Seattle Weekly, the Seattle Times's Thursday "Tempo" section, and the Seattle Post-Intelligencer's Friday "What's Happening" section.

RADIO STATIONS

AM

570	KVI	Talk radio
710	KIRO	News
950	KJR-AM	Sports
1000	KOMO	News
1090	KPTK	Talk radio

FM

92.5	KLSY	Rock
94.1	KMPS	Country
94.9	KUOW	Public radio
97.3	KBSG	Oldies
98.1	KING	Classical
99.9	KISW	Oldies
102.5	KZOK	Rock
107.7	KNDD	Alternative

RESTAURANTS

Reservations are necessary for most popular restaurants, and it's best to book far in advance for the hottest dining spots such as **Rover's** and **Wild Ginger**. In general, jackets and ties are not required (except at the poshest of places), and most establishments accept credit cards.

SHOPPING

Galleries and antiques stores abound in the Pioneer Square area. Downtown, **Rainier Square** and the **US Bank Centre** offer several upscale shops; Fifth and Sixth Avenues are also lined with specialty stores. There's Pike Place Market for fresh produce, seafood, flowers, and souvenirs. Bargain hunters will want to head for

Fremont's resale shops; shopaholics, for the **Bellevue Square Mall**.

SMOKING

Health-conscious Seattle has a low threshold of tolerance for smokers. Smoking is prohibited in all restaurants, bars, and public establishment, as well as within 25 feet of their entrances.

STREET PLAN

You can generally tell the location of a place by the directional reference tacked on to the street name: For example, a place in Ballard will have an *NW* somewhere in its address, whereas an address in the **Seward Park** area will have an *S*. Most north–south roads in Seattle are avenues, and their compass directions are listed *after* their name or number. East–west thoroughfares are usually streets, and their compass directions appear *before* their name or number. Aberrations are the occasional ways, which usually run diagonally to the city grid, and I-5, which slices right through the city.

If you're lost, remember that Seattle is shaped like an hourglass, with downtown smack in the middle. Puget Sound is always west of the city, and **Mount Rainier** rises up to the southeast.

TAXES

Washington State sales tax is a hefty 8.8% on all purchases except groceries; it is 9.3% in restaurants and bars. The hotel tax is 15.3%.

TELEPHONES

The area code for Seattle itself is 206. Nearby areas have two new codes: 425 for regions east and north of Seattle (such as Bellevue, Kirkland, Bothell, Redmond, and Everett), and 253 for communities to the south, including Tacoma. When calling from 206, 425, or 253, these 10-digit calls are not long distance, so be sure not to dial 1 before them; you'll have to pay long-distance charges if you do.

In addition, the 360 area code has been assigned to the rest of coastal Washington. **Phone numbers in this book have the 206 area code unless otherwise specified.** If you have trouble reaching attractions listed here, contact either directory assistance or the Washington State Convention & Trade Center (800 Convention Place, at Eighth Avenue; 461.5840).

Local pay-phone calls (including those from Seattle to Bainbridge Island and the Eastside) cost 35 cents. *Note:* Hotels generally impose a steep charge for outgoing calls, so it may be worthwhile to dial from a public phone booth.

TICKETS

Two clearinghouses offer tickets to a variety of performing arts and venues. **Ticket Ticket** sells half-price, cash-only, day-of-show tickets from several locations (call 324.2744 for more information). **Ticketmaster** (628.0888) is a computerized charge service for concerts and sports that sometimes offers discounted tickets; there are several cash-only centers

around town. Some theaters schedule special discount performances, and many offer reduced-price preview tickets.

TIME ZONE

Seattle is in the Pacific Time Zone, 3 hours earlier than New York City.

TIPPING

A 15% to 20% tip is standard in restaurants and taxis, and $1 per bag is expected by hotel porters. Concierges anticipate tips based on the quality of their service: $20 for a week's worth of consistently good advice would be a healthy thanks, although some guests prefer to give $1 per service.

TOURS

The city's most popular tour is **Underground Seattle** (682.4646; www.undergroundtour.com), an hour-long excursion literally beneath the streets of Pioneer Square. When this district was rebuilt after the Great Fire of 1889, the decision was made to raise the land higher above water level to improve drainage and expand buildable acreage. To allow for this regrading, structures adopted double sets of entrances—one at the original ground level and another one story up, where sidewalks eventually would be laid. Engineers finally made the roads and the sidewalks even, but they did so without destroying the lower-level pedestrian ways. The remaining "underground city" is what you'll see on this entertaining and unusual expedition. Tours leave from **Doc Maynard's Public House** (610 First Avenue, between James and Cherry Streets) and last about 1.5 hours; they're available from late morning until midafternoon most days of the year. In July and August, tours run daily between 10AM and 8PM; the schedule varies the rest of the year, so call ahead.

Chinatown Discovery Tours (425/885.3085; www.seattlechinatowntour.com) is a company that escorts visitors through Seattle's International District, taking in such attractions as a fortune-cookie factory and an herb dispensary and breaking for a dim sum lunch. **Show Me Seattle** (633.2489; www.showmeseattle.com) takes visitors on 3-hour tours of downtown, the waterfront, Pioneer Square, residential neighborhoods, the **Hiram M. Chittenden Locks**, the giant **Fremont Troll**, and other offbeat sights. See Seattle Walking Tours (425/226.7641; www.see-seattle.com) trek through the Pike Place Market, along the waterfront, and through Pioneer Square and **Chinatown**. **Gray Line** (626.5208; www.graylineofseattle.com) offers a variety of sight-seeing excursions, including runs along Seattle's waterways and, in the summer, out to Mount Rainier, **Snoqualmie Falls**, and the tiny town of **North Bend**. **Argosy** (623.1445; www.argosycruises.com) schedules cruises through the Hiram M. Chittenden Locks and around Lake Washington and historic Elliott Bay.

The *Spirit of Washington Dinner Train* runs up and down the east-side length of Lake Washington, features 1930s railcars and engines on a 45-mile round trip that's just under 4 hours, and includes dinner and a winery tour. The trip starts and ends in **Renton**, at the south end of Lake Washington (425/277.RAIL or 800/ 876.RAIL; www.spiritofwashingtondinnertrain.com).

THE MAIN EVENTS

Seattle residents, ever the aspiring extroverts, love to party. Inspiration may come from occasions as noble and mystical as the return of salmon to northwest spawning grounds or as ignominious as the approach of fall and winter rain showers. Calendars in this area weigh heavily with annual fests, sporting events, and artsy convocations. Some of the most popular celebrations throughout the year are the following:

January

Chinese New Year The International District comes alive with lively fairs, colorful dragon-dense parades, and cultural displays. Festivities celebrating the symbolic expulsion of demons used to last a month, but West Coast Chinese have whittled their schedule of events down to about a week. Seattle's is held in either January or February, depending on the lunar calendar. Call 382.1197 for more information.

February

Fat Tuesday Pioneer Square jiggles with jazz, rock, and Cajun melodies, plus a waiter/waitress race and a wild (by local standards) parade, as Seattle presents its own spin on Mardi Gras. Events begin Wednesday of the week preceding Fat Tuesday (the day before Ash Wednesday and the beginning of Lent). For details, call 622.2563.

Tet Nguyen Dan Festival, the most important festival of Vietnamese culture, symbolizes the lunar new year and new beginnings. This 2-day festival at Seattle Center involves ancestral rituals, art exhibits, folk music, traditional dance, and martial arts demonstrations, as well as a vibrantly colored dragon weaving intricate patterns for the Lion Dances while noisy fireworks welcome visitors and salute the spirit of spring. There's plenty for kids to do and enjoy as well. And of course lots of Vietnamese food. For details, call 684.7200.

Northwest Flower and Garden Show This veritable Eden of horticulture seems to grow each year, feeding Seattle's much-written-about fondness for gardening. Hundreds of demonstration plots, supply sales booths, statuary displays, and lectures by landscapers and gardening writers round out the schedule. The event takes place at the Washington State Convention & Trade Center; admission is charged. For information, call 789.5333; www.gardenshow.com/nw.

March

St. Patrick's Day Downtown resounds with bagpipe music and the beat of dancing feet as an annual parade follows a special green stripe painted down **Fourth Avenue** from the **Municipal Building** to Westlake Center; call 623.0340 for more information. Meanwhile, runners participating in the popular 4-mile St. Patrick's Day Dash leave from **T.S. McHugh's** (21 Mercer Street, at First Ave North), bound for **F.X. McRory's** (419 Occidental Avenue South, at South King Street) in Pioneer Square; call 223.3608 for details.

Whirligig An indoor 3-week carnival for kids between ages 2 and 10 features rides (including a giant slide), family-oriented performances, and music. The fun takes place at the **Center House** in the Seattle Center; call 684.7200.

Mainly Mozart Festival The **Seattle Symphony** schedules three concerts honoring the genius of Wolfgang Amadeus Mozart. Admission is charged, and performances take place at the **University of Washington's Meany Hall**. For schedules, call 543.4880.

April

Cherry Blossom & Japanese Cultural Festival This celebration of cherry blossom season features performances of Japanese music and drama, as well as art exhibits and other cultural events. The 3-day festival is held at the Seattle Center; for more details, call 684.7200 or 723.2003, extension 2.

Daffodil Festival The warm-up act for **Skagit Valley's Tulip Festival** later in the month, this more-than-60-year-old tradition includes a parade of flower-bedecked private boats along with some navy craft and a giant floral parade that marches through four towns—**Tacoma**, **Puyallup**, **Sumner**, and **Orting**—all in the same day. The mid-April event is free; call 253/627.6176.

Skagit Valley Tulip Festival It is not always easy to gauge precisely when the 1,500 acres of tulip fields north of Seattle will bloom, but it's guaranteed that thousands of Washingtonians will rush to see them when they do. Because **Skagit Valley** roads are regularly jammed with flower lovers during this time, the best plan of action is to catch one of the well-posted shuttles through the fields; you'll even be able to tiptoe through the tulips. Capitalizing on the floral draw, the adjacent town of **Mount Vernon** celebrates tulip season with parades and a street fair. And **La Conner** almost explodes at the seams as tourists finish off their visit with a stroll through that burg's many small shops. Salmon barbecues, pancake suppers, and formal bike tours may also be on the docket. Watch newspapers for the official blooming announcement. The tulip fields are located outside of Mount Vernon, 60 miles north of Seattle on I-5. Call 360/428.5959 for additional information and schedules; www.tulipfestival.org.

May

Opening Day of Yachting Season This is a big deal in a city that claims one boat for approximately every 12 people. On the first Saturday in May, you can watch a ceremonial regatta on **Lake Union**, races to showcase the talents of the University of Washington rowing team, and lots of Sunday sailors catching the breezes and trying to steer clear of collisions on Lake Washington.

Call the **Seattle Yacht Club** at 325.1000 for more about this free event. The gathering point for the ceremonial blessing of the fleet is at **Seattle Fishermen's Memorial**, which is held on the first day of the fishing season. For more information, call 283.3366.

Northwest Folklife Festival With booths offering handmade crafts, banjo players, gospel performances, storytelling sessions, and clog-dancing exhibitions, this free 4-day hootenanny—which is said to be the country's largest folkfest—strives to show that Seattle hasn't sold out completely to glitz. Like most major functions at Seattle Center, it's dominated by food booths. Attendees are asked to help defray administrative costs by purchasing commemorative event pins. The festival is held every Memorial Day weekend; call 684.7300; www.nwfolklife.org.

Pike Place Market Festival One of the city's most boisterous neighborhood hooplas, this free festival offers live-music stages, plenty of food and drink, clowns, and an activities area set aside specifically for children. The festival is held every Memorial Day weekend at Pike Place Market; for details, call 587.0351.

Poulsbo Viking Fest Break out your horned helmets and help celebrate the Scandinavian heritage of Puget Sound's most deliberately Norwegian village. Expect live music, traditional dancing, and a group of iron-stomached guests engaging in a contest to see who can eat the most *lutefisk* (cod soaked in brine and spices). The free event is held in **Poulsbo**, on the **Kitsap Peninsula**, 12 miles northwest of the **City of Bainbridge Island** on **Route 305**; call 360/779.4848 for further information.

Seattle International Film Festival Founded in 1976, this is supposedly the best-attended film festival in North America, showing more than 160 new works from around the world at several Seattle theaters. Screenings run from mid-May through early June. Series tickets go on sale in January. Call 324.9996 for information; www.seattlefilm.com.

University Street Fair Fed by a colorful cross section of University of Washington students and well woven with curious arts and crafts booths, this free 2-day street party, begun in 1970, is always worth a look. There are lots of mimes, musicians, and street eats, plus great people watching. It's usually held the third full weekend in May on University Way. For more about the fair, call 632.9084 or 547.4417; www.udistrictstreetfair.org.

June

Summer Nights Spend a summer evening listening to such acts as Hootie and the Blowfish, Nina Simone, Robert Cray, John Lee Hooker, Ringo Starr, or Ziggy Marley against the backdrop of sailboats and the sun setting over the Olympic Mountains. Summer Nights takes place at Gasworks Park on Lake Union and runs throughout the summer. Call 628.0888; www.summernights.org.

Fire Festival More than a century after the Great Fire of 1889, which completely flattened downtown, the city can commemorate that blaze without pangs of loss. Fire equipment parades along First Avenue, live entertainment heats up **Occidental Park**, and historical exhibits teach the dangers of pyromania. Pioneer Square marks the center of activity; call 667.0687.

Fremont Fair Fremonters show up by the thousands for this eclectic neighborhood celebration featuring not only food and crafts booths but also live music by plenty of street performers. It takes place on **34th Street**, just north of the Fremont Bridge. For more about the fair, call 694.6706 between January and June; www.fremontfair.com.

Out to Lunch Summer is officially declared when the sounds of midday concerts (from jazz to calypso) begin resounding from downtown's canyon-lands. The series is free and usually continues through early September. Call 623.0340 for specific locations.

Seattle Gay Pride Parade The Northwest's largest parade (or, more correctly, the Lesbian/Gay/Bisexual/Transgender [LGBT] event) provides fantastic floats, "dykes on bikes," acres of male skin, shiny leather, and Broadway tunes galore, as it processes from Westlake Mall to Seattle Center for the winter-long Seattle Gay Pride Festival. www.seattlepride.org.

July

Bite of Seattle Here's yet another shameless opportunity to eat yourself silly in public, as 50 or more local restaurants serve their specialties from open-air booths. Don't forget the Tums. This foodfest takes place at the end of July at the Seattle Center; 425/283.5050; www.biteofseattle.com for details.

King County Fair Enjoy 5 days of rodeo, pig racing, and music headliners at the state's oldest county fair beginning the third Wednesday in July. The **King County Fairgrounds** are in **Enumclaw**, just 40 miles southeast of Seattle; take I-5 south to **Route 18**, east to **Auburn**, then head southeast on **Route 164**. For more about this event, call 360/825.7777.

Mercer Island Summer Celebration Booths display arts and crafts, jugglers perform, children are invited to participate in distracting building projects, and Saturday night swings with a live band beside the dance floor. This event takes place the second weekend of July at various venues in the **Mercer Island** central business district; call 236.7285.

Olympic Music Festival The rather incongruously named **Philadelphia String Quartet** (which has been based in Seattle since 1966) joins other musicians in an 11-weekend series of chamber-music performances, held in a turn-of-the-19th-century barn on the nearby Olympic Peninsula between late June and early September. Bring blankets to sit on. Admission is charged, and the festival is held in **Quilcene**, 11 miles west of the **Hood Canal Bridge** on **Route 104**; call 527.8839.

Pacific Northwest Arts and Crafts Fair Bellevue upstages Seattle with this exhibition of performing arts, crafts displays, and a juried show of visual arts in **Bellevue Square** and the **Bellevue Square Garage** (NE Eighth Street and Bellevue Way). It's free and takes place the last weekend of July; for additional information, call 425/519.0770.

San Juan Island Dixieland Jazz Festival Ferries chugging to San Juan Island are especially full when Dixieland lovers swarm toward one of this area's finest summer musical events. The 3-day festival features continuous entertainment presented on three outdoor stages. Music includes traditional jazz, New Orleans–style jazz, swing, gospel, and blues. The shows take place in the town of **Friday Harbor**. Warning: Lodging reservations can be hard to find in the San Juan Islands during this time (late July), so call *very* early to get a room. Individual-day and full-festival passes are available. Catch the ferry at Anacortes, 78 miles north of Seattle; your best bet is to leave your car there and walk onto the ferry. Call 360/378.5240 or 888/825.9390 for more about the festival.

Seafair features the old-style **Seafair Pirates**—and since 1950, milk-carton boat races on **Green Lake**, a torchlight parade, hydroplane races on Lake Washington, and a demonstration of acrobatic flying by the **Blue Angels**. This event is mostly free, and it's held from the third weekend of July through the first Sunday in August at various venues; for details, 728.0123; www.seafair.com.

WOMAD USA More than 30 legendary musicians, dancers, performers, and visual artists from Africa, Asia, Australia, and Europe, as well as North and South America, gather for an annual 3-day festival (World of Music, Arts and Dance) of global rhythms, cultural celebration, and fun in a lovely rural setting. **Marymoor Park** is 13 miles and about 25 minutes east of Seattle, via Route 520; take the **West Lake Sammamish Parkway** exit. Thrill to the likes of Ravi Shankar, Ashley MacIsaac, King Sunny Ade, Abdullah Ibrahim, and Yungchen Lhamo. Daily tickets are available, as are 3-day special prices. There's no charge for kids age 12 or younger, and parking is free. For information, call King County Parks at 296.2966; for tickets, call 628.0888; www.womad.org.

Lake Union Wooden Boat Festival Events include music, food, toy boat building, races, regattas, and demonstrations of boat restoration. Admission is free. More information at 382.2628; www.cwb.org.

August

Evergreen State Fair Animal shows, stock-car races, a chili cook-off, totem-pole carving, and cow-milking contests are all part of this 11-day show-and-tell in the backwoods hamlet of **Monroe**, 30 miles northeast of Seattle. The fair takes place from late August through Labor Day, and there is an admission charge; 360/805.6700; www.evergreenfair.org.

KOMO Kidsfair Jointly sponsored by local radio station **KOMO** and the Seattle Center, this day-long fair presents a roster of outdoor activities for the entire family, including pony rides, face-painting, miniature train rides, and the "clown bounce," where kids bounce up and down on a gigantic inflated apparatus. For more information, call 684.7200.

September

Bumbershoot Seattle's premier entertainment event, playfully taking its name from a British slang term for *umbrella*, is a 4-day extravaganza of music, art shows, literary readings, and food, food, food. The Seattle Center fills with crafts booths, fortune-tellers, balloon artists, and the riffs of nationally known musicologists. Admission is charged, and it's held Labor Day weekend; 684.7200; www.bumbershoot.org.

Western Washington Fair Most folks just call this country fest the "Puyallup Fair," as in the slogan "Do the Puyallup" (pronounced Pew-*al*-up). For 17 days, children can stuff themselves silly on cotton candy and then bump along on carnival rides. Adults watch rodeos and livestock shows and listen to well-known country-and-western musicians. The smells of livestock and the grunts of pigs abound. The fair takes place at the **Puyallup Fairgrounds**, 31 miles south of Seattle. For more information, call 253/841.5045; www.thefair.com.

October

St. Demetrios Greek Festival Lovers of bouzouki music and gyro sandwiches, take note. This partially covered

Brochures for most tour companies can be found at the tourist information booth on the galleria level of the Washington State Convention & Trade Center (800 Convention Place, at Eighth Avenue) and at Sea-Tac International Airport (lower concourse, baggage claim area).

Visitors' Information Offices

There are two main visitors' information centers: on the galleria level of the Washington State Convention & Trade Center (800 Convention Place, at Eighth Avenue; 461.5840) and at Sea-Tac International Airport (lower concourse, baggage claim area). Both are open Monday through Saturday.

ethnic tribute to Rain City's 10,000-plus Greek descendants, held at **St. Demetrios Church** (2100 Boyer Avenue E, at 19th Avenue), thrives on dancing, heaped plates of Athenian cuisine, wonderfully sticky baklava, and arts-and-crafts exhibits. Long lines form at the food booths, so come early. Admission is charged. The date varies, based on parking availability due to University of Washington (UW) **Huskies** football games; call 325.4347.

Issaquah Salmon Days This free 2-day event, held the first weekend of October, commemorates the annual return of the Northwest's premier sporting fish to its spawning grounds with a parade, salmon bake, hydroplane races on **Sammamish Lake**, and live entertainment. Pony rides and face-painting are favorites for children. Events are held all over **Issaquah**, 15 miles east of Seattle on **Interstate 90**; call 425/392.0661.

November

KING 5 Winterfest A free 5-week holiday jamboree beginning Thanksgiving weekend offers entertainment for children, ice skating, symphony concerts, senior dances, holiday music, and, of course, jolly old St. Nicholas. Sponsored by local TV station **KING**, it runs through early January at the Seattle Center. Call 684.7200 for details.

December

Christmas Ships The Christmas Ships sail over Elliott Bay and Lake Washington, sparkling with colorful lights and adding a festive spirit to Seattle's holiday season.

Bonfires are set up on local beaches to watch the show. For site information, call 684.4075.

The Messiah This is one of very few American performances of Handel's celebrated work to employ authentic instrumentation. Call early (323.1040) for reservations, as tickets always sell out. The performances are held from early to mid-December at **St. Mark's Episcopal Cathedral** (1245 10th Avenue E, between Highland Drive and Blaine Street).

The Nutcracker The **Pacific Northwest Ballet**'s rendering of this classic fairy tale might be only vaguely recognizable to Russian Tsar Nicholas II, for whom Tchaikovsky first staged his ballet in 1892. The set designs, by renowned Seattle artist Maurice Sendak, help make this production both more whimsical and more memorable than its competitors. Tickets go on sale in October; call 441.2424.

New Year's Eve at the Space Needle As many as 20,000 chilled and damp celebrants huddle on three levels of the **Needle** (on the observation deck, in the **Space Needle Restaurant**, and at the skyline level) to offer toasts and kisses. Local bands hold forth at the tower's base. As midnight approaches, a spectacular fireworks display rises from the bottom, pours out from the sides, and crowns the needle at the beginning of the new year. Admission is charged; for details, call 443.2100. Tens of thousands watch the show free from the **Seattle Center** grounds, from nearby hills, or on television.

Phone Book

EMERGENCIES

AAA of Washington	448.5353
Ambulance/Fire/Police	911
Auto Impound	684.5444
Auto Theft	684.8940
Dentist referral service	443.7607
U.S. Healthworks	682.7418
Hospitals	
Harborview Emergency	731.3074
University of Washington	548.3300
Locksmith (AAA 24-hour)	325.1515
Pharmacy (24-hour)	
Bartell's Pharmacy	284.1354
Poison Control Center	526.2121

VISITORS' INFORMATION

American Youth Hostels	622.5443
Amtrak	800/872.7245
Better Business Bureau	431.2222
Convention and Visitors Bureau	461.5800
Greyhound Bus	628.5526, 800/231.2222; www.greyhound.com
Metro Transit	553.3000; www.transit.metrokc.gov
Time	464.6400
US Customs	553.0770
US Passport Office	808.5700
Washington State Convention & Trade Center	461.5840
Washington State Ferries	464.6400
Weather	526.6087

A MINIGUIDE TO SEATTLE

In a perfect world, you would have all the time you needed to explore Seattle thoroughly, but in reality, you'll be here for only a few days and will have to pick and choose which sights to visit. What follows is our short-stay list of the outstanding attractions here to help you make the most of your time.

Pioneer Square/International District

Start with a dim sum lunch at **House of Hong** (409 Eighth S, between Jackson and King Streets; 622.7997), and then walk down to **Uwajimaya** (600 Fifth Avenue S, between S Dearborn and S Weller; 624.6248) one of the best Asian supermarkets in the country. If you're up for a long stroll, continue west down **Jackson Street** toward **Occidental Avenue**. Take the time to look into some of the galleries and boutiques here. Finish your shopping trip with a browse through the **Elliott Bay Book Company** (101 S Main Street, at First Avenue; 624.6600), then enjoy a coffee or a beer at the **Elliott Bay Cafe** (682.6664) on the premises. From there, walk two blocks north to **Doc Maynard's Public House** (610 First Avenue; between James and Cherry Streets; 682.4649) and take the tour of **Underground Seattle**.

Business District

Park at the Seattle Center (Fifth Avenue N, between Broad and Mercer Streets) and take the Monorail to Westlake Center (Fourth Avenue and Pine Street). Take a peek inside **Nordstrom**, then head north along Fifth Avenue. Stop at an espresso stand (there's one about every 50 feet in this area) and pick up a *latte* and a pastry to take to **Freeway Park** (Seneca Street, between Eighth and Sixth Avenues). Relax and enjoy the greenery, and then walk west on **Seneca Street** downhill to **Second Avenue**. Turn left and head south through the financial district, making sure to check out the fantastic terra-cotta architecture of the older buildings—especially the walruses on the **Arctic Building** (700 Third Avenue, at Cherry St).

Pike Place Market/Waterfront

If you have only a little while, spend it all in the Pike Place Market. There is no area more quintessentially Seattle, not only because of its pioneer spirit and laid-back atmosphere but also because of its history. Start your tour at the corner of Pike Street and **Pike Place** under the big **Market Clock**. Wander through the **Main Arcade** (Pike Place between Pike Street and Western Avenue) and watch the goings-on at **Pike Place Fish** (682.7181, 800/542.7732; fax 682.4629) as the

vendors fling salmon and crab back and forth over their customers' heads. At the northernmost end of the arcade, cross Pike Place and watch the street performers in front of the **Soames-Dunn Building** (Pike Place, between Stewart and Virginia Streets). The **Triangle Building** (Pike Place and Post Alley), the **Sanitary Market Building** (Pike Place and Post Alley), and the **Corner Market Building** (Pike Place and Pike Street) are also worth a look. Good dining choices include **Chez Shea** (Corner Market Building; 467.9990), **Il Bistro** (Lower Post Alley, between Union and Pike Streets; 682.3049), and **Maximilien-in-the-Market** (Main Arcade; 682.7270).

Belltown/Seattle Center

If you have tots in tow, spend your time at the Seattle Center (Fifth Avenue N, between Broad and Mercer Streets), especially the **Pacific Science Center** (443.2880; recorded information, 443.2001), the **Children's Museum** (441.1768), and the **Charlotte Martin Theatre** (441.3322), home of the **Seattle Children's Theatre** (**SCT**). The best restaurant choices here include **Flying Fish** (2234 First Avenue, at Bell Street; 728.8595), **Lampreia** (2400 First Avenue, at Battery Street; 443.3301), and **Queen City Grill** (2201 First Avenue at Blanchard Street; 443.0975).

Capitol Hill to Seward Park

Start your exploration of this area in or around **Volunteer Park** (1247 15th Avenue E, at Highland Drive). While you're here, spend some time in the small but beautiful **Conservatory** (E Highland Drive, between 15th and Federal Avenues; 684.4743) and visit the **Seattle Asian Art Museum** (1400 E Prospect Street, between 15th and Federal Avenues; 625.8900), which features one of the most comprehensive collections of Chinese and Japanese art in the country. Leave the park and walk up 15th Avenue to **Louisa Boren View Park** (E Garfield Street and 15th Avenue) to enjoy the view of the University of Washington, the **Montlake Cut**, the **Arboretum**, and Lake Washington. Then wander through the **Lake View Cemetery** (15th Avenue E, between Highland Drive and Howe Street; 322.1582); father-and-son movie stars Bruce and Brandon Lee are interred here. Walk back through Volunteer Park, and then turn right onto **Prospect Street**. Take a left on **10th Avenue**, which becomes **Broadway**. Follow Broadway south, people-watching and shop-browsing as you go, then turn left on **Denny** for the amazing **Cal Anderson Park**. Then grab a coffee at **B&O Espresso** (328.3290).

West Seattle

Exit the **West Seattle Freeway** onto **Admiral Way** and go up the hill to **Belvedere Viewpoint** (SW Olga Street and Admiral Way) to watch planes land at **Boeing Field** and ships unload at **Harbor Island**. Back in the car, follow Admiral Way through West Seattle, past **Schmitz Park**. Take a right on **63rd Avenue** and park near **Alki Beach**. Walk along the beach to **Duwamish Head**; on your way, stop to eat at **Spud Fish and Chips** (2666 Alki Avenue SW, between 59th and 60th Avenues; 938.0606).

Queen Anne/Magnolia

Take the **Garfield Street** viaduct to **Galer Street** in **Magnolia**. Follow Galer to **Magnolia Park** (1461 Magnolia Boulevard W, between Galer and Howe Streets), taking in the fantastic view along the way. Follow Howe west to **Magnolia Boulevard**, then continue to its end at **Discovery Park**. Wander through the park, stopping at the **Daybreak Star Indian Cultural Center** (285.4425) and the 19th-century **West Point Lighthouse**. Exit the park via **Government Way**, which turns into **Fort Street** and, farther east, **Gilman Avenue**; when you reach **Emerson Place**, turn left and cross the railroad tracks. Continue along Emerson Place to **15th Avenue**, passing **Fishermen's Terminal**, where you can observe hundreds of ships moving in and out of the port. Head south on 15th Avenue (which eventually becomes **Elliott Avenue**), then turn left onto Mercer Street. Take Mercer to the foot of **Queen Anne Hill** and turn left up the **Queen Anne Counterbalance** (Queen Anne Avenue N, between Roy and Galer Streets). Have lunch at **The 5-Spot** (1502 Queen Anne Avenue N, between Galer and Garfield Streets; 285.7768) or dinner at the excellent **Ponti Seafood Grill** (3014 Third Avenue N, between Florentia and Etruria Streets; 284.3000) or **Canlis** (2576 Aurora Avenue N, north of Halladay Street; 283.3313).

Fremont/Wallingford

If your time is limited, spend it exploring the fascinating anachronism that is Fremont. Park your car along the **Lake Washington Ship Canal** on 34th Street. Take a look at the sculpture *Waiting for the Interurban*, then head north on **Fremont Place**, poking into **Fritzi Ritz** (3425 Fremont Place N, at 35th Street, 633.0929) and **Deluxe Junk** (3518 Fremont Place N, between 35th and 36th Streets; 634.2733) retro shops on your way. Stave off hunger pangs at the **Triangle Lounge** (3507 Fremont Place N, between 35th Street and Evanston Avenue; 632.0880), or pick up an espresso at the funky **35th Street Bistro** (709 N 35th Street, between Woodland Park and Fremont Avenues;

547.9850). Return to your car and drive east on 36th Street, tipping your hat to the famed **Fremont Troll**.

Green Lake/Greenwood/North Seattle

If you're an animal lover, spend the afternoon at the **Woodland Park Zoo** (5500 Phinney Avenue N, between 50th and 59th Streets; 684.4800); if you're more interested in humans, the entire Green Lake area is great for people watching. In warm weather, sit on the grass at the edge of the lake and enjoy a treat from the **Urban Bakery** (7850 E Green Lake Drive N, at Stroud Avenue; 524.7951). More substantial (and excellent) meals can be had at the **Santa Fe Cafe** (5901 Phinney Avenue N, at 59th Street; 783.9755) or **Mae's Phinney Ridge Cafe** (6412 Phinney Avenue N, between 64th and 65th Streets; 782.1222).

University District/Ravenna

The choice here is simple: Spend your time on the UW campus. Go to the **Thomas Burke Memorial Washington State Museum** (NE 45th Street, between Memorial Way and 15th Avenue; 543.5590), then wander over to the **Suzzallo/Allen Library** (Central Plaza) and visit the **Graduate Reading Room**. From the library, walk southeast toward **Husky Stadium** (3800 Montlake Boulevard NE, between Pacific Street and Walla Walla Road; 543.2200), passing the *Drumheller Fountain* along the way. If you feel like shopping, check out the **University Book Store** (4326 University Way NE, between 43rd and 45th Streets; 634.3400). For food, try the **Continental Restaurant** (4549 University Way NE, between 45th and 47th Streets; 632.4700) or **Mamma Melina Ristorante** (4759 Roosevelt Way NE, at 50th Street; 632.2271).

Eastside

Kirkland is the most walker-friendly town on the Eastside. Park your car in the downtown center, which is an easy stroll from beach parks, art galleries, restaurants, and elegant shops. Top sights include **Shamiana** (10724 NE 68th Street, at Sixth Street S; 425/827.4902), a popular Indian restaurant, and the **Gunnar Nordstrom Gallery** (127 Lake Street S, between Second and Kirkland Avenues; 425/827.2822), exhibiting noteworthy abstract art. If time permits, take the walk to look at the public art around the city. If you're in Bellevue, check out the beautiful **Bellevue Botanical Gardens** (12001 Main Street, between 124th Avenue NE and 118th Avenue SE; 425/462.2749) or the **Bellevue Downtown Park** (102nd Avenue NE, between First and Fourth Streets); get a taste of the Christmas season at **Christmas House** (11024 NE Second Street, between 111th and 108th Avenues; 425/455.4225), and grab a pizza at **Spazzo** (10655 NE Fourth Street, between 108th and 106th Avenues; 425/454.8255).

PIONEER SQUARE/ INTERNATIONAL DISTRICT

In the middle of a parched summer in 1889, when Seattle had been an incorporated city for a mere 20 years, its business district—now known as **Pioneer Square**—started burning beyond control. Thirty central city blocks, a total of 64 acres, were leveled before the Great Fire of 1889 fizzled amid tidelands where the

former **Kingdome** stadium stood. Amazingly, not a single person is known to have perished in the blaze.

No sooner did the smoke dissipate than civic boosters began to see the calamity as a boon for Seattle, a second chance to become a showplace and commercial cap-

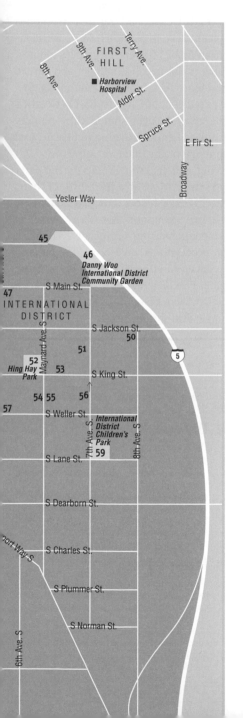

ital. The fledgling city immediately began to rebuild—this time instituting regulations requiring that all new downtown buildings be constructed of brick, stone, and iron. And the structures were constructed on higher ground.

Ever since claims had first been staked on **Elliott Bay** in 1852, city engineers had used dredging and landfill to both expand Seattle's commercial acreage and lift it above water level. After the fire, this strategy was adopted for Pioneer Square as well; much of the area was filled in with excess earth graded down from the nearby hills, burying the first stories of many buildings and creating what has become known as **Underground Seattle**.

Thanks in large measure to James J. Hill, who designated Seattle as the western terminus for his **Great Northern Railroad**, the town was back in business less than two years later—more populous and optimistic than ever. Then came the beginning of the Alaskan Gold Rush in 1897, which transformed Seattle into a wealthy embarkation point. Pioneer Square celebrated a commercial heyday until after the turn of the 19th century.

In about 1900, the city began to develop northward, and Pioneer Square was left with honky-tonk taverns, bawdy houses, and transient hotels. Opium dens and, during Prohibition, speakeasies sprang up in the shadowy tunnels created by regrading. During the Depression, the area became totally decrepit, and by 1966 the proposal was made to level it to make room for more parking lots and new offices.

Architects and preservationists were incensed. So was well-known local newspaper columnist Emmett Watson. "I swear, my friends," Watson lamented in print, "progress is going to be the death of this city yet!" But Pioneer Square escaped death once again. Banks initiated incentive loan programs to revive the neighborhood, and businesses moved in to restore its sturdy buildings. Today, approximately 88 acres of offices, restaurants, art galleries, and specialty stores populate what was the city's first historic district.

The **International District** (or I.D., as locals say), bordering Pioneer Square on the east and encompassing the city's Chinese and Japanese enclaves, has a similarly troubled but far different heritage. Seattle's original **Chinatown** was actually centered at **Second Avenue** and **Washington Street**, smack in what was then the middle of the city. Its inhabitants had come to **Puget Sound** to work on railroads and in lumber mills or mines. Later, they developed successful cigar-making and dry-goods businesses, but by the mid-1880s, as unemployment rose in the Northwest, white laborers came to resent the Chinese and their "cheap labor." In February 1886, mobs of Sinophobes (including, it's said, many police officers) invaded Chinatown and herded almost all of the city's 350 to 400 Chinese residents to steamships bound for San Francisco. Martial law was declared to halt the expulsion, but at least half of Seattle's Chinese population left anyway, fearful of the consequences should they remain. Only well after the Great Fire of 1889 did the Chinese begin returning to Seattle, and by then new Japanese immigrants had filled up much of the labor vacuum.

Chinatown relocated to the blocks around **King** and **Jackson Streets** in the early 1900s. Meanwhile, the Japanese immigrants had settled in an area just north of there, which they called Nihonmachi. By 1910 Nihonmachi housed more than 6,000 Japanese residents. But World War II took a toll on both Asian communities. Many Japanese were interned in camps all over the West. Low-income housing subsequently invaded the south end of downtown, and condemnation proceedings were brought against a number of older structures. But in the 1970s, a concerted effort went into revitalizing the I.D., and much of it has since been renovated. Families started to move back in, parks were laid out, and new businesses—especially Asian restaurants—attract visitors as well as residents from all parts of town to sample dim sum or sushi.

PIONEER SQUARE

1 SEATTLE MYSTERY BOOKSHOP

Proprietor Bill Farley carries an abundance of new and used and collectible works, paperback and hardcover, including some detective and spy novels that just don't seem to turn up elsewhere in town. There are special sections for Sherlock Holmes and for Puget Sound crime novelists, such as Earl Emerson, J.A. Jance, Robert Ferrigno, K.K. Beck, G.M. Ford, and Mary Daheim, and books by many others. Mailings alert regular patrons to signings by well-known authors. ♦ M-Sa, 10AM-5PM; Su, noon-5PM. 117

Cherry St (between Second and First Aves). 587.5737. www.seattlemystery.com

2 LOWMAN BUILDING

The only French Renaissance eclectic-style tower at Pioneer Place, this building (finished in 1900) is quite a standout from the parade of Romanesque piles. The principal designer was **August Heide**, an import from back east who worked primarily in the nearby town of Everett. The Lowman now includes renovated studio apartments. ♦ 107 Cherry St (at First Ave). www.lowmanbuilding.com

3 MARIO'S PIZZA

★★$ Seattle is certainly not short on pizza joints, but few can beat the crust on the pies created in this pizzeria. Ingredients are liberally apportioned, and the crusts are thick and chewy. The GASP (a wonderful concoction of garlic, artichoke hearts, sun-dried tomatoes, and pesto) is the house specialty. For more tender palates, there's the soothing Zorba, which is like a flat, open gyro sandwich, with beef, onion, feta cheese, green olives, and homemade *tzatziki* (yogurt, herb, and cucumber sauce). You can get your pizza to go or eat at one of the outdoor tables. And, of course, they deliver. ◆ Pizza/takeout ◆ Daily. 616 First Ave (between James and Cherry Sts). 621.8500. &

3 OLD TIMER'S CAFE

★$ The wood-and-brass décor are Pioneer Square clichés, and the boxcar narrowness of this tavern ensures it will seem crowded even when there are only a few people inside. The draw is the nightly performances by local blues and jazz musicians. The food is of a Southern bent, including gumbo, barbecue ribs, catfish, and mustard greens. ◆ Southern ◆ Cover. Daily, lunch and dinner; music until 2AM. 620 First Ave (between James and Cherry Sts). 623.9800

4 TRATTORIA MITCHELLI

★★$$ Owner Dany Mitchell defies Seattle's reputation for rolling up its sidewalks before 10PM. Late-movie crowds, Pioneer Square's after-theater clientele, and a jolly assortment of famished insomniacs end up at this festive, noisy joint at all hours of the night. Crave a heaping plate of ravioli in butter and garlic at 2AM? A tasty Italian breakfast frittata at 3AM? Step this way—your table's waiting. Plentifully apportioned lunches and early dinners are also served, but people-watching before the *Tonight Show* is less interesting. The service is often tardy, but who notices after midnight? ◆ Italian ◆ Daily, breakfast, lunch, and dinner (dinner until 4AM, F and Sa only.) 84 Yesler Way (at Post Ave). 623.3885. www.mitchellis.com

5 MAGIC MOUSE TOYS

This must be where all stuffed animals pray they'll wind up, and hundreds of them do, especially teddy bears. The store's high-quality selection also includes wooden train sets, art supplies, children's books, and more than enough bathtub gizmos to occupy the kids. ◆ Daily. 603 First Ave (at Yesler Way). 682.8097

5 MUTUAL LIFE BUILDING

Additions can often detract from an architect's vision, but in this case they seem to have enhanced the look of this grand box, which sits where Seattle's first "restaurant"—Henry Yesler's cookhouse—once did business. Most critics agree that the basement and first floor were designed by **Elmer Fisher** and finished around 1892. Upper stories, completed in 1897, are slightly contrasting creations from the partnership of **Robertson and Blackwell**. Another 30-foot hip was added to the west side in 1904, and a 1983 renovation cleaned up the old elevator cars, gave the exterior a swabbing of postmodern hues, and modernized the lobby. ◆ 605 First Ave (at Yesler Way)

5 RAGAZZI'S FLYING SHUTTLE

The front windows of this shop are filled with lots of handwoven clothing and offbeat jewelry—great for browsing from the sidewalk. Many wonderful designer-made women's clothes are here to sigh over. Or tempt yourself further: Go in and try on some of the stylish pieces. ◆ Daily. 607 First Ave (between Yesler Way and Cherry St). 343.9762. www.ragazzisflyingshuttle.com

6 PIONEER PLACE PARK

Ⓟ The spiritual hub of Pioneer Square was once a disregarded and clumsy intersection called Yesler's Corner. Only after the fire of 1889 did it become a landmark. This cobble stoned triangle is home to many panhandlers and pigeons, but it's also a good spot for people watching or studying the surrounding architecture.

A red cedar totem pole has stood on this spot since 1899. The original, carved by Tlingit Indians, was chopped down and taken as a "souvenir" from Alaska's Tongass Island by an excursion party from Seattle. After an arsonist damaged the monolith in 1938, it was shipped back to its home, where local carvers (apparently unperturbed by Seattle's filching of the original) crafted the current replica. A drinking fountain and bust of Chief Sealth, designed by James A. Wehn and installed in 1909, are also here. A cast-iron-and-glass pergola was erected at the park's southwestern tip in 1909 (and rehabilitated

---

Restaurants/Clubs: Red | **Hotels: Purple** | **Shops: Orange** | **Outdoors/Parks: Green** | **Sights/Culture: Blue**

in 1970) to serve as a shelter for pedestrians waiting to board passing trolleys. Sadly, the pergola was demolished in a 2001 accident; it was rebuilt with the help of Seildelhuber IronWorks, who did an amazing job of salvaging the damaged pieces. The pergola also marked the entrance to Seattle's first public rest room (opened in 1909)—a lavish underground hideaway of Alaskan marble and skylights that offered shoe shines and a newspaper stand until plumbing problems forced its closure in 1939. The facility still exists, but it's accessible now only through a manhole. So far the city has refused all requests to reopen the rest room. ◆ First Ave (between Yesler Way and Cherry St)

7 PIONEER BUILDING

Two years after this structure was completed in 1892, the American Institute of Architects labeled it "the finest building west of Chicago." Commissioned by Seattle pioneer and entrepreneur Henry Yesler (whose first home sat on the same property), and designed by Massachusetts emigrant **Elmer Fisher**, the building is a paradigm of this neighborhood's architecture. (Fisher would go on to create some 50 other buildings in and around Pioneer Square, lending it a homogenous but hardly disagreeable look.) Its style is Romanesque Revival, as developed and refined by such visionary architects as **Henry Hobson Richardson** and **Louis Sullivan**. A rusticated stone base and Roman archway give way to progressively different window treatments in the upper stories. The structure was originally endowed with a pyramid-topped central tower, but that was taken down (along with other towers and cornices in the district) as a precautionary measure after an earthquake rumbled up from Olympia to clobber Seattle in 1949. Although the building houses private offices, you can stop in the lobby and take a peek at the Italian red-marble interior and atrium. ◆ 606 First Ave (between James and Cherry Sts)

7 ZASU RESTAURANT AND BAR

★$ Within its brick walls and elegant Art Deco black-and-red décor, this spacious two-story establishment serves up some nicely executed lunches: The herb-roasted chicken and salmon poached in white wine are delicately seasoned. On Friday and Saturday nights, **Zazu** turns into a disco. ◆ American ◆ Cover for disco F, Sa. M-F, lunch. 608 First Ave (between James and Cherry Sts). 682.1200

7 DOC MAYNARD'S PUBLIC HOUSE

★$ This restored pub is high on atmosphere (check out the magnificent carved bar), and on a sunny day, its outdoor tables invite you to take a seat and wet your whistle. The menu is pedestrian, running to sandwiches and bar munchies, but the pub does offer a lively repertoire of rock and R&B bands on Friday and Saturday nights. It shares a joint cover charge with nine other Pioneer Square places, creating a bargain for the fleet of foot. It's also the jumping-off point to tours of **Underground Seattle**, a long-buried maze of corridors that were once the sidewalks and first floors of Pioneer Square. ◆ American ◆ Cover F, Sa. Daily, 9AM-4PM, 8PM-2AM. 610 First Ave (between James and Cherry Sts). 682.4646, 888/608.6337. www.docmaynards.com

8 SECOND & JAMES PARKING GARAGE

In an earlier era, one of the city's first and finest hotels occupied this triangular block. The **Occidental Hotel** opened in the 1860s with 30 rooms. But in 1865, as the Civil War was ending, an entrepreneur named John Collins arrived in Seattle, unstrapped $3,000 in gold dust from his waist, and purchased a one-third interest in the ivory-hued hostelry. Collins would go on to write Seattle's first charter, serve on its first city council, develop coal fields on the east side of Lake Washington, and start the Seattle Gas Light Company, as well as serve a term as mayor. His hotel was no less ambitious. While Collins was sitting in the first session of the Washington Legislature (1883–1884), he had the hotel completely rebuilt in ostentatious style, complete with an elevator; Collins hyperbolically proclaimed the property the "leading hotel in the Northwest," and guest capacity was expanded to 400. But then came the Great Fire of 1889. Collins tried to save his hotel by buying up the surrounding clapboard structures and blowing them to smithereens, but the transactions couldn't be made fast enough, and the hotel went up with most of the rest of old Seattle. Collins went on to build a third incarnation of the hostelry, which he later renamed the **Seattle Hotel**; it stood on this site until the early 1960s. Today it's a parking garage shaped like a ship's prow. ◆ James St and Second Ave

9 AL BOCCALINO

★★★$$ Gone is Luigi DeNunzio, the former co-owner and effervescent front man who, for so long, made it a pleasure just to walk through this restaurant's door. (He walked out that same portal in 1992 to create **La Buca**, on Cherry Street.) The chefs continue, however, to use the robust recipes that DeNunzio brought over from his Italian hometown. Try creamy risotto or moist *vitello* (veal) or perfectly sautéed *gamberoni* (prawns). Intimate rooms and brick walls with stained glass make this the ideal setting for a romantic rendezvous. ♦ Italian ♦ M-F, lunch and dinner; Sa, Su, dinner. Reservations recommended. 1 Yesler Way (at Alaskan Way S). 622.7688

10 PIONEER SQUARE HOTEL

$$ The only hotel actually in Pioneer Square, this small, elegant property is a surprisingly good value. Built in 1914, the brick structure has been beautifully restored and offers 75 rooms and suites decorated with period reproductions. The location is convenient too—within walking distance of all the sights of Pioneer Square. There's no restaurant, but a continental breakfast is included in the rate. Room service may be ordered from **Al Boccalino**. ♦ 77 Yesler Way (between First and Western Aves S). 340.1234, 800/800.5514. & www.pioneersquare.com

11 YESLER BUILDING

During a flag-waving tour of the Northwest in 1891, President Benjamin Harrison speechified from the balcony of this small, granite-based structure, which stands where Henry Yesler once had a dance hall. Erected in 1890, this **Elmer Fisher** creation was damaged during the 1949 quake and later repaired. It now houses private offices. ♦ 95 Yesler Way (at First Ave S)

12 COW CHIP COOKIES

Only the very hungry or metabolically advantaged snackers will be able to tackle one of the gooey, mammoth munchies served at this chain outlet. Scientific researchers studying the effects of sugar overload are also welcome. ♦ M-Sa. 102 First Ave S (between Washington St and Yesler Way). 292.9808. & www.cowchipcookies.com

13 MERCHANT'S CAFE

★$ Originally, a wooden drugstore occupied this spot, and upstairs was a gallery displaying work by E.M. Sammis, Seattle's first resident photographer. Then, in the late 1890s, it became a tavern where Klondike gold miners swilled 5-cent beers or patronized the high-class brothel upstairs. More wild and uproarious tales and outright whoppers have been swapped in this joint than beer has been spilled on its wooden floors. The city's oldest tavern, it is also one of its most democratic: Down-and-outers occupy bar stools right next to newcomers, but somehow every discussion winds around to "the way Seattle used to be." There's often good live blues music in the evenings, and on summer days black-clad university students

gather at sidewalk tables to smoke, eat burgers and other pub grub, and generally chill out. With its wonderful decorative glass and sputtering neon sign out front, this long-time establishment is a genuine spot of Seattle history and style. ♦ American ♦ Daily, lunch and dinner. 109 Yesler Way (between Occidental and First Aves S). 624.1515

14 YESLER WAY

Arriving in Seattle in April 1852, pioneer Henry Yesler was enthusiastically embraced by the town's few inhabitants when he announced his desire to build a sawmill in what is now West Seattle. The enterprise was deemed too important to be located so far away, and Yesler was given this ribbon of property running from the waterfront up to his claim of 320 forested acres. First called **Mill Street**, the strip of land eventually assumed the nickname **Skid Road**, for the skids used to transport the logs from Yesler's property to the sawmill. Then, in the early 20th century, it acquired another nickname: **the Deadline**, or simply **the Line**. "Bawdy houses and low theaters were expected to stay south of the Line," explains Murray Morgan in his history *Skid Road*. But the nickname Skid Road predominated. After World War II, when businesses all but abandoned Pioneer Square, the whole quarter came to be known as Skid Road. So did other down-at-heel urban areas throughout the country, although it mutated into *skid row*. Today it's home to various commercial establishments. ♦ Between I-5 and Alaskan Way

14 INTERURBAN BUILDING (SMITH TOWER ANNEX)

The exceptional brick masonry, stone carving, and terra-cotta trim make this oft-overlooked office building another excellent example of Pioneer Square's Romanesque-Victorian style. Fenestration carefully orchestrated from floor to floor gives rhythm and a fine scale to the architecture. The corner entrance is ornamented with a lion's head. Not surprisingly, the architect who designed this 1890 building, **John Parkinson**, was a contemporary of **Elmer Fisher**. Until 1920, this was the **Interurban Railway Depot**. And during World War II, Boeing had its headquarters here. ♦ 102-08 Occidental Ave S (at Yesler Way)

15 DELMAR BUILDING (STATE HOTEL)

Pioneer Square preservationists managed to save some of the city's classic neon signs and painted billboards. One of the most endearing still hangs from the former **State Hotel**, an excellent brick-and-terra-cotta pile that went up in 1890 and was once a popular stop for gold-seekers coming back from Alaska and lumberjacks rolling into Seattle on a bender. "Rooms 75 Cents," it reads. Penny-pinchers will be disappointed to learn that the hotel went out of business in 1962. ♦ 114-16 First Ave S (between Washington St and Yesler Way)

Within the Delmar Building:

NEW ORLEANS CREOLE RESTAURANT

★$ Internationally recognized jazz bands are generally showcased here on weekends, but this restaurant-cum-honky-tonk is hardly quiet during the remainder of the week. Monday nights feature traditional swing from the house band, Tuesday is swing, jazz, and blues, and Wednesday is designated for contemporary jazz. Ragtime, zydeco, and R&B artists all make periodic showings. The food is good but not especially memorable. Gumbo and crawfish are distinctive picks, but the catfish can be oily. An adjoining dark-wood bar is the only place in town where mint juleps ("the South's revenge for losing the war," as one wit put it) are regularly featured on the drinks roster. ♦ Cajun/Creole ♦ Cover F, Sa. Daily, lunch and dinner. 622.2563. www.neworleanscreolerestaurant.com

16 MAYNARD BUILDING

One of the more sophisticated structures in the area, this building illustrates the wide range of possibilities within the Romanesque Revival style. Compared with the bombast of **Elmer Fisher**'s **Pioneer Building**, this structure, designed in **Richardson** Romanesque style by **Albert Wickersham** in 1892, is a whisper of refined detail. The exterior's handsome sandstone is from Bellingham Bay, to the north of Seattle, and the gray brick was shipped by rail from St. Louis. Window designs in the upper stories show an expressiveness similar to **Louis Sullivan**'s. In the lobby, the frame of an elevator shaft flaunts a brilliant bouquet of cast iron, and the staircase shows exquisite wood detailing. For years, the building was a banking center; since its 1975 rehabilitation, however, it has been occupied by many different businesses. ♦ 117 First Ave S (between Washington St and Yesler Way)

17 RIALTO MOVIE ART

When you come upon the brightly painted sandwich board, look to your side and venture down those colorful steps. You could spend hours looking into all the nooks and crannies filled with movie and pop culture memorabilia. Reminisce over a *Bewitched* Samantha doll or fondly remember your *Partridge Family* lunchbox as you spot them. This store has been in business since 1986, and it feels as though they've been hoarding all they can since then. ♦ W–Su, 11AM-4PM. 81 S Washington St (between First Ave and Alaskan Way). 622.5099

18 J&M CAFÉ & CARDROOM

★$ Pioneer Square's most popular saloon has the longest lines, and no amount of fast-talking will get you past the Gibraltar-size door sentries. The hamburgers and nachos are worth every cent you fork out for them, but the beer selection is skimpy, and the ambient noise level inside almost requires you to use sign language to communicate. The café prospers on its hip rep and the fact that it does have one of the snazziest wooden bars this side of San Francisco. The building and tavern date back to 1900, when it was a gambling and dancing hall. ♦ American ♦ Daily, lunch and dinner. 201 First Ave S (at Washington St). 292.0663

19 WASHINGTON COURT BUILDING

What historian Bill Speidel called "the most glorious and sumptuously furnished palace of sin in the city" once operated from this unpretentious, four-story brick Victorian. The madam was Lou Graham, a strong-willed businesswoman who took this site in about 1888, rebuilt it after the Great Fire, and for another dozen years entertained well-to-do gents and their scions. So successful was her business, writes historian Paul Dorpat, that "Graham and her ladies . . . helped keep the city solvent through the hard times of the mid-1890s." The building is now rented mostly by lawyers. ♦ 221 S Washington St (at Third Ave)

20 CENTRAL SALOON

What kind of place would tout itself as "Seattle's only second-class tavern"? It's got to have a sense of humor, and this joint—dating back to 1889 and looking not quite every year of its age—definitely does. It also has live music 7 nights a week starting at 9PM; mostly rock, blues, and R&B. ♦ Cover. Daily, 11AM-2AM. 207 First Ave S (between Main and Washington Sts). 622.0209. www.centralsaloon.com

21 FIREWORKS GALLERY

Unusual, outrageous, artistic, humorous, bizarre, beautiful—pick an adjective; they all work for the creations in this gallery. They have items in the categories of new, home, office, kids, Judaica, and ineffables. In the ineffables category, there are critters, potty humor, a bevy of Buddhas, and so on. Cosmic clocks, wildly creative jewelry, and artistic picture frames are among the fine and often one-of-a-kind items in this store. ♦ Daily. 210 First Ave S (between Main and Washington Sts). 800/505.8882, 682.9697. www.fireworksgallery.net. Also at numerous locations throughout the city

22 GRAND CENTRAL ARCADE

What a long, strange trip it's been for this site! In the 1870s arms magnate Phil Remington acquired it and several other nearby blocks on speculation. He was subsequently bought out by his entrepreneurial son-in-law, Watson C. Squire, who in 1879 opened the three-story **Squire's Opera House**—Seattle's first *real* theater—on the property. President Rutherford B. Hayes, visiting the West Coast in 1880 (which no sitting president had done before), was given a warm reception at the theater, but he had to shake some 2,000 hands before being released for the evening.

Two years later, Squire remodeled the top two floors into the **Brunswick Hotel**. Of course, the Great Fire of 1889 burned it down (an estimated $9 million loss), but Squire was one of the first business leaders in town to announce his intention to rebuild. In 1890, the new **Squire-Latimer Building** was completed on the same site. The facility supplied central heating and lighting to many other establishments in the district and reportedly made a profit doing so. Yet when the Alaska Gold Rush took off in 1897, Squire again decided that a hotel would be even more of a moneymaker; he called the new venture the **Grand Central**.

Meanwhile, Squire had become a politician. When Seattle's anti-Chinese riots broke out in 1886, it was Washington Territorial *Governor* Squire who declared martial law. After Washington earned statehood in 1889, Squire was one of its first US senators. The hotel was ultimately less successful. It declined with the rest of the old city and, during the Depression, became a flophouse. Only after 1970, when the Pioneer Square National Historic District was founded, did the hotel again receive attention. It was one of the square's first major restoration projects and now bustles with two levels of mall shops. ♦ Daily. 214 First Ave S (between Main and Washington Sts). 623.7417

Within the Grand Central Arcade:

DAVID ISHII BOOKSELLER

Would that everyone in the world could adopt the laid-back demeanor of proprietor David Ishii. At just about any time of the business day, it seems, you can walk by his antiquarian bookstore and see him slouched in a chair, reading his own dusty merchandise. Ishii's two passions are fly-fishing and baseball, so if you share his interests, you're likely to find just the obscure volume you're seeking in this small, cluttered shop. Books about other subjects are stocked capriciously. ♦ Daily. First floor. 622.4719

GRAND CENTRAL BAKING CO.

The bakery situated on one side of **Grand Central**'s chandelier-festooned main foyer is famous for its rustic breads and fragrant cinnamon rolls; it also supplies the bread that's enjoyed in many of Seattle's best restaurants. Across the way, an affiliated deli does some of its best work with hearty soups and well-endowed salads (although the sandwiches can be somewhat lackluster). Seating is available in the foyer. ♦ Daily. First floor. 622.3644. www.grandcentralbakery.com

MEGAN MARY OLANDER FLORIST

Fresh blooms abound, but it's even more interesting to see how many delicate and beautiful arrangements have been made of dried flowers. Lots of money could be spent here, but the sales staff is also very good at working within minuscule budgets. ♦ M-Sa. First floor. 623.6660

THE BLACKSMITH SHOP

An ideal anachronism for an area steeped in history, this establishment rings all day long with the pounding of metal on metal. Owner Mike Linn has been in this business for more than 20 years, designing and making custom furniture, candlesticks, hooks and brackets, and similar pieces. A sign out front, however, makes it clear that whatever else he does, this blacksmith "does not do horseshoes." Visitors can watch Linn work through a glass wall that separates his work area from the retail side of the shop. ♦ Tu-Sa. Basement. 623.4085

23 GREG KUCERA GALLERY

It's a small space, but this gallery has a big reputation. Exhibits range from the works of nationally known artists—photographs by William Wegman, paintings by Jane

---

Hammond or Terry Winters, prints by Motherwell or Frankenthaler, sculpture by Deborah Butterfield—to the work of such local artists as Darren Waterston, Roger Shimomura, and Mark Calderon. The exhibits are always thought-provoking, and sometimes controversial. ◆ Tu-Sa. 212 Third Ave S (between Main and Washington Sts). 624.0770. www.gregkucera.com

24 FOSTER/WHITE GALLERY

Established Northwest talents, such as Morris Graves and Mark Tobey, are represented here. Some Pilchuck glasswork is also on display. ◆ 220 Third Ave S (between Main and Washington Sts). 622.2833. Also at 1331 Fifth Ave (between University and Union Sts). 583.0100. www.fosterwhite.com

25 WATERFALL GARDEN

Filled with crashing waterfalls and benches perfect for lunch breaks, this corner plot is a soothing escape from the business world. Yet its very existence is rooted in business, specifically the United Parcel Service. UPS grew from a packaging and delivery enterprise that opened in a basement under this spot in 1907. The company's principal founder, James Emmett Casey, was a Nevada boy who delivered his first parcel on behalf of a Seattle department store in 1899. ◆ S Main St and Second Ave

26 COMEDY UNDERGROUND

Nationally known standup comics, as well as local Seinfeld- and Roseanne-wannabes, show up at this joint tucked below **Swannie's** bar and restaurant. Sunday and Monday are open-mic nights for amateurs, Tuesday is nonprofit comedy night, and the pros entertain Wednesday through Saturday. ◆ Cover. Shows Su-Th, 8PM; F, Sa, 8PM, 11PM. Reservations recommended. 222 S Main St (between Second Ave Extension and Second Ave). 628.0303. www.comedyunderground.com

27 BREAD OF LIFE MISSION

Victorian in style, with projecting bays but flat fenestrated detailing, this building stands on the site of Seattle's first store, founded in 1852 by pioneer David "Doc" Swinton Maynard. The building is now one of several help centers for elderly and disadvantaged residents of the Pioneer Square neighborhood. ◆ 301 First Ave S (at Main St). www.breadoflifemission.org

28 EARL D. LAYMAN STREET CLOCK

Time doesn't stand still, the saying goes, and neither has this fine pedestal timepiece. It used to decorate the sidewalk at the corner of Fourth Avenue and Pike Street, in front of **Young's Credit Jewelers**, but then it was moved in 1984 and dedicated to the city's first historic preservation officer (who held office between 1973 and 1982). ◆ S Main St and First Ave

28 ELLIOT BAY BOOK COMPANY

Opened in 1973 in what used to be the **Globe Hotel** (and before that was the site of Seattle's first hospital), this is the city's second-largest bookstore; its name is known to bibliophiles across the country. (**University Bookstore**, off the tourist-beaten path in the University District, is the largest.) The store enjoys a great deal of intellectual cachet, thanks in part to its very popular series of readings by well-known authors. It even publishes its own quarterly paper, *Book Notes*, full of staff reviews. History, current affairs, cooking, poetry, fiction, and mystery—all are well represented here. Travel books have their very own level; works for children occupy a separate and substantial chamber. Staffers are knowledgeable and wonderfully responsive. If there's anything to quibble about, it's shortages in the architectural history and nature-lit departments. Author readings and/or signings are held every evening. The readings are free, but you'll want to get there nice and early, because seats are limited. ◆ M-Sa, until 11PM; Su, until 6PM. 101 S Main St (at First Ave). 624.6600. www.elliottbaybook.com

Inside the Elliott Bay Book Company:

ELLIOTT BAY CAFE

★★$ Could anything be more civil than buying a new book and then trotting downstairs to read it in this brick-and-book-lined retreat? The food runs the gamut, from sandwiches to rather overpriced (or is it just undersized?) desserts; beer and wine are available, as are steaming cups of coffee, just the right accompaniment for a dive into the latest Crichton. ◆ American ◆ Daily, breakfast, lunch, and dinner. 682.6664

29 BOWIE & COMPANY, INC., BOOKSELLERS

The only way this shop could survive next door to **Elliott Bay Book Company** is by attracting a completely different audience; and that's what it does, with its shelves of first editions and cases of incunabula. Prices range from under $10 to several thousand dollars. Old maps and postcards are also available, as are mail-order catalogs. ◆ Daily. 314 First Ave S (between Jackson and Main Sts). 624.4100

30 Café Hué

★★$ Created by a Vietnamese husband-and-wife team, this café (the latter part of whose name is pronounced *way*) serves cuisine that reflects that country's colonial past. Vietnamese dishes display definite French touches, such as escargots seasoned with ginger. And the spring rolls and soups are not to be missed (try the filling crab soup). Chef Kieutuy Nguyen was trained in Saigon by a French baker, so it's no wonder that desserts here (including the wonderful Parisian éclairs, amandines, and traditional napoleons) are so plentiful and rich. Everything is presented with artistry. Service is fast and efficient, and there's no high-turnover mentality here. ◆ Vietnamese/French ◆ M-Sa, lunch and dinner; Su, lunch. 312 Second Ave S (between Jackson and Main Sts). 625.9833

31 Seattle Metropolitan Police Museum

Seattle Police veteran Jim Ritter established this tiny, nearly hidden museum in partnership with local law enforcement agencies. The exhibits explore the highs and lows of 140 years of Seattle Police history. In addition to historical displays, the museum offers an interactive children's area, a full-size replica of a jail cell, and a room available for community events. ◆ Tu-Sa, 11AM-4PM. Adults, $3; kids, $1.50. 317 Third Avenue S (between S Jackson and S Main Sts). 748.9991. www.members.aol.com/smpmuseum

32 Wood Shop Toys

Keepers of this shop like to play with their own toys, which is always a good sign. At least one salesperson has been seen delighting young customers with a dog hand puppet. In fact, it's hard to find an (always) friendly hand without a puppet on it. Shelves of any kind of animal you've heard of and other sturdy toys charm even adults. The goods come from around the world range from Russian nesting dolls to Indonesian hanging figures. ◆ Daily. 320 First Ave S (between Jackson and Main Sts). 624.1763

32 Bud's Jazz Records

Don't be afraid to open the metal gate and descend the narrow staircase from Jackson Street—there are a lot of ghosts down here (well, in a manner of speaking, anyway). Chicago émigré and jazz aficionado Bud Young has created what must be the largest selection of jazz and jazz-related CDs, tapes, and records this side of the Windy City—some 150,000 titles. Whole afternoons could be spent in the cluttered atmosphere, flipping through racks of works by John Lee Hooker, Dizzy Gillespie, Stanley Turrentine, Robert Johnson, Lightnin' Hopkins, and an eclectic lineup of other musicians who created the basis of contemporary jazz and blues. Music searches are accepted and jazz trivia questions are happily fielded by employees. ◆ Daily. 102 S Jackson St (between Occidental and First Aves). 628.0445

33 Occidental Avenue

At the turn of the 19th century, railcars clanked and wobbled down **Occidental Avenue**, bound for Tacoma. Exclusive parlor cars for spendthrift passengers willing to shell out 85 cents, rather than the regular fare of 60 cents, brought up the rear. First Avenue (then known as Front Street) was Seattle's oldest thoroughfare, but aged photographs show commercial Occidental Avenue being just as busy during Pioneer Square's post-fire renaissance. Both streets eventually fell on hard times, but after the district earned national landmark status, Occidental Avenue's revitalization was a top priority. Cobblestones were retained, two blocks were closed to cars, and plane trees were planted from Jackson Street to Yesler Way to lend the new mall, called **Occidental Park**, a leisurely Parisian-boulevard atmosphere. Today, food and art vendors gather here on weekends, and starry-eyed couples are often seen strolling the stones hand in hand. There's a handsome, old-fashioned shelter at the corner of Occidental and Main where you can hitch a ride on a streetcar running from the Waterfront up to the International District. And a shady plaza between Main and Washington Streets contains totem poles and a horse trough that can be converted to a drinking fountain simply by cupping your hand over it. Sadly, many tourists and even more Seattleites avoid this plaza, fearful of its ubiquitous panhandlers; and the street's northernmost block, between Washington Street and Yesler Way, has never quite overcome the shabbiness of pre-1970 Pioneer Square.

34 Klondike Gold Rush National Historical Park

On 17 July 1897, the steamship *Portland* arrived almost empty in Seattle. But after word spread that it was carrying 2 tons of gold found in the Klondike region of Canada, a full complement of passengers signed up for the return voyage—prospective gold miners who thought they could make a profit from the Northwest's biggest gold rush, and prospective gold diggers—women of questionable virtue who knew they could mine the pockets of any men who actually struck it rich. This gold rush couldn't have come at a more propitious time for Seattle. Like the rest of the nation, the town was still trying to overcome the hard times that followed the infamous Panic of 1893, so it took full advantage of its position as a principal embarkation point for prospectors (or sourdoughs, as they were called then). Hotels sprang up almost overnight to accommodate the thousands of men funneling through Puget Sound on their way north, and a number of mining schools also opened. Local outfitters, capitalizing on a Canadian law that required gold seekers to bring along a year's worth of goods, grew rich from the hundreds of dollars each would-be miner had to spend on the provisions. The chamber of commerce even hired Erastus Brainerd, a hucksterish former editor of the *Seattle Post-Intelligencer*, to cement commercial links between this city and the Klondike. Magazines such as *Frank Leslie's Popular Monthly* bought right into Brainerd's game. "The eyes of the civilized world today are turned upon two points—namely the gold fields of Alaska and the City of Seattle," the magazine wrote. A government assay office was established on Seattle's Ninth Avenue in 1898. During its first 4 years of business, its scales weighed more than $174 million in gold. The **Klondike Gold Rush National Historical Park** is a highfalutin name for what is really a colorful storefront museum (the *real* park is in Skagway, Alaska). Through old photographs, walking tours of Pioneer Square, and films, the museum does basically what Erastus Brainerd did so well a century ago: It proves that Seattle was indeed "the gateway to the Klondike." ♦ Free. Daily. 319 Second Ave S (at S Jackson St). 220.4240. www.nps.gov/klse

35 PACIFIC MARINE SCHWABACHER BUILDING

An honest-to-goodness cornerstone of Seattle's development, this was the city's original hardware store. The exquisite brick structure from 1905, by **Leonard L. Mendel** and English-born architect **Charles Bebb** (who later established a partnership with renowned Seattle designer **Carl Gould**), only punctuates the store's success and stature in the community. Notice especially the terra-cotta frieze around the front door. Details like this used to be commonplace, decoration to dress up relatively plain-faced commercial buildings. ♦ 401 First Ave S (at S Jackson St)

36 NORTHWEST GALLERY OF FINE WOODWORKING

For people who thrill to the feel of soft, smooth wood, this place is heaven on earth. The gallery showcases locally made woodcrafts in a simple, well-lighted, inviting space without hype or pressuring sales-people. Imagine how the elegant chairs, desks, dressers, and assorted boxes might look in your home—then steel yourself before looking at the price tags. ♦ Daily. 101 S Jackson St (at First Ave). 625.0542. www.nwfinewoodworking.com

37 EBBETS FIELD FLANNELS

This factory outlet is not what you would expect when you hear the words "flannel" and "outlet." Started in 1987 by Jerry Cohen, this company specializes in accurate reproduction vintage baseball jerseys and caps. Over the years, they have expanded into sports like football and hockey, but if you were ever itching for a 1949 Brooklyn Bushwicks or a 1940 Habana Leones ball cap, this is the place. ♦ M–F, 7AM–5PM. 404 Occidental Ave S (between S King and S Jackson Sts). www.ebbets.com

38 ZEITGEIST COFFEE & ART

A great break from the local coffee moguls, Zeitgeist offers a space of inspiration and industrialized/beat sensibilities. How can a space so grand feel so comfy? The walls are often covered with rotating art shows, and the music will have you asking the barista for the name of the CD. Sit in the big corner window to people watch, as you sip your beverage and enjoy a snack. ♦ M–F, 6AM–7PM; Sa, Su, 8AM–7PM. 171 S Jackson St (between Second Ave S and Occidental Ave S). 583.0497. www.zeitgeistcoffee.com

39 TERRAZZO CARMINE

★★★$$$ There's so much deliberate sophistication here you can cut it with a knife . . . if you aren't already using that particular utensil to slice off pieces of the marvelous venison medallions. The veal piccata with a reduction of capers and lemon has a large number of local fans, as has sweetbreads with prosciutto and peas, gently smothered in a wonderful light wine sauce. Floor-to-ceiling drapes block out the sun and prying eyes, but on pleasant summer days, the patio out back is available and refreshingly airy. ♦ Italian ♦ M-F, lunch and dinner; Sa, Su, dinner. Reservations recommended. 411 First Ave S (between King and Jackson Sts). 467.7797. www.ilterrazzocarmine.com

40 F.X. MCRORY'S STEAK, CHOP AND OYSTER HOUSE

★★$$ Talk about a split personality: On one hand, this spot wants to be a high-class establishment, serving grilled meats, succulent bivalves, and substantial dinner salads. On the other hand, it dearly loves being a party place, full of rambunctious college kids and young professionals who drop by after night games. The latter identity better matches the food, which, though tasty, is not awe-inspiring. And don't wait for a table in the dining room. Eat in the atmospheric high-ceilinged bar, with its full-mirrored wall of liquor bottles and its Leroy Neiman art. There's a good selection of Northwest microbrews and an outdoor seating area for bright afternoons. ♦ American ♦ Daily, lunch and dinner. 419 Occidental Ave S (at King St). 623.4800. www.fxmcrorys.com

41 KING STREET STATION

Still operating as a railroad depot, this neoclassical station was built in 1906 for James J. Hill's **Great Northern Railroad**. In 1910, 62 passenger trains pulled up on the tracks adjacent to this depot every day, disgorging 3,500 passengers. And recently, after decades of decline, rail travel is picking up again, with new **Amtrak** trains being scheduled and commuter light rail on the horizon. Minnesota architects **Reed and Stem**, who designed the building, created New York City's Grand Central Station in 1913. The brick exterior has hardly changed since day one, but the interior was modernized. Fortunately, a massive renovation, now under way, promises to return this station to its earlier splendor. Notice the clock tower; it was modeled after the Piazza San Marco campanile in Venice, Italy. ♦ 303 S Jackson St (between Second Ave Extension and Second Ave)

42 TRIANGLE HOTEL BUILDING

C. Alfred Breitung was born in Austria and trained as an architect in Europe before he arrived in Seattle in 1900. Like many other young designers, Breitung was attracted to Puget Sound's turn-of-the-19th-century prosperity and the reputations of such people as **Elmer Fisher**. His name is now familiar because of several large constructions in Seattle, including the **Good Shepherd Center** in Wallingford. This hotel was certainly one of his more unusual commissions. When it was completed in 1907, the building housed an eight-room hotel on the second floor, said to be the West Coast's smallest such hostelry. Today it is full of offices. ♦ 551 First Ave S (at Railroad Way)

43 SEAHAWKS STADIUM & EXHIBITION CENTER

The new home to the Seattle Seahawks opened in July 2002. An open-air stadium in Seattle? Yes, indeed, but over 70% of the 72,000 seats will be covered. A Paul Allen company built the publicly owned stadium and hopes to use it for major-league, World Cup, and collegiate soccer in addition to NFL and college-bowl football. The plans for the stadium include over $1 million worth of art from local and national artists and a public plaza and amphitheater to accommodate 5,000 people for public events. ♦ 800 Occidental Ave S. www.stadium.org

44 SAFECO FIELD

Many Seattleites doubted the wisdom, fiscal and otherwise, of demolishing the crumbling **Kingdome** in favor of separate, publicly funded baseball and football stadiums. But **Safeco Field**, home of the **Mariners**, is already much cherished by Seattleites; in combination with a popular winning team, the new stadium has produced record-breaking attendance. Safeco Field holds more than 47,000 seats, from which fans can view Puget Sound, the Olympic Mountains, and the downtown skyline; the retractable roof guarantees cover when it rains. While at a game or on one of the daily tours, visitors enjoy works of art such as a sculpture of 1,000 translucent bats, a bronze statue of a mitt, and the logos of each of the major-league teams made out of soldered soda cans. In addition, there are 2 restaurants, 62 food stands, a pub looking

---

Restaurants/Clubs: Red | Hotels: Purple | Shops: Orange | Outdoors/Parks: Green | Sights/Culture: Blue

into the bullpen, the Mariners' Team Store, and a children's playfield. ♦ 1250 First Avenue South. 206.622.HITS. www.seattlemariners.com

INTERNATIONAL DISTRICT

45 NIPPON KAN THEATER

A reminder of Seattle's historic Japantown, opened in 1909 as the **Astor Hotel** and later a performance hall for Kabuki theater, this redbrick building was renovated in 1981 and is now best known for its Japanese Performing Arts Series, which runs from October through May. ♦ Box office daily. 628 S Washington St (east of Sixth Ave). 224.0181

46 DANNY WOO INTERNATIONAL DISTRICT COMMUNITY GARDEN

On one side, facing south, these 1.5 acres provide an excellent panorama of the old south end, from Smith Tower past **Union Station**. On the opposite side, however, at the top of the slope, I-5 charges by in a smelly roar. Luckily, it's possible at most points in this garden to enjoy the former without enduring the latter. Established in 1975 and expanded 5 years later, the site contains about 120 individual growing areas, each managed by a resident of **Chinatown**. But passersby are invited to climb the garden's graveled paths, sniff the fragrance of the many fruit trees, and admire a giant stone lantern at the hilltop, given to Seattle by the Japanese city of Kobe during the 1976 US bicentennial. Benches are available for afternoon reading. A few transients hang about, but they're less obtrusive than in Pioneer Square. ♦ S Main St and Seventh Ave

47 MANEKI RESTAURANT

★★$$ It looks rather shabby outside, notched into the ground floor of what used to be the **Northern Pacific Hotel** (built for rail passengers in 1914 by Seattle architect **John Graham Sr.**, who later designed downtown's stately **Dexter Horton Building**), but this edifice boasts what may well be Seattle's first sushi bar. The selections are fresh and tasty. Call ahead for reservations, and for a large group, reserve a private tatami room. ♦ Japanese ♦ Tu-Su, dinner. 304 Sixth Ave S (between Jackson and Main Sts). 622.2631

48 CHAUS CHINESE RESTAURANT

★$ The standard Cantonese dishes are okay, but this place really earns its nickel with its seafood. Try the steamed oysters in garlic sauce or the Dungeness crab, and don't be shy about ordering Seattle's favorite bivalve, geoduck (but pronounce it "goo-ee duck" if you don't want to advertise your tourist status). It's not available everywhere you go, nor is it always as well prepared as it is here. ♦ Cantonese ♦ M-F, lunch and dinner; Sa, Su, dinner. 310 Fourth Ave S (between Jackson and Main Sts). 621.0006

49 UNION STATION

In 1911, Eastern railroad scion Edward Henry Harriman opened this barrel-vaulted stopping point for his **Union Pacific Railroad** above the tidelands of Jackson Street. The last passenger train pulled away from here 60 years later. Ever since, the depot (designed by San Francisco architect **D.J. Patterson**) has been used for antiques shows and a range of catered events. The **Great Hall** has been renovated to restore it, like its neighbor the **King Street Station**, to its original historical condition. The regional transit (light rail) offices are headquartered in this lovely station. Unfortunately, at present the building is not open to the general public. The southernmost entry to Seattle's downtown bus tunnel is located next door. ♦ S Jackson St and Fourth Ave

50 HOUSE OF HONG

★★$$ With tantalizing displays of barbecued duck, pork loin, and chicken hanging in the front window, it's hard not to be drawn into this large restaurant decorated in ornate chinoiserie. Lunch and dinner menus are extensive, and everything is good. House of Hong's pot stickers are the best in town. For dim sum (daily until 3PM) try crispy shrimp puffs, succulent barbecued pork, and their terrific *hum bao*. ♦ Chinese ♦ Daily, lunch and dinner. 409 Eighth Ave S (at S Jackson St). 622.7997. www.houseofhong.com

51 WING LUKE MUSEUM

Wing Luke was Seattle's first Chinese-American city council representative, elected in 1962, and the first Asian-American elected to public office in the continental United States. He died in a plane crash in 1965, but his interest in meshing the Asian-American experience into Northwest history lives on in this small cultural center, which is full of old photographs, antiques, and Chinese artifacts. ♦ Admission; free Th. Tu-Su; Th until 7PM. 407 Seventh Ave S (between King and Jackson Sts). 623.5124. www.wingluke.org

52 HING HAY PARK

With its trees and maybe a little rare sunshine, this small park is one of the nicest places to relax in the I.D. The colorful, traditional Chinese pavilion is a gift from the people of Taipei, Taiwan, and the huge dragon mural that decorated the back of the old **Bush Hotel** was designed by John Woo. ◆ S King St and Maynard Ave

53 PHNOM PENH NOODLE HOUSE

★$ Though this restaurant's menu boils down to seven variations of rice-noodle soup, each bowl has distinctive characteristics that appeal—especially to the local Cambodian population, some of whom probably will be waiting in line for a table along with you. ◆ Cambodian ◆ Daily, lunch and dinner. 660 S King St (between Seventh and Maynard Aves). 748.9825

54 ADAMS–FREEDMAN BUILDING

Elaborate façades, with cast-stone canopies at the entrances and an intriguing hierarchical arrangement of windows, make this one of the neighborhood's more elegant structures. Built in 1910 as a hotel, it's been rehabbed with apartments and commercial space. ◆ 515 Maynard Ave S (between Weller and King Sts)

Within the Adams–Freedman Building:

CHOY HERBS

A native of Hong Kong, Kai Chiu Choy has been in this country since 1974, dispensing herbal medicine in a state where such a specialty is neither generally recognized by physicians nor licensed. Choy's diagnostic methods include taking a patient's pulse, looking at his or her tongue, and carefully examining the face and eyes for signs of internal disorders. (The eyes, it seems, are more than windows on the soul; according to Choy, they reveal kidney or liver problems.) ◆ M-Sa, 2-5PM. 624.8341

55 HONEY COURT SEAFOOD RESTAURANT

★★$$ Octogenarian Luk Sing Hing used a term of endearment for her late husband as the name for this much-written-about restaurant. Surely he would have approved of the 160-plus menu items here. Cantonese and Hong Kong styles are integrated to produce inexpensive curries of chicken or beef with rice, as well as the favored plates of barbecued pork over vermicelli with slivered ginger. The service is not fantastic and the atmosphere leaves something to be desired, but the food is awesome. ◆ Chinese ◆ Daily, lunch and dinner. 516 Maynard Ave S (between Weller and King Sts). 292.8828

56 SEA GARDEN

★★★$$ In a town jam-packed with great seafood restaurants, this place stands out. The dining room itself is nothing fancy, but the subtly flavored, mildly spiced Cantonese food is wonderful, and the prices are reasonable. Top choices include crab with ginger and green onions, clams with black-bean sauce, and braised black cod. ◆ Chinese ◆ Daily, lunch and dinner. 509 Seventh Ave S (between Weller and King Sts). 623.2100. ♿

57 SHANGHAI GARDENS

★★★$$ Locals, who would otherwise go to Vancouver, British Columbia, can now get high-level Chinese cuisine right here. Mr. Su's menu is huge, ranging from the simply but wonderfully prepared chow mein to such exotica as fungus soup and hog maw. Anything made with pea vines or hand-shaved noodles must be tried. Simply put—everything is terrific. ◆ Chinese ◆ Daily. 524 Sixth Ave S (at Weller St). 625.1689. ♿

58 UWAJIMAYA

Here is a big, efficient, clean supermarket, where you can even buy live fish that's ready to be sliced and served as sushi. This store may be the largest Japanese emporium on the West Coast; it's certainly the hub of Seattle's Japanese community. Founded in 1928 by Fujimatsu Moriguchi, the business moved into this gigantic location in 2001, but is still owned by the Moriguchi family. It's a great cultural experience, even if you don't purchase any of the fresh vegetables, porcelain pieces, or appliances on sale. A branch of **Kinokuniya Books** (587.2477), Japan's second-largest book chain, is also within the store, as is **Isami at Uwajimaya**, serving a menu of pan-Asia offerings, from sashimi to lo mein, in a stylish space. ◆ Daily, until 10PM. 600 Fifth Ave S (between S Dearborn and S Weller Sts). 624.6248. Also in Bellevue. 15555 NE 24th St (at Bel.Red Rd), 425/747.9012. www.uwajimaya.com

59 INTERNATIONAL DISTRICT CHILDREN'S PARK

Ⓟ If your offspring need a break from touring the city, give them some time out at this quiet corner with its long curving slide and bronze dragon sculpture designed by Seattle artist George Tsutakawa. ◆ S Lane St and Seventh Ave

---

Restaurants/Clubs: Red | Hotels: Purple | Shops: Orange | Outdoors/Parks: Green | Sights/Culture: Blue

Downtown Seattle is a geographical ambiguity. Technically, the center of town is at **University Street** and **Fourth Avenue**. But the city's true heart is split between **Pike Place Market** and **Pioneer Square**. What lies between the two sites is a high-tide area bounded on the south by **Yesler Way**, on the north by **Virginia Street** and **Denny Way**, on the west by **Second Avenue**, and on the east by **Inter-state 5**. Seattle's financial, shopping, and entertainment operations moved here after the Great Fire of 1889 destroyed the original city center. Downtown's post-fire move north can be tracked through the age and character of its architecture. The area first developed along Second Avenue, dropping enough banks in its wake to create the closest thing Seattle had to a real financial district. A building boom during World War I brought many of the magnificent terra-cotta structures that still stand on Second and **Third Avenues** (for more about these buildings, see "Terra-cotta Town" on page 84). After development of the boxy, modern **Seattle-First National Bank Tower** (now called **1001 Fourth Avenue Plaza**) in 1969, a great fence of high-rises ascended north along Fourth Avenue, and the area declared itself Seattle's new financial district.

Walt Crowley, a local TV commentator and longtime civic activist, pointed out some years ago that Seattle "is really a confederacy of neighborhoods. People don't identify so much with downtown as they do with the specific area in which they live. In Portland, Oregon, downtown is everybody's neighborhood. But in Seattle, everybody's neighborhood is their downtown."

Seattleites venture downtown to work, of course. And they come here to shop for special presents and to show out-of-town visitors the sights. But efforts to keep the business core thriving 24 hours a day by transforming old hotels or commercial buildings into condominiums have seen only limited success. Explore the central Business District on a weekday, when street musicians perform, espresso carts steam, and people watching is at its best. Weekend activities gravitate to the Waterfront and Pioneer Square, with some spillover into **Westlake Center**, whereas "downtown" goes into siesta mode until Monday morning.

1 RE-BAR

This club certainly boasts the liveliest disc jockeys (don't miss Queen Lucky if she's in town). The crowd is mixed straight and gay. You'll hear lots of Diana Ross and industrial dance—it all depends on the DJ. Live bands and theater performances are scheduled irregularly; call ahead for information.
♦ Cover. Daily, until 2AM. 1114 Howell St (between Boren and Minor Aves). 233.9873

2 HOTEL MAX

$$ Built in 1926 by the Vance Lumber Company as a stopover for visiting lumber brokers and other dealmakers, this hotel was pretty seedy when the WestCoast chain decided to spend $7 million in 1990 on its restoration. The exterior was not meant to be breathtaking, but it does include fine terra-cotta detailing near street level and a nicely polished dark lobby. The 165 rooms tend to be smaller than normal but still pleasant, with the best views of the **Space Needle** from above the fifth floor on the north side. The **Yakima Grill** is also open. 441.4340 ♦ 620 Stewart St (at Seventh Ave). 728.6299. www.hotelmaxseattle.com

3 ICON GRILL

★★$$ No matter where you look in this restaurant, you see glass art, posters, knickknacks, bric-a-brac, and gewgaws. The menu is just as surprisingly varied—pasta, pizza, seafood entries, chicken, steak, you name it. And all of it is good. Comfort food taken to a very high level! ♦ American ♦ 441.6330. M-Sa, lunch and dinner. 1933 Fifth Ave (at Virginia St). www.icongrillseattle.com

4 WESTIN HOTEL

$$$$ You can't miss this place: It's the one with the round twin pillars of guest rooms that look like corncobs. Each of the 891 rooms features a balcony (though the best vistas are from above the 20th floor). Guests enjoy spacious and well-lighted accommodations but contrastingly plain furnishings. Some of the rooms are "guest offices," equipped with handy business features. In addition, local, 800-number, and credit-card calls are free. The convention facilities are plentiful and spread over several levels. There's a large pool, an exercise room, and a lounge. ♦ 1900 Fifth Ave (at Stewart St). 728.1000, 800/228.3000. &. www.westin.com

Within the Westin Hotel:

COLDWATER BAR & GRILL

★★$$ A contemporary dining experience. Chef Renatto Medranda has created a varied menu focusing on Northwest flavors and influences. Seafood of all kinds is the specialty. Try a Washington Apple Martini from the bar. ♦ Daily, breakfast, lunch, and dinner. 256.7697

5 TRENDWEST CAMLIN HOTEL

$$ Money to finish this brick-and-terra-cotta tower in 1926 was actually embezzled by a pair of ambitious bankers, Adolph Linden and Edmund Campbell, who were subsequently prosecuted and sent to Walla Walla State Penitentiary in eastern Washington. The architect was **Carl J. Linde** of Portland, Oregon, a onetime brewery designer from Wisconsin who had worked under noted Oregon architect **A.E. Doyle**. Most of Linde's efforts were concentrated on the hotel's Ninth Avenue façade. The basic style was Gothic, complete with lions' heads and other decorative gargoyles. Interestingly, the 11-story structure is only *half* a hotel. A second, 14-story establishment, to have been built just north of the existing hotel (where a parking lot now stands), never made it past the drawing board. This hotel was isolated to the northeast of downtown when it opened in 1926, but it has since been engulfed by the expanding city. A $2 million restoration in 1985 brought in double-paned windows, so that noise (even from the **Paramount Theater** down the street) isn't a problem in the 136 large guest rooms, each of which is decorated in various shades of beige, with exposed pipe fixtures in the bathrooms and overstuffed chairs. Just try to avoid the gloomier cabanas. ♦ 1619 Ninth Ave (between Pine St and Olive Way). 682.0100, 800/426.0670

6 TIMES SQUARE BUILDING

It was no coincidence that this flatiron structure and the irregular intersection to its immediate west came to be known as Times Square. First off, the building housed the *Seattle Times* newspaper between 1916 and 1931. Second, the intersection bears a strong resemblance to Manhattan's Times Square. Constructed of terra-cotta and granite, with fine Beaux Arts detailing (note the elegant eagles decorating the roofline), the structure was one of the earliest downtown works by architect **Carl Gould**. A graduate of the Ecole des Beaux Arts in Paris who apprenticed with the famous New York City firm of **McKim, Mead & White** before heading west for his health, the architect would eventually give Seattle a series of landmarks, including the original **Seattle Art Museum** on Capitol Hill and the **Suzzallo Library** at the **University of Washington**. ♦ Olive Way and Stewart St

7 PACIFIC PLACE

Adjacent to **Nordstrom** (see page 34) and connected to it by a sky-bridge is this block-square, self-proclaimed "upscale shopping, dining, and entertainment destination complex"—five floors of retailers, including **Tiffany & Co**, **Cartier**, **Ann Taylor**, and **Williams-Sonoma**, plus several restaurants and the predictable gigantic multiscreen movie complex. There's parking underneath for 1,200 cars. The complex is just part of a huge redevelopment and revitalization of the downtown area north and northwest of the **Convention Center**. ♦ Bounded by Seventh and Sixth Aves and by Pine St and Olive Way. www.pacificplaceseattle.com

Within Pacific Place:

EDDIE BAUER, INC.

Eddie Bauer was born to Russian immigrant parents on Orcas Island, north of Seattle, in 1900. Always enchanted with fishing and hunting, he seemed to move naturally into a sporting-goods sales career and was wildly successful at it. He inevitably opened his own store in Seattle in 1922, attracting customers with his demanding policies about quality and his interest in improving what was already on the market. It was the latter that led him to invent the down jacket. While fishing on Washington's Olympic Peninsula in 1934, Bauer almost froze to death because he didn't bring along an appropriate jacket. He started thinking about how to make both warmer and lighter outerwear and remembered a tale his uncle had told about surviving the Russo-Japanese War of 1904 by wearing goose-down quilted undergarments. Bauer took some of the down he was already importing from China for use in fly ties and shuttlecocks, quilted a few jackets for himself, and when friends declared them a hit, patented both the jackets and their manufacturing process. There are now about 200 stores across the country that bear his name.

Although it's now owned by Spiegel Inc., the company still sells the well-known goose-down fashions, as well as sleeping bags, backpacking equipment, knives, sunglasses, and some of the coziest wool socks available anywhere. The store is known for offering hefty price reductions on the Bauer line. ♦ Daily; F, until 8PM. 622.2766. ఈ. www.eddiebauer.com

8 PARAMOUNT HOTEL

$$ Another member of the WestCoast chain, this hotel is just down the block from its namesake theater and close to the **Washington State Convention & Trade Center** and midtown shopping (**Westlake Center**, **Pacific Place**, and **City Center** are all within a few blocks). Its modest size (146 guest rooms) and "European château" ambience will appeal to those weary of giant, anonymous megahotels. Standard guest rooms are nicely appointed, though rather small. ♦ 724 Pine St (at Eighth Ave). 292.9500, 800/663.1144. ఈ. www.paramounthotelseattle.com

Within the Paramount Hotel:

DRAGONFISH ASIAN CAFE

★★★$$ This highly acclaimed pan-Asian bistro is decorated with metal sculpture, a 20-foot ceramic undersea mural, brightly colored origami-like mobiles, *pachinko* machines, a koi tank—and a menu with Thai, Korean, Chinese, Japanese, Vietnamese, and Indonesian accents. The place is lively, noisy, and flashy, and so is the food, much of it following a local trend toward numerous small dishes to be shared. With more than half the dishes costing $6 or less, executive chef Michael Weeks's wares (he's a veteran of **McCormick & Schmick's**) can be a reasonable proposition—though you may well be tempted to keep ordering more and more. ♦ Pan-Asian ♦ Daily, breakfast, lunch, and dinner. 467.7777. ఈ

9 PARAMOUNT THEATER

This theater and its smaller sister space in Portland, Oregon, were modeled after the Paramount in New York City. Again, **B. Marcus Priteca** was the architect, but here, 13 years after construction of the **Coliseum Theater** (now **Banana Republic**), he played a more reserved hand. Its monumental proportions—from the high-rise brick façade to the tall arched windows out front and

roofline decorations—were all meant to emphasize the theatricality and fantasy of screen and stage drama. Where vaudeville performers used to tread the boards, the spotlights now fall mostly on rock musicians. A group of deep-pocketed investors, headed by former Microsoft marketing exec and arts-management consultant Ida Cole, purchased the theater in early 1993, renovated and added to the structure, and replaced low-income housing units in the upper stories with commercial spaces. Free tours of this beautiful theater are offered the first Saturday of the month at 10AM, beginning in front of the main entrance. ♦ Box office opens 1 hour prior to show time. No credit cards. 901 Pine St (at Ninth Ave). 682.1414; Ticketmaster, 628.0888. www.theparamount.com

10 MOORE THEATRE

For many years, pioneer Arthur Denny had reserved 6 acres here in hopes that Seattle might one day capture the Washington state capitol building (which was eventually built in Olympia). But in 1888, he decided to fill the site with a first-class hotel—something the city desperately needed after the Great Fire of 1889. The national depression of 1893 stalled construction of this multitowered edifice, and it was finally completed a decade later by Seattle developer James A. Moore. (President Teddy Roosevelt was the first guest at the new hotel when it opened in 1903.) Almost immediately, Moore had bigger dreams for this area. He wanted to erect the most artistic and beautiful theater in the West. Sure enough, an adjoining playhouse (designed by prolific Seattle architect **E.W. Houghton**) went up in 1908. But in the meantime the hotel was razed to make possible the re-grading of Denny Hill. James Moore fell on hard times not many years later, and so did his theater. Its vaguely Egyptian Revival–style interior is still intact, but the likes of Marie Dressler and John Barrymore no longer perform here. Now the hall is used mostly for concerts. ♦ Box office hours vary; call ahead. 1932 Second Ave (at Virginia St). www.themoore.com

11 MAYFLOWER PARK HOTEL

$$ The 171 rooms here are furnished in antiques, but they're sometimes small—that's the tradeoff for accommodations right in the heart of the downtown shopping district. Just be sure to ask for a room high up in this handsome 1927 tower, where you'll see a slice of the city past surrounding building walls. An antiques-filled lobby provides access to a commodious, high-ceilinged bar

and to the neighboring **Westlake Center**.
♦ 405 Olive Way (at Fourth Ave). 623.8700, 800/426.5100. www.mayflowerpark.com

Within the Mayflower Park Hotel:

ANDALUCA

★★★$$ Glowing rosewood booths, fresh flowers, and deeply jewel-toned walls create a romantic setting for lusty, flavorful dishes. Chef Wayne Johnson combines Northwest ingredients with flavors of the Mediterranean: crab tower (with avocado, palm hearts, and gazpacho salsa), smoked lamb loin, *zarzuela* (shellfish stew), *cabrales*-crusted beef tenderloin (with Spanish blue cheese and bread crumbs). Desserts are as lovely as they are tasty. ♦ Northwestern/ Mediterranean ♦ M-F, breakfast, lunch, and dinner; Sa, Su, breakfast and dinner. 382.6999. ₲. www.andaluca.com

12 WESTLAKE CENTER

Downtown's $250 million version of a suburban shopping mall offers little in the way of a downtown park—a component that its creators, the Maryland-based **Rouse Company**, promised their center would go out of its way to provide. Overall, the glitzy mall feels little connected to the architectural and social character of Seattle's nexus. And it seems aggressively unconnected to the town's history, even though it stands at what has long been an important hub, which, until 1931, held a glorious flatiron building called the Hotel Plaza. Yet, because Seattle has no real civic center, this complex has succeeded in becoming a focus of activity. The third floor's carnival of food counters is awash during weekday lunchtimes with workers from the surrounding office hives. Among the businesses in Westlake Center are **Jessica McClintock Boutique**, **Godiva Chocolatier**, **Fireworks Gallery**, and **Made in Washington**. A rather stark public plaza out front stays lively with T-shirt vendors, street musicians, hellfire-and-brimstone preachers, and a fountain that you can actually walk through. And it doesn't hurt business any that the monorail from **Seattle Center** has its endpoint here, or that one of the downtown transit tunnel's five stations sits beneath the center.
♦ Fourth Ave and Pine St. ₲. www.westlakecenter.com

Within Westlake Center:

MILLSTREAM

This place takes it to the max in promoting the natural attributes of Seattle and the Pacific Northwest: There are walls of ferry and whale pictures, salmon sculptures, and a trickling fountain just to establish the proper peaceful mood. Even jaded natives have been known to fall under the shop's spell. ♦ Daily. 233.9719. www.millstreamseattle.com

MONORAIL

This is the beginning (or end) of the 1.2-mile overhead journey to **Seattle Center**. Trains depart every 15 minutes, and the 90-second trip is over before you know it. Still, how many other cities have monorails?
♦ Free. ♦ Daily. Third floor. 441.6038. ₲. www.seattlemonorail.com

13 NORDSTROM

The department-store chain may have spread nationwide, but Seattleites still consider this locally owned store very much theirs and the Nordy's label a symbol of cachet. The store is famous for its generous customer-service policy; this is one place where returns are no big deal. Salespeople are attentive without being cloying, and they're knowledgeable about current fashion trends. A personal-shopper service accommodates people who haven't the time or the inclination to browse through all the racks themselves. Valet parking is also available. In 1998, **Nordstrom** moved into this $100 million renovation of the elegant 1919 building that once housed the **Frederick & Nelson** department store (see "Terra-cotta Town" on page 84). This Seattle landmark and flagship of the Nordstrom line contains a 380,000-square-foot shop, with the company's corporate headquarters above it. Several annual sales are much anticipated: the store's anniversary (July), and the two semiannual sales for women (June and November) and men (June and January). ♦ Daily. 500 Pine St (at Fifth Ave). 628.2111. www.nordstrom.com

14 THE ROOSEVELT: A COAST HOTEL

$$ When this 20-floor hotel (then the tallest in town) originally threw open its doors in 1930, the *Seattle Daily Times* could hardly contain its enthusiasm. The building's entryway received particular attention: "The ornately furnished lobby was virtually a tower of flowers as guests and well-wishers trooped into it last evening. Visitors were given the freedom of the house and were enabled to inspect the lounge, decorated in French Moderne style and furnished in highly polished ebony and hardwood, and saunter up a winding staircase past the orchestra balcony to the mezzanine." Unfortunately, that lobby—with its strip skylight and several levels—was lost during a 1987 renovation. The present low-ceilinged space, appointed pleasantly with light gray décor and glass blocks, was at one time the **Rough Rider Lounge**, sporting a disco dance floor where a baby grand

The Best

Jean Godden

Seattle City Councilmember

Seattle owes its existence to **Elliott Bay**, a spectacular deepwater harbor. It's the natural wonder that first drew settlers to its shores, and it's one of the best places to begin exploring the Northwest's largest city. You can start at the **Seattle Art Museum**'s recently opened **Sculpture Garden**, a fabulous outdoor attraction on the waterfront's north end.

From the Sculpture Garden, walk back along the waterfront. You'll see freighters, cruise ships, and container vessels loaded with cargo from afar. You can visit the world-famous **Seattle Aquarium**, browse through import shops, take a waterfront tour on one of the Argosy sightseeing ships, and, when hunger strikes, dine on fish and chips at a sidewalk café.

From the waterfront, take the **Hillclimb**, a stairway across from the Aquarium, and head up the hill to the **Pike Place Public Market**. Founded in 1907, the colorful farmers' market hosts truck farmers, greengrocers, artisans, street musicians, specialty shops, and restaurants. Fishmongers toss king salmon to one another, warning visitors to "beware of flying fish."

Three blocks east of the Market lies **Westlake Park**, an urban triangle where civic events and rallies are staged. Don't miss **Macy's**, the region's largest department store, or **Nordstrom**, the apparel chain's flagship store. Save time to explore **Pacific Place** and

Westlake Center; both complexes are home to a splashy array of shops.

While downtown, you'll want to pay a visit to the newly reopened **Seattle Art Museum (SAM)**. A giant 48-foot statue titled *Hammering Man* guards the building, pounding away two and a half times a minute. Permanent exhibitions at SAM include North Coast Indian art and priceless works from African and Pacific Rim countries.

Another must-see is **Pioneer Square**, Seattle's first neighborhood. Many of its handsome masonry buildings date from just after 1889's Great Seattle Fire; others were built during the boom times of the Alaskan Gold Rush. To learn something of the city's history, pay a visit to the National Park Service's **Klondike Museum** or take the kitschy-but-fun **Underground Tour**, which tells the story of how Seattle raised its low-lying streets to avoid flooding at high tide.

Make sure to include the **Hiram Chittenden Locks**, often called the **Ballard Locks**. Second in size only to the Panama Canal, the Locks serve as a marine elevator, boosting vessels from the salt water of Shilshole Bay to the fresh water of the Lake Washington Ship Canal. Be sure to stroll across the Locks for a view of salmon swimming past a glass-sided fish ladder.

Finally, go to dinner at a restaurant on nearby **Shilshole Bay**, **Ray's Boathouse** or **Anthony's Homeport**. You can dine on seafood, sip the Northwest's prize-winning wines, and watch tiny tugs sail past pulling giant barges, while the sun sinks behind the snow-capped **Olympic Mountains**. Truly it doesn't get any better than this.

piano now rests. Designed by architect **John Graham Sr.**, the hotel used to be a warren of 234 small rooms. The floors have been divided to allow for only 151 larger accommodations, each decorated with subtle and comfortable furnishings. Superior-class rooms also boast Jacuzzis. The 19th floor (with a skylight enclosing its outdoor landing) is a town house for one of the building's owners. The top level has a single deluxe guest room, with what is perhaps the structure's best view of the city. ♦ 1531 Seventh Ave (at Pine St). 621.1200, 800/716.6199. ♦. www.coasthotels.com

Within The Roosevelt:

Von's Grand City Cafe

★★$ Occupying the hotel's old main lobby space, this clubby restaurant serves an assortment of sandwiches, fish, and steaks. But it's best known for dispensing quality martinis—and lots of them. ♦ American

♦ Daily, breakfast, lunch, and dinner. 619 Pine St. 621.8867. ♦

15 The Elliott Grand Hyatt Seattle

$$$$ The main entrance of the **Elliott**, which opened in the summer of 2001, is graced by Willem de Kooning's original bronze sculpture *The Reclining Figure*, setting the tone of elegant luxury for this hotel (425 rooms, including 113 suites). All rooms feature original art, mahogany furnishings, onyx lighting fixtures, and cherry wood shoji doors with opaque glass panels. State-of-the-art technology and a fully equipped health club are also available to guests. The fact that the Elliott is immediately adjacent to the **Washington State Convention & Trade Center** is a plus, as is the 950-space parking garage. ♦ 721 Pine St (between Eighth and Seventh Aves). 774.1234. www.seattlegrand.hyatt.com

Restaurants/Clubs: Red | Hotels: Purple | Shops: Orange | Outdoors/Parks: Green | Sights/Culture: Blue

Within the Elliott Grand Hyatt Seattle:

RUTH'S CHRIS STEAKHOUSE

★★★$$$$ This company has been renowned for over 40 years for its excellent steaks, expertly prepared seafood, and New Orleans–inspired appetizers. Bar snacks, though small, are tasty and affordable; the fare is expensive, but you get what you pay for. 624.8524. www.ruthschrisnw.com

16 MACY'S

Seattle now has its own Macy's, having taken over the building that once housed the venerable Bon Marché. Upholding the tradition of department stores, Macy's wants to be everything to everybody. Clothes, cosmetics, china, shoe repair, furniture, candy, liquor—they're all here. Merchandise is well selected and stocked, and prices are often more moderate than at similar stores in town. ◆ Daily. Third Ave (at Pine St). 344.2121. www.macys.com

17 METRO BUS TUNNEL

It's not exactly the London Underground, but Seattle's 1.3-mile transit tube isn't a gloomy bat cave, either. Buses passing through here are converted temporarily from diesel to electric power. On a cold or rainy day, shoppers appreciate the interior walkways (just above the bus platform level) that connect **Westlake Center** with **Nordstrom** and **Macy's**. About $3 million was spent by **Metro** on public art for the five bus stations. At the **Westlake stop**, check out the multicolored terra-cotta tiles that carry leaf and vine patterns. (The **Pioneer Square Station** features large clocks made from masonry remnants and a mural that captures aspects of Seattle history in tile. Origami designs spark up the **International District** bus terminal.) ◆ Ticket window: M-F, 5AM-11PM; Sa, 10AM-6PM. Pine St (between Fourth and Third Aves). 553.3000. www.transit.metrokc.gov

The first concert on the Internet was performed on 10 November 1994 by a Seattle-based rock band called Sky Cries Mary.

Bertha Landes, elected mayor of Seattle in 1913, was the first woman in the US to hold that office.

The Big Snow of 1880 marked the worst winter this city ever experienced. Snow began to fall on 5 January and within a week was heaped in 6-foot-high drifts. The *Seattle Post-Intelligencer* confessed that "we shall have to admit hereafter that snow does occasionally fall in this country." The 64-inch snow total from that week brought the city (including vital railroad lines) to a complete standstill.

18 MERIDIAN WEST AND MERIDIAN EAST

Yet another megamall that occupies almost an entire square block. Some Seattleites think it's a sign that the city has come of age, whereas others see it as an ostentatious harbinger of Seattle's imminent decline. The complex, composed of the 65,000-square-foot **Meridian West** and the 96,000-square-foot **Meridian East** across the way, boasts mostly chain shops and restaurants, including **Niketown** (447.6453), **The Original Levi's Store** (467.5152), **Sega Gameworks** (featuring high-tech, interactive, and virtual reality entertainment), and **Cineplex Odeon**, with 16 screens and seating for 3,200 people. ◆ Daily. Sixth Ave (between Pike and Pine Sts)

Washington State Convention & Trade Center

19 WASHINGTON STATE CONVENTION & TRADE CENTER

With its recent expansion, this huge complex, which covers several square blocks, has 102,000 square feet of dedicated meeting and exhibition space. The center includes four ballrooms, two conference lobbies, and a spectacular four-story, glass-enclosed atrium entrance at the corner of Seventh and Pike. A bridge within a block-long arched glass canopy connects new and existing exhibition halls. This arch, which is four stories above Pike Street between Seventh and Eighth Avenues, is, according to some, a stunning downtown landmark, and, according to others, a monstrous, view-blocking intrusion. ◆ 447.5000. www.wsctc.com

There's also a **Visitors' Center** providing all the usual tourist information. ◆ M-F. 800 Convention Pl (at Eighth Ave). 461.5840

20 KEY BANK TOWER (OLYMPIC TOWER)

This 1929 Art Deco specimen features a polygonal crown and restored terra-cotta facing. It was the creation of local architect **Henry Bittman**. ◆ 217 Pine St (at Third Ave)

21 SHARPER IMAGE

Across from the **Westlake Center** in the **Century Square Building** is a browser's delight and a gadgeteer's dream. This catalog-come-to-life is full of high-tech sound equipment, full-body massage tables, adult toys, and fancy watches. ◆ Daily. 1501 Fourth Ave (at Pike St). 343.9125. www.sharperimage.com

22 BANANA REPUBLIC

This used to be the **Coliseum Theater**, an Italian Renaissance relic. The first theater in the world designed specifically to show motion pictures, it was commissioned by Joe Gottstein, an ambitious 23-year-old Seattle native who believed people would flock to the movies if they could enjoy them amidst some class and comfort. So in 1916, **B. Marcus Priteca**, personal architect to vaudeville magnate Alexander Pantages, took on the assignment of creating an opulent film palace. The resulting 1,700-seat theater, with its terra-cotta façade detailed with grotesque masks, festoons of fruit, and bullocks' heads, was a huge success. But later in its life, the venue fell on hard times, languishing in virtual disuse. In 1994, the theater was purchased and faithfully renovated by **Banana Republic**, and it has reopened as the flagship store of this international chain. The shop occupies the entire lower level, including the former lobby, and guided tours of the restored theater upstairs are given on request. Ask the store manager, if you're interested in taking one. ◆ Daily. 1506 Fifth Ave (between Pike and Pine Sts). 622.2303. www.bananarepublic.com

23 SEATTLE SHERATON HOTEL AND TOWERS

$$$ This modern hotel is a convenient retreat for businesspeople attending events at the **Washington State Convention & Trade Center**, just up Pike Street from here. An expansive lobby is decorated with Dale Chihuly glass art. Meeting rooms are plentiful. Most of the 838 guest rooms are cramped by comparison, lacking all but the most essential components. Four VIP floors (31-34) offer more elaborate rooms and a separate concierge. A health club and pool on the 35th floor are open to all guests. **Pike Street Cafe**, a casual, well-lighted restaurant off the lobby, offers a sumptuous buffet luncheon. Parking is available for a fee. ◆ 1400 Sixth Ave (at Union St). 621.9000, 800/325.3535. &. www.sheraton.com

24 KREIELSHEIMER PLACE/ EAGLES AUDITORIUM

When completed in 1925, architect **Henry Bittman**'s Renaissance Revival–style home for the Fraternal Order of Eagles was among the country's most distinguished fraternal buildings. The block, a fine example of Seattle's ornate terra-cotta façades, is the home of **A Contemporary Theatre**. This Equity theater company puts on a wide variety of modern and contemporary works. Their annual holiday performances of *A Christmas Carol* are popular. The season runs May through December. ◆ Box office: daily, noon to 6PM. 700 Union St (at Seventh Ave). 292.7676. www.acttheatre.org

25 US BANK CENTRE

Although it's a hefty hunk of California glitz and post-Postmodernist doodads staked into downtown Seattle, this building (formerly the **Pacific First Centre**) draws Seattleites with its nationally known retailers in **City Center**. The smaller shops here are also worth a browse. ◆ 1420 Fifth Ave (between Union and Pike Sts). &

Within the US Bank Centre:

ANN TAYLOR

In the same way that **Brooks Brothers** purveys timeless fashions for men, so this fine chain courts the women's trade. It's conservative and expensive but reliable. ◆ Daily. First floor. 623.4818. &

DESIGN CONCERN

With high-design office supplies and tableware, Japanese clocks, and a broad selection of obscure gadgets, this is a great place to browse and shop for gifts. ◆ Daily. Second floor. 623.4444. &

PALOMINO

★★★$$ Leave your jeans and T-shirts in the closet. Like owner Rich Komen's other restaurants (**Cutter's Bayhouse** in **Pike Place Market** and **Palisade** in Magnolia), this gleaming, highly stylized spot draws a beautiful crowd of designer-suited gents and women in fancy dresses. Dale Chihuly glassworks sparkle under the directional lights. The kitchen and open oven area produce excellent king salmon, garlic chicken, and pork loin. Pizzas are thin-crusted and, alas, also thinly covered. The bar fills up quickly with an after-work crowd, but the people watching is even better here than in the dining area. There's a decent selection of microbrews on tap; have the knowledgeable bartenders advise you on which new varieties to try. Be warned: Service can be very poor, and don't sit near the door. ◆ Mediterranean ◆ M-Sa, lunch; daily, dinner. Reservations recommended. Third floor. 623.1300. ᕘ. www.palomino.com

26 FOURTH AND PIKE BUILDING

Designed by the architectural firm of **Lawton and Moldenhour**, this 1926 skyscraper of cream-colored terra-cotta was one of the last commercial high-rises built before the Great Depression brought downtown construction to a screeching halt. The impressive lobby here somehow survived relatively intact while other downtown buildings were having theirs regrettably "modernized." ◆ 1424 Fourth Ave (between Union and Pike Sts)

Within the Fourth and Pike Building:

DASHASA STUDIO

Jeweler Daniel Shames has a fondness for intensely colored opaque stones, and he crafts them into gorgeous pendants and rings. Pieces are hand-assembled to order; the prices are high (starting from $500), but considering the labor involved, not unreasonably so. ◆ Daily. Appointment recommended. Suite 807. 623.0519. www.dashasa.com

SEATTLE PEN

This intimate shop sells only writing instruments—new models and exquisitely kept older specimens. Repairs and engravings are available too. ◆ M-F; Sa, until 3PM. Suite 527. 682.2640

27 BUTCH BLUM

Sophisticated, high-fashion men's clothing by classically influenced yet contemporary European and American designers (such as Donna Karan, Ermenegildo Zegna, and Calvin Klein) is the specialty of this upscale boutique. The service is warm, personal, and attentive without being intrusive. ◆ Daily. 1408 Fifth Ave (between Union and Pike Sts). 622.5760

28 1411 FOURTH AVENUE BUILDING

Textural details spun from Celtic motifs and Art Deco flourishes enliven the façade and lobby of this **Robert C. Reamer** office tower that opened in 1929. The stone facing represented a move away from the brick and terra-cotta that were so common to other structures in the neighborhood. Note the elegant entrance sign created by Lloyd Lovegren (who went on during the 1940s to design the Lacey V. Murrow Bridge across Lake Washington). ◆ Between Union and Pike Sts. ᕘ

29 TULLY'S

★$ Far more than your average coffeehouse, this elegant and spacious establishment boasts a grand piano playing softly and art on display from the well-known Pratt Fine Arts Center. The flagship of the *other* local name in coffee, Tully's corporate statement identifies a commitment to ambience and friendliness in an upscale environment; they've certainly succeeded here. Their significant charity and community involvement is well known to Seattleites. ◆ Coffeehouse ◆ Daily, until 7PM. 1401 Fourth Ave (at Union St). 625.0600, 800/96-TULLY. ᕘ. Also at numerous locations throughout the city

30 BROOKS BROTHERS

"BB" has made some changes in the last few years, but this store (the clothier's only outpost north of San Francisco) doesn't seem to have lost a smidgen of its traditional demeanor. A wealth of inventory, including some elegant women's wear, is presented in a refined manner; the salespeople are helpful but not intrusive; and those overseeing the men's suits department might have learned their manners from valets to the Duke of Windsor. It's worth waiting until June and right after Christmas for the annual sales. ◆ Daily. 1330 Fifth Ave (between University and Union Sts). 624.4400. www.brooksbrothers.com

30 FOX'S GEM SHOP

This is a sophisticated and refined environment that's all glittering stones, a finely tailored clientele, and steep prices. There's lots of sterling silver jewelry and a boutique selection of Tiffany products. ◆ M-Sa. 1341 Fifth Ave (at Union St). 623.2528. www.foxesgemshop.com

31 SKINNER BUILDING

What does this block-long, tile-roofed Mediterranean palazzo from 1926 have to do with the monumental Old Faithful Inn in Yellowstone National Park and the Canyon Hotel at the Grand Canyon? They were all designed by **Robert C. Reamer**. Born in Ohio in 1873, Reamer started with an architectural firm in Detroit and moved from there to Cleveland, Chicago, San Diego, and Wyoming. He came to Seattle during World War I to become chief architect for the Metropolitan Building Company. Considered at one time to be a supreme practitioner of his art—a Richardsonian in his architectural aesthetics and a romantic by inclination—Reamer has all but disappeared from Seattle history books. Yet his buildings (this structure, the **Meany Tower Hotel** in the University District, the **Seattle Times Building** on John Street, and the **1411 Fourth Avenue Building** downtown) are some of the most intriguing around. ◆ 1326 Fifth Ave (between University and Union Sts)

Within the Skinner Building:

FIFTH AVENUE THEATER

Behind the Skinner's Wilkeson sandstone exterior is Seattle's loveliest performance space, said to be patterned after the imperial throne room in Beijing's Forbidden City. Gustav Liljestrom, a Norwegian artist trained in China, was responsible for the interior of this former vaudeville house, which features a coiled dragon painted on the ceiling. The theater was restored in 1980, and now it hosts various touring Broadway shows. Don't miss a chance to venture inside. ◆ Box office: M-F. 625.1900

32 SEATTLE HILTON

$$$ It's rather confusing that this hotel's lobby sits on the ninth floor rather than at ground level (to make way for a parking garage). But that may be the only unusual thing in this cookie-cutter member of the Hilton chain. Furnishings are tasteful but hardly memorable, and color schemes in the 237 rooms are benign, reflecting the aesthetics of a 1980s redo. A view restaurant, the **Top of the Hilton**, specializes in local seafood and attracts a mostly business clientele to its lounge. (As with most view restaurants, the prices are as high as the elevation.) Very convenient for conventioneers, the hotel is connected by an underground passage to the **Washington State Convention & Trade Center**, **Rainier Square**, and the **Fifth Avenue Theatre**. ◆ 1301 Sixth Ave (at University St). 624.0500, 800/Hiltons. www.hilton.com

33 FREEWAY PARK

How better to defy noisy freeway canyons than to cover them with something as peaceful as this 5-acre park? Developed in 1976 under the direction of Lawrence Halprin, this $13.8 million greensward on a large overpass atop I-5 features small ponds, flower beds, an engagingly irregular array of stairs leading from level to level, and a concrete abstraction of a waterfall that audibly separates the park from its hectic surroundings. Relax with a good book and

imagine the blood pressures escalating on the freeway below you. ◆ Seneca St (between Eighth and Sixth Aves)

34 WILD GINGER

★★★$$ The satay bar here was the first of its kind in the nation and continues to be a main event. You can just hang out, enjoying the grilled chunks of chicken, beef, prawns, or veggies on skewers that are served with a zingy peanut or soy and black-vinegar sauce, or take a place in the antique-filled dining room and order them as appetizers. Among the soups, *laksa* (a coconut-based bouillabaisse buoying tender chunks of scallops and seafood) is a must. The fragrant Wandering Sage soup is another house specialty. The seafood, particularly the scallops, is delicious, as are the beef curry and a sweetly flavored duck. Specials are influenced by cooking from around the Pacific Rim and are based on what's seasonally fresh. Paintings by local artists hang on the white walls. ◆ Asian ◆ M-Sa, lunch and dinner; Su, dinner; satay bar until 1AM. 1401 Third Ave (at Union St). 623.4450. www.wildginger.net

35 NORTHWEST PENDLETON

If consumption of woolen goods has tapered off since the 1980s owing to the increased use of synthetic materials, it has only made Oregon's Pendleton Woolen Mills more determined to promote its durable line of jackets, sweaters, and accessories beyond the Beaver State. This entire business evolved from the lowly Pendleton blanket, first crafted in eastern Oregon by Thomas Kay, an Englishman who'd studied in the textile mills of Philadelphia and came out west in 1863 to borrow native blanket designs for his own products. ◆ M-Sa. 1313 Fourth Ave (between University and Union Sts). 682.4430. www.nwpendleton.com

36 RAINIER TOWER

First-time visitors are often caught staring up at this striking white high-rise, alternately wondering how it balances on its 12-story pedestal and whether it might topple down on them. Not to worry. The principal designer, **Minoru Yamasaki**, knew what he was doing. Born in Seattle, the architect presented his hometown not only with this building but also with another landmark: the **Pacific Science Center** complex at **Seattle Center**. His reputation spread beyond Puget Sound, and he designed the Century Plaza Towers in Los Angeles, the World Trade Center in New York, and corporate offices worldwide. In all his work, Yamasaki once

---

Restaurants/Clubs: Red | Hotels: Purple | Shops: Orange | Outdoors/Parks: Green | Sights/Culture: Blue

POCKET-SIZE PARKS

Most people know about Seattle's major parks, including **Discovery**, **Volunteer**, **Seward**, and the **Washington Park Arboretum**. Their large size and abundant greenery ensure that they'll be noticed and appreciated. But scattered here and there throughout the city are several small, out-of-the-way green spaces that also feature lovely scenery and panoramic views—and you'll be more likely to have them to yourself. A number of these parks are named after prominent local people, giving you a taste of history along with the scenery. The following spots are worth taking time to visit.

On **Queen Anne Hill**, there's a steep, multilevel layout called **Bhy Kracke Park** (Comstock Place, just southeast of Bigelow Avenue N). It was named after its owner, Werner H. "Bhy" Kracke (1902–1971), a bank auditor, world traveler, and gardener. A winding path through the park affords terrific views; one vantage point at the top shows off downtown Seattle, **Lake Union**, the **Space Needle**, and **Capitol Hill** to fine advantage. There are also several landscaped gardens with ivies, azaleas, and rhododendrons.

The **Schmitz Memorial Overlook** (4503 Beach Drive SW, at Oregon Street) in **West Seattle** was a gift to the city in 1945 from the wealthy Schmitz family. The panoramic view here includes **Bainbridge Island**, **Kitsap Peninsula**, and **Vashon Island**.

Another spot with a historical background is **Jose Rizal Park** (S Judkins Street and 12th Avenue), which was named for a 19th-century Filipino patriot who was active in political and social reform in his home country (the city paid this tribute to him at the urging of its sizable Filipino population). It boasts a sweeping view that encompasses **Elliott Bay**, the **Olympic Mountains**, and the city skyline.

Then there's **Louisa Boren View Park** (E Garfield Street and 15th Avenue), named after the last surviving member of the party that founded Seattle in 1851. High above **Interlaken Park**, it faces northeast, with views of **Montlake**, the **University of Washington**, **Lake Washington**, and the **Cascades**.

The formal **Parson's Gardens** (W Highland Drive and Seventh Avenue) is the perfect setting for a quiet stroll or picnic. Located across the street from **Betty Bowen Viewpoint**, the tiny space affords a vista that takes in Elliott Bay, downtown Seattle, and even **Mount Rainier** in the distance. It's especially stunning at sunset.

Enjoy sunset views from **Magnolia Park** (1461 Magnolia Boulevard W, between Galer and Howe Streets), a 16-acre area on a bluff overlooking the Olympic Mountains, and **Sunset Hill Park** (NW 77th Street and 34th Avenue), from which you can see **Puget Sound**, **Shilshole Bay**, and the Olympics.

Kobe, Japan, one of Seattle's sister cities, donated the cherry trees and antique 4-ton stone lantern that decorate **Danny Woo International District Community Garden** (S Main Street and Seventh Avenue). The lantern is named Yukimidoro, which means "view of the snow" in Japanese. You get to see much more than just snow from here, though: There's a fine panorama of the **Duwamish Valley** to the south and **Harbor Island**, Elliott Bay, and West Seattle to the west and southwest.

For a different perspective on the city, head for **South Passage Point** (Fuhrman and Fairview Avenues E), located between the pillars of the **I-5 Bridge**, looking onto the many boats traveling the watery passage between **Portage Bay** and Lake Union. Peaceful and quiet, it's the ideal spot for relaxation and a moment of introspection.

---

said, he strove to offer "delight, serenity, and surprise." He certainly succeeded here in this upside-down pencil of a skyscraper, locally known as the "beaver building" because it looks as if a beaver had chewed it. Two levels of shops, collectively known as **Rainier Square**, anchor the pedestal. ♦ Fifth Ave and University St W

Within Rainier Square at Rainier Tower:

CREPE DE PARIS

For an evening of musical comedy, book a table at this cozy cabaret, which puts on six to eight shows a year, from humorous productions like *Waiter, There's a Fly in My Latte* to Gershwin revues. ♦ Cover. Shows Th-Sa, 8PM. Reservations required. Second level. 623.4111

37 BENAROYA HALL

After a long wait, the **Seattle Symphony** is at last in a home suited to its needs and reputation. More than 100 years old, the orchestra, one of the most recorded and admired in the world, will be the primary tenant and manager of this new hall owned by the city. The lovely exterior of the building is clad in gray-green granite, buff-colored Kasota limestone, and anodized metal panels in light and dark gray. The facility is state-of-the-art in concert hall design. With ideal acoustic features, it follows the principles of the great traditional concert halls, such as Vienna's Grosser Musikvereinssaal. The Benaroyas, a local family who provided much of the money to build the hall, contribute extensively to the arts, human services, and medical research. In addition to hosting the symphony, visiting orchestras, and other classical music performing arts groups, it will host performances by jazz, country, popular, and folk musicians. ◆ 200 University St (at Second Ave). 215.9494; ticket line, 215.4700. www.seattlesymphony.org

38 COBB BUILDING

This august imposition of brick and terra-cotta, completed in 1910, is the last survivor of a once-grand midtown scheme. In 1861, Seattle pioneers Arthur and Mary Denny and Charles and Mary Terry dedicated this corner, along with the surrounding 10-acre knoll (all of which was on the outskirts of town at that time), as the site of a territorial university. Thirty years later, school regents determined that their original institution was no longer sufficient and moved the **University of Washington** to its present site at the north end of Lake Union. The city then proposed to develop this knoll as a park. But UW had other ideas: Regents signed a 50-year agreement with the Metropolitan Building Company to improve the acreage for commercial use. The New York architectural firm of **Howells & Stokes** was engaged, and a program was developed to raise uniform 11-story façades along both sides of Fourth Avenue, with a central plaza and residential apartments on Fifth Avenue. Both this building and the **White-Henry-Stuart Building** were completed before the plan began to unravel. Later neighboring structures, such as the **Olympic Hotel** (now the **Four Seasons Olympic Hotel**) and the **Skinner Building**, were compatible with the architectural plan but deviated from its uniformity. In the 1960s, a contrasting design scheme took control of the tract, and the White-Henry-Stuart Building was razed to make room for the Popsicle-ish **Rainier Tower**. But the **Cobb** remains, and it is still very impressive. Note the Beaux Arts–inspired ornamentation, particularly the Indian heads attributed to sculptor Victor G. Schneider. ◆ 1305 Fourth Ave (between University and Union Sts)

39 FAIRMONT OLYMPIC HOTEL

$$$$ Seattle newspapers printed special photo sections touting this hotel's virtues when it opened in 1924. Men and women showed up in fancy cars and fancier dress, eager to celebrate their city's newfound sophistication. The hotel's designers—**George B. Post**, **Carl Gould**, and **Charles Bebb**—had created an Italian palazzo, with a base of rusticated stone, a terra-cotta face, and such details as Roman arches and

dentils. It was a landmark by which Seattle could judge its prosperity. After half a century, though, the declining hotel only narrowly escaped demolition. Sale to the Four Seasons chain and a 1982 rehabilitation by **NBBJ** brought grandeur back to both the interior and the exterior. Public rooms, including the cavernous lobby, now showcase lots of marble, thick carpeting, comfortable armchairs, and giant potted plants. A balcony around the lobby features some delightful historical photos of the hotel. The 450 guest rooms are somewhat less ostentatious, but they're still large and attractively appointed with 1920s reproduction furniture. Valet parking, 24-hour room service, and complimentary shoe shines all add to that pampered feeling. **Shuckers**, a clubby oyster bar on the Fourth Avenue side, is excellent for winding down after work. The refurbishment added the large-windowed **Garden Court**, above the University Street entrance, where you can enjoy a light lunch or high tea, or dance to swing bands on carefree weekend evenings. ◆ 411 University St (between Fifth and Fourth Aves). 621.1700, 800/223.8772. ₺. www.fairmont.com

Within the Fairmont Olympic Hotel:

THE GEORGIAN

★★★★$$$$ With its chandeliers and tall windows, this restaurant looks like a ballroom in a French manor house. Into this classically elegant space, chef Gavin Stephenson has introduced an unexpected menu catering to diners who are health-conscious yet still want sophisticated presentation. There is, for example, a yellow chanterelle and heirloom squash soup with shaved white truffles as an appetizer. Popular entrées include venison medallions, red wine–poached lady apple, Oregon truffle yams, and red cabbage. Less health-conscious diners can also find rack of lamb or prime Angus tenderloin as well as fish dishes here. For about $20 extra, the sommelier will select wines that complement each course, adding to the delights of your meal. ◆ Continental ◆ M-Sa, dinner; Su, breakfast and dinner. Reservations recommended. 621.7889. ₺

40 CROWNE PLAZA HOTEL

$$$ What it lacks in architectural character, this 415-room hotel tries to compensate for in its services. Upper-level rooms, dressed up in appealing reddish hues, have access to a special lounge and their own concierge and receive free newspapers. Guests staying on some of the lower floors, unfortunately,

find less distinctive accommodations. There's a café that serves breakfast, lunch, and dinner. The lobby is comfortable and the staff helpful, but in a downtown full of historic establishments, this hotel just isn't all that interesting. ◆ 1113 Sixth Ave (between Spring and Seneca Sts). 464.1980, 800/980.6429. www.ichotelsgroup.com

41 FINANCIAL CENTER

The designer of this 1972 rough-concrete tower, with its appealing, punch-card-like fenestration, was **Don Winkelmann**—the same man who did the dark **1001 Fourth Avenue Plaza** building three years before. In the 1970s the architect was sometimes called "Mr. Fourth Avenue" because of the towers he was lining up along that thoroughfare. Despite his influence on the Seattle cityscape, Winkelmann appreciated the city's old architecture as much as he did his own. So taken was he with the nearby **Seattle Tower**, for instance, that he insisted his new financial center not block any of its views. His solution, unfortunately, was to lay down a fairly lifeless plaza to one side of the center. ◆ 1215 Fourth Ave (between Seneca and University Sts)

42 SEATTLE TOWER

Being surrounded by more contemporary skyscrapers only enhances the nobility of this 26-story Art Deco tower, completed in 1929. Faced with earth- and rock-colored gradations of brickwork—darker at the bottom, becoming lighter as the building ascends—the tower was intended to remind viewers of Northwest mountains. Principal designer **Joseph Wilson** tapered the structure upward to emphasize its verticality and made the most of setbacks to bring light to a maximum of offices. At one time, those setbacks were filled with more than 200 floodlights, which simulated an aurora borealis across the building face. The Third Avenue lobby continues the mountain theme, achieving a cavernlike ambience with its dark marble walls and gilt ceiling. Look for such interior details as Indian headdresses, stylized evergreens, and abstract Chinese characters. ◆ 1218 Third Ave (between Seneca and University Sts)

43 BROOKLYN SEAFOOD STEAK & OYSTER BAR LOUNGE

★$$$ When land was being cleared to erect **1201 Third Avenue**, the splendidly refitted brick building that houses this dining spot somehow survived the wrecking ball. The interior is quite handsome—lots of wood and shiny metal, plenty of big booths, and chic café tables surrounded by stools. But the menu—given to steaks and seafood—isn't innovative or consistent enough to make a special trip here, although anything having to do with oysters can't go wrong. Appetizers tend to be too small, too expensive, or both, and service can be slow. ◆ Steak/seafood ◆ M-F, lunch and dinner; Sa, Su, dinner. Reservations recommended. Valet parking. 1212 Second Ave (between Seneca and University Sts). 224.7000. www.thebrooklyn.com

44 1201 THIRD AVENUE

For a while, this tapered, 55-story eye-grabber (formerly known as the **Washington Mutual Tower**) was wildly popular in Seattle. The much-ballyhooed New York firm of **Kohn Pedersen Fox** had bundled it up with historical references: a cruciform floor plan, for instance, harking back to Greek cross churches of the Renaissance, and a stepped-back profile that reminded critics of the Empire State Building. No one seemed to care that it barely related to the surrounding architecture and presented nothing better than a cliff face at sidewalk level. With an exterior of pink Brazilian granite, its playful pyramidal top (inspiring jokes about this being Seattle's largest pencil), and a lobby resplendent in mahogany, the 1988 structure seemed a significant and relieving departure from decades of almost featureless glass boxes. ◆ At Seneca St

45 W SEATTLE

$$$$ Clad in pre-cast concrete with black granite insets, this luxurious and modern 26-floor facility belongs to the Stanwood chain of boutique-style business hotels. There's a state-of-the-art fitness center, 24-hour room service and concierge, and a complete array of business amenities and services, including a business center and in-room equipment on request. ◆ 1112 Fourth Ave (between Spring and Seneca Sts). 264.6000. ♿. www.whotels.com

Within the W Seattle:

EARTH & OCEAN

★★★$$ This restaurant, developed by New Yorker Drew Nieporant of Nobu and Tribeca fame, offers a unique dining experience, featuring a lineup of dishes from around the world that make use of local ingredients. Currently under the creative direction of executive chef Adam Stevens, the menu changes monthly. ◆ Japanese ◆ Daily, breakfast; M-F, lunch; M-Sa, dinner. 264.6060. www.earthocean.net

46 HOTEL VINTAGE PARK

$$$ Well-known San Francisco hotelier Bill Kimpton has given the formerly disheveled **Kennedy Hotel** a refurbished lobby, some

elegant furnishings, and a too-quaint-for-words Washington wine theme (the 126 guest rooms are named in honor of wineries and vineyards throughout the state). It's all part of Kimpton's usual "discount luxury" package. Rooms are decorated in splashy textiles but subtle colors, and if they offer some unnecessary accoutrements (direct-dial phones in the bathroom?), their general comfort, as well as the hotel's convenience to downtown, is undeniable. As at other Kimpton properties on the West Coast, complimentary local wines are poured each afternoon in the lobby. Ask for a room on a high floor or on Spring Street, as Fifth Avenue is a funnel for rush-hour traffic. On-site parking and 24-hour room service are available. ♦ 1100 Fifth Ave (at Spring St). 624.8000, 800/853.3914. ಈ. www.hotelvintagepark.com

Within the Hotel Vintage Park:

TULIO RISTORANTE

★★★$$ In the midst of high-rise downtown, patrons here enjoy the pleasant conviviality of an Italian neighborhood gathering spot. The ambience suggests a Mediterranean villa, with cream-colored walls, wood paneling, and white tablecloths. Tables are set out on the sidewalk in warm weather. Chef Walter Pisano directs a kitchen staff that cures its own meats, makes its own bread and pasta, and even stretches its own mozzarella. The smoked-salmon ravioli in lemon cream sauce is a winner, and many regulars favor the roasted lemon chicken risotto. ♦ Italian ♦ Daily, breakfast, lunch, and dinner. 624.5500. ಈ. www.tulio.com

47 PACIFIC PLAZA HOTEL

$$ An older property (built in 1929, refurbished in 1989), this is a pleasant surprise in the middle of Big-Bucks Hotel Land. The 159 rooms aren't luxurious, and they're often too small for families, but the hotel's central location (only five blocks from **Westlake Center**) is real hard to beat at the price. The rate includes a complimentary continental breakfast. The hotel's restaurant also serves lunch and dinner. ♦ 400 Spring St (at Fourth Ave). 623.3900, 800/426.1165. www.pacificplazahotel.com

48 HOTEL MONACO

$$$ Award-winning interior designer Cheryl Rowley has given a bright, Mediterranean look to what was not so long ago the corporate headquarters for Pacific Northwest Bell. The domed lobby features white marble floors, images of old-time steamer trunks, and a nautical mural of cavorting ancient Greek dolphins. The 189 boldly designed rooms all have wet bars, coffeemakers (with Starbucks coffee), irons and ironing boards, and terry-cloth robes. ♦ 1101 Fourth Ave (at Spring St). 621.1770, 800/945.2240. ಈ. www.monaco-seattle.com

Within the Hotel Monaco:

SAZERAC

★★★$$ The first question answered first: Sazerac is a New Orleans cocktail made with Old Overholt rye whiskey. Yes, chef and owner (self-nicknamed Big Dawg) Jan Birnbaum is from there originally and is a master of New Orleans cooking variants. This is a grand space, with high ceilings, chandeliers, the warmth of purple velvet and mahogany, and touches of whimsy. The open kitchen at the rear is where Birnbaum and executive chef Jason McClure preside over earthy, wood-fired cooking. The menu changes frequently, but there's always a strong Creole influence on catfish, ribs, pulled pork, and spicy andouille sausage. ♦ Southern ♦ M-Th, until 7PM; F, Sa, until 11PM. 624.7755. ಈ. www.sazeracrestaurant.com

49 SEATTLE PUBLIC LIBRARY

Covering a square block (bounded by Fourth and Fifth Avenues and Madison and Spring Streets), this new structure is the third version of Seattle's downtown library to occupy the same site, after the Carnegie building (1906) and the midcentury modernist structure (1960), which featured such innovations as a drive-up-and-drop-off window, the first escalators in any American library, and electric typewriters. The new 362,987-square-foot building, designed by Dutch architect Rem Koolhaas, a crystalline steel-and-glass structure featuring five platforms and a large central "book spiral," is already a source of local controversy. The weird form of the building, with cantilevered sections jutting out, has already upset many library patrons, but Deborah Jacobs, the city librarian, is pleased at how "it reflects the building's program. It also happens to be incredibly cool." The new downtown library houses 1.4 million volumes on 10 floors and features underground parking, close to a million dollars' worth of art, and all the latest in library technology. ◆ M-Th, 10AM-8PM; F, Sa, 10AM-6PM; Su, noon-6PM. 386.4636. www.spl.org

50 RENAISSANCE MADISON HOTEL

$$$ Despite its proximity to the I-5 gully, this property manages to project a sense of quiet. Maybe it's the regal color scheme, or the muted lighting, or the marble and rich wood that decorate the 553 guest rooms. Perhaps it's the peaceful views from both sides (Elliott Bay on the west, the Cascade Mountains on the east). Luxury addicts can book rooms on the **Club Floors** (25th to 27th), which offer special check-in services, a complimentary continental breakfast, a library, and free in-town transportation. A 40-foot-long rooftop pool and Jacuzzi will work out the jet-lag kinks. There's indoor parking (for a fee), and a soothing bar right off the lobby. ◆ 515 Madison St (at Sixth Ave). 583.0300, 800/546.9184. ㅎ. www.marriott.com/hotels

51 1001 FOURTH AVENUE PLAZA

When this modernist bronze monolith was completed in 1969, professional journals hailed it as among the most technologically advanced buildings of its time. **Don Winkelmann**, the partner in the **NBBJ Group** who was responsible for the design, rhapsodized for the *Seattle Times*: "You see a jet move across the horizon above this building and [the] two are compatible. It all fits with rockets to the moon." Many Seattleites took a dimmer view of the 50-story corporate headquarters for Seattle—First National Bank. One popular derisive comment was that the building was the box that the **Space Needle** came in. Others criticized it as a dark birthmark on the predominantly white terra-cotta hand of Seattle, and they didn't like the fact that it so overwhelmed the beloved **Smith Tower**, which is only 42 stories tall. But time has quieted the cavils, as did a 1986 revitalization that added small shops and a glass-enclosed **Wintergarden**, making the building more people-friendly. English sculptor Henry Moore's bronze *Three-Piece Sculpture: Vertebrae* is the most prominent feature of the plaza. ◆ 1001 Fourth Ave (at Madison St)

52 FIRST UNITED METHODIST CHURCH

I-5 severed this church from First Hill to the east, the neighborhood it had served for most of the 20th century. Now it stands out as a handsomely domed anachronism amid the field of central city skyscrapers. Designed by **James Schack** and **Daniel R. Huntington** (the latter served as city architect for many years), this 1907 building combines Roman and Palladian Renaissance qualities, a departure from the Gothic cathedral designs then so popular in America. In addition to its usual religious activities, the church also occasionally serves as a lecture hall. ◆ 811 Fifth Ave (between Columbia and Marion Sts). 622.7278. www.firstchurchseattle.org

53 RAINIER CLUB

Architect **Kirtland K. Cutter** is not as well known here as in his adopted hometown of Spokane, Washington (where he designed, for instance, the eclectic old Davenport Hotel). Yet this building, opened in 1904, is indeed one of the most startling and handsome juxtapositions to the skyscrapers of Seattle's central business district. Cutter modeled this males-only club after English men's clubs, with rustic brickwork and curvilinear gables drawn from Jacobean, or late English Renaissance, style. (A separate guest entrance for women was tucked away on the Marion Street façade.) In 1929 the prestigious partnership of **Charles Bebb** and **Carl Gould** added 54 feet to the south end of the building, all in character with the original design. The club was created as a haven for the city's meritocracy, a place for them to gather and chat over cigars and brandy. Today it's still private, though the membership is no longer restricted to men. From the outside, little has changed: Many Seattleites don't even know what goes on inside these brick walls, for there's no sign outside announcing the building's use. ◆ 810 Fourth Ave (between Columbia and Marion Sts)

54 MCCORMICK AND SCHMICK'S SEAFOOD RESTAURANT

★★$$ Decorated with lots of polished wood, brass, and greenery, this restaurant tends to attract an older, conservative, and loyal clientele. Younger drop-ins usually come from City Hall or one of the other government beehives nearby and wind up in the convivial bar. The offerings are pretty reliable and the quality consistent—the menu features simple preparations of seafood, with selections changed daily. ◆ Seafood ◆ M-F, lunch and dinner; Sa, Su, dinner. Reservations recommended. 722 Fourth Ave (at Columbia St). 682.3900. ㅎ. www.mccormickandschmicks.com

55 COLUMBIA BANK OF AMERICA CENTER

Seattleites love to hate this 76-story cloud-ripper that is so out of scale with the rest of downtown. You can't help but notice this

CAREFREE (AND CAR-FREE) SIGHTSEEING: SEATTLE BY BUS

One of the most convenient and least expensive ways to tour Seattle is by taking the regular commuter buses operated by **Metro Transit** (553.3000; www.transit.metrokc.gov). You can cover a lot of ground in a short time, and you don't have to worry about navigating through traffic or getting lost. The routes cover most of the city, and several offer spectacular views of both Seattle's glorious natural surroundings and its architectural splendors. Traveling by bus is also a great way to get in touch with the daily routine of local residents, making you feel less like a stranger. All of the routes listed below leave from downtown, and maps and schedules can be found at libraries, hotels, ferry terminals, and tourist offices. Your journey will be much more relaxing if you avoid the morning and evening rush hours (7 to 10AM and 4 to 6PM, Monday through Friday). To save money, purchase an All-Day Pass (allowing a day's unlimited travel on weekends and holidays on all **Metro Transit** buses) from the driver.

West Seattle

Two bus routes cover this area. **No. 37** travels over the **Duwamish River** for a view of the harbor and downtown skyline before heading out along the shoreline around **Duwamish Head** and along the beach past **Alki Point**; vistas of **Puget Sound**, offshore islands, and the **Olympic Mountains** unfold before you. **No. 56** goes over the West Seattle ridge, showing off the **Space Needle**, **Queen Anne Hill**, **Magnolia**, the harbor, and downtown.

Magnolia

No. 19 reverses the West Seattle routes by going north, then west up a steep viaduct to the crest of **Magnolia Bluff**. As the bus travels along the bluff, you can see downtown, West Seattle, Puget Sound, **Bainbridge** and **Vashon Islands**, and, in clear weather, the breathtaking sight of **Mount Rainier** filling the southeastern horizon.

West Queen Anne/Madrona Park

No. 2 gives you a choice of two different views: from downtown, up the steep **Counterbalance** to the top of Queen Anne Hill for fabulous views of the city in all directions; or up over **First Hill** (affectionately called "Pill Hill" because of the many hospitals and clinics here) and out through the **Madrona** neighborhood to **Lake Washington**. A sign on the front of the bus indicates which destination it's going to.

Madison Park/Ferry Terminal

No. 11 runs in a straight diagonal line along the 4-mile width of the city, from the harbor to Lake Washington. It takes you through commercial and residential areas, including the trendy **Madison Valley** area, the **Washington Park Arboretum**, the exclusive **Broadmoor** residential enclave, and the charming **Madison Park** neighborhood.

Colman Park

No. 27 goes from downtown along **Yesler Way**, then descends precipitously to the shoreline of Lake Washington. From the lake, it continues past **Leschi Park** to **Colman Park**, passing by the **Evergreen Point** and **Lacey V. Murrow Floating Bridges**, the wooded **Seward Park** peninsula, **Mercer Island**, and Mount Rainier, as well as several long beachfront stretches of the Olmsted green belt.

U-District/Sand Point

No. 74 begins downtown; then it takes a scenic tour of the **University of Washington** before heading east and north on **Sand Point Way** to the **National Oceanic and Atmospheric Administration**'s **Western Regional Center**. You can transfer there to **No. 75**, which will take you to **Northgate Shopping Center**.

exclamation point of steel and glass; built in 1985, it's the tallest building in town. **Chester L. Lindsey Architects** achieved an unusual vertical and monumental sense by sheathing the center in black glass; a lighter face would have revealed individual floor levels and thus perceptually diminished the building. Alternating concave and convex exterior surfaces, as well as the skyscraper's stair-stepped arrangement, create more complex light patterns than would be possible on a straight-sided tower. Forget the lower-level shopping floors, which are a bit dingy. An observation deck on the 73rd floor, however, provides a broad panorama of the city and is in many ways superior to the **Space Needle**—it's higher and more private, its view is better, and its admission charge is much lower. ♦ Fee to observation deck. Observation deck: M-F. 701 Fifth Ave (at Cherry St). 386.5151

Restaurants/Clubs: Red | Hotels: Purple | Shops: Orange | Outdoors/Parks: Green | Sights/Culture: Blue

56 METROPOLITAN GRILL

★★★$$$ Proving that not all Seattleites are worried about their fat and cholesterol intakes, this restaurant turns out thick mesquite-grilled steaks accompanied by baked potatoes or pasta. The clam chowder makes a good starter, and the burgers and onion rings are tasty too. An adjacent big-windowed bar is comfortable until 5PM, when financial district habitués start streaming in. "The Met" is popular with Japanese businesspeople, who can request a special translated menu. ◆ American ◆ M-F, lunch and dinner; Sa,Su, dinner. Reservations recommended. 820 Second Ave (between Columbia and Marion Sts). 624.3287. ઇ. www.themetropolitangrill.com

57 CHAMBER OF COMMERCE BUILDING

An Italian Romanesque basilica notched into the contemporary downtown area? Leave it to the local chamber of commerce to plumb ostentatious associations. This 1924 design was allegedly inspired by a trip to Europe that the principal architect, **Harlan Thomas**, took to view 12th-century Lombardy churches. The chamber moved out of its faux cathedral years ago, and the structure is now occupied in large part by the architectural group **TRA**, which rehabilitated the building in 1970 and is the direct descendant of **Schack, Young & Myers**, the firm that assisted Thomas in the structure's conception. A sculptural frieze called *Primitive & Modern Industries* by Morgan Padelford extends to the left side of the main entrance and refers to aspects of Northwest history. ◆ 219 Columbia St (between Third and Second Aves)

58 ARCTIC BUILDING

The tusks of the 25 terra-cotta walrus heads that stud the façade here are not the same ones that garnered public attention in 1917, when the prestigious old Arctic Club first opened this building. It seems the original tusks were removed during the 1950s, owing to public fear that they'd break off and spear passing pedestrians. Not until the early 1980s, when a restoration of this **A. Warren Gould** edifice took place, did the walruses get their tusks back, this time cast of a special epoxy. Unfortunately, the life-size polar bear that formerly crowned the building's Third Avenue entrance was not replaced. Currently undergoing a $9 million restoration, this building will reopen as a 117-room luxury hotel. ◆ 700 Third Ave (at Cherry St)

59 CHERRY STREET PARKING GARAGE

Although it isn't usually on the city tour, this arch-windowed structure was showman John

Mary Ann Conklin (1821–1873) ran Seattle's first hotel, the Felker House, at Main Street and First Avenue S. Her profane vocabulary and fiery temper earned her the moniker "Mother Damnable," which later transmuted into "Madame Damnable" when she diversified the hotel business by adding a brothel on the upper floor. She died in 1873. Felker House burned to the ground in the Great Fire of 1889.

Let's Make Ourselves a Park!

Cal Anderson Park is unique, not only because it represents an imaginative solution to an engineering problem and is the product of innovative landscape design, but also because it came about as the result of determination on the part of neighborhood activists.

The Olmstead brothers (son and stepson of Frederick Law Olmstead, the designer of New York City's Central Park) completed a comprehensive park plan for Seattle in the very early years of the 20th century. In addition to a proposed chain of parks linked by boulevards, they designed **Lincoln Park** around Seattle's first water pumping station and open-to-the-air reservoir. By the 1990s that park, with a chain-link fence surrounding the crumbling reservoir and the paths given over to drug dealers and their often unsavory customers, no longer functioned as an attractive green space in the heart of Seattle's most densely populated neighborhood.

Meanwhile, Seattle's Public Utilities Department developed a plan to provide better control of water quality and safety than the open-air holding pond had done. The reservoir was to be replaced by two huge underground tanks. Hower, a determined group of local residents organized, lobbied, and harangued. They pushed for grants and matching funds—and finally got the city to include the park in a city-wide bond issue, which succeeded, providing necessary funding for a huge renovation.

The Berger Partnership, which had already been working with the community on design concepts for the park, was chosen by the city as the landscape architects for the project—which would involve not only laying out a park that would go over the lid of the underground tanks, but also a significant renovation and upgrading of the rest of this 12-acre park, which at the time consisted of various playfields, a children's play area, and decrepit, vandalized public rest rooms.

A grassy park was constructed on the lid of the new, covered reservoir. Doug Hollis, in conjunction with the Berger Partnership, designed gradual, low-grade hills, sinuous paths, and a spectacular water feature—water spews from the top of a stone-covered cone (reminiscent of the volcanic cone of Mt. Rainier), drops into a sloping pool, then ripples along a rocky incline and comes to a stop in a still pool. The original Beaux Arts–style pump house has been integrated into the design, a graceful gesture toward the Olmstead design of more than a hundred years earlier.

Cal Anderson Park was renamed in memory of a popular community activist, the first openly gay person to be elected to the state legislature. The park is now a kind of village green for the vibrant community surrounding it. People come to walk, picnic, toss Frisbees, and wade in the shallow pool. Children play on swings and slides, and teams compete on the fields. It is a lovely and active place, a tribute to what dogged community persistence, imaginative planning, and a willing city can achieve, a park the community has every reason to be proud of.

Cort's **Grand Opera House**, the "finest theater in the city" when it opened in 1900. Here Seattleites used to gather along two huge balconies to take in turn-of-the-20th-century culture. (Note what looks like the vestige of a grand entrance.) ♦ Third Ave and Cherry St

60 ALASKA BUILDING

Opened in 1904, this 14-story structure (designed by the St. Louis firm of **Eames & Young**) was the first in Seattle to employ steel-frame construction. That technology, developed in Chicago office towers as early as the 1880s, allowed exterior masonry to be ornamental rather than strictly load-bearing. Thus, buildings could be made bigger and taller without becoming as heavy as the Romanesque piles of Pioneer Square. The penthouse here was once home to the Alaska Club, a social circle for Last Frontier emigrants, many of whom came south after the 1897 gold rush. Today the building houses municipal offices.

♦ 618 Second Ave (between James and Cherry Sts)

61 KING COUNTY COURTHOUSE

Between the 1890s and 1916, the county's center of legal activity was several blocks east of this intersection of Third Avenue and James Street. Where **Harborview Hospital** now perches, an old "cruel castle" of a courthouse then loomed, its imposing pillared mass lifting to a dome visible all over town. The current courthouse was designed by **A. Warren Gould**. His concept broke away from the notion of a monumental temple of justice, calling instead for a 22-story, H-shaped skyscraper with a pyramid-topped tower in the center. Only six stories were erected initially, with another five added in 1930 under the direction of **Henry Bittman** and **John L. McCauley**. The planned tower and additional floors were never built. ♦ 516 Third Ave (between Yesler Way and James St)

Restaurants/Clubs: Red | Hotels: Purple | Shops: Orange | Outdoors/Parks: Green | Sights/Culture: Blue

PILLARS OF THE COMMUNITY

That tourists regard Seattle as home to so many totem poles is an odd quirk of taste and history. Native Americans of the Seattle area, after all, did not create this detailed form of columnar art, but Seattleites took a shine to it way back in the 19th century. Ever since, totem poles have been imported, duplicated locally, or stolen for their aesthetic attributes rather than for their regional relevance. Poles around town are generally the work of the Tlingit people of southeastern Alaska, the Haida of the Queen Charlotte Islands, or the Kwakiutl and Tsimshian Indians of southwestern British Columbia. They symbolize this city's reputation as the gateway to the north.

Totem poles originated as memorials, grave posts, and architectural supports. Their designs included creatures of nature transformed into specific mythological figures—Raven, Frog, Coyote, and others—each with its own temperament, style, and power. The representations were stacked on a totem pole in ways that retold bits of Native American history or legends, with the top figure identifying the clan whose story was being told.

The 50-foot-tall western red cedar pole in **Pioneer Place Park** (First Avenue, between Yesler Way and Cherry Street) is Seattle's best-known totem. The original monolith, a Tlingit pole stolen by a Seattle expeditionary party during the 19th century, stood in that park from 1899 until it was damaged by dry rot and arson in 1938. What exists today is a replica, also carved by Tlingit. This totem symbolizes not one but three myths, the predominant legend involving the cunning Raven (a figure depicted at the top of the totem), who stole the sun and the moon from Raven-at-the-Head-of-Nass and brought them to the world.

In **Pioneer Square**'s peaceful **Occidental Park** (Occidental Avenue S, between Jackson and Washington Streets) is a totem called *Sun and Raven*, a 32-foot pole carved by artist Duane Pasco for the 1974 World's Fair in Spokane. Three other Pasco pieces—*Man Riding on Tail of Whale*, *Tsonoqua* (a mythical giant of the deep forest), and *Bear*—are also in the park. And at **Seattle Center** (Fifth Avenue N, between Broad and Mercer Streets), near the **Center House**, you can see a 30-foot Pasco pole with four main figures: Hawk, Bear (holding a salmon), Raven, and Killer Whale.

The carved cedar pole at the intersection of **South Washington Street** and **Alaskan Way** was commissioned by the Port of Seattle to commemorate links between Seattle and Alaska. This 1975 piece, created at the Alaska Indian Arts Center in Haines, Alaska, includes several symbols of the 49th state. Eagle, representing the main Tlingit tribe, sits at the top; below him is Brown Bear holding a coin, symbolizing Alaska's great size and wealth, and Killer Whale, representing tenacity and strength; and at the pole's base is the figure Strong Boy, which stands for the state's youth and vigor.

The more traditional of the two poles in **Victor Steinbrueck Park** (Western Avenue and Virginia Street), at the north end of **Pike Place Market**, does not depict a legend but includes mythical figures inspired by Haida Indian designs, which stand for qualities of strength and abundance. The other, a nontraditional unadorned totem pole, was apparently inspired by a pole found near Ketchikan, Alaska, that features Abraham Lincoln; Seattle's version is topped by two figures of a farming couple standing back to back. These pieces were designed by Quinault Indian artist Martin Oliver and Seattleite James Bender.

A 1937 example of the art, carved originally for a fish cannery in Waterfall, Alaska, by a Haida Indian, can be seen just east of the **Montlake Bridge** on **East Shelby Street**. After many years of greeting fishers returning to Alaska, this pole was stored in a Seattle warehouse until it could be purchased and reassembled by philanthropic locals. The obelisk tells about a very old woman whose brother, a Haida chief, considered her worthless. When the chief moved his people, he ordered that his sister be left behind without food or fire. She, however, called on the spirits for help, and her prayers were answered by an eagle that brought her food each day. When a bear tried to steal the raptor's gifts, the woman again appealed to the spirits, who sent someone to kill the thieving bruin.

Two other fine examples of totem art are located in **Vancouver**'s **Stanley Park**. Charles James carved the turn-of-the-19th-century house posts, both of which depict Thunderbird at the top. They were designed to serve as architectural supports for communal homes.

62 SMITH TOWER

When it opened on 4 July 1914, this was the tallest building outside of Manhattan—42 floors, 522 feet—and for 48 years it remained the highest west of the Mississippi River. (The record was broken in 1969 by the 50-story, 609-foot-high **Seattle–First National Bank Tower**—now **1001 Fourth Avenue Plaza**.) Bankrolled by Lyman C. Smith, the armaments entrepreneur turned typewriter baron, the building was also Seattle's first fireproof steel structure, decorated with terra-cotta facing and cornices. Visiting Seattle in 1909 to do some real-estate speculation, Smith saw it as ripe ground on which to demonstrate the depth of his success; he commissioned the firm of **Gaggin & Gaggin** to build a skyscraper that would anchor downtown Seattle near its starting place. (A forlorn hope: Commercial construction moved farther and farther north, fashionably away from the "old city.") Smith also wanted a building that wouldn't be exceeded in height during his lifetime. That wish came true in a twisted way: He died before this building was completed. His two-stepped legacy remains Seattle's best-loved, if not loftiest, construction. An observation deck on the 35th floor provides a panorama of downtown; on the same floor can be found the teak-ceilinged **Chinese Room**, which Smith conceived especially for his daughter's marriage and where weddings are still held. The West Coast's only manually operated elevators (complete with original-style levers) are also to be found in this building. And don't miss the enchanting carved Indian heads above the first-floor elevator doors. ♦ 506 Second Ave (at Yesler Way). www.smithtower.com

63 CITY HALL PARK

Seattle's **City Hall** stood on this tiny treed triangle until 1909. When that was leveled, Mayor George Dilling established this historic but now rather seedy site as the city's first downtown park, originally known as **Court House Park**. The surrounding area was the site of the "Battle of Seattle," an 1856 skirmish during the Indian War in which the frigate *Decatur* peppered the area east of Third Avenue with cannon fire to root out some natives who were hiding there. This conflict was the culmination of years of tension between white settlers and the Klickitat, Muckleshoot, and Nisqually people who were here originally. Cannonballs from this episode have been uncovered in the park as recently as 1995. ♦ Yesler Way and Third Ave

64 OLD PUBLIC SAFETY BUILDING

Young Seattle took a long time to erect a City Hall to match its optimism and ambition. (For that matter, the city still lacks such a centerpiece, tolerating instead that glass-walled Kennedy-era monstrosity on Fourth Avenue known as the **Municipal Building**.) But in the early days of the 20th century, local burghers hired architect **Clayton Wilson** to erect a new administration building on this triangular block. Comparisons with New York City's Flatiron Building are inevitable, but Wilson did more than just copy it. His five-story structure with a penthouse, faced with brick and sandstone and boasting a curved copper roofline, was properly formal without being pretentious. City government moved in immediately, but only 7 years later, it had to relocate again to larger digs in the **King County Courthouse** on Third Avenue. Wilson's structure subsequently housed a hospital, a jail, and a police station. Still later, after abuse as a parking garage and as an unofficial sanctuary for the homeless, it was converted back into office space. ♦ 400 Yesler Way (at Fourth Ave)

The market is a kinetic profusion of people, energy, and individual enterprise. Flowers for sale. Pottery. Pastries. Scarves. Cigars. Seascapes. T-shirts. Teacups. Fish peddlers toss huge flounder above the heads of awed customers. A ragtag band coaxes a lively rendition of Jimmy Buffett's "Pencil-Thin Mustache" from time-distressed instruments. A hawker at First and Pike News shouts, "*P-I! Seattle Post-Intelligencer! Seattle Times! New Yo-o-o-rk Times! LA Times! We've got the Times!*" Shoppers jockey with automobiles along the two-and-a-half-block stretch of **Pike Place**, with drivers almost invariably losing out. As many as 40,000 people visit this bazaar daily.

There's no guarantee you'll find the freshest produce here, but for urban color, **Pike Place Market**–the oldest continuously operating farmers' market in the country–is unbeatable. *New York Times* correspondent Timothy Egan called it the "Marrakech of the Northwest." Artist Mark Tobey, who haunted the market frequently, beginning in the 1920s, once described it as "a refuge, an oasis, a most human growth, the heart and soul of Seattle."

The market began in 1907, when food wholesalers formed a Produce Row along **Western Avenue**. Farmers who couldn't take the time off to sell their crops relied on wholesalers to do the job for them. But local growers suspected (quite rightly, in many cases) that these intermediaries were cheating them of a fair price for their goods and, at the same time, gouging customers with excessive fees. The city's response was to establish a *true* farmers' market. The location was based primarily on convenience (aggressive re-grading had recently leveled the land at **Pike Street**'s western end, and newly planked Western Avenue connected it with the Waterfront). On opening day, 17

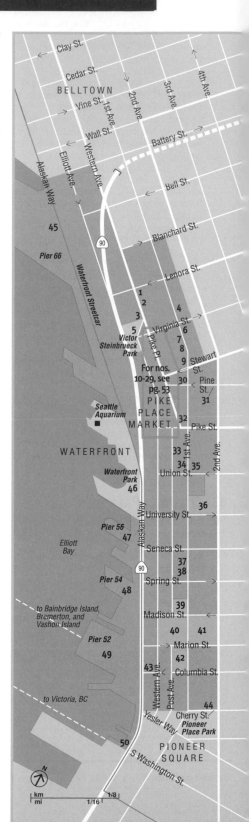

August 1907, fewer than a dozen wagons showed up (and one of those, driven by a Japanese farmer, was ransacked), but thousands of Seattleites came, eager to buy. The next week, 70 wagons took positions on the Pike Place curb. Fishmongers soon infiltrated the neighborhood, as did other small businesses. Stall sizes had to be reduced to fit everybody in, and canopies were built to keep commerce chugging along through the Seattle rains. Several proposals called for Pike Place Market to grow into a grandiose commercial complex spilling down from its bluff on **Elliott Bay** into a railroad and marine terminal on the Waterfront. But residents voted to keep the market small and personable: exuberant with Italians, Japanese, and Sephardic Jews hawking their goods; replete with local characters like Horseradish Jerry, who ground roots into relish, or the old-timers who droned tall tales of the Klondike Gold Rush. Within 10 years, the market had become Seattle's funky equivalent of a community square.

The 1929 Depression exacted its toll on Pike Place Market. So did the World War II internment of Japanese farmers; the decline of **First Avenue**, from a workers' mall to a strip of peep shows and honky-tonks; and the insurgence of supermarkets. By 1963, with the market and indeed all of Seattle in wan condition, planners encouraged the city to bulldoze the market in favor of a parking lot and high-rise development. Only a concerted effort by preservationists, politicians, local architects (among them, the persistent **Victor Steinbrueck**, who had designed the **Space Needle**), and—eventually—voters saved the heart and soul of Seattle. A seven-acre Market Historical District was established in 1974.

Regular guided tours will give you an overview of the market, but the best way to get a feel for it is to wander about its well-preserved edifices, exploring the alleys, stairways, and ramps where the many buildings have been strung together throughout the years. However, it would take years to fully appreciate all the attractions and rhythms of the place; in fact, even most natives know it only in passing. Pike Place Market (which is also referred to as the Public Market) is open daily early May through December, and Monday through Saturday the rest of the year. Individual shops hours vary, as do the seasonal schedules of businesses not contained completely within market buildings.

Because Pike Place Market achieved historic status, every one of its buildings has been renovated or reconstructed. Unfortunately, less attention has been paid to Seattle's Waterfront. This was once the center of local commerce, a strip alive with the shouts of merchants and the jibs of the **Mosquito Fleet**, an early ferry service. But several decades ago, the Waterfront was severed from the rest of downtown by the **Alaskan Way Viaduct** and—except for the estimable **Seattle Aquarium** and the too-small **Waterfront Park**—has since been all but completely given over to fast-food joints and kitschy emporiums. Hope for its revitalization is now centered on the **Bell Street Pier**, an 11-acre span of urban shoreline that has been developed as a convention center, dining complex, marina, and museum.

1 PHOENIX RISING GALLERY

Simultaneously playful, pricey, and *very* crowded with merchandise, this shop is decorated with table after table of contemporary glassworks, jewelry, business gifts, and home accessories. ♦ Daily. 2030 Western Ave (at Lenora St). 728.2332. www.prgallery.com

2 SEATTLE ATHLETIC CLUB

On the edge of the **Pike Place Market**, this 2,400-member health club features all the usual exercise equipment and free weights, as well as a pool, indoor track, basketball, racquetball, squash courts, and aerobics classes. A number of downtown hotels offer

Restaurants/Clubs: Red | Hotels: Purple | Shops: Orange | Outdoors/Parks: Green | Sights/Culture: Blue

their guests temporary club memberships here. ♦ Daily. 2020 Western Ave (between Virginia and Lenora Sts). 443.1111. www.twogreatclubs.com

2 ETTA'S SEAFOOD

★★★$$ Formerly a sports bar, this place has green-backed booths, a long counter and bar, and plenty of friendly noise. There is a small, quiet dining room as well. Not really the spot for beef eaters, Its specialty definitely is seafood in a variety of forms. Entrées include oysters on the half-shell, and Maine lobster and local Dungeness crab steamed or wok-seared in chile and black bean sauce. Part of the Tom Douglas chain of restaurants, Etta's presents an inspired, ever-changing menu. ♦ Seafood ♦ Daily, lunch and dinner; Sa, Su, brunch. Reservations recommended. 2020 Western Ave (between Virginia and Lenora Sts). 443.6000. ⑤. www.tomdouglas.com/ettas

3 CUTTER'S BAYHOUSE

★$$$ People either love this place or they would sooner swear off *lattes* for life than dine here again. The problem isn't the food; like its sister establishments (**Palisade** in Magnolia, **Palomino** downtown), this one shows skill in the kitchen. So what if the menu is all over the map—a little Chinese, some Cajun, a dash of Italian—as long as the pasta, seafood, and the garlicky focaccia remain impressive. No, the problem here is the clientele: lots of competitive yuppies (and wannabes), lots of fatless body fanatics, and everybody checking out everybody else's vital stats. ♦ International ♦ Daily, lunch and dinner; bar (serving light meals): daily, until 1:30AM. 2001 Western Ave (between Virginia and Lenora Sts). 448.4884. www.cuttersbayhouse.com

4 VAIN

Owner Victoria Thomas brings to Seattle a new way of thinking and acting upon life and community. She wants to inspire a do-it-yourself attitude and readily promotes freedom of expression. Known for cutting-edge hairstyling and fashion, this space is often filled with a variety of beautiful muses. Host to many fundraisers and fashion shows, Thomas also helps keep Seattle on the forefront of art and beauty. She has restored this three-story structure, turning the space into part gallery, part salon, part retail space, and 20 artists' studios. ♦ 2018 First Ave (between Virginia and Lenora Sts). 441.3441. www.vain.com

5 VICTOR STEINBRUECK PARK

🛈 It's fitting that such a lively spot (designed in 1982 by both **Steinbrueck** and **Richard Haag**) should be dedicated to an architect who sought to maintain the vibrancy of **Pike Place Market**. This grassy viewpoint bustles on warm days with businesspeople lunching, tourists pondering the passage of ferries on the Sound, and the usual Seattle complement of panhandlers. A pair of Northwest Indian totem poles designed by Quinault tribe member Marvin Oliver were carved with the assistance of James Bender. The bad news is that right below the park rushes the interminably noisy Alaskan Way Viaduct. ♦ Western Ave and Virginia St

6 PETER MILLER BOOKS

Specializing in architecture and design books (new as well as out-of-print titles), with such nifty accessories as build-it-yourself paper replicas of the **Space Needle**, this bookstore is a great place to while away an hour. There's a mail-order catalog too. ♦ Daily. 1930 First Ave (between Stewart and Virginia Sts). 441.4114. www.petermiller.com

7 VIRGINIA INN BAR

A favorite hangout for newspaper and magazine types, this tavern has anchored the corner of First Avenue and Virginia Street since about 1908. Unlike many similar pubs, it never closed during Prohibition but was converted temporarily into a card- and lunchroom. Knife-scarred wooden booths hug a corner near the door, leaving the remaining floor space to a maze of little round tables and a long elegant bar that can barely be seen through the mass of revelers on weekdays after 5PM. The choice of craft beers and wines, although not extensive, is select. There's not much in the way of pub grub, although the platter of smoked salmon and bread provides a reasonable light lunch. Art on the brick walls changes frequently. The rest rooms are worth a peek: *True Detective* motif in the men's john, and lip prints next door for women. ♦ Daily, until 2AM. 1937 First Ave (at Virginia St). 728.1937

7 LE PICHET

★★★$$$ The ultimate Seattle French restaurant, with lots of terrines, pâtés, charcuterie, and entrées like *moules frites*, a perfect combination of mussels and fries that is unlike anything you've ever tasted—and more fabulous.
♦ Daily, breakfast, lunch, and dinner. 1933 First Ave (between Stewart and Virginia Sts). 256.1499. www.lepichetseattle.com

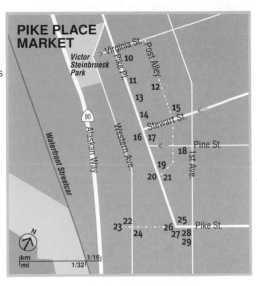

8 PENSIONE NICHOLS

$$ Prices at Lindsey Nichols's bed-and-breakfast establishment are extremely reasonable for the location—just a block off Pike Place and convenient to a superfluity of restaurants and shops. It's easy to miss the entrance: It's just a single doorway off the sidewalk that opens onto a cliff of stairs. The *pensione* occupies two floors up the stairs; check in at the desk on the third floor. The eight guest rooms and two suites are brightly painted, cozy, and overlook either First Avenue or Elliott Bay; the latter are slightly quieter, but the former seem more intimate. A large third-floor sitting room embraces views of Elliott Bay and is replete with soft couches for reading or clandestine romancing. Guests (save for those in the suites) must share bath and rest room facilities, but they are quite comfortable and well maintained. A continental breakfast is included in the room rate. Although the establishment has collected national raves, local attention has been far more stingy. Overshadowing it has been the nearby **Inn at the Market**, a higher-priced and more expensively retailed hostelry. Also weighing against it may be the fact that the *pensione* is located directly above a porno-movie house. Whatever the reason, the slight is unfortunate, for Nichols manages a secret uptown gem. ♦ 1923 First Ave (between Stewart and Virginia Sts). 441.7125. www.pensionenichols.com

8 ISADORA'S

Owner Laura Dalesandro has been providing Seattle with elegant, high-end vintage evening wear, men's accessories, and estate/antique jewelry for over 30 years.

You'll swoon at the gorgeous gowns and pieces as you are transported back to a time when women and men epitomized the idea of glamour. ♦ 1915 First Ave (between Stewart and Virginia Sts). 888/ISADORA. www.isadoras.com

9 ZEBRA CLUB

This store carries sporty and lightweight unisex street attire for those who favor the ultracasual look. Ubiquitous video equipment heightens the youth-oriented tone. ♦ Daily. 1901 First Ave (at Stewart St). 448.7452

10 PIKE & WESTERN WINE MERCHANTS

This shop stocks a wide range of wines, specializing in vintners from the Northwest; the selection of French and German vintages is also well chosen. ♦ Daily. 1934 Pike Pl (at Virginia St). 441.1307. &. www.pikeandwestern.com

11 LOUIE'S ON THE PIKE

Although most market shops specialize, here is a general-interest grocery store—*the* place to shop if you're looking for something so pedestrian as a bottled soft drink or an ice-cream bar. There's also a decent deli counter inside. ♦ Daily. 1926 Pike Pl (between Stewart and Virginia Sts). 443.1035

12 POST ALLEY

Horse-drawn hearses once clattered down this uneven brick path to deposit corpses in the basement crematorium of the Butterworth Mortuary, now home to **Kell's Restaurant & Pub** (see page 54). This is still

---

Restaurants/Clubs: Red | Hotels: Purple | Shops: Orange | Outdoors/Parks: Green | Sights/Culture: Blue

the only section of Post Alley open to vehicular traffic. ♦ Between Stewart and Virginia Sts

Along Post Alley:

GLASS EYE GALLERY

Mount St. Helens's volcanic eruption in 1980 proved a big boom to some of the Northwest's novelty glassmakers. The co-owners of this shop, Rob Adamson and Dale Leman, caught on early to the possibilities (they're still riding the trend) and incorporated the peak's ashen and slightly iridescent detritus into their hand-blown glass pieces. Look here for dishware, blown-glass fruit, and shapely vases. ♦ Daily. 441.3221. www.gcgallery.com

THE PERENNIAL TEA ROOM

For all the coffee talk in Seattle, there is the occasional tearoom, and this is one to remember. It features lovely teapots, ranging from what you'd expect in the parlor of a proper English home to outrageous and funky. The shop also is well stocked with biscuits, teas, tea cozies, and all manner of things to accessorize your afternoon sip. ♦ Daily. 448.4054. ♿

KELL'S RESTAURANT & PUB

★$$ This hidden-away pub is easy to miss, but don't. It's everything a pub should be: Aged and full of smoke-darkened woods and sporting prints, this is a place where patrons aren't afraid to argue and maybe fight for their politics. Guinness is available on tap, or dip into a pint of one of the Northwest's assertive brews. The menu complements the Irish ambience with homemade stews, lamb pies, and traditional soda bread. There's also a gift shop that ships worldwide. And live Irish music is featured Wednesday through Saturday nights. In summer, a small outdoor dining area is cordoned off in the alley. ♦ Irish ♦ Cover F and Sa nights. Daily, lunch and dinner; bar: daily, until 2AM. 728.1916. www.kellsirish.com

MILAGROS

A beautiful shop filled with handcrafted Mexican folk art. Not only will you find wonderful works of art, such as Day of the Dead sculptures and *santos* from Guerrero, but you also might find yourself a new Lucha Libra key chain. ♦ 464.0490. www.milagrosseattle.com

THE PINK DOOR

★★$$ Although some summer visitors know this place solely for its alfresco dining, this high-ceilinged trattoria serving inexpensive Italian fare is romantic year-round—at night, candles illuminate the surroundings. Servers can be forgetful, and sometimes you have to wield sharp elbows to find lunchtime seating, but such dishes as fettuccine with clam sauce and lasagna are hard to beat. ♦ Italian ♦ Tu-Sa, lunch, afternoon antipasto, and dinner; bar: Tu-Sa. 443.3241. www.thepinkdoor.com

13 SOAMES-DUNN BUILDING

Two adjoining structures from 1918—one held Dunn's Seeds, the other the Soames Paper Company, which peddled paper bags to market merchants—were combined to make this building. A 1976 rehabilitation was accomplished by architect **Arne Bystrom**. ♦ Pike Pl (between Stewart and Virginia Sts)

Within the Soames-Dunn Building:

EMMETT WATSON'S OYSTER BAR

★★$ A former semipro baseball player, Watson is now retired from being the city's curmudgeonly columnist (with the *Seattle Times*, after an early stint with the competing *Post-Intelligencer*). He was the journalist who discovered and notified the world that Ernest Hemingway's 1961 death in Ketchum, Idaho, was a suicide. More recently, he's led the "Lesser Seattle" movement, endorsing slow or no growth for the city and railing against the influx of Californians. This oft-crowded restaurant named in Watson's honor has earned institution status for its consistently fresh and varied selection of oysters. Salmon soup and hearty helpings of fish and chips can also be had, if you're not keen on bivalves. Wash your food down with something from the ample beer roster. One warning: Niched beside a courtyard at the back of the building, the restaurant can be hard to find. ♦ Seafood ♦ Daily, lunch and dinner. 448.7721

THE SOAP BOX

Indulge your inner child with the bath oils and rubber duckies that are sold here. ♦ Daily. 441.5680. www.soapboxltd.com

THE SOUK

Foods and spices from the Middle East, Pakistan, India, and Africa stock these shelves. ♦ Daily. 441.1666

STARBUCKS

★$ According to an old Turkish proverb, "Coffee should be black as hell, strong as death, and sweet as love." Well, the ancient Turks would be shocked at the way their heady brew is treated around here. The ol' black magic has all but disappeared from the coffee in the Seattle area, where ordering a cup of regular, "unmilked," unadorned java will earn you the kind of bug-eyed stares usually reserved for asylum escapees. The caffeine craze in Seattle can mostly be attributed to this chain, which grew to ubiquity (not only in Seattle but throughout the country) after this storefront opened in 1971. It's always crowded on weekends, when classical violinists perform from time to time just outside the front door. ♦ Coffeehouse ♦ M-Sa, from 7:30AM; Su, from 8:30AM. 448.8762. &. www.starbucks.com. Also at numerous locations throughout the city

14 STEWART HOUSE

A working person's hotel, built in stages between 1902 and 1911, this place was closed in the 1970s for failure to meet city housing codes. A 1982 renovation by **Ibsen Nelsen & Associates** rehabilitated the wooden structure and included a four-story brick-faced addition. Studios for senior citizens and people with disabilities are located above the street-level shops. ♦ Stewart St and Pike Pl

Within the Stewart House:

LE PANIER

Warm, fragrant French breads are the main attraction, but once you're inside, the pastries are no less an enticement. This is no place to be worried about your waistline. ♦ M-Sa, from 7AM. 441.3669. www.lepanier.com

MARKET TOBACCO PATCH

Owner Bill Coulson defies political correct- ness to maintain Seattle's premier pipe and cigar emporium. Pipe tobacco is available in a splendid variety, and Coulson keeps 60 to 80 types of cigars in stock. But the real treat here (for smokers, at least) is stepping inside the climate-controlled cigar humidor and inhaling deeply. ♦ Daily. 728.7291

15 94 STEWART

★★$$ Chef/owner Celinda Norton's approach is Mediterranean, but she does her own thing with it. For lunch try the appetizer platter, which might include cured meats, duck roulette, pickles, peppers, cheese, and homemade duck pâté. The house specialty is lumps of fresh avocado, rolled in panko, flash-fried, and served warm with fresh crab and chive-infused oil. Then there's crab cakes, crab chowder, and crab sandwiches. Lunch is served until 5PM; dinner main dishes change with the seasons. ♦ Tu-Su, lunch and dinner. 94 Stewart St (between First Ave and Pike Pl). 441.5505. www.94stewart.com

15 ANTIQUES AT PIKE PLACE

In business for over 15 years, this 5,000- square-foot place is bound to have the perfect treasure for you. With over 100 dealers displaying collectibles, it's easy to spend a couple of hours wandering up and down the aisles and peering into the crevices of this mini-mall. The range is huge, from a 1920s copy of *Dr. Jekyll and Mr. Hyde* to a high-end piece of Art Deco jewelry, and everything in between. ♦ M-Sa 10AM-6PM; Su 12PM-5PM. 92 Stewart St (between First Ave and Pike Pl). 441.9643. www.antiquesatpikeplace.com

16 NORTH ARCADE

This has become one of the slowest-moving pedestrian areas in the market, as everybody stops to look at the tables piled with hand- knit sweaters, homemade jellies and jams, and arrangements of dried flowers. On warm days, merchants even stretch out north along the sidewalk, selling some of the more interesting T-shirts available here, as well as jewelry and pottery. ♦ Pike Pl (between Pike St and Western Ave)

17 GARDEN CENTER

Originally an egg market, this building became the place for flowers and plants in 1946. ♦ Pike Pl (between Pine and Stewart Sts)

Within the Garden Center:

SEATTLE GARDEN CENTER

Potted plants decorate the sidewalk outside, and indoors are planters, tools, birdhouses, and more seed packets than most people would think to use in a lifetime, but dedicated gardeners will love perusing them all. Polish up that green thumb. ♦ Daily. 448.0431

SUR LA TABLE

Shirley Collins's hillside lodestone for butchers, bakers, and candy-stick makers represents the height of kitchen chic. Even amateurs can appreciate the shiny and varied wealth of gadgets, dishware, picnic baskets, and kitchenware here. The staff is knowledgeable, and there's a wide assortment of pricey cookbooks to further expand your culinary expertise. Just watch out for weekends and lunch hours, when the cramped aisles seem to become all feet and elbows. ♦ Daily. 448.2244, 800/243.0852

Restaurants/Clubs: Red | Hotels: Purple | Shops: Orange | Outdoors/Parks: Green | Sights/Culture: Blue

18 POST ALLEY MARKET

Designed in 1983 by **Bassetti/Norton/ Metler**, this building is strictly functional (unlike some of the other nearby structures). Shops at the bottom give way to offices on top. ♦ Post Alley and Pine St

Within the Post Alley Market:

MADE IN WASHINGTON

Here's the place to get just the souvenir gift to send or take to someone back home. Everything in this store is, as the name says, made locally. Choose from among jewelry, glass artwork, pottery, wall art, T-shirts, and other clothing. There's also a wide selection of smoked salmon, mussels, and oysters, and much more. ♦ Daily. 467.0788. www.madeinwashington.com

SBC

★$ It's the rare Seattleite who would remember this, but Jim Stewart began selling roasted coffee in 1970, when he had an ice-cream parlor called the **Wet Whisker** in Coupeville on Whidbey Island. He opened his first store with his brother, Dave, in 1971 at Pier 70. Ten years later, **Stewart Brothers Coffee** began business in Bellevue Square. By 1989, when the name changed to **SBC Coffee** (defined archly as "Seattle's Best Coffee"), Jim Stewart had locations on both sides of Lake Washington, including the **Westlake Center**. (And even though Starbucks bought out SBC, all SBC outlets serve their own roast, not Starbucks.) This contemporary corner shop in **Pike Place Market** was designed by architects **Olson/Walker**. On warm days, the alley side wall opens and patrons spread onto the sidewalks. Both bulk coffee beans and cups of espresso variations are available. ♦ Coffeehouse ♦ Daily, from 7AM. 467.7700. www.seattlesbest.com

SISTERS EUROPEAN SNACKS

★$ In summer, the glass front opens to the elements so patrons sitting along the counter can eavesdrop on alley strollers. And year-round, this is a bright and warm-hearted establishment, specializing in grilled sandwiches served on focaccia. The Corsica (Black Forest ham, artichoke hearts, fontina cheese, and tomato) and the Gesundheit (sun-dried tomato, cream cheese, avocado, and alfalfa sprouts) are faves. Black-bean chili and borscht are good winter warmers, and the apple-mint tea is especially refreshing in summer. Breakfast waffles, selected deli meats, and cheeses are served all day. ♦ European deli ♦ Daily, until 5PM. No credit cards accepted. 623.6723. &

19 TRIANGLE BUILDING

When this building was constructed in 1908 as home to the South Park Poultry Company, shoppers used to browse here among the stripped chickens that hung from the ceiling. The structure was rehabilitated in 1977 by architect **Fred Bassetti**, along with the adjoining **Silver Oakum Building** to the north. ♦ Pike Pl and Post Alley

Within the Triangle Building:

CINNAMON WORKS

The signature cinnamon rolls here may be filling, but the chocolate chocolate-chip cookies are some customers' secret weakness. ♦ Daily, from 7AM. No credit cards accepted. First floor. 583.0085

MR. D'S GREEK DELICACIES

★$ Fast food, Aegean style, with *spanako-pita* (spinach and feta cheese wrapped in phyllo), juicy gyros, and Greek pastries to go. There are a few tables in the back where you can chow down. ♦ Greek deli/takeout ♦ Daily. No credit cards accepted. First floor. 622.4881

MEE SUM PASTRIES

The service can be a bit surly, but it's a small price to pay for the fine Chinese pot stickers and *hum baos* (meat- or vegetable-filled doughy buns) here. ♦ Daily. No credit cards accepted. First floor. 682.6780

COPACABANA CAFE

★$$ This restaurant was opened in 1963 by Ramon Pelaez, a writer, former owner of Bolivia's largest radio station, and long-time political activist. Pelaez died in 1979, but his daughter and son-in-law continue to run the city's only Bolivian restaurant, using many Pelaez family recipes. Look up one level as you stride the bricks of **Pike Place** and you're likely to spot the crowded, two-tables-wide deck that surrounds this place—a favorite summer dining option. Service is often slow, but the food is worth missing a meeting or two. Best choices from the regular menu are the filling paella and the *pescado a la Española*, a delicate halibut steak with onions and tomatoes in a mild saffron sauce. Order the shrimp nachos (with a side of beer) as an appetizer. ♦ Bolivian ♦ M-F, lunch; Sa, Su, lunch and dinner. Second floor. 622.6359. &

20 MAIN ARCADE

Frank Goodwin's first market building, dating from 1907, reflects a simpler

IN THE MARKET FOR A GOOD TIME?

Think of **Pike Place Market** as a separate village within a city, one that claims its own rules of conduct, its own traditions, its own unique style and pace. You really need a kindly old uncle or aunt to show you the ropes, but barring that option, here are a few tips for getting the most out of Seattle's spiritual nexus.

● Show up here early in the morning (between 7AM and 8AM) to see the farmers and craftspeople setting up their colorful stalls. If your goal is to find the best choice of fresh foodstuffs, come between 8AM and 11AM, before lunchers descend on the market. And if you're hoping to score last-minute discounts on the day's still-unsold edibles, arrive at about 4:30PM.

● Vendors new to the market don't have enough seniority to earn display space on weekends, so they tend to bring their novel works to the market Monday through Friday. You'll find more familiar, longtime craftspeople here on weekends.

● Just as it is impolite in foreign countries to bargain for goods and then choose not to buy them, it also is considered gauche in the market to listen to street musicians for any length of time without contributing at least a few coins to their buckets or violin cases.

● Despite ongoing discussions about making Pike Place a car-free zone, the market just wouldn't be the same without the constant jockeying of humans and autos here. If you're happy to move at slug speed, stay on the crowded sidewalks. Otherwise, step right onto the brick-covered street

and walk with the cars. Just keep a wary eye out for drivers wheeling in and out of the angled parking spaces.

● The odds of finding a parking spot anywhere around Pike Place are poor at best. Try, instead, the 550-space **Market Garage** just west of the **North Arcade**, off Western Avenue, which allows free parking with shopping validations from many market merchants. On-street parking is easiest to find heading north of the market, between Bell Street and Denny Way. Avoid parking lots along First Avenue, as they tend to be overpriced.

● Do not depend on market merchants to choose your produce. The best way to get the quality you pay for is to paw lightly over the foodstuffs yourself—no matter how much sellers try to discourage this practice.

● Two sets of public rest rooms are available in the market. One is at the south end of the **Main Arcade**, downstairs from **Pike Place Fish**. The other can be found at the Main Arcade's north end, by descending the ramp adjacent to **City Fish**.

● One-hour tours of the market are scheduled on Saturday mornings, at either 9AM or 10:30AM, depending on the availability of guides. They set out from the **Market Information Booth**, at First Avenue and Pike Street. The charge is $5 per person, and reservations are required. Call 682.7453 for weekly schedules and to sign up for an informative walk, or visit www.pikeplacemarket.org.

---

architectural style than he applied to his reworking of the **Economy Market**. About 50% of the market's fish and produce stalls are located here, with many others just across the street. Take a look at the engraved floor tiles covering the arcade's main level, laid out as part of a fund-raising project in the mid-1980s. Seattleites paid $35 apiece to have their names imprinted on these tiles; Ronald and Nancy Reagan are also represented here, although they didn't pay anything for the privilege. Two floors (making up what used to be called the **Labyrinth**) descend from street level and are known simply as First Floor Down Under and Second Floor Down Under. ♦ Pike Pl (at Post Alley). www.pikeplacemarket.org

Within the Main Arcade:

PIKE PLACE FISH

In 1947, the Seattle City Council forbade singing by market vendors. But wait until you hear the bellowing hawkers here, whose voices positively explode from beneath the **Market Clock**. Crowds of tourists gather to observe the iced beds of crab and to gape as fishmongers hurl salmon over customers' heads for weighing behind the counter. Founded in 1930, the store ships fresh fish anywhere in the US. ♦ Daily, from 6:30AM. Main floor. 682.7181, 800/542.7732. www.pikeplacefish.com

---

Restaurants/Clubs: Red | Hotels: Purple | Shops: Orange | Outdoors/Parks: Green | Sights/Culture: Blue

Down the staircase behind Pike Place Fish:

PLACE PIGALLE

★★★$$ Early in the 20th century, this place was essentially a bar frequented by men (many were patrons of the **LaSalle Hotel** bordello) who drank with their hats on. Now it's one of the most pleasant dining spaces in the market—the floor is covered in alternating black-and-white tiles, and the outlook on Puget Sound is wondrously unobstructed. The menu includes whatever is seasonally fresh, leaning heavily toward seafood. A porch is available for outdoor dining during the summer. ♦ Continental/Northwestern ♦ M-Sa, lunch and dinner. Reservations recommended. 81 Pike St. 624.1756

MARKET SPICE

Olfactory overload! More than a hundred flavors of tea, bulk coffee beans, and giant jars of seasonings can be found here, as can tea-brewing paraphernalia and boxes of fine sweets. Head first to the free-tea dispenser, just beside the cashier's counter and usually filled with the popular house blend (developed by the wife of a pharmacist in the 1970s). Then roam the aisles with an open mind . . . and an open nose. Mail orders accepted. ♦ Daily. Main floor. 622.6340. &

MAXIMILIEN-IN-THE-MARKET

★★★$$$ You've got to admire the ego of a restaurant that showcases a review written in French. Are you just to *assume* that the report is favorable, or should you simply allow yourself to be seduced by the old-fashioned charm and exceptional Puget Sound views here? Owned and operated since 1997 by host Axel Macé and chef Eric Francy, this restaurant is proud of its Frenchness, but that doesn't translate to haughtiness; in fact, staff members are pleasant and attentive. Entrées include shellfish-rich bouillabaisse, fresh salmon and mussels, and the classics, such as onion soup. The bar is a fine redoubt from winter chills. ♦ French ♦ Tu-Sa, lunch and dinner; Su, brunch. Reservations recommended. Main floor. 682.7270. &. www.maximilienrestaurant.com

If visitors from San Francisco feel a bit more at home in Seattle than the rest of us, it may be because part of their city is here. A good portion of the land used to regrade the waterfront area came from Telegraph Hill. The dirt had been brought over on ships from San Francisco as ballast, then dumped here.

ATHENIAN INN

★★★$ Opened in 1909 as a Greek bakery-luncheonette, and later operated as a bar (it received one of Seattle's earliest liquor licenses, in 1933), this is among the market's most friendly and democratic restaurants. Fishermen hunker up to the bar counter while designer-suited sales reps wait in line for tables with great views of Puget Sound. The menu hits all the local standards—from grilled oysters to fat burgers—with the breakfast faves being red-flannel hash (with beets, corned beef, green peppers, and potatoes) and sweet-potato turkey hash. The breakfast menu is available all day long, and the bar has upwards of 20 beers on tap and stocks more than 300 brews. ♦ American ♦ M-Sa, breakfast, lunch, and dinner until 6:30PM. Main floor. 624.7166. &

CITY FISH

This busy stall was started by the city in 1918 to offer Seattleites fresh fish at reasonable prices. Newspaper reports of overcharging had led Mayor Hiram Gill to make his health commissioner responsible for setting up a market space stocked with dirt-cheap hatchery fish. Prices began at one third to one quarter of what was being charged elsewhere for fish. For four years, this operation was profitable, but as sales waned, the city sold out. David Levy, one of the first Sephardic Jews to arrive in Seattle, bought the stall in 1926 and quickly earned the nickname "Good Weight Dave" for keeping his thumb off the scale. The business was bought from the Levy family about 5 years ago by Jon Daniels, a commercial fisherman who continues to sell high-quality fish and also offers overnight shipping to any location in the continental US. Look for the well-preserved **City Fish Market** sign on Pike Place. ♦ Daily, from 7:30AM. Main floor. 682.9329. www.cityfish.com

LOWELL'S RESTAURANT

★$ Substantive—though not surprising—dishes (try the fried oysters and the Monte Cristo or Reuben sandwiches) are served at this classic cafeteria and restaurant. It was opened as a coffee shop in 1908 by brothers Edward and William Manning, who did something early on that much later would become a Seattle signature: They started selling roasted coffee beans in bulk. Three

floors of Puget Sound Views. ◆ American/ seafood ◆ Daily, breakfast, lunch, and dinner until 5PM. Main floor. 622.2036. &. www.eatatlowells.com

Golden Age Collectables

This crowded corner store carries the city's largest selection of comics, everything from standards such as *Spider-Man*, *Legends of the Dark Knight*, and *Green Arrow* (the last now drawn by local talent Mike Grell and set in Seattle); to *Aliens*, *Swamp Thing*, *Bikini Confidential*; to some of the more obscure titles from the Dark Horse publishing house of Portland, Oregon. There's a wide array of vintage comics, too, plus science-fiction novels, models, sports cards, and binders full of classic movie-star publicity stills. Special orders are taken. ◆ Daily. First Floor Down Under. 622.9799. www.goldenagecollectables.com

Market Magic Shop

Common thrills here are the impromptu performances by owners Darryl Beckmann and Sheila Lyon, who always seem willing to open their bags of tricks. With professional paraphernalia and joke props, replicas of old Houdini posters, and juggling clubs, this is an ideal spot to conjure up an afternoon's escape—mental, if not physical. ◆ Daily. First Floor Down Under. 624.4271. www.generalrubric.com

Old Seattle Paperworks

With the feel of a richly cluttered attic, this is a narrow storehouse of old postcards for sale, classic black-and-whites from Seattle's early years, and piles of dusty *National Geographic* magazines like the ones your grandparents have held onto for half a century. ◆ Daily. First Floor Down Under. 623.2870

Grandma's Attic

One of several collectibles outlets on the arcade's lowest level, this one is filled with delicate, feminine vintage outfits and knickknacks. ◆ Daily. Second Floor Down Under. 682.9281

Yesterdaze

Intriguingly cluttered with well-kept old hats, ties, and jewelry but especially known for its period military clothing, this shop is a perfect stop for collectors. ◆ M-Sa. Second Floor Down Under. 521.0572

21 Sanitary Market Building

The name derives from the fact that this was the first building in the market that didn't allow horses inside. It was four stories tall when erected in 1910, but the upper floors were destroyed by a fire 31 years later, one of several conflagrations to sweep through the market since its inception. City architect **Daniel R. Huntington** redesigned it in 1942 as a two-story edifice with rooftop parking. The building was rehabilitated again in 1981 by **Bassetti/Norton/Metler**. ◆ Pike Pl and Post Alley

Within the Sanitary Market Building:

Jack's Fish Spot

$ Behind the fresh shellfish tanks (the only ones in the market) is a walk-up seafood bar. Try the cioppino or the fish and chips, considered by some the best in town. ◆ Seafood ◆ Restaurant: daily, lunch; fish market: daily, from 7:30AM. First floor. 467.0514. &. www.jacksfishspot.com

Three Girls Bakery

★$ Its roots are in the **Corner Market Building**, where it opened in 1912, but this bakery is now an institution at its current location. You can tell by the crowded lunch counter and the line weaving from its take-out window down the sidewalk. In addition to the baked goods, a delicious assortment of homemade soups and sandwiches is featured; the corned beef and the ham are savvy buys. ◆ Deli/bakery ◆ M-Sa, breakfast and lunch. First floor. 622.1045. &

22 Kasala

A glass-walled corner location provides a cheery showplace for contemporary and high-style (but surprisingly comfortable) furniture for office and home. There are lots of high-tech floor lamps and other European accessories. Salespeople are readily available but usually leave you alone to browse. ◆ Daily. 1505 Western Ave (between University and Virginia Sts). 623.7795. www.kasala.com. Also at 1014 116th Ave NE (between Eighth and 12th Sts), Bellevue. 425/453.2823

23 Hillclimb Corridor

In the market's early days, a wooden pedestrian overpass (built in 1912) connected **Pike Place** with Waterfront piers, an essential link. Many sellers at the market arrived by boat, often on craft belonging to the old **Mosquito Fleet**, an armada of 70 small steamers that hustled people and products to 350 ports on Puget Sound. In 1973, after the market gained historical status, those rickety steps were replaced with these landscaped stairs (designed by **Calvin/Gorasht and**

Sanders) down to the Waterfront and the **Seattle Aquarium**. The incline is steep (some refer to it as Cardiac Gulch), yet the **Hillclimb** has proved a magnet for both shops and shoppers.

In the Hillclimb Corridor:

EL PUERCO LLORON

★$ It looks like a cafeteria decorated by collectors of cheesy Tijuana trinkets, but the authentic hand-made tortillas, tamales, and exceptional *chiles rellenos* more than make up for the decorative deficiencies. Beware of the salsas: It's always best to taste first before pouring them over your meal.
♦ Mexican ♦ Daily, lunch and dinner. 1501 Western Ave. 624.0541. &

PROCOPIO

Treat yourself to a delicious homemade gelato sans artificial anything. Appropriately enough for this city, flavors include cappuccino and mocha. ♦ M-Th, until 10PM; F-Sa, until midnight. No credit cards accepted. 1501 Western Ave. 622.4280

24 THE SPANISH TABLE

Passionate about paella? Transported by tapas? Chomping for *chorizo*? This store has everything for the lover of Spanish and Portuguese cooking. There are kitchen tools, cookbooks, and hard-to-find specialty foods and wines. The shop also has a widely used mail-order service.
♦ Daily. 1426 Western Ave. 682.2827. www.spanishtable.com

25 CORNER MARKET BUILDING

One of the things about **Pike Place Market** that most fascinates architects is that so little of the development here can be ascribed to professional designers. An exception is this formal structure built in 1912 and conceived by **Harlan Thomas**, designer of the **Sorrento Hotel** and **Harborview Hospital**, both on First Hill, and the Byzantine **Chamber of Commerce Building** downtown on Columbia Street. A three-story brick structure, this building is best recognized by its graceful arched top-level windows. The first tenant was **Three Girls Bakery**, which now operates in the **Sanitary Market Building**. Also housed here was the Northwest's first homegrown grocery chain: Herman Eba moved from the **Main Arcade** stall he had occupied since 1910 to the **Corner Market** in 1929; 6 years later, he adopted the business name **Tradewell**, a label that later became familiar to supermarket shoppers around the region. This was the first market landmark to be rehabilitated (1975).
♦ Pike Pl and Pike St

Within the Corner Market Building:

THE CRUMPET SHOP

★$ This cozy, very British dining room prepares its own spongy crumpets, which are great topped with raspberry jam, marmalade, or even ricotta cheese. This is a wonderful choice for a unique and inexpensive breakfast; lox or ham on crumpets is available at lunch, as are more conventional sandwiches. The space can be packed with take-out patrons early on weekday mornings, but it's a comforting crowdedness—really.
♦ Teahouse/takeout ♦ Daily, breakfast, lunch, and afternoon tea. First floor. 682.1598. &

LEFT BANK BOOKS

It takes a while to acquaint yourself with the categorization here (books written by men, for instance, are separated from books by women), and the array of new and used volumes tends to be more funky than complete. But there's an endearing, antiquarian nature to this place, buttressed by a lack of computerization and a pack-rat mentality. The bent is toward liberal, sometimes revolutionary works. ♦ Daily. First floor. 622.0195. www.leftbankbooks.com

PIKE PLACE BAR & GRILL

★$$ Sandee and Gordy Brock's joint is a market standard, not flashy but satisfying. Newcomers usually wind up at the restaurant end, filling themselves with sandwiches (thumbs up, especially for the French dip) or pleasing pasta and fish specials. Seattleites gravitate to the noisier bar, which has the best views of the market. ♦ American ♦ Daily. Second floor. 624.1365. www.pikeplacebarandgrill.com

CHEZ SHEA

★★★$$$$ This restaurant is especially romantic late at night, when candlelight is the principal illumination, and the half-moon windows allow a softened perspective on the market below and the ferries gliding over Puget Sound. Chef Jeremy Bund presents original and inspired eight-course, prix-fixe dinners, and there are always vegetarian alternatives, such as vegetable paella (broad beans, rice, roasted peppers, black olives, tomatoes, and saffron). The menu changes seasonally, and the service is always excellent. The wine list represents both top West Coast and European vintages. There's also a lounge serving libations and a bistro-style menu. ♦ Continental/Northwestern ♦ Tu-Su, dinner. **Shea's Lounge** is open Tu-Th and Su, 4:30PM-midnight; F, Sa, 4:30PM-2AM. Bistro menu is available 10PM-midnight. Third floor. 467.9990. www.chezshea.com

MATT'S IN THE MARKET

★★$$ If you're visiting Seattle, you have to go to Pike Place Market. This tiny spot overlooks the Farmer's Market sign and the brass pig, a landmark. Matt's has the best luches, and the dinner menu is equally good. The cook creates from portable burners and in hardly any space to speak of, turns out food that makes you grateful to be hungry. It ranges from complex little salads to hearty soups and fish sandwiches. There is also a nice selection of beer and wine to choose from. ♦ 467.7909

26 MARKET CLOCK

Rising from the elbow that connects the **Economy Market** to the **Main Arcade**, this timepiece and the **Public Market** sign that surrounds it are supposed to be the oldest examples of public neon in Seattle, dating back to the 1920s or 1930s. The clock is a favorite among visiting photographers, and on New Year's Eve, crowds of happily tipsy Seattleites gather below it to celebrate at the stroke of midnight. ♦ Pike St and Pike Pl

26 RACHEL, THE MARKET PIG

This overgrown piggy bank is the Market Foundation's friendliest fund-raiser. More than $35,000 has been dropped into her belly since she took up her position below the **Market Clock** in 1986. ♦ Pike St and Pike Pl

27 LOWER POST ALLEY

This was once a major commercial route connecting the market with Western Avenue's Produce Row, the Waterfront, and

In a backlash against the Seattle hype of the 1980s, Emmett Watson, the *Seattle Times*'s longtime columnist and curmudgeon, resorted to half-truths and a few pointed prevarications regarding Seattle's resolute smugness, its notorious rainfall, and its general backwardness. "Plainly," Watson stated, "only a fool would want to live in Seattle, fools like me . . ."

Pioneer Square. Guttering beneath the main market sign and clock, the alley is now pretty much ignored, yet it is supposedly the only completely restored cobblestone street in the Northwest. The glass-walled bridge above the alley's entrance off First Avenue was known historically as the Bridge of Sighs. Apparently, from here south, the alley used to be lined with bars, and sailors would stop in at each of them for a nip before shipping out of town. It's said that from the bridge women would watch their men amble slowly away and, presumably, sigh. ♦ Between Union and Pike Sts

Along Lower Post Alley:

IL BISTRO

★★★$$$ Trimmed in dark woods and set off by arches, this quiet dining spot is like a European *cave* or wine cellar. People come here after work to decompress, sipping wine or whiskey in the bar or chatting over dinner in the more secluded reaches. Italian dishes got this place off the ground, and although a variety of seafood plates have been introduced with varying degrees of success, pasta is still instrumental in keeping it popular. Both the veal piccata and the outstanding rack of lamb will satisfy your appetite. The cioppino is also a standout. Leave room for the Marquis—it's a sublime chocolate dessert. ♦ Italian ♦ Restaurant: daily, dinner; bar: until 2AM. 93A Pike St. 682.3049. www.ilbistro.com

LASALLE HOTEL

This bay-windowed building beside the **Public Market** sign was the first bordello north of Yesler Way and survived to become the last of this city's big-time bawdy houses. Erected in 1909 as the **Outlook Hotel**, prior to World War II it was owned by a Japanese family who catered to frugal workers and the elderly. After the 1942 internment of Japanese residents, the hotel was taken over by Nellie Curtis (née Zella Nightengale), who had run orderly disorderly houses across Canada before moving to Seattle in 1931. Small and birdlike, she drove Cadillacs, kept her money in drawers rather than banks, wore ermine shawls, and collected hats with the same superfluousness with which Imelda Marcos would later gather shoes. As Alice Shorett and Murray Morgan recall in their jolly history, *Pike Place Market: People, Politics, and Produce*, the hotel even had "enough rooms so that some could be used for legitimate purposes, thus providing a cover for more profitable activities."

Shortly after business got under way here, some of Nellie's "girls" went down to the

---

Restaurants/Clubs: Red | Hotels: Purple | Shops: Orange | Outdoors/Parks: Green | Sights/Culture: Blue

Waterfront to meet incoming ships and hand out business cards: "LaSalle Hotel—Friends Easily Made." That night, hundreds of libidinous wharf rats and sailors tried to anchor in one of the hotel's 57 berths, attracting attention not only from the local military but from reform Mayor William Devin, who ordered a prostitution crackdown. But Nellie's fortunes went undisturbed.

It was only in 1949, after her nephew botched a temporary management of the place and Seattle had been shaken by its first major earthquake, that Nellie decided to sell the hotel. The buyers were a Japanese-American couple, George and Sodeko Ikeda, who had trouble convincing some of Nellie's old clients that there were no longer any "working girls" in the hostelry. The Ikedas subsequently sued Nellie for overstating profits to be made from the property. Not only did Nellie lose $7,500 in court but she also finally attracted the attention of the Internal Revenue Service. The hotel was rehabilitated in 1977 and now contains commercial space as well as low-income housing.

28 MARKET INFORMATION BOOTH

Market maps and other visitor info are happily dispensed here. This is the starting point for tours of the neighborhood. ♦ Daily. Pike St and First Ave. 682.7453

29 ECONOMY MARKET

Promoter and investor **Frank Goodwin** was an eccentric who played heavily with penny stocks, put together an early steam-powered automobile, and practiced a strict vegetarian diet. He bought heavily into Pike Place real estate and was the man who finally brought the market in out of the rain in 1907, when he constructed the **Main Arcade**. An amateur architect, Goodwin designed and built a multistory expansion of the market down Pike Place bluff to Western Avenue. In 1916 he obtained a lease on the

Bartell Building (completed in 1900) at the corner of First Avenue and Pike Street, transforming it into today's Economy Market. Look for his design work in this building's Doric columns and the plaster garlands of fruit and flowers. Preservation architect **George Bartholick** headed a rehabilitation of the market in 1978. The angled ramps in the atrium used to be trodden on by horses, which were checked through here on their way to the main market. ♦ Pike St and First Ave

Within the Economy Market:

SASQUATCH

Whether descended from prehistoric primates or born from human imagination, Sasquatch (or Bigfoot, if you prefer) has become the Northwest's signature monster. Its appearances hark back to the tribal mythology of virtually every native people from coastal British Columbia to northern California. The name *Sasquatch* comes from *sas-kets*, a term used by Salish-speaking tribes of southwestern British Columbia to describe the hairy, humanlike giants they said lived in the Fraser River Valley and communicated via whistles and shrill screams. More than 2,500 Sasquatch sightings have been recorded since the 1960s, most of them in Washington State. This brooding sculpture was carved by artist Richard Beyer. ♦ Atrium

THE GREAT WIND-UP

Follow the noise of barking dogs, growling dragons, and hopping bunnies to this toy-filled corner shop. While children gather ideas for Christmas, adults can enjoy a table filled with windup kangaroos, chattering teeth, and mince-stepping eyeballs. Other perennial favorites include ducks on bikes, collectible tin toys, candle boats, yo-yos, and Wheelos. ♦ Daily. Atrium. 621.9370. www.thegreatwindup.com

TENZING MOMO

Come to this herbal apothecary—the oldest herb store on the West Coast—to buy a stick of incense or herbs in bulk. You can also pick up fluid extracts, Chinese nostrums, earwax candles, or books on witchcraft. The store's name, translated from Tibetan, means "illustrious dumpling." This is holy ground for worshipers in the temple of natural health. ♦ M-Sa. Atrium. 623.9837. www.tenzingmomo.com

FIRST & PIKE NEWS

This is one of the two best-stocked newsstands in this city (the other contender is **Bulldog News** in the University District). The inventory here reflects a walloping diversity of American and international periodicals. Expect everything from *Popular Mechanics* to *Sassy*. Looking for the *International Herald Tribune* or the *Nome Nugget*? They're here too. ♦ Daily, 7AM-7PM. Main floor. 624.0140. www.firstandpikenews.com

DAILY DOZEN DOUGHNUTS

Snag a sack with a baker's dozen of miniature doughnuts—plain, powdered-sugar, or cinnamon. Then hope nobody witnesses your abject gluttony. ♦ M-Sa. No credit cards accepted. Main floor. 467.7769

DELAURENTI'S SPECIALTY FOODS

Exotic Mediterranean canned goods, meats, and wines are shoehorned into a space barely big enough to contain them all. Though the history of this shop is commonly traced back to owners Pete and Mamie DeLaurenti in the 1940s, Mamie's very Italian mother, Angelina Mustelo, had opened a small store on the market's lower level in 1928. ♦ M-Sa. Main floor. 622.0141. 425/454.7155. www.delaurenti.com

30 INN AT THE MARKET

$$$ What finer location for a Seattle hotel than smack dab in the midst of its famous market district? And in most aspects, this 65-room hotel, wrapped about a surprisingly peaceful courtyard, will live up to your expectations. There's a well-respected restaurant located right downstairs, a large deck overlooking the market and Elliot Bay, blessedly little chance that you'll be surrounded by conventioneers (thanks to a shortage of facilities in the hotel for their use), separate floors for nonsmokers, and a warm, European personality. The rooms are good-sized and attractively decorated with sculptures and flowers. Though the hotel doesn't have a kitchen, the restaurant provides room service. The downside is that the same thing that makes the market a wonderful place to be—the bustle and the attendant noise—can also detract from the intimacy and comfort. Rooms on the west side have the best views, but there's disruptive noise for most of the day; those on the east, or First Avenue, side suffer traffic noise. This is a hotel for lovers of the urban experience. ♦ 86 Pine St (at First Ave). 443.3600, 800/446.4484; fax 448.0631. ♿. www.innatthemarket.com

Within the Inn at the Market:

CAMPAGNE

★★★★$$$ Romantically appointed, with Oriental rugs and a satisfying view of Elliott Bay, this restaurant is noted for its gracious host and fine servers. On the level beneath the restaurant is the stylish **Cafe Campagne**, serving bistro cuisine in an informal setting. ♦ French ♦ Restaurant: daily, dinner; lighter fare served until midnight; bar: daily until 2AM. Café: M-Sa, breakfast, lunch, and dinner; Su, brunch. Jacket required. Reservations recommended. 86 Pine St (at First Ave). 728.2800. ♿. www.campagnerestaurant.com

DILETTANTE CHOCOLATES

Formulas for making this shop's sweet temptations were passed down from Julius Rudolph Franzen, who created pastries for Emperor Franz Josef of Austria and was master candy maker to Nicholas II, the last czar of Russia. Just before the czar was assassinated, Franzen immigrated to the US, where he educated his American brother-in-law, Earl Davenport, in the chocolatier's art. Now Davenport's grandson produces some of the most tempting truffles, butter creams, and dragées (nuts or dried fruits dredged through dipping chocolate) you'll ever try. ♦ Daily. 728.9144. Many other locations. 329.6463. ♿. www.dilettante.com

31 A.E. DOYLE BUILDING

Built as a department store in 1915, this unobtrusive terra-cotta edifice, designed in

---

Restaurants/Clubs: Red | Hotels: Purple | Shops: Orange | Outdoors/Parks: Green | Sights/Culture: Blue

the Venetian Renaissance palazzo style, was remodeled in 1973 and now carries the name of its original architect, a prominent figure in early 20th-century Portland, Oregon. ◆ Pine St and Second Ave

Within the A.E. Doyle Building:

M. Coy Books and Espresso

More selective than comprehensive in his collection of books, proprietor Michael Coy is usually on top of the latest best-sellers, as well as new regional publications. General fiction is well represented, and there's a mind-engaging array of nonfiction available, but the range within any genre (particularly mystery and science fiction) is, for the most part, fairly narrow. Fortunately, employees are helpful and ready to take special orders. A small coffee shop in the back contributes a relaxed and contemplative atmosphere. ◆ Daily. 117 Pine St. 623.5354

32 Metsker Maps

Joseph Conrad captured the appeal of maps in *Heart of Darkness*, when Marlowe explained: "Now, when I was a little chap, I had a passion for maps. I would look for hours at South America, or Africa, or Australia, and lose myself in all the glories of exploration." Marlowe might have begun many a voyage at this shop, which sells hundreds of maps as well as guidebooks and assorted travel paraphernalia to satisfy the hunger of wanderlust. ◆ M-Sa. 1511 First Ave (between Pike and Pine Sts). 623.8747. www.metskers.com

33 Pike Pubs and Brewing Company

This establishment has sold fresh hops, malted barley, and home-brewing supplies since 1921. Beer-making classes are offered several times a year, covering the basics as well as fermentation, bottling, and stylistic variations. ◆ 1415 First Ave (between Union and Pike Sts). 622.6044. www.pikebrewing.com

34 South Arcade

This tower, a jarring, neon-highlighted contrast to the sedate **Pike Place Market**, was designed in 1985 by **Olson/Walker**. ◆ 1411 First Ave (between Union and Pike Sts)

Within the South Arcade:

Undercover Quilts

This store has a lot of authentic antique quilts, some dating as far back as the 1850s, as well as a large collection of new quilts made by artists from all over the US. Owner Linda Hitchcock will even make a quilt to your specifications. Also in stock here are fabrics, one-of-a-kind dolls, and Christmas decorations made from vintage quilts. ◆ Daily. 622.6382. www.undercoverquilts.com

World Class Chili Incorporated

★★$ Arguments about what chili is and what it isn't could (and do) fill whole cookbooks. Joe Canavan, who collected recipes for years before he opened this small place, has decided to give purists and bean lovers something to sink their spoons into. Here the Texas-style bowl, dense with beef and chiles, leads the herd. Other versions mix beef and pork with ingredients like chocolate and cinnamon, substitute chicken for red meat, or throw out the meat altogether in favor of lentils and veggies (sacrilege!). ◆ Chili ◆ M-Sa, lunch and dinner until 6PM. No credit cards accepted. 623.3678

35 Union

★★★$$$ Chef-owner Ethan Stowell is on fire—his place is always busy. Located just down First Avenue from Pike Place Market and near the newly remodeled Seattle Art Museum, Union offers a selection of inventive dishes using seasonal ingredients. From Dungeness crab to artichokes and morel mushrooms to seared sea scallops with lentils and ham hocks, its menu captivates and entices the senses. But don't get too attached to any particular dish, because the menu changes every day. ◆ 1400 First Ave (at Union St). 838.8000. www.unionseattle.com

36 Seattle Art Museum (SAM)

Asked to explain the intent behind his firm's design of the **Seattle Art Museum**, which was relocated downtown in 1991, Philadelphia architect **Robert Venturi** said he wanted to create a "current urban art museum that is popular yet esoteric, closed but open, monumental yet inviting, an accommodating setting for the art, but a work of art itself." In other words, a little bit of everything: a sophisticated but unimposing juxtaposition of convex and concave curves, all faced in fluted limestone and terra-cotta ornament. The corner of University Street and First Avenue is enlivened by sculptor Jonathan Borofsky's *Hammering Man*, a black, 48-foot-tall mechanical piece that took a spill during its installation and had to be repaired before final placement. Working within zoning requirements that dictated view corridors to Puget Sound, Venturi, his partner **Denise Scott Brown**, and their associates created a waterfall of an outdoor staircase along the south wall that's almost mirrored by a processional stair inside.

By the beginning of the 21st century, it was clear that a significant expansion was necessary in order to display the more than

23,000 objects in the permanent collection and have space enough to accommodate major traveling shows. Hence the addition of four stories and 70% more gallery space immediately north of and adjacent to the 1991 structure of First Avenue. **Brad Cloepfil** (of **Allied Works Architecture**, a firm that has designed are museums for New York, Ann Arbor, Dallas, and St. Louis) has seamlessly connected the expansion to the Venturi section. The shimmering glass and stainless-steel structure has a new main entrance at First and Union; a second entrance has been opened up on Second Avenue so that people can flow down the existing processional stairway and into the civic space, a two-story area open free to the public, where artworks and educational tools serve the mandate of SAM to integrate art and the community. ♦ Admission; free for children age 12 and younger, for members, and on the first Thursday of each month; discount for senior citizens and students. Tu-Su; Th, until 9PM. 100 University St (at First Ave). 654.3100. www.seattleartmuseum.org

37 GRAND PACIFIC HOTEL

Displaying a stone and arched face that would have been more familiar in Pioneer Square than this far north on First Avenue, this building (known upon opening in 1898 as the **First Avenue Hotel**) was at no time a luxury inn. Its tenants were miners, sailors, and businessmen of modest means, in the early years many of them blowing through town on their way to the gold fields of the Klondike. But the structure, with its Romanesque stone footing, arched windows along the third floor, and fine detailing on its brick upper façade, doesn't lack class or style. Now restored, it's been attached to the neighboring **Colonial Hotel** and divided into residential units. ♦ 1115-17 First Ave (between Spring and Seneca Sts)

38 WATERMARK TOWER

This sculpted 20-story edifice (designed by **Bumgardner Architects** in 1983) bursts upward from the preserved terra-cotta façade of the 1915 **Colman Building** (conceived by **Carl Gould** and **Charles Bebb**). Pay special attention to the dynamic entry arch on Spring Street.♦ First Ave and Spring St

Within Watermark Tower:

McCORMICK & SCHMICK'S

★★$$ Waiters in black bow ties add a touch of class to this restaurant that specializes in seafood and grilled meats. The lamb chops don't disappoint, nor do the salmon dishes. Enjoy a preprandial cocktail in the comfortable, dark-wood barroom. The Irish coffees served here are better than most. ♦ Seafood ♦ M-F, lunch and dinner; Sa, Su, dinner. Reservations recommended. 1103 First Ave. 623.5500. www.mccormickandschmicks.com

39 ALEXIS HOTEL

$$$ Designed in 1901 by architect **Max Umbrecht**, this building was renovated in 1982 as part of a large-scale, privately

---

Restaurants/Clubs: **Red** | Hotels: **Purple** | Shops: **Orange** | Outdoors/Parks: **Green** | Sights/Culture: **Blue**

THE BEST

Jeanne Anderson

CEO, Early Learning Foundation

Green Lake: This most popular park in the state is used by more than 10,000 people per day much of the year for walking, jogging, swimming, boating, soccer, rugby, inline skating, and basketball. Join us.

Shopping the **REI** flagship store is an adventure in itself!

In the friendly neighborhood of Wallingford, I enjoy **Wide World Books & Maps**, which takes you around the world through books, guides, and maps. Everything to know about travel is here.

The **Spirit of Washington Dinner Train** is a fine way to see the length of Lake Washington, enjoy a lovely dinner, and tour a winery, all in just under 4 hours on a beautifully restored train.

For the energetic, there's **Vertical World**, a fabulous indoor rock climbing club near Fisherman's Terminal.

I like the variety of the monthly **First Thursday Art Walk** through the many galleries in and around **Pioneer Square**. They're open in the early evening, for the occasion.

From the **Inn at the Market**, it's nice to see the early morning opening of the stands and stalls and watch the ferries come and go across **Elliott Bay**.

People come from all over the city to join the locals eating at **Mona's**, near Green Lake. Great food, great atmosphere.

Watch boats both big and small go up or down the "water elevator" of the **Hiram M. Chittenden** (we all call it the **Ballard Locks**).

Head out to **Golden Gardens** for views of **Puget Sound**, the Olympic Mountains, and the many local folks basking in the summer sun.

---

funded project that also fixed up several nearby edifices. The property was re-furbished again in 1996, doubling in size. Convenient to **Pike Place Market**, the **Seattle Art Museum**, and Pioneer Square, the hotel now boasts 109 guest rooms, two restaurants, a fitness center, and spa services. Trapped between the revolting Alaskan Way Viaduct and noisy First Avenue, the hotel has no views to speak of, but a handful of balcony rooms face an interior courtyard and thus provide the most peace and quiet. Suites are outfitted with Jacuzzis, wood-burning fireplaces, and marble fixtures. Complimentary services include shoe shines, sherry in your room, continental breakfast, and a morning newspaper. "Discount luxury" hotel operator Bill Kimpton, who also owns the **Hotel Vintage Park** in the business district, is now at the helm. Parking around here can be a problem. ♦ 1007 First Ave (between Madison and Spring Sts). 624.4844, 800/426.7033. www.alexishotel.com

Within the Alexis Hotel:

THE LIBRARY BISTRO AND BOOKSTORE BAR

This is actually a better taproom than it was a bookstore. With its shelves full of literature, the place still maintains a bit of the feeling of its previous incarnation. The atmosphere is conducive to political discussions and after-work jousts with colleagues. ♦ M-Th, until midnight; F-Su, until 2AM. 624.3646

THE LEGACY

The collection of historic baskets, masks, and carvings from Northwest Indians and

Eskimos here is rounded out with newer native merchandise. ♦ M-Sa. 624.6350. www.thelegacyltd.com

Old Federal Office Building

North Market Street Graphics

40 OLD FEDERAL OFFICE BUILDING

Looking very much like a snowcapped mountain range, what with its brick facing topped by terra-cotta detailing, this memorable stepped-back Art Deco structure (which recently received an extensive

Pier 54, now the Waterfront home of Ye Olde Curiosity Shop, is remembered by old-timers as the place where, in 1940, Two-Ton Tony Galento, a 350-pound boxer, climbed into a tank of seawater to wrestle a 75-pound octopus. Brokered by late Seattle restaurateur Ivar Haglund, the bout ended in a draw.

Late journalist and broadcaster Alistair Cooke once characterized Seattle as "a rain-soaked fishing village midway between San Francisco and Alaska."

renovation) was one of the few projects raised in downtown during the Depression. The architect was **James A. Wetmore**.
♦ 909 First Ave (between Marion and Madison Sts)

41 HENRY M. JACKSON FEDERAL OFFICE BUILDING

The original building on this site was the **Frye Opera House**. With a mansard roof and brick walls, featuring 1,400 seats and a stage with seven trapdoors, the theater was once Seattle's most ostentatious landmark. The Great Fire of 1889 began at this intersection, in a woodworker's basement, and the Frye went up in smoke. After the fire, **Elmer Fisher** designed the Victorian-style **Burke Building** here, which in turn was torn down in 1974 to make room for the current structure, boasting a hipped and tiled roof and a fenestration of interlocking prefab concrete segments. This tower (designed by **Fred Bassetti**, along with **John Graham & Company**) gives off a Mediterranean palazzo feel. The lobby appeals with its wood finishes, but the star of this building is its outdoor cascading hillside stairs, which include remnants from the Burke Building. Sculptor Isamu Noguchi contributed an abstract grouping of pink granite blocks, called *Landscape of Time*, to the Second Avenue plaza here.
♦ 915 Second Ave (between Marion and Madison Sts)

42 COLMAN BUILDING

Scottish immigrant James M. Colman's namesake structure had trouble getting off the ground in more ways than one. A mechanic and a steam-mill operator, Colman first acquired this property by running a ship aground here long enough to earn legal title; he planned simply to build over the hull. But Colman's original, very ornate design (conceived by architect **Stephen Meany** before the Great Fire of 1889) was stunted by his business caution after the blaze. He went ahead with only the concept's first two stories, waiting to see what demand there was for more office and commercial space in the rapidly rebuilding city. Not until about 1904 did architect **August Tidemand** completely revamp these two floors in brownstone style; he then added four more austere brick stories above those to form the basic edifice you see today. In 1930 Seattle architect **Arthur B. Loveless** performed another remodeling that incorporated several Art Deco elements into the glazed street canopy and lobby. ♦ 811 First Ave (between Columbia and Marion Sts)

43 CURRENT

The high-style Moderne furniture that turns up in these expansive showrooms is unquestionably elegant. There are pieces for every room in the house, with a special focus on sconce lighting. The prices, unfortunately, can be quite steep. ♦ Daily. 629 Western Ave (at Columbia St). 622.2433.
www.currentonline.com

44 BAKEMAN'S RESTAURANT

★$ Tucked beneath the historic **Hoge Building**, famous for a pride of lion heads along its cornice, is a lunchtime fave among office workers—400 to 500 get lunch here every day. Sandwiches (especially the turkey and meat loaf varieties) are thick enough to defy easy gripping (or biting), and the soups are renowned. ♦ American ♦ Restaurant: M-F, breakfast and lunch; bar: M-F, until 7:30PM. No credit cards accepted. 122 Cherry St (at Second Ave). 622.3375

WATERFRONT

45 WATERFRONT STREETCAR

Seattle's original trolleys were stripped from service decades ago, but, for nostalgia's sake, **Metro Transit** imported these vintage machines from Australia to make the clattering 15- to 20-minute run from Pier 70 through Pioneer Square to the International District.
♦ $1.25 at peak times (M-F, 6-9AM and 3-6PM); $1 off-peak; children younger than 5 admitted free. Daily. 553.3000. www.transit.metrokc.gov

45 BELL STREET PIER

Seattle's latest effort to reclaim its forgotten north waterfront area is this enormous complex, a combination of convention space, marina, museum, and restaurant. The **Bell Harbor International Conference**

On 26 January 1700, at about 9PM Pacific Standard Time, a gigantic earthquake occurred 60 to 70 miles off the Pacific Northwest coast. The quake violently shook the ground for 3 to 5 minutes and was felt along the coastal interior of the Pacific Northwest, including present-day King County. A tsunami formed, reaching about 33 feet high along the Washington coast, traveled across the Pacific Ocean, and hit the east coast of Japan. Japanese sources documented this earthquake, which is the earliest documented historical event in King County.

Restaurants/Clubs: Red | Hotels: Purple | Shops: Orange | Outdoors/Parks: Green | Sights/Culture: Blue

Seattle Aquarium

Patti Kahler / North Market Street Graphics

Center, cunningly designed to look and feel like a part of the "working waterfront" that surrounds the pier, has full conference facilities geared to international business (including a multilingual staff and five simultaneous translation booths). Above the center is a public viewing space complete with comfortable benches and free telescopic sights; it's a great spot to sit and watch the harbor and street activity. Visitors' gastronomic needs are satisfied by **Anthony's Pier 66 & Bell Street Diner** (448.6688), a complex of three restaurants that forms the newest link in the **Anthony's Homeport** chain of seafood eateries. Other facilities here include a small short-stay marina and a cruise-ship dock. ♦ Pier 66. www.portofseattle.org

On the Bell Street Pier:

ODYSSEY, THE MARITIME DISCOVERY CENTER

This huge, hands-on, high-tech, interactive facility lets kids and their families explore fishing, sea trade, and the maritime environment in four different galleries, each of which involves a variety of exhibits, theater offerings, and interactive experiences. Operate remote-control miniature tugboats, climb aboard a fishing boat especially constructed for kids, check out the latest in nautical technology and oceanographic mapping, or take a simulated kayak ride through **Elliott Bay**. It's a great way to have fun while learning about the marine life of Puget Sound and all the local and international commercial activities associated with it. ♦ Admission.

Daily. 2205 Alaskan Way. 374.4001. ♿ www.ody.org

46 WATERFRONT PARK

A soothing "boardwalk" hugging **Elliott Bay**, the elevated walkways here give visitors a better perspective on the city and the Sound. It's a good place for picnics, offering a superfluity of fish, hot dogs, and ice-cream parlors nearby. Long gone is adjacent Pier 58, where the first cargo of tea from the Orient arrived in 1896 and where the steamer *Portland* anchored in 1897 with the first news that gold had been discovered in the Klondike; a plaque here recalls the beginning of Alaska's gold rush. The minipark was designed in 1974 by the **Bumgardner Architects**. ♦ Piers 57 and 59

Within Waterfront Park:

SEATTLE AQUARIUM

Seattle's waterfront area incurred serious damage during the Nisqually Earthquake of 2001. The Alaskan Way Viaduct, for example, had to be extensively repaired and then strengthened against further earthquakes. Then, as if that weren't enough, an inspection revealed that significant damage to the wooden supports of the seawall along the waterfront had been done by wood-chewing crustaceans called gribbles. The city decided to take the opportunity, while funding basic structural support repair, to launch a major renovation of the ever-popular waterfront aquarium.

The aquarium has gained 18,000 square feet of display space. At its heart is the **Puget Sound Great Hall**, a three-story, light-filled building with interactive educational kiosks, seal-life art, and thought-provoking conservation exhibits, focused on Puget Sound's ecosystems. At the end of the Great Hall stands **Window on Washington Waters**, a 17- by 39-foot, 120,000-gallon showcase evoking Neah Bay's rock blades filled with salmon, colorful rockfish, vibrant sea anemones, and other marine life swimming in a kelp-filled sea. New visitor amenities include a full-service café and gift store, and second-floor viewing platforms for a three-dimensional look into the Washington Waters exhibit. An open 40- by 6-foot wave tank lets visitors hear the surging waves and see how marine animals and plants survive in swirling rough water. Expect to spend at least three hours at the aquarium. ♦ Admission; children age 2 and younger admitted free; discount for senior citizens, disabled persons, children ages 3 to 5, King County residents, and groups of 10 or more. ♦ Daily. Pier 59. 386.4320. www.seattleaquarium.org

47 ELLIOTT'S OYSTER HOUSE & SEAFOOD RESTAURANT

★$$$ Water views, fast (bordering on indifferent) service, and some of the best oysters in town are featured here. Huge desserts are also worth sampling. ♦ Seafood ♦ M-Sa, lunch and dinner. Pier 56. 623.4340

48 YE OLDE CURIOSITY SHOP

A mecca for tourist-trinket junkies, founded in 1899, this carnival-flavored shop sells rubber slugs, Seattle T-shirts, Russian nesting dolls, seashells, scrimshaw, and shrunken heads—they're all here, alongside such Barnumesque oddities as a bottled pig with eight legs, three eyes, three mouths,

and a pair of tails. Most popular is Sylvester the Desert Mystery: a mummified murder victim found in the Arizona sandflats in 1895 with a bullet through his stomach and with mustache and fingernails still intact. ♦ Daily; Th-Sa, until 9PM. Pier 54. 682.5844. www.yeoldecuriosityshop.com

48 IVAR'S ACRES OF CLAMS AND FISH BAR

★★$$ Ivar Haglund, who died some years ago, was Seattle's quintessential promoter. He's remembered for his corny commercial slogan (Keep Clam), his guitar playing and storytelling, and the carp wind sock that he ran up the flagpole on **Smith Tower** when he owned that building, beginning in 1976. This full-service restaurant offers a variety of seafood; tried-and-true choices include the clam nectar and the cod and chips. The outdoor seating can hardly be beat for Seattle charm. And to add to the waterside mood, a sentimental statue of Ivar feeding gulls holds court nearby. ♦ Seafood ♦ Daily, lunch and dinner. Pier 54. 624.6852. www.ivars.net

49 COLMAN DOCK

Elliott Bay's worst docking collision occurred here in April 1912, when the ocean liner *Alameda* charged right into this pier, toppling its previously elegant clock tower into the drink. The *Alameda* suffered barely a scratch. The clock from the tower was retrieved after the collision and restored; you can see it inside. It wasn't the first time this dock was rebuilt, nor would it be the last. The original wharf went up by order of Scottish immigrant James Colman in 1882. The current modern incarnation is its sixth and least interesting form, dating only to 1966. **Washington State Ferries** leave from here many times daily, bound for Bainbridge Island and Bremerton (call 464.6400 for the schedule). ♦ Pier 52. www.wsdot.wa.gov

50 WASHINGTON STREET PUBLIC BOAT LANDING

Built in 1920 from a design by city architect **Daniel R. Huntington**, this iron-and-steel pergola—much less ornate than the older Pioneer Place pergola only two blocks to the east—was intended to house Seattle's harbor master and be the entry point for visiting seamen. Now rehabilitated, it is more a curiosity than anything else, being located near Pier 48 but away from other Waterfront landmarks. Watch for it on the **Waterfront Streetcar** ride. ♦ Alaskan Way S and Washington St

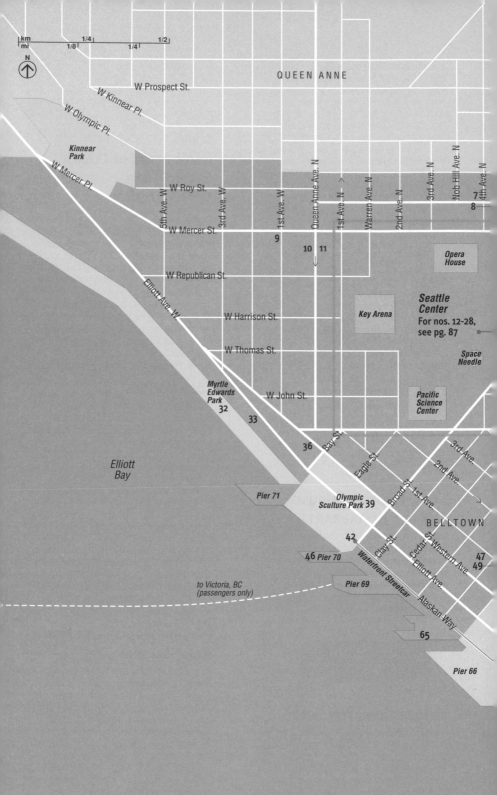

km
mi
1/4
1/8
1/4
1/2

N

QUEEN ANNE

W Prospect St.

W Kinnear Pl.

W Olympic Pl.

Kinnear
Park

W Mercer Pl.

W Roy St.

5th Ave. W

3rd Ave. W

W Mercer St.

1st Ave. W

Queen Anne Ave. N

1st Ave. N →

Warren Ave. N

2nd Ave. N

3rd Ave. N

Nob Hill Ave. N

4th Ave. N

7

8

9

10 11

Opera
House

W Republican St.

Elliott Ave. W

Seattle
Center
For nos. 12-28,
see pg. 87

W Harrison St.

Key Arena

W Thomas St.

Space
Needle

Myrtle
Edwards
Park

W John St.

Pacific
Science
Center

32

33

36

Bay St.

Eagle St.

3rd Ave.

2nd Ave.

Elliott
Bay

Pier 71

Olympic
Sculture Park 39

Broad St.

1st Ave.

BELLTOWN

42

46 Pier 70

Clay St.

Cedar St.

Western Ave.

Elliott Ave.

47

49

to Victoria, BC
(passengers only)

Pier 69

Waterfront Streetcar

Alaskan Way

65

Pier 66

No matter what you call it—Belltown or the **Denny Regrade District**—this area just north of downtown is Seattle's boulevard of forgotten dreams, at least those of an urban development nature. During the late 19th century, one of Seattle's first settlers, William Bell, hoped to create a commercial center here, but he died before his plans could amount to much. Between 1906 and 1911, city engineer Reginald H. Thomson ordered that 300-foot-high **Denny Hill**, which loomed up from the corner of **Second Avenue** and **Virginia Street**, be sluiced into **Elliott Bay**. The regrading was supposed to inspire business development by making the neighborhood flatter and thus easier to traverse. That notion, however, fell on deaf ears.

In 1911, engineer Virgil Bogue unveiled a plan that would have made the intersection of **Fourth Avenue** and **Blanchard Street** the nexus of a new and improved downtown Seattle. Bogue proposed the construction of a civic center that would stretch from this intersection all the way to **Lake Union**. It would feature boulevards, federal buildings, a courthouse, library, art museum, 15-story memorial tower, and subway, all of which would transform dowdy downtown Seattle into a major metropolitan center. Bogue was an urban visionary and, like those of most visionaries, his ideas were rejected.

It wasn't until 1962, with construction of the Century 21 Exposition and the landmark **Space Needle**, that Belltown made the leap into the future. This World's Fair was *The Jetsons* incarnate, a spectacle that *Life* magazine called "out of this world." Attorney General Robert Kennedy, actors John Wayne and Danny Kaye, Prince Philip of Britain, and even Lassie showed up to take a gander. Elvis Presley arrived amid a wail of shrieking teenagers to shoot a mediocre movie called *It Happened at the World's Fair*.

The fairgrounds have now become the **Seattle Center** (renovated not long ago to the tune of more than $200 million), the closest thing the city has to a community center. Thousands of people crowd in here year after year for a variety of events ranging from the Northwest Folklife Festival to the Bumbershoot. Parents bring their children to visit the museums; teens hang out with friends at the amusement park, gobble pizza in **Center House**, and attend dances and karaoke competitions; and the Space Needle remains a popular upscale dating destination. Sporting events, ranging from professional basketball (the **Seattle SuperSonics**) to high school football, take place in the **Key Arena** (formerly the **Coliseum**) and at **High School Memorial Stadium**. Several stages deliver theater and musical productions.

For several decades, Belltown was a bohemian and artistic zone. Secondhand shops, bookstores, art galleries, and coffeehouses occupied buildings long vacated by more conventional businesses, and Belltown became a focus of Seattle's dance-club scene, attracting a wide roster of rock bands. This is all still true, but to a lesser degree. Belltown now chimes along nicely in a major transition. Restaurants, which once ignored the neighborhood as just too far from the city's critical office mass, have moved in. Now this is where many upscale and highly designed eateries are opening, among the rapidly sprouting condominiums that are changing the neighborhood tone. The result is an interesting medley of the city's elements.

1 I Love Sushi

★★$ The beloved menu of the popular sushi palace of the same name in Bellevue is now offered at this outpost. Tuna, eel, and Dungeness crab remain ever-popular selections. Master chef Tadashi Sato wields the knives here. ♦ Japanese ♦ M-F, lunch; Su-Th, dinner. 1001 Fairview Ave N (at Ward St). 625.9604. www.ilovesushi.com. Also at 11818 NE Eighth St (between Bellevue-Redmond Rd and 116th Ave), Bellevue. 425/454.5706

CHANDLER'S
CRABHOUSE
AND FRESH FISH MARKET

Seattle, USA ♦ Yokohama, Japan

2 Chandler's Crabhouse and Fresh Fish Market

★$$$ One in a series of nosheries that round the southern end of Lake Union and attract a business crowd at lunch, a cross-section of Seattle at dinner, and tourists. This spot does its best with crab in a multitude of variations. There's also a daily fresh-fish roster and a satisfying Sunday brunch. ♦ Seafood ♦ M-Sa, lunch and dinner; Su, brunch and dinner. 901 Fairview Ave N (between Valley St and Minor Ave). 223.2722. &

2 Duke's Lake Union Chowderhouse

★$ In the lower corner of the **Chandler's Cove** retail complex, this spot is rather hard to find. But the view of Lake Union can't be beat, even when the sun is bright enough to pierce your retinas, and the deck dining area makes a terrific after-work hangout. (The interior is often too noisy for a pleasant chat.) Fresh seafood is available daily, but the sandwiches and fries fit equally well with the yacht-club atmosphere. ♦ American ♦ Daily, lunch and dinner. Bar: daily. 901 Fairview Ave N (between Valley St and Minor Ave). 382.9963. & www.dukeschowderhouse.com

3 Jillian's Billiard Club

This pool hall, in what was once a Toyota showroom, offers 29 tables and a munchies menu, along with beer, wine, champagne, and espresso drinks. A bar at one end of the club provides a windowed retreat. It's a dress-up joint, not your classic dark pool hall. Billiards lessons are available. It was nominated in 2001 as best sports bar. ♦ Daily, until 2AM. 731 Westlake Ave N (between Broad and Aloha Sts). 223.0300

4 Wawona

Harking back to Seattle's maritime heritage is this tri-masted, 468-ton schooner built in 1897. For 3 decades, beginning in 1914, the ship sailed north to hunt for cod in the Bering Sea. Ironically, those fish that ended their lives on the *Wawona* actually helped extend this ship's own life, preserving the inner hull with their oils. In 1970, it was the first US ship to be declared a national historic site. ♦ The $1 fee goes toward the ship's upkeep. Daily. Northwest Seaport Dock, 1002 Valley St (between Fairview and Westlake Aves N). 447.9800

4 Center for Wooden Boats

A historical museum and boat-rental dock are rolled into one, with many vintage and replica craft on view. The center also offers classes in sailing, sail repair, boat-building, and other maritime skills. ♦ Fee for boat rentals. Museum/gift shop: M, W-Su. Boat rentals: daily. 1010 Valley St (between Fairview and Westlake Aves N). 382.2628. www.cwb.org

5 Daniel's Broiler

★★★$$$ Daniel's is the only major Seattle steak house to serve USDA prime beef exclusively. The restaurant offers spectacular views of Lake Union from every table and outside waterfront dining in warmer weather. The steaks are excellent; Daniel's puts many of the big-name steak houses in Seattle to shame. It's pricey but well worth it. ♦ 809 Fairview Pl N (on the corner of Valley St and Fairview Ave). M-F, lunch; daily, dinner. Also at Bellevue Place, 10500 NE Eighth St (between 106th Ave and Bellevue Way), 21st floor, Bellevue. 425/462.4662; and 200 Lake Washington Blvd (at E Alder St). 329.4191

6 Lincoln Towing "Toe Truck"

Another stop on the official "Outrageous, Never to Be Sanctioned by the Chamber of Commerce" kitsch tour features this company's pink pickup truck with a gargantuan toe protruding from its roof. Get those cameras ready! ♦ Mercer St and Fairview Ave N. 622.0415

7 Bamboo Garden Vegetarian Cuisine

★$$ A decidedly odd vegetarian experience, but one not to be missed, this restaurant (aka the "fake-meat palace") lists items on its Hong Kong–style menu according to which meats they simulate. The only thing to avoid is the faux beef—trust us on this one. ♦ Vegetarian/Chinese ♦ Daily, lunch and dinner. 364 Roy St (between Fourth and Nob Hill Aves N). 282.6616. ♿

7 MEDITERRANEAN KITCHEN

★$ Vampires will want to keep clear of this garlic-heavy Middle Eastern restaurant, but budget diners will praise the ratio of price per pound of food. It's unusual *not* to see patrons exiting here with a carton or more of leftovers, maybe the remains of the superb Farmer's Dish (tart lemon chicken on rice) or a helping of lamb shank with couscous, carrots, and potatoes. Dinners come with soup and salad. Owner Kamal Aboul-Hosn also offers tempting appetizers (the *baba ghannouj* and hummus both deserve plaudits), but only those with big appetites could eat all this and an entrée too. ♦ Middle Eastern ♦ Daily, dinner. 366 Roy St (between Fourth and Nob Hill Aves N). 285.6713

8 BAHN THAI

★★$ Zesty but not overpowering Thai fare is served in an ornately overdecorated setting within a converted house. The curry of the day is usually an excellent choice, as is the chicken satay. Only menu listings with more than two or three stars are hot. It's a good idea to make reservations. ♦ Thai ♦ M-F, lunch and dinner; Sa, Su, dinner. 409 Roy St (between Fifth and Fourth Aves N). 283.0444

9 OZZIE'S

★$ A burger joint with attitude for the 1990s (they call it vegetarian-friendly), this place boasts chrome and neon fixtures, shimmering color schemes, design angles so acute you don't want to bump against them, neo-1950s and 1960s kitsch décor, and a pool table. If you don't want a hamburger, try a nut-burger (they're actually better). The fries are fine, and so are the desserts and breakfasts. Service—so-so. ♦ American ♦ Daily. 105 W Mercer St (between First and Second Aves). 284.4618. ♿

10 UPTOWN ESPRESSO

★$ One of the best cups of espresso available in Seattle (and that's saying a lot) is served with pizzazz and cutting-edge attitude. The **Uptown Bakery**, offering great baked goods, was recently added to the premises. ♦ Coffeehouse ♦ Daily. 525 Queen Anne Ave N (between W Republican and W Mercer Sts). 285.3757

11 MECCA CAFE

★$ Originally opened 1 July 1930, this eatery used to be popular with older people and working-class residents. Lately, however, it's become the meeting place of choice for grunge rockers and other young Seattle bohemians who come for late-night eating and drinking and early-morning hangover cures. It tends to be rather loud, and staff members and regulars can get quite vehemently opinionated when discussing local issues. There's also a bar. It's a good place to hang out, enjoy well-prepared (if standard) American diner food, and people-watch. ♦ American ♦ Daily, lunch and dinner until 2AM. 526 Queen Anne Ave N (between Republican and Mercer Sts). 285.9728. ♿

11 KEYSTONE CORNER CARDS

Baseball and other sports-card aficionados share a deep respect for this place. ♦ M-Sa. 534 Queen Anne Ave N (between Republican and Mercer Sts). 285.9277

12 LARRY'S MARKET

The Belltown link in this chain of upscale food emporiums offers a staggering selection of the freshest produce, meat, seafood (including sushi), and other grocery items. The décor is quasi-industrial, with exposed ventilation pipes, rafters, and metal racks. There's also a huge underground parking garage. ♦ Daily, 6AM-midnight. 100 W Mercer St (at First Ave N). 213.0778. Also at 10008 Aurora Ave N (at 100th St). 527.5333. www.larrysmarkets.com

13 T.S. MCHUGH'S PUBLIC HOUSE

★$$ Owned by formula restaurateur Mick McHugh, this is an American place masquerading as a British pub, with the required (but faux) time-darkened façade outside and the rich wood appointments inside. There's an Old World conviviality at the bar, where the bartenders chat up the customers and help them expand their knowledge of liquors and local microbrews. Skip the dining room and stay at the bar, where you can order a hefty sandwich or burger, accompanied by terrific fries, and sample the plentiful stash of beers. ♦ American ♦ Daily. 21 Mercer St (at First Ave N). 282.1910. www.tsmchughs.com

14 CHUTNEYS

★★★$$ This friendly Indian restaurant is named after the spicy condiment, which comes to your table in two varieties—cilantro and mint, and garlic and tomato—along with a complimentary appetizer called *papadum*, a lightly fried sheet of pressed lentils. (Those with sensitive palates be warned: These chutneys are pretty fiery.) Standouts on the generally excellent menu include rack of lamb and *aloo gobi* (potatoes and cauliflower prepared in a rich and heavily spiced yogurt sauce). There's also a bargain all-you-can-eat lunch buffet, whose dishes are much milder than their counterparts at dinner (but you can ask for extra chutneys to spice things up, if you wish). The décor features traditional fabrics and 39 bas-relief images of Indian gods on the walls. ♦ Indian ♦ M-Sa, lunch; F-Su, dinner. Reservations recommended. 519 First Ave N (between Republican and Mercer Sts). 284.6799; fax 284.6901. &. www.chutneysbistro.com. Also at 605 15th Ave E (between Mercer and Roy Sts). 326.1000. &; and 1815 N 45th St (between Burke and Wallingford Aves). 634.1000

15 MARIAN OLIVER McCAW HALL

Some of the finest cultural offerings to be found in Seattle cross the stages of this large structure along Mercer Street. The building used to be Seattle's **Civic Auditorium** but was remodeled for the World's Fair by **B. Marcus Priteca** and **James J. Chiarelli**. It is now home to the **Seattle Opera** and the **Pacific Northwest Ballet**. ♦ www.seattleopera.org

The **Seattle Center Foundation** completed a $140 million renovation of the old Seattle Opera House in the summer of 2003 and renamed it Marion Oliver McCaw Hall. The new facility has 100 fewer seats, but better sight lines for the 2,900 remaining. It is more spacious in backstage and storage areas, and, significantly, a much needed doubling of the rest rooms over the old facility should cut down the legendary lines.

James Fitzgerald's refurbished and graceful *Fountain of the Northwest* stands in front of the **Intiman Playhouse**, home to the theater troupe of the same name, and the **Bagley Wright Theatre** hosts the **Seattle Repertory Theatre** company. The quality of productions at these venues ranges widely, but they are all first-rate houses. ♦ 321 Mercer St (between Fifth and Warren Aves N). www.seattlerep.org; Pacific Northwest Ballet, 292.2787; Intiman Playhouse, 269.1900; Bagley Wright Theatre, 443.2222. www.intiman.org

16 INN AT QUEEN ANNE

$ Former studio apartments have been converted into 37 suites with small kitchens—nothing fancy, but very functional. Long-term rentals are available as well. It's located across the street from the **Seattle Center** and a major grocery store, **QFC**, which is good because there's no restaurant here. ♦ 505 First Ave N (at Republican St). 282.7357. www.innatqueenanne.com

17 INTERNATIONAL FOUNTAIN

From its inception, this fountain possessed an endearing hideousness. With its long, pointed water spouts on a metal hill, sharp marble and granite boulders, and steep-sided cement crater, it was not only aesthetically displeasing but also dangerous to the many children who played around it. In addition, many of the spouts were broken. But the city has recently given the entire structure a makeover: Its metal hill is now smooth, the spouts have been repaired, the concrete crater has a less steep grade, a computerized sound and lighting system has been added, and the boulders are gone. There's even a curving ramp leading to the foot of the fountain—great for wheelchair users and stroller-pushing parents. The result is a safer and far more inviting attraction.

18 FUN FOREST AMUSEMENT PARK

Originally called the **Gayway** in World's Fair days, this facility is only so-so, although kids in the middle of their second Sno-Kone and fifth Tilt-A-Whirl ride won't care. For the old-at-heart, there's a carousel and classic bumper cars. Call ahead for hours and special offers. ♦ Fee for rides. Daily, noon-11PM Memorial Day–Labor Day; hours vary off-season. 728.1585

19 EXPERIENCE MUSIC PROJECT (EMP)

The outer shell of this surreal-looking structure designed by **Frank Gehry** consists of undulating stainless steel and 21,000 aluminum shingles shimmering in shades of silver, gold, purple, red, and blue. It looks a bit like a smashed electric guitar, which Gehry himself says was an early influence on the design. It is located near the Center stop of the monorail, which runs right through the EMP building.

EMP is a one-of-a-kind museum combining interactive and interpretive exhibits to tell the story of rock 'n' roll, from its roots in jazz, soul, gospel, country, and the blues to its influence on hip-hop, punk, and other recent genres. Here you can see guitars that belonged to Bob Dylan, Bo Diddley, Muddy Waters, and Kurt Cobain, take in the world's largest collection of Jimi Hendrix memorabilia, play an instrument, and perform your own music. ♦ 325 Fifth Ave N, at the foot of the Space Needle, between Broad and Harrison Sts. 770.2702. Also in the EMP: Paul Allen's Science Fiction Museum and Hall of Fame. Closed Tu. 770.2702, 877/SCIFICT. www.sfhomeworld.org

---

Restaurants/Clubs: Red | Hotels: Purple | Shops: Orange | Outdoors/Parks: Green | Sights/Culture: Blue

20 CENTER HOUSE

A $6 million face-lift has given this center a much more contemporary look. The plaza on the south side of the building is inlaid with brightly colored bricks and ribbons of steel; there's also a new walkway from there to Center House itself. On the side of the building is a quartet of acrobats created by sculptor Timothy Siciliano. Many cultural festivals are held here throughout the year. The inside of the center is less interesting—mostly overpriced fast-fooderies—but there is the newly expanded **Seattle Children's Museum** (441.1768), located on the lower level. With its exhibit space tripled in size, the museum provides special multicultural programs as well as the permanent **Playcenter**, a supervised play area. ♦ Daily. 305 Harrison St (west of Fifth Ave N). 684.7200

21 MONORAIL

The **Seattle Center** marks this train's northern terminus. From here, it departs every 15 minutes to **Westlake Center**. ♦ Fee. Daily. 905.2620. www.seattlemonorail.com

22 POTTERY NORTHWEST

Most of this building is devoted to studio space for local artisans. A small gallery lets visitors in on what residents are up to, which is often interesting, brightly colored work. Some classes are held here too. ♦ Tu-Sa. 226 First Ave N (at Thomas St). 285.4421. www.potterynorthwest.org

23 CHARLOTTE MARTIN THEATER

Designed by **Mahlum & Nordfors McKinley Gordon**, this $10.4 million building is the home of the popular **Seattle Children's Theatre (SCT)**. Artist Garth Edwards's functional art delights the eye even as it serves a structural purpose: Images from smiling cacti to fanciful sea creatures adorn handrails, archways, even heating grills. ♦ Box office: M-F. Second Ave N and Thomas St. 441.3322. www.sct.org

24 SEATTLE CENTER

Site of the 1962 Century 21 Exposition, this sprawling complex of buildings on 74 acres of land just north of Belltown has recently emerged from a 5-year, $204 million refurbishing. Much of that money has gone toward the renovation of the pyramid-shaped **Coliseum** (now called the **Key Arena**), featuring a larger seating capacity, a state-of-the-art video scoreboard, and a new parking garage. Other improvements include a total redesign of the façade of **Center House**, including the construction of a colorful outdoor plaza leading to the south entrance, the expansion of the **Children's Museum**, the addition of several pieces of modern art, and the enhancement of the lighting and sound systems. ♦ Fifth Ave N (between Broad and Mercer Sts). 684.8582. www.seattlecenter.com

24 SPACE NEEDLE

"Back when we were in school, if you wanted attention, you put up your hand. That is what the **Space Needle** will do for the [1962 World's] Fair and Seattle." Those words were spoken by Joe Gandy, used-car salesman and president of the Century 21 Expo. His enthusiasm was not unfounded: In its three-plus decades, the Space Needle has become the supreme symbol of Seattle, the city's equivalent to San Francisco's Golden Gate Bridge. If it seems absurd at first, don't worry—it will grow on you. This monument was the brainchild of World's Fair organizer Eddie Carlson. He scribbled his idea on a napkin one night, an image that looked like a flying saucer on a tripod. Architects **Victor Steinbrueck** and **John Graham Jr.** gave it a kind of *Amazing Stories* reality. Construction proved to be an enormous project. Consider some of the stats: The foundation is 30 feet deep and weighs 5,850 tons; what you see above ground weighs 3,700 tons; the legs are anchored by some 74 bolts, the dimensions of which are 4 inches by 32 feet; the tower claims 24 lightning rods and can endure winds of up to 150 miles per hour; and it stands more than 600 feet high. The elevator takes 43 seconds to reach the peak (and it's literally a breathtaking experience). The restaurant floor at 500 feet turns a single revolution every hour, thanks to a 1-horsepower motor. And the view is magnificent from the **Observation Deck**, particularly on clear days. Check it out. ♦Fee for the Observation Deck. Daily, until midnight. 219 Fourth Ave N (just north of Broad St). 443.2111, 800/937.9582. ₺. www.spaceneedle.com

Within the Space Needle:

SKY CITY RESTAURANT

★$$$ It's sad to say, but this casual restaurant and the swankier top-of-the-tower **Emerald Suite** ($$$$) don't measure up to their lofty positions on the Needle. It's understood, of course, that you're paying for the view, and it is a very fine one. But the cost is just too steep for the meals served here, which have a reputation for dipping to mediocre and barely rising to good. Both restaurants specialize in Northwestern fare, especially seafood. Diners ride the elevator free of charge. A dress code (no T-shirts, tennis shoes, or jeans) is enforced at the Emerald Suite. ♦ Northwestern ♦ M-Sa, breakfast, lunch, and dinner; Su, brunch and dinner. Reservations recommended. Sky City Restaurant: 443.2100. ₺; Emerald Suite: 443.2150. ₺

25 PACIFIC SCIENCE CENTER

It's an interesting stop for adults, but with the hands-on exhibits and full slate of activities and programs (about dinosaurs, for instance, and whales), this place is even better for children. It's a sort of minicampus with six interconnected buildings. Designed for the World's Fair by well-known Seattle-born architect **Minoru Yamasaki**, along with **Naramore, Bain, Brady & Johanson**, it claims a wonderfully tranquil and inviting space outside, full of pools and soaring arches. ("It is as if Venice had just been built," crowed Alistair Cooke when the complex opened.) But the inside all too often feels cramped and constricted. There's a fine planetarium, a laser theater, and an IMAX theater. ♦ Admission. Tu-Su. 200 Second Ave N (between Denny Way and Thomas St). 443.2880; recorded information, 443.2001. www.pacsci.org

26 CHAMPION WINE CELLARS

The selection of wines here is both imported and domestic, and staffers are helpful, knowledgeable, and bewilderingly happy to answer your every oddball query. The store also stocks a selection of imported beers. ♦ M-Sa. 108 Denny Way (between Warren and First Aves N). 284.8306. www.championwinecellars.com

27 CAFFÈ MINNIE'S

★$ Although most of the city's restaurants still shut down pretty early (9PM during the week and 11PM on weekends), this informal eatery decorated in a funky style (pink walls with maroon trim, glass-topped tables) dares to go its own way, serving a full menu of international specialties 24 hours a day. So, if you're dying for a bowl of gazpacho or a Dutch Baby (a puffy baked pancake with custard reportedly invented in Seattle) at 3AM, **Minnie's** is the place to go. ♦ International ♦ Daily, 24 hours. 101 Denny Way (at First Ave). 448.6263. &

28 CHIEF SEATTLE FOUNTAIN

This bronze memorial to the city's namesake (who was actually called Chief Sealth, not Seattle, by the way) was the first public artwork commissioned by the City of Seattle. With the Alaska-Yukon-Pacific Expo approaching in 1909, local business leaders prevailed on the city to set aside a triangle of property where they proposed to commemorate the friendship between the white settlers and Native Americans of Elliott Bay. The symbol of that friendship was to be a life-size rendition of Chief Sealth, the leader of the Duwamish and Suquamish tribes who had negotiated the treaty that gave up title to what's now much of northwestern Washington state. The sculptor was James A. Wehn, who 2 years later would design the fountain and bust of Chief Sealth at **Pioneer Place Park** and go on to establish the sculpture department at the **University of Washington**. Disputes over which foundry should cast the work delayed the statue's unveiling, but it was finally put on view in 1912. For many years after that, it stood green from advanced oxidation. In 1989, the city discovered while cleaning it that the statue had a very thin gold plate that now lends it an extra sheen. ♦ Denny Way and Fifth Ave

29 ST. SPIRIDON ORTHODOX CHURCH

The city's first Russian Orthodox church was established in 1898, the same time Americans were rushing through Seattle on their way to gold fields in the old Russian outpost of Alaska. This tiny church, conceived by architect **Ivan Palmoy** (who also designed **St. Nicholas Russian Orthodox Church** on Capitol Hill), came along much later—in 1938—yet it contains all of the arresting clichés of Eastern churches. Drivers on I-5 are often bewildered to see its white-and-blue onion domes. ♦ Harrison St and Yale Ave N. 624.5341

30 *SEATTLE TIMES* BUILDING

One of the city's two major newspapers occupies a lesser-known building among those designed by architect **Robert C. Reamer** (who was also responsible for the **Skinner Building** and **1411 Fourth Avenue Building** downtown). Completed in 1930 but added to since, this Moderne-style headquarters is notable for the grillwork at its entrance and the understated sign cut along its façade. ♦1120 John St (at Fairview Ave N)

Get outside yourself.

31 REI

Founded in 1938, **Recreational Equipment Inc.** has become a Seattle institution, as well as the nation's largest consumer cooperative, with more than 80 stores across the US and more than 1 million active members worldwide. In 1996, it moved from its original 11th Avenue location to this huge flagship store with 80,000 square feet of retail space. Everything you'll need for your

---

Restaurants/Clubs: **Red** | Hotels: **Purple** | Shops: **Orange** | Outdoors/Parks: **Green** | Sights/Culture: **Blue**

next expedition to the Himalayas or just a jog around the block is here: gear and clothing for backpacking, climbing, water sports, cycling, and skiing. The new space also features a 65-foot freestanding indoor climbing pinnacle (the world's largest), an indoor trail where you can "test walk" your hiking boots before you buy them, and a 20,000-square-foot courtyard that boasts a mountain bike trail, a stream, vegetation, and a waterfall. There's even an adventure-travel booking service and a mail-order catalog that is circulated around the world. ◆Daily. 222 Yale Ave N (between John and Thomas Sts). 223.1944. www.rei.com

32 MYRTLE EDWARDS PARK

Ⓟ Situated on the Waterfront just north of downtown and west of the **Seattle Center**, this spot makes for a spectacular city stroll. On nice days, catch an unmatched view of the Olympic Mountains, Mount Rainier, the Seattle skyline, and more along the rolling greensward's mile-long walkway. On less nice days (for which a rain slicker is strongly recommended), it offers a moody sky and coal-gray churning waters. This is a favorite place for picnickers, in-line skaters, and lunchtime runners. ◆ Along Elliott Ave W.

33 *P-I* GLOBE

At least as tacky as the **Elephant Car Wash**'s pink proboscidean (see opposite) is this revolving neonized world atop the *Seattle Post-Intelligencer*'s offices. It's easily visible from many points on **Elliott Bay** (including the ferry routes and harbor tours), as well as, suddenly and unexpectedly, from many parts of Belltown, **Seattle Center**, and the Queen Anne neighborhood. Locals have come to rely so much on the regularity of this landmark's spin that when mechanical problems cause a halt, you can almost see the psychological pall it casts. ◆ 101 Elliott Ave W (between Bay St and Third Ave W)

34 DENNY PARK

Ⓟ In 1884, pioneer David Denny and his sister Mary donated the land on which this two-block-size oasis of trees was established. It is the city's oldest park. Previously, it had been **Seattle Cemetery**. (The dear departed are now at **Lake View Cemetery** on Capitol Hill.) ◆ Bounded by Ninth and Dexter Aves N and by Denny Way and John St

35 13 COINS

★$$ Although other swankier joints have failed, this culinary institution just keeps going and going. What's the secret? Probably a combination of the facts that it stays open 24 hours; has a huge menu of pasta, grilled meats, and fish entrées; and

serves a dynamite Caesar salad. The portions are generous, and the people watching in the wee small hours is some of the best around. ◆ American ◆ Daily, 24 hours. 125 Boren Ave N (between Denny Way and John St). 682.2513. ᕗ. www.13coins.com

36 BOAT STREET CAFÉ

★★★$$ A touch of Provence down a ramp where Western converges with Denny. It's a beautifully appointed room, with consistently good food that is dazzling in its simplicity and good prices—what more could you ask for? Try the foamy carrot soup spiked with star anise, and the steamed salmon with lemon tarragon cream (served with caramelized brussel sprouts). And for dessert, try their fabulous amaretto bread pudding. M-F, lunch; Sa, Su, brunch; Tu-Sa, dinner. 3131 Western Ave (between Bay St and Denny Way). 632.4602. www.boatstreetcafe.com

37 ELEPHANT CAR WASH SIGN

A tacky fave among locals, this blinking and revolving pink sign won a 1956 design contest held by car wash owners. It has since proliferated (several replicas now adorn branches from here to Puyallup) and become almost as renowned a symbol of Seattle as the **Space Needle**. *Cosmopolitan* magazine even suggested that single women of the 1990s should be on the lookout for this pink pachyderm, as the establishments it decorates tend to be hangouts for eligible men. ◆ 616 Battery St (at Seventh Ave)

38 GROUP HEALTH BUILDING (*P-I* BUILDING)

The New York firm of **Lockwood-Greene** was responsible for most of the architecture of this three-story block, and the landscaped top level was added in 1978 by Seattle's **Naramore, Bain, Brady & Johanson** (now the **NBBJ Group**). The *Seattle Post-Intelligencer* newspaper moved out of the building in the late 1980s, taking along the giant revolving globe that had capped the rounded tower. The *P-I* now operates from a glass cliff on Elliott Avenue, whereas Group Health Cooperative has taken over this structure. ◆ 521 Wall St (at Sixth Ave)

39 OLYMPIC SCULPTURE PARK

This unusual park space, which opened in January of 2007, connects Belltown with Puget Sound via a series of shifting perspectives as its zigzag path frames views of the Sound, the Olympic Mountains, and the downtown skyline. This project brings together three properties as it crosses over a busy roadway and working railroad tracks, bridging from Western Avenue all the way down to a narrow now-reclaimed strip of beach some three blocks away.

The New York firm of **Weiss/Manfredi Architects**, who won the Seattle Art Museum's design competition in 2001 (from a field of contestants that included Richard Meier and Rem Koolhaas), have integrated all aspects of their design: the café furniture, the light fixtures along the pathways, the pleated stainless-steel shell of the pavilion, and the shifting folds of concrete boundary walls, their pleats and folds echoing the path's shape. Sculptors represented among the 21 pieces in the permanent collection include Richard Serra, Alexander Calder, Louise Bourgeois, Mark Dion, Roxy Paine, Claes Oldenburg, and Mark di Suvero.

Turning a former fuel storage and oil transfer site into a green space with a gradually descending pathway down to the water struck a chord with many in this environmentally conscious city. Another satisfying benefit: A 2001 earthquake had damaged the seawall, threatening a habitat for migrating salmon. The museum recruited engineers and aquatic scientists to buttress the seawall with stepped terraces to restore the migratory path along the shore. ♦ 2901 Western Ave. 654.3100. www.seattlemuseum.org

40 ENGINE HOUSE NO. 2

A fire station has occupied the corner of Fourth Avenue and Battery Street since 1890, although the original wooden building—**Engine House No. 4**—sat across Battery Street from where architect **Daniel R. Huntington**'s 1920 brick structure now stands. Unlike **No. 4**, which had to depend on horse-drawn fire engines, the new **No. 2** was the talk of the town during the Jazz Age for its "motor-powered apparatus." ♦ 2334 Fourth Ave (at Battery St)

41 ART/NOT TERMINAL

After four initial years operating in a space converted from a **Trailways** bus station (hence the name), this co-op gallery-shop moved into more upscale digs. Shows change each month, though some stay longer. Exhibits draw from the work of about 200 member artists, including sculptors, photographers, and painters. The nonprofit gallery is good to its artists, taking an uncharacteristically small percentage from the sales, and customers can even work out layaway plans with individual artists. New show openings, with live music and refreshments, are usually scheduled the Saturday immediately following the first

Thursday of each month. ♦ Daily. 2045 Westlake Ave (at Lenora St). 233.0680. &.

42 WATERFRONT STREETCAR

Seattle's original trolleys were stripped from service decades ago, but for nostalgia's sake, **Metro Transit** imported these vintage machines from Australia to make the clattering 15- to 20-minute run from Pier 70 through Pioneer Square to the International District. ♦ $50 at peak times (M-F, 6-9AM and 3-6PM); $1.25 off-peak; children under 5 free. Daily. 553.3000

43 TWO BELLS TAVERN

★★$ Belltown's great altar of burger worship is almost impossible to get into at lunchtime, when the suits mix with the bohemians in the booths and at the bar. Come for one of the Paul Bunyan–size decks of beef covered in fried onions, with a sidecar of chunky potato salad. It's messy but worth the dry-cleaning bill. The lemonade and the salads are also recommended. Small rock groups or solo singer/songwriters appear here on Saturday nights, beginning at 10PM. All in all, it's a good place to see and be seen. ♦ American ♦ Restaurant: daily, lunch and dinner; bar: daily, until 2AM. 2313 Fourth Ave (between Bell and Battery Sts). 441.3050

44 DIMITRIOU'S JAZZ ALLEY

Longtime jazz producer John Dimitriou owns this club, a genuine treasure for blues and jazz fans alike. Some of the most significant names in the genre have graced the room: Harry Connick Jr. used to play here before he was famous, and Diane Shuur has been a regular performer through the years. Expect to see such entertainers as Charles Brown, Ray Brown, and Maynard Ferguson every week, Tuesday through Saturday (local performers appear on Monday). The food is nothing special, but the room is excellent, with comfortable seating. If you're a music fan, don't miss this place. ♦ Cover. Daily, from 6PM. Reservations recommended. 2033 Sixth Ave (at Lenora St). 441.9729. www.jazzvalley.com

45 SIXTH AVENUE INN

$$ One step above a motel (some rooms even have brass beds, and room service is available), this 166-room hostelry is reasonably priced and centrally located, is fairly convenient to both the downtown core and the **Seattle Center**, and has a basic restaurant for quick meals. Street noise can be a problem, though, especially

---

Restaurants/Clubs: Red | Hotels: Purple | Shops: Orange | Outdoors/Parks: Green | Sights/Culture: Blue

on the Sixth Avenue side. ♦ 2000 Sixth Ave (at Virginia St). 441.8300. www.sixthavenueinn.com

46 PIER 70

The **Ainsworth & Dunn Wharf** has stood at the north end of the Waterfront for nearly a hundred years—a marvelous building, with wide-plank flooring, rough-hewn log walls, and cavernous open spaces. (A history of this fine structure is mounted just inside the entrance.) It now houses a variety of curio, candy, and T-shirt shops for tourists, as well as some restaurants.

47 EL GAUCHO

★★★$$$ Once a favored refuge of the downtown martini-and-steak crowd, **El Gaucho** has been resurrected on this site by Paul Mackay (of **Ponti Seafood Grill** and **Flying Fish** fame). Dark and classy, with neo–Art Deco lighting and curved teak railings separating the tiered dining areas, the restaurant boasts both romantic intimacy and an exhibition kitchen. Dazzling tableside preparations of salads, specialty items, flaming swords of shish kebab, and flambéed desserts are executed by tuxedo-clad servers with flair and elegance. This up-to-date old-style steak house (it even features a cigar lounge) was voted one of the nation's best new restaurants of 1997 by *Esquire* magazine. ♦ American ♦ Daily, dinner. Reservations required. 2505 First Ave (between Wall and Vine Sts). 728.1337. & www.elgaucho.com

48 SHIRO

★★★$$ Chef Shiro Kashibo, brings his highly acclaimed talents to the menu here. Naturally the sushi and sashimi are superb, and so are the appetizers (particularly the soft-shell crab and asparagus salad). There are even a few exotic items to tempt the more adventurous palate, like squid tentacles and cured seaweed. The place itself seems rather formal, with its blond wood paneling and immaculate linen tablecloths and napery, but the staff is warm and friendly. ♦ Japanese ♦ M-F, lunch and dinner; Sa, Su, dinner. Reservations recommended. 2401 Second Ave (at Battery St). 443.9844. &

49 ACE HOTEL

$ From the street, one might not even notice that there is a hotel in this small brick building, save for the modest plaque near the door. The 35 rooms offer vaulted ceilings, brick walls, and hardwood floors. For a moderate price, you will have a sink and vanity in the room, with shared bathrooms down the hall; for a bit more, rooms with private bathrooms are available. Local art museums often books guests and visiting artists in this sleek, quiet hotel. Located near some of the city's most popular clubs and restaurants. ♦ 2423 First Ave (between Battery and Wall Sts). 448.4721. www.theacehotel.com

50 MACRINA BAKERY

Many people's favorite, this is Belltown's neighborhood bakery, turning out excellent rustic breads and coffee cakes, muffins, scones, and tarts. For lunch they carry fine sandwiches and freshly made salads. ♦ 2408 First Ave (between Battery and Wall Sts). 448.4032. www.macrinabakery.com. Also at 615 W McGraw St (at Sixth Ave N). 283.5900

51 LAMPREIA

★★★★$$$$ This sleek, spare restaurant seems even more elegant in comparison with its gritty Belltown surroundings. Chef Scott Carsberg marries highly seasoned Italian oils and sauces with fresh Northwest produce to create such appetizers as *pizzelle* (crisp little waffles with thin slices of marinated tuna and pesto). Entrées are similarly inspired: Think cannelloni stuffed with Dungeness crab or braised saddle of rabbit wrapped in pancetta. Dessert lovers will not want to pass up the chocolate *feuilleté* (thin alternating layers of chocolate and praline), particularly because portions of everything are extremely small. ♦ Italian ♦ Tu-Sa, dinner. Reservations recommended. 2400 First Ave (at Battery St). 443.3301. &

52 RENDEZVOUS

The primary battleground for the hearts and minds of Belltown, the bar here is worth a look, but in general steer clear of it unless you're into knocking back triple scotches. Instead, head straight to the **Jewelbox Theater** in back, which is somewhat shabby but elegant and comfortable. The entertainment consists of a wildly uneven menu of live music but was nominated for Best

The Arctic Building's walrus heads had their tusks removed more than 30 years ago for fear they'd fall off and mortally wound passersby. During a 1980s restoration, however, the walruses got their tusks back.

THE BEST

Rabbi Jonathan Singer and Rabbi Beth Singer
Temple Beth Am

Walking **Green Lake** on a sunny day with a *latte* from the **Urban Bakery** in hand.

Mae's Cafe on Phinney Ridge, complete with bovine décor and tremendous portions of good food.

Feeding the koi fish at the Japanese garden in the **Washington Park Arboretum**.

Window shopping at **University Village** and enjoying Mexican food there at **Burrito Loco**.

Browsing in the **Tree of Life** bookstore in **Ravenna**.

A summertime zoo concert on the lawn with your children or a romantic **Chateau Ste. Michelle** evening concert without them.

Ice-cream sundaes at **Dilettante's** on **Capitol Hill**, followed by reading in the **Bailey-Coy** bookstore.

Jukebox in 2001. ♦ Cover. Daily. 2320 Second Ave (between Bell and Battery Sts). 441.5823. ♿

53 PALACE KITCHEN

★★★$$$ Soaring ceilings, an open wood-fired grill, multicolored chandeliers, an enormous horseshoe-shaped bar, plus lush fabric and colors set the scene for a long list of imaginative, tasty, crowd-pleasing appetizers (the better to share) and rustic and hearty entrées. Tom Douglas's third Seattle creation (he owns both the **Dahlia Lounge** and **Etta's Seafood**) is as much an upscale bar as a fine restaurant, serving food until 1AM. The desserts (for which Douglas's other two restaurants are justly famous) are produced in the kitchen here. ♦ Fusion ♦ Daily, dinner. 2030 Fifth Ave (between Virginia and Lenora Sts). 448.2001. ♿

54 MONORAIL

Walking along Fifth Avenue north of Pine Street after dark, when the ghostly monorail flashes by overhead, is one of Seattle's finest urban experiences. The monorail is very quiet, with faces peering out of the lighted windows. The slingshot-shaped concrete supports make for a fine Hitchcock scenario, with generous geometric lines and shadows. Locals who've pushed for the monorail's removal—so a clear view of the **Space Needle** can be opened along Fifth Avenue—don't appreciate the drama of this silver-skinned dinosaur. Director Alan Rudolph did, however, and he made plentiful use of it in

his 1985 film *Trouble in Mind*. Be on your guard, though, especially at night: This stretch of Fifth Avenue is not heavily populated. www.seattlemonorail.com

55 ODD FELLOWS HALL/AUSTIN A. BELL BUILDING

The connected brick structures you see here, plus the **Hull Building** kitty-corner across First Avenue, are about all that remain of an ambitious 19th-century scheme to develop Belltown as a commercial hot spot. The architect was **Elmer Fisher**, who put his stamp all over Pioneer Square, but the plan was the brainchild of pioneer William Bell and his son, Austin Americus Bell.

In 1883, William Bell erected the impressive four-story, mansard-roofed **Bell Hotel** (subsequently renamed the **Bellevue Hotel**) at the corner of Battery Street and what's now First Avenue. Four years later, Bell died from a "softening of the brain" that had brought on fits and confusion. His son came north from his home in California to attend the funeral and claim his inheritance. In 1888, while architect Fisher was working on a new hall for the Odd Fellows fraternal group two doors south of the hotel, Austin commissioned him to design a compatible apartment building that would fit between the hall and the hotel. This was to be Austin's first big mark on Seattle and, though he'd suffered from periodic depression, he seemed enlivened by the project. But in the spring of 1889, after a hearty breakfast and a stroll to his office, he wrote a shaky note to his wife and shot himself in the head. He was 35, the same age his father had been when he carved out the clearing that would become Belltown. His wife, Eva, completed Austin's handsome structure and named it in his honor.

The Bellevue Hotel has long since vanished, and the **Odd Fellows Hall** is now the **2320 First Avenue Building**, its upper stories

---

SELLING SEAFOOD BY THE SEASHORE

When it comes to supplying savory salmon and other seafood delectables, Seattle is not only Washington's largest seaport but Alaska's as well. The salmon, halibut, and sablefish caught in Alaskan waters generally pass through this city to be processed or shipped to international markets. Seattle also has easy access to seafood from all around Washington State: mussels from **Penn Cove** on **Whidbey Island**, pink swimming scallops from the **San Juan Islands**, octopus from **Puget Sound**, Pacific oysters from the **Hood Canal** and **Willapa Bay**, Olympia and Kumamoto oysters from southern Puget Sound, and Dungeness crab from offshore waters. The big favorites here are oysters and salmon, and there are so many species of each available—all with different flavors and textures—that it can easily boggle the mind of the average landlubber. Here's a reference guide to the local catch.

Oysters

Four varieties of oysters are commonly found in Seattle-area restaurants and seafood markets, from the native Olympia to the often pricey European Flat. In general, these oysters are in season from late October through May or June—as long as the Puget Sound waters remain cold. Oysters prepare to spawn and turn milky and soft during warm weather, which is why they are usually not at their best during the summer months (but that's all right, because summertime is when salmon is most abundant in local waters). Each kind is best served raw on the half shell.

European flat oyster Often erroneously called belon, after the most famous French beds of this delectable mollusk, they have a delicate yet satisfying flavor. Primarily raised in the pristine waters off San Juan Island, supplies are limited (and the prices for these oysters often are higher than for the other varieties raised hereabouts), so feast on them whenever they are available. (Some Seattle restaurants serve a related oyster, the Chiloë, in midsummer when local oysters are out of season.)

Olympia oyster The tiny oyster's superb taste—which makes the Olympia much in demand—more than compensates for its drab exterior. This is the Northwest's only native oyster; all other species were first raised from spawn shipped in from Asia or Europe.

Kumamoto oyster Deeply cupped, thus better preserving their tasty juices, the Kumamotos have a complex and subtle flavor. At their best, they surpass the renowned Olympia.

Pacific oyster Seattle's primary commercial variety is a plump, lusciously flavored bivalve, originally imported from Japan but now ubiquitous in Washington's inland waters. Fatter than other shellfish, they have a rich, satisfying flavor that's excellent raw or cooked. Pacific oysters are often named after the areas they're grown in, such as **Samish Bay**, Hood Canal, **Shoalwater Bay**, and **Skookum Inlet**.

Salmon

There are five species of salmon caught in Seattle's local waters. The earliest to migrate are the spring salmon, which are also the last to spawn. Sockeyes run in August, silver salmon in August and September, pinks in summer, and chums in fall. These dates are important

---

warrened with offices. But the **Austin A. Bell Building** has been boarded up, a disheveled ghost of a tormented man's dream. ◆ 2320 First Ave (between Bell and Battery Sts)

56 CASCADIA

★★★★$$$$ This is the very classy result of Bruce McCaw's dream, from sterling silver salt cellars to the Limoges china. And of course, the billionaire chose Kerry Sear as chef to create his amazing creations to celebrate everything Northwest. Sear serves only what he can get in the Cascadia region—the lush area between the Cascade Mountains and the Pacific Ocean. He and his staff turn what they find into subtly flavored dishes. You can watch them through windows or even go inside. For example, there is air-dried duck with stuffed squash blossoms and warm peaches, or seared halibut in chanterelle broth with chickweed. And then there's pastry chef Kristina Bartleson's desserts: examples are Chocolate Catch of the Day and warm spice cake with roasted pear and wildflower ice cream. For those with sophisticated palates seeking adventure or those who just want the best, Cascadia is definitely worth a visit. ◆ Northwest ◆ 2328 First Ave (between Bell and Battery Sts). 448.8884. www.cascadiarestaurant.com

57 MAMA'S MEXICAN KITCHEN

★$ Every inch of wall space here is a witty adventure, overdecorated with Mexicana; there's even an Elvis Room, with some memorabilia of the singer and videos of his movies. Is there a stick of furniture in the place that matches any other? Probably not.

to know, because most local salmon are caught just before they enter the rivers to spawn.

When buying salmon, look for fish with red gills, a complete coat of scales, and bright, unclouded eyes. To avoid buying fish that has turned sour, smell the stomach cavity. The flesh should be firm, glossy, brightly colored, and resilient to the touch (meaning your finger shouldn't leave an impression when you poke it). Atlantic and silver salmon can be farmed, but try to buy wild fish whenever possible for their superior texture and flavor. **University Seafood & Poultry** (1317 NE 47th St, at University Way; 632.3900) and **Mutual Fish Company** (2335 Rainier Ave S, between McClellan and College Sts; 322.4368) are among those markets that sell the best seafood in town.

Because it's often difficult to tell salmon apart in the markets, a few identification tips may prove helpful:

Spring salmon These fish, also called chinook or king, have gray or brown spots on the upper body, tailfin, and head (other salmon don't have spotted heads). The flesh is rich in oil and often deep red in color, but it may be white or even streaked with white, red, and pink (particularly in the rainbow king variety). Whatever the color, spring salmon make for great eating.

Silver salmon Also known as coho, they have dark spots on the back and upper tail and are smaller and more slender than spring salmon. Silvers are commonly featured on local menus because they are farmed in Washington and caught in the wild. Farmed silver salmon are smaller than others but are still very flavorful, and they're especially good served with sauces made from fresh, tart berries.

Chum salmon They're similar in shape to silver salmon but have a more deeply forked tail with a rounded slender base. Sometimes sold as silverbrite, chum is low in oil and should be grilled or smoked.

Steelhead Large oval spots on the tail and back and small scales are the predominant features of these fish. Steelhead flesh is low in oil. It's delicious when smoked.

Sockeye salmon These are the oiliest and most richly flavored of salmon. Their flesh is deep red and the bodies are slender, with a few tiny specks on the back but none of the spots found on other salmon. Consider yourself lucky if you see Fraser River sockeyes in a Seattle seafood market; they're brought in from British Columbia.

Seafood Served Here

If you prefer to have your oysters shucked by a professional or want to have the catch of the day cleaned and cooked for you, Seattle offers a wide assortment of first-rate seafood restaurants. For example, **Elliott's Oyster House & Seafood Restaurant** (Pier 56; 623.4340) on the **Waterfront** is renowned for its oysters on the half shell. **Ray's Boathouse** (6049 Seaview Ave NW, just west of 38th Ave; 789.3770; &) specializes in salmon dishes, whereas its neighbor, **Anthony's Homeport** (6135 Seaview Ave NW, between 38th Ave and 67th St; 783.0780; &), features a superbly rich Yukon River king salmon in the spring. And for salmon and other entrées, you'll want to try **Restaurant Zoë** (2137 Second Ave, at Blanchard St; 256.2060).

Food comes in huge portions, with lots of taco and burrito plates and rice and beans on the side—a carbo-loader's fantasy. Come here on a warm summer's night to get a table outside and eat basket upon basket of the saltless tortilla chips, washing them down with Corona beer. ♦ Mexican ♦ Daily, lunch and dinner. 2234 Second Ave (at Bell St). 728.6262. &

57 LAVA LOUNGE

If you're in the mood for a dry martini or an exotic drink in a relaxed nightclub, this is the place for you. This lounge is a popular, laid-back hangout for people who come to sit in the plush red booths, drink, and listen to live performances by up-and-coming artists and groups or play shuffleboard. There's also a

menu of bar-type munchies. ♦ Daily, until 2AM. 2226 Second Ave (between Blanchard and Bell Sts). 441.5660. &

58 FOURTH AND BLANCHARD BUILDING

Affectionately known by locals as the Darth Vader Building for its resemblance to the *Star Wars* villain, this dark, 440-foot-tall glass monolith was designed by the same folks who brought you the **Columbia Seafirst Tower** downtown (**Chester L. Lindsey Architects**). It's all astonishing surfaces, with dramatic angles at the top that make it eerily reminiscent of New York architect **Philip Johnson**'s Pennzoil Place in Houston. In the nearby courtyard, adorning two benches across from each other, are *He* and

TERRA-COTTA TOWN

The raging fire that destroyed early Seattle in 1889 was a tragic event, but this very same fire also had a lot to do with how the city's architecture developed over the following five decades. Just trace the growth northward from **Pioneer Square**. Starting at **Smith Tower**, the handsome but weighty Romanesque Revival style of brick and stone gives way to paler, more gracefully ornamented terra-cotta towers that were believed (correctly) to be more structurally sound than their precursors. These buildings were also a kind of insurance policy for Seattle: Terra-cotta, it had been proved, was more fire-resistant than many other building materials. Perhaps more significant, however, is that for most of the 20th century these towers would characterize Seattle as a great white city on the water.

Terra-cotta became an accepted building material for Chicago's large-scale projects shortly after that city suffered its own skyline-devastating blaze in 1871. The enriched clay eventually became the facing of choice among early American skyscraper builders, including such architects as **Louis Sullivan** and **Daniel Burnham**, who discovered they could use it to create higher and slimmer towers. They achieved this by assembling steel skeletons to bear most of a building's weight, then sheathing the structure with a lighter skin of terra-cotta (which weighs about 70 pounds per cubic foot, compared to 170 pounds for granite).

It could also be modeled easily into an infinite variety of shapes before it was hardened by firing—a bottom-line plus during a period when the expense of traditional ornamental stonework was on the rise. As architect **Frank Lloyd Wright** later remarked, terra-cotta "takes the impression of human imagination. . . . It is in the architect's hand what wax is in the sculptor's hand." The material allowed designers to more fully express themselves in the sort of Beaux Arts embellishments popular during the early 20th century. Gargoyles, cartouches, French nymphs, and a ribbon of walrus heads could all be produced cheaply and quickly and in numerous shades to enhance a structure.

Of course, the Northwest's damp climate forced special requirements on terra-cotta manufacturing. More porous versions might have been fine for California, but here the clay renderings had to be highly glazed, a fact that contributed greatly not only to their waterproofing but also to their general longevity. (The Capitol Theater in Yakima, Washington, for instance, was hit by a fire some years back that destroyed the interior but left the distinguished terra-cotta façade standing.)

One of the earliest architects erecting terra-cotta–sheathed edifices in Seattle was **Charles Bebb**, an Englishman who'd worked in Chicago with **Louis Sullivan**'s firm. In about 1890, he moved to Seattle to serve as an engineer for an early terra-cotta company owned, at least in part, by pioneer Arthur Denny. Bebb formed his own architectural practice in 1898, subsequently linking up with **Leonard L. Mendel** and talented New Yorker **Carl Gould** to create some of Seattle's most significant terra-cotta structures. They were joined in their taste for terra-cotta by local architects **John Graham Sr.**, **Henry Bittman**, **A. Warren Gould**, and theater designer **B. Marcus Priteca**, an experimental stylist who created molds for classical ornamental motifs that became catalog items and eventually detailed buildings all down the West Coast.

Not until 1930 did the demand for terra-cotta suffer a decline, brought on by the Depression, escalating production costs, and changes in architectural taste. By then, however, Seattle—as well as Portland, Oregon, and San Francisco—displayed a rich diversity of terra-cotta works.

Unfortunately, some of the finest examples have been victims of the wrecking ball (including the old **Rhodes Building** and the **Orpheum Theater**, both once in downtown Seattle), but others are still standing and are definitely worth seeing. A few of the more interesting examples are listed below.

Alaska Building Downtown's first steel-girdered high-rise, it was designed in 1904 by **Eames & Young**.
♦ 618 Second Ave (between James and Cherry Sts)

She, two life-size bronze statues by Howard Garnitz. ♦ 2101 Fourth Ave (at Lenora St)

59 WARWICK HOTEL

$$$ Too large to be considered intimate but too small to feel corporate, this hotel is an odd beast. The 229 rooms are comfortable and large, with balconies that offer decent downtown views. There's a pool (albeit a shallow one) in the health club, and the piano lounge provides entertainment nightly. Front-desk personnel are friendly and efficient, and a 24-hour courtesy van will whisk you to downtown engagements. Room rates, however, are steep for accommodations so far from the heart of the city; even the reduced corporate tariffs aren't exactly a bargain. The **Brasserie Margaux** restaurant serves breakfast, lunch, and dinner. ♦ 401 Lenora St (at Fourth Ave). 443.4300, 800/426.9280. www.warwickhotel.com

60 FLYING FISH

★★$$ Owner and chef Christine Keff presents an imaginative, frequently

Arctic Building Designed in 1917 by A. Warren Gould, this ivory-colored terra-cotta structure has "confectioner's touches of aquamarine and rose," as one architectural guide puts it. The walrus heads lining the edifice speak well of the artistic possibilities in this clay construction. ♦ 700 Third Ave (at Cherry St)

Banana Republic Formerly the **Coliseum Theater**, a 1916 structure by **B. Marcus Priteca**, this is one of downtown's most beautifully detailed buildings despite its decline over the last two decades. Although it now houses the flagship branch of Banana Republic, it has been completely restored to its original appearance. ♦ 1506 Fifth Ave (between Pike and Pine Sts)

Corona Hotel When designing this 1903 structure, Bebb & Gould paid homage to Louis Sullivan, who inspired the façade's woven floral ornamentation of unglazed terra-cotta. ♦ 608 Second Ave (between James and Cherry Sts)

Dexter Horton Building Like the **Arctic Building** before it, this 1922 tower (by **John Graham Sr.**) is ivory-hued—a nationally popular color at the time. But it's more sternly businesslike in conception, with giant Doric columns of granite on the north side that express the original height of its lobby. ♦ 710 Second Ave (between Cherry and Columbia Sts)

Fischer Studio Building Bebb & Mendel designed the building in 1912; two years later, Bebb and his new partner Gould added five stories onto the original three and integrated the façade into a continuous whole. The seventh and eighth floors, blank on the exterior except for Venetian-inspired detail, were built to house a Renaissance Revival–style music hall. ♦ 1519 Third Ave (between Pike and Pine Sts)

Four Seasons Olympic Hotel Designed in 1929 by **George B. Post**, an important New York architect, with Bebb & Gould administering the construction, this brick-clad building has terra-cotta ornaments. ♦ 411 University St (between Fifth and Fourth Aves)

Medical-Dental Building In 1925, John Graham Sr. designed this building as a physical and spiritual extension of his 1919 **Frederick & Nelson** department store. But although the drama of the former F & N is apparent at all heights, most of the building's interest doesn't begin until the 14th floor, where Venetian filigrees and a series of setback penthouses and towers are located. ♦ 505 Olive Way (between Sixth and Fifth Aves)

Sailors Union of the Pacific A creation of **T. Bohannon** and **K. Better**, this 1954 edifice is a particularly late and simplistic example of terra-cotta design. ♦ 2505 First Ave (between Wall and Vine Sts)

Bank of America A former department store, this building designed in 1908 by **J.J. Baillargeon** has an arched entrance, lion heads decorating the corners, and shell-patterned window frames adorning the ground level. ♦ 1100 Second Ave (at Spring St)

Securities Building This John Graham Sr.–designed 1912 structure has a Greco-Roman design, executed in terra-cotta. Pay special attention to the ornamentation, including playful green cartouches, along **Third Avenue**. ♦ 1904 Third Ave (between Stewart and Virginia Sts)

Smith Tower Owing to terra-cotta's light weight, this early skyscraper (designed in 1912 by **Gaggin & Gaggin**) could be built taller than was previously possible. ♦ 506 Second Ave (between Yesler Way and James St)

Terminal Sales Building This 1923 building by **Henry Bittman** has facing of tan brick and terra-cotta, with English Gothic ornament that stands out pleasantly against its Art Deco profile. ♦ 1934 First Ave (at Virginia St)

Woolworth Building The designer, **Harold B. Hamhill**, built this Moderne-style structure around 1935 using Woolworth's standard design. It was the only new terra-cotta building constructed in downtown Seattle during the 1930s and 1940s. ♦ 301 Pike St (at Third Ave)

changing menu of mainly seafood dishes. Keff's fusion cuisine shows influences and flavors drawn from all over the world, particularly Thailand, Mexico, and Catalonia. Especially recommended are the Thai crab cakes, lobster risotto, and grilled escolar. The vibrant décor, featuring bright, tropical colors and hand-painted tables, nicely complements the food. Catering to late-night diners, the kitchen stays open until midnight. ♦ Seafood ♦ Daily, dinner until midnight. Reserva-

tions required. 2234 First Ave (at Bell St). 728.8595 &

61 CROCODILE CAFE

During the day, this café is an only moderately successful diner. But at night, it turns into one of Seattle's most adventurous and intriguing rock clubs, booking cutting-edge acts from the city and elsewhere in the country. Kitsch art crams every cranny and literally drips off both the

Restaurants/Clubs: Red | Hotels: Purple | Shops: Orange | Outdoors/Parks: Green | Sights/Culture: Blue

ceiling and walls, even in the rest rooms. One of the more creative displays is the salad-fork mélange in the men's room.
♦Cover. Daily. Call for music schedule. 2200 Second Ave (at Blanchard St). 441.5611. www.thecrocodile.com

62 RESTAURANT ZOË

★★★$$$ Decorated with warm tones of yellow and green with soft lights, it's a nice airy place until the door opens. Make sure you take your coat. Chef Scott Staples, with a reputation for great seafood, is in charge here. Currently on Zoë's menu are a fresh artichoke salad, sautéed mussels in a tomato-infused broth, pan-seared sea scallops, and salmon with browned butter, balsamic vinegar, and beets—all worthy of awards. The grilled romaine salad with bleu cheese, apples, and smoked bacon is also very good. Some of the other items are perhaps too creative to work perfectly; stay with seafood. Reservations are recommended. ♦ American/seafood ♦ 2137 Second Ave (at Blanchard St). 256.2060

63 BRASA

★★★$$$ Trying to convey a Mediterranean village, this restaurant has several dining venues set apart from each other by a curved terrazzo path and iron railings. The lounge pulls in a younger crowd, whereas the middle-aged gravitate toward the dining room and the hippest prefer the gallery-level tables looking down on the main floor. Noted chef Tamara Murphy is definitely in control. The lounge has its own menu of steak frites, pizzas, fried oysters, pasta, and even cinnamon-scented quail in black-bean sauce. Dining-room fare has such items as skate wing (with arugula, lemon, capers, and sweet-potato fries), pleated ravioli (with aged Piedmontese cheese, porcini jus, and currants), and grilled squab (with fingerling potatoes, caramelized onions, and foie gras vinaigrette). Murphy's cooking tends toward hearty simplicity; nothing is fussy or contrived. ♦Mediterranean ♦Daily, dinner and bar. 2107 Third Ave (between Lenora and Blanchard Sts). 728.4220. www.brasa.com

dahlia lounge

64 DAHLIA LOUNGE

★★★$$$ After 10 years, Dahlia moved a block north into a larger space, where the new digs define Northwest palate in a deep crimson room with Chinese lanterns hanging from exposed beams. Owner Tom Douglas has done it again! Chef Matt Costello continues the tradition of innovative dishes with such gems as white gazpacho, thick and rich with hazelnuts and touched with mint, and foie gras with lavender-caramel and figs. Entrées are stellar versions of classic dishes: for example, flat-iron steak with green beans and melting bleu cheese. Desserts are also impressive, whether you go for the famous coconut cream pie or the "fancy chocolates" done three ways. ♦ Northwestern ♦ M-F, lunch and dinner; Sa, Su, dinner. Reservations recommended. 2001 Fourth Ave (at Virginia St). 682.4142. &

65 HOTEL EDGEWATER

$$$ Several of the 235 rooms here literally hang out west over Puget Sound, affording marvelous scenery during the day and fresh salt air at night. At one time this hotel rented fishing poles to guests who wished to wet a line from their rooms (the Beatles were supposed to have indulged in this sport during an early visit here). But too many people made a mess while cleaning their catches, so the service was discontinued. In 1988, the hotel was remodeled to give a mountain-lodge ambience. Waterside rooms are the quietest, but city-view rooms are also fine—and cheaper. Parking is free, and there's a good restaurant with a piano lounge. ♦ Pier 67. 728.7000, 800/624.0670. www.edgewaterhotel.com

66 BELLTOWN BILLIARDS

★★$$ People don't generally think of pool halls as high-class, but this isn't a pool hall with cheap beer and people you'd rather not know. It was named one of the "Nation's Top Five Billiard Rooms" in *Billiards Digest*. At this trendy place, the beers and wines are of good quality, and there's champagne ready to celebrate a winning game. Instead of the usual pub food, chef Hugo Huesca has created a full

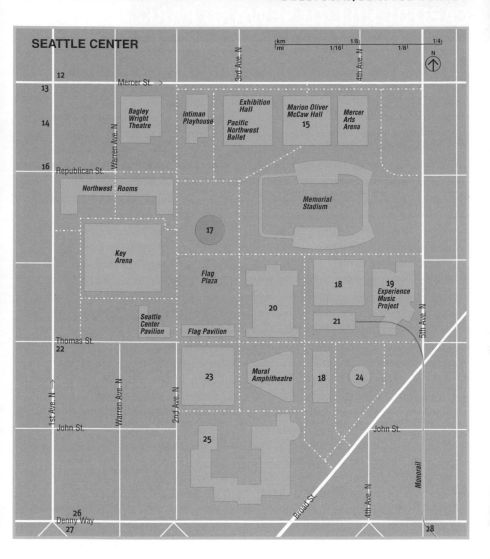

menu of southern Italian cuisine. And if you buy lunch, you can play pool free until 4PM. ◆ Italian ◆ 90 Blanchard St (between Western and First Aves). 448.6779. Tu-F, 11:30AM-2AM; Sa-M, 4PM-2AM.

66 QUEEN CITY GRILL

★★$$ A rich mahogany bar, several small dining booths, and burnt-sienna walls all combine to create a chic yet casual and warm atmosphere. Credit for the success of this stylish grill goes to co-owners Peter Lamb (who is also responsible for **Il Bistro** in **Pike Place Market**) and Steven Good, as well as to chefs Allan Davis and Michael Martino, who do marvelously simple but wonderful things with grilled fish or meats and garlic. Another plus: Dinner is available

until quite late. ◆ American ◆ M-F, lunch; daily, dinner. 2201 First Ave (at Blanchard St). 443.0975. &

67 BETHEL TEMPLE

Erected around 1915, this elegantly appointed terra-cotta edifice originally housed the ritzy **Crystal Swimming Pool**; it's now a Pentecostal church. Where the corner of this structure now drops back to glass doorways and a lighted sign at Second Avenue and Lenora Street, a huge metal dome used to rise over a pillared base. Model T's would drive up and drop youngsters here for an afternoon dip. The only hint of this building's early purpose may be the stylized green dolphins that decorate its roofline. ◆ 2033 Second Ave (at Lenora St)

Restaurants/Clubs: Red | Hotels: Purple | Shops: Orange | Outdoors/Parks: Green | Sights/Culture: Blue

CAPITOL HILL TO SEWARD PARK

In a city of diverse neighborhoods, those areas lying just east of downtown—along the hilly ridge that separates downtown skyscrapers from placid **Lake Washington**—are by far the most diverse. The wealth of old Seattle is entrenched here, but these streets are also home to penniless refugees, leather-clad punks with bright hair, and, in August, crowds drawn to Seafair's annual hydroplane competition.

The 2000 census identified distinct racial and/or ethnic groups in this enormous area, including European-Americans, African-Americans, and Asian-Americans. Latinos and Native Americans also appear in significant numbers. Diversity reaches its apex on Capitol Hill, where any given block may be home to young singles, blue-collar Boeing workers, members of the gay and lesbian community, and émigrés from a half-dozen nations. If there is a minority group in this part of town, it might be the white families with children that predominate throughout the rest of the city.

There's no real central focal point here, and indeed the neighborhood boundaries are ill-defined; even City Hall may find itself divided as to whether a given residence is located in, say, **Leschi** or **Madrona**. Outside of a few isolated areas, there's not much nightlife on these tree-lined streets. **Broadway** on Capitol Hill is pretty lively, especially on weekend evenings. The Pike–Pine Corridor—the several blocks of **Pike and Pine Sts** east and west of Broadway—is crowded at night with up-and-coming trendy types, a large gay community, and many pierced and tattooed young folks, all patronizing small bookstores, cafés and coffeehouses, clubs and bars, restaurants and microbreweries. And with the construction of lofts and condos, it's feeling like a new Belltown.

Madison Park hosts an impressive enclave of stately and well-preserved mansions, surpassed only by **Millionaires' Row** and the **Harvard-Belmont Historic District** on Capitol Hill. In addition, **Madison Valley** is home to two of Seattle's best restaurants, **Rover's** and **Cafe Flora**.

First settled by Italian farmers, the nearby **Central District** became more urban and residential during World War II, as African-Americans from the South arrived to work in Seattle's booming economy. In recent years, much of the neighborhood has fallen into disrepair, and vice and violence have crept in. But there's also a closeness felt by the residents here, people bravely fighting modern urban plagues.

There is a plethora of parks in the area—from the traditionally styled **Volunteer Park** and the innovative **Cal Anderson Park** on Capitol Hill to the urban wilderness of Seward Park on Lake Washington. The lake draws flocks of citizens to its shores in warm months and is used year-round for fishing and boating. **Washington Park Arboretum** will captivate both the casual stroller and the professional botanist. And these are just the largest greenswards; perhaps a dozen smaller (but no less charming) acreages—such as the **Louisa Boren View Park**—are tucked away, known to neighborhood residents and waiting to be discovered by the visitor.

1 ROMIO'S PIZZA

★★$ A relatively young entry in the pizzeria chain, this branch is more spacious but less homey than its brethren. It's hard, though, to complain about a place that serves pizza as fabulous as this. ◆ Pizza/takeout ◆ Daily, until 11PM. 3242 Eastlake Ave E (at Fuhrman Ave). 322.4453. &.

Also at numerous locations throughout the city

2 MONTLAKE BRIDGE

Built in 1925, with distinctive Gothic-inspired towers (visually linking it to the nearby **University of Washington**), this span was designed by the university's architect, **Carl**

km 1/2 1
mi 1/4 1/2

N

Union Bay

Fuhrman Ave. E

E Roanoke St.

EASTLAKE

E Lynn St.

Montlake Bridge

E Hamlin St.

Portage Bay

Foster Island

Evergreen Point Floating Bridge

520

Eastlake Ave. E

5

Washington Park Arboretum

MADISON PARK

24th Ave. E

Boyer Ave. E

Louisa Boren View Park

Interlaken Park

10th Ave. E

E Galer St.

23rd Ave. E

Lake Washington Blvd. E

Arboretum Dr. E

Broadmoor Dr. E

Parkside Dr. E

43rd Ave. E

E Garfield St.

McGilvra Blvd. E

Volunteer Park

E Prospect St.

E Aloha St.

CAPITOL HILL

MADISON VALLEY

For nos 1-81, see pgs. 90-91

Bellevue Ave. E

Belmont Ave. E

E Republican St.

E Thomas St.

E John St.

E John St.

Broadway

E Denny Way

E Denny Way

Florence Ct.

Cal Anderson Park

E Pine St.

31st Ave.

FIRST HILL

E Union St.

CENTRAL DISTRICT

Madison St.

12th Ave.

15th Ave.

19th Ave.

23rd Ave.

M.L. King Jr. Way

34th Ave.

35th Ave.

Madrona Park Bathing Beach

E Cherry St.

82

Cherry St.

James St.

E Alder St.

83

Lake Washington

Boren Ave.

Harborview Hospital

Leschi Park

85 86

84

E Yesler Way

16th Ave. S

S Jackson St.

Frink Park

87

YESLER TERRACE

S Dearborn St.

Jose Rizal Park

12th Ave. S

Lakeside Ave. S

Lacey V. Murrow Floating Bridge

90

S Holgate St.

BEACON HILL

Colman Park

Mercer Island

S Lander St.

Airport Way

5

88

900

89

West Seattle Fwy.

4th Ave. S

S McClellan St.

34th Ave. S

167

Lake Washington Blvd. S

Industrial Way S

S Spokane St.

Beacon Ave. S

Jefferson Park Golf Course

900

M.L. King Jr. Way S

Rainier Ave. S

90 Stan Sayres Memorial Park

Genesee Playfield

S Genesee St.

S Columbia Way

15th Ave. S

Columbia Park

42nd Ave. S

38th Ave. S

MOUNT BAKER

Lake Washington Blvd. S

Andrews Bay

91
↓

92
↓

51st Ave. S

93
Seward Park

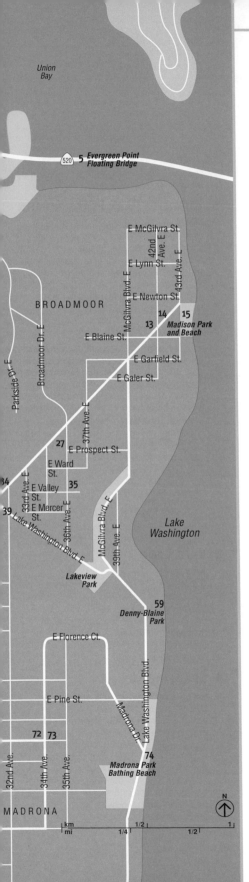

Gould. At that time, the need for a bridge had existed for only 8 years, because the ship canal, finally linking Puget Sound with Seattle's "inland sea," plowed through what had originally been an isthmus. An earlier, more easily crossed canal (about 100 yards south of the present Montlake Cut, and filled long ago) had been completed in 1884 but was used only for logs and the occasional canoe, as it was too narrow to carry ships. Completion of the UW stadium in 1920 initiated interest in a bridge; in fact, in preparation for the stadium's first football game (UW and Dartmouth), a graduate manager at the school tied a row of barges together near this point to allow fans easy passage north from the Montlake neighborhood. Three elections later, this bridge was built. A pleasant walkway runs along the south side of the canal and beneath the bridge.

3 SEATTLE YACHT CLUB

A water-oriented city, Seattle has a long list of yacht clubs—some spiffy, some not. This 3,000-member organization is the largest, the oldest (founded in 1892), and the hardest to get into (you must be nominated by a current member). It sponsors Seattle's traditional raft of events revolving around the opening day of yachting season, which is the first Saturday in May. The clubhouse was designed around 1920 by architect **John Graham Sr.** Facilities also include four docks full of well-oiled teak and mahogany. ♦ 1807 E Hamlin St (between Montlake Blvd and W Park Dr). 325.1000. www.seattleyachtclub.com

4 MUSEUM OF HISTORY AND INDUSTRY (MOHAI)

Opened in 1952, the city's premier repository of the past had a long gestation period. In 1911, historians began efforts to erect a permanent museum, but sufficient funds weren't gathered until the late 1940s. After locating choice property on the current site, however, museum backers faced opposition from the **University of Washington**, which owned the land—or thought it did, anyway. It turned out that a portion of the property was under federal control; museum supporters lobbied for its use and won. The museum now chronicles the city's heritage with displays of fire engines, a cable car, and numerous artifacts from the lumber, shipping, and fishing industries. Seattle is the birthplace of the Boeing Company, so it's no surprise to find a 1920s Boeing mail plane here. The museum also boasts a rich maritime collection—the model ships and figureheads are popular with children—and one of the state's most extensive arrays of

historic photographs from the region.
♦ Admission. Daily. Reservations required to visit the photo archives. 2700 24th Ave E (at Rte 520). 324.1125. www.seattlehistory.org

At the Museum of History and Industry:

FOSTER ISLAND WALK

At the bottom of **MOHAI**'s parking lot is the start of the largest wetlands trail system left in Seattle. A 20-minute nature walk starts off along wooden plankways and winds through a tangle of tall grasses, marshland exposed after the opening of the Lake Washington Ship Canal lowered the lake by 20 feet. The trail leads to Foster Island, a historic burial ground for the Union Bay Indians, now a pleasant picnic spot. From this point, you may gaze at the regular parade of boats crisscrossing the canal from Lake Washington to Lake Union. It's very soothing here—walk at water's edge past the white water lilies, yellow irises, and cattails and listen to the sounds of song sparrows, red-winged blackbirds, and marsh wrens. Dreamy as it is, your powers of reverie must be able to block out the discordant howl of traffic and the unsightly concrete of nearby Route 520. Neither pets nor jogging is allowed on this quiet trail, which continues past Foster Island another half-hour to the **Washington Park Arboretum**.

5 NELLIE CORNISH MEMORIAL SCULPTURES

Artist Parks Anderson's 1989 stylized windmills, jutting up from the waters of Lake Washington at the western end of the Evergreen Point Floating Bridge (Route 520), were installed in honor of longtime Seattle arts advocate Nellie Cornish, founder of Capitol Hill's **Cornish College of the Arts**. Each tower consists of four steel legs rising from a concrete base and topped with two bronze wind-wheels that rotate in opposite directions. Above these, and not visible except from boats that can get closer than cars to these sculptures, is a tiny bear, balanced whimsically on a golden ball, with another smaller ball perched on its nose. Fountains used to shoot eight-foot-tall sprays of water up the legs but not any more, since the spray interfered with nearby freeway traffic; the sculptures are lighted at night and create an eerie spectacle.

6 ROANOKE PARK PLACE TAVERN

This is a prime watering hole for the just-over-21-and-frisky set down from Capitol Hill. It's lively and good for people watching but definitely *not* the place to go if you're feeling your age. Burgers and beer are the two essential food groups. ♦ Daily, until 2AM. 2409 10th Ave E (between Miller and Roanoke Sts). 324.5882. &

7 14 CARROT CAFE

★$ It's a popular place, and on weekends you may have to cool your heels outside the front door with a newspaper. The menu features such dishes as vegetarian lasagna and self-designed omelets. ♦ American ♦ Daily, breakfast and lunch. 2305 Eastlake Ave E (at Lynn St). 324.1442. &

8 CAFÉ LAGO

★★★$$ The chefs at this bistro pride themselves on their gnocchi, but the real prize here is the antipasti selection. Top choices are the eggplant marinated in garlic and olive oil and the lasagna. Reservations recommended. ♦ Italian ♦ Daily. 2305 24th Ave E (between Lynn and McGraw Sts). 329.8005. &. www.cafelago.com

9 SERAFINA

★★$$ A few taverns have always been present in Eastlake, plus the odd used-books outlet and some totally forgettable office buildings, but such refined establishments as this place have greatly enhanced the neighborhood's profile in recent years. Begin your meal with a few small appetizers in the tapas style—the *vitello tonato* (veal scallopini chilled and served with a traditional tuna and caper sauce) is particularly good. Among the entrées, *linguine alla Cubana* (fresh linguine with prosciutto in a spicy tomato cream sauce,

---

Most cities have only one sister city (if any) elsewhere in the world; Seattle has quite a few, including Beersheba, Israel; Bergen, Norway; Chongqing, China; Christchurch, New Zealand; Galway, Ireland; Kōbe, Japan; Limbe, Cameroon; Managua, Nicaragua; Mazatlán, Mexico; Mombasa, Kenya; Nantes, France; Reykjavík, Iceland; Tashkent, Uzbekistan; and Taejŏn, South Korea. And there are local committees for each one of them; for more information, call City Hall at 386.1511.

The 39 inches of rain that Seattle receives in a year is in fact less than what falls on New York or Boston or Atlanta. Miami actually puts up with a whopping 58 inches annually.

topped with fresh arugula) and *pollo di pietro con morelli* (chicken breast stuffed with fontina cheese, morel mushrooms, and asparagus) are both delicious. This popular place is often crowded, and on busy nights the service can be slow. When there aren't a lot of patrons, it can be a romantic setting, especially with the occasional addition of live piano music. There's a wonderful patio out back, where diners at a handful of tables can relax and eat in a tranquil garden setting. ♦ Italian ♦ M-F, lunch and dinner; Sa, Su, dinner. Reservations recommended. 2043 Eastlake Ave E (at Boston St). 323.0807. &. www.serafinaseattle.com

Arboretum

10 WASHINGTON PARK ARBORETUM

This 200-acre woodland, planned in 1936 and stretching south from Lake Washington's Union Bay, is the city's jewel in a necklace of parks designed by the Olmsted Brothers landscaping firm of Massachusetts.

The arboretum was a long time in the making. After putting the area aside as parkland in 1904, the city developed Lake Washington Boulevard E (the narrow, curving thoroughfare that cuts through the park) as a scenic entryway to the 1909 Alaska-Yukon-Pacific Exposition, held on the **UW** grounds. But it didn't develop the park until the university agreed to help manage it. The arboretum first featured native plants (despite the Olmsteds' historical antipathy toward Northwest flora), but in the 1940s, it expanded to include species from all over the globe. Today more than 5,500 kinds of trees, shrubs, and flowers flourish on the grounds.

Visitors to the park can find a spot to fit almost any mood: Toss a Frisbee across the broad, open meadows; stroll through the ornamental gardens; or enter into the serene, otherworldly atmosphere of the tea garden. A harmonious collaboration of natural elements and human stewardship prevails throughout the park. Many plants have identification tags, but the thickly wooded grounds have none of the fussy feeling of some public gardens. There are several hours' worth of trails to explore. Dogs love to romp in this park, but the city's leash laws should at least be acknowledged, if not followed to the letter.

Within the Washington Park Arboretum:

GRAHAM VISITORS' CENTER

The park's focal point offers trail maps, botanical pamphlets, and a small gift shop and bookstore. The center schedules two large sales during the year, one of plants (in April) and another of bulbs (in October), when you may see normally serene local gardeners locked in combat for possession of a bewildered baby rhododendron. Just outside the front door, several hiking trails lead to wooded areas. ♦ Daily. Group tours of the park Saturday and Sunday at 1PM (except in December). 2300 Arboretum Dr E (between Lake Washington Blvd and Foster Island Rd). 543.8800

Adjacent to Graham Visitors' Center:

WINTER GARDEN

Plants that thrive in the mild Northwest climate and bloom between October and March are displayed here. Witch hazel and viburnum are prominent attractions. In early spring, the tall cornelian cherry shrubs burst forth with their small yellow flowers, set against an under-planting of Lenten roses. ♦ 543.8800

AZALEA WAY

This wide, grassy three-quarter-mile path was the site of a raceway for harness horses in Seattle's pre-auto era but is now considered too fragile to withstand even joggers—it's for walkers only. Crowds gather along the path on weekends from April through June to see flowering cherry trees, azaleas, and the dogwoods. Farther along is the **Rhododendron Glen**, where a pond reflects a riot of colors.

JAPANESE TEA GARDEN

Designed in the Momoyama style in 1960 by Japanese architect **Juki Iida**, this 3.5-acre garden is a tranquil world of Asian and Northwest plantings, rookeries, bridges, granite lanterns, waterfalls, and glassy pools. Believed to be one of the most authentic outside of Japan, the tea garden's construction required transporting more than 500 massive granite boulders, each wrapped in bamboo matting to prevent scratching, from high in Washington's Cascade Mountains. The original cypress-and-cedar teahouse, hand-constructed in Japan, was destroyed by fire in 1973, then rebuilt following the original plans. The teahouse offers demonstrations in Chado, the highly ritualized Japanese tea ceremony (on the third Saturday of the month at 1PM from April to October). ♦ Admission. Daily, Mar–Nov. 1502 Lake Washington Blvd E (between Arboretum Dr and Foster Island Rd). 684.4725; tea ceremony demonstrations, 324.1483. www.seattlejapanesegarden.com

11 LOUISA BOREN VIEW PARK

Pike Place Market hero **Victor Steinbrueck** designed this small park in 1975. Looking north, it commands views of Portage Bay, the **UW** campus, Lake Washington, and the Cascade Mountains. The park was named after Louisa Boren Denny, the last survivor of the 1851 Alki Point settlers. The large untitled Cor-Ten steel sculpture, composed of 10 interlocking blocks rusted to an even brown color, was created by artist Lee Kelly. ♦ E Garfield St and 15th Ave

12 INTERLAKEN PARK

This park is really just a serpentine, tree-lined street with a few shady footpaths that are frequented by neighborhood residents. It was originally the route of a short-lived bicycle path, built during a Seattle bike craze around the turn of the 19th century. Interlaken Boulevard now connects the **Washington Park Arboretum** and Lake Washington Boulevard with Capitol Hill, before heading northwest to the Eastlake neighborhood. ♦ Interlaken Blvd (between Lake Washington Blvd E and Delmar Dr E)

13 MADISON PARK GARDEN SHOP

Yes, there are lots of plants and supplies here, plus a frosting of paraphernalia, toys, and baskets. But the bonus is proprietor Lola McKee, the unofficial mayor and historian of Madison Park, who has become a tenacious advocate for preservation of this community's many charms. ♦ M-Sa. 1837 42nd Ave E (at Madison St). 322.5331. ♿

14 RED ONION TAVERN

This is a classic neighborhood joint where the never-rowdy clientele grows younger as the night wears on; by closing time, young singles predominate. The pool tables are bumpy, and the pizza is filling but mediocre. However, a fireplace does much to promote lingering conversation. ♦ Daily, until 2AM. 4210 E Madison St (between 43rd and 42nd Aves). 323.1611

14 CACTUS

★★$$ Popular traditional Spanish and Mexican specialties are served here, authentic right down to the use of fish flown in from the Yucatán. But the primo draws are the invitingly displayed and spicy tapas. ♦ Spanish/Mexican ♦ M-Sa, lunch and dinner; Su, dinner. Reservations recommended for groups of five or more. 4220 E Madison St (between 43rd and 42nd Aves). 324.4140. www.cactusrestaurant.com

15 MADISON PARK AND BEACH

Not a component in the Olmsted Brothers' greenbelt scheme but linked to it by later planners, this is the northernmost in a continuous string of parks that lines Lake Washington's western banks. There are roped-off swimming areas and lighted tennis courts, and on steamy summer afternoons, droves of sun worshipers jam the beach.

In the 1890s, the **Madison Street Cable Car Company** ran a line out here to a small amusement park with a 500-seat pavilion, boathouse, ballpark, and racetrack. Boat cruises around the lake began from this spot, and summer vacationers came to mount big canvas tents on specially constructed platforms.

In preparation for the AYP Exposition, $30,000 was spent on improvements to the amusement park, which was then called **White City**, and a ferry line to Mercer Island and other nascent Eastside communities was added. But it all fell into disuse after the Expo ended. One remaining remnant of those days is **Pioneer Hall**, which is listed on the National Register of Historic Places. Built in 1910, the structure now houses a museum (with very limited hours) that displays pioneer artifacts, period costumes, and 19th-century photographs. In 1919, the city bought the streetcar line, along with the park and its entertainment facilities. Twenty years later, the city initiated a Works Project Administration landscaping program to take advantage of new waterfront space created here after the ship canal lowered Lake Washington by 20 feet. ♦ Pioneer Hall: free; 1-4PM on the second of the month. 2300 43rd Ave E (between E Newton and E Blaine Sts.)

16 EGAN HOUSE

This triangular oddity may well be the most unusual residence in Seattle. Built in 1958, the house is the work of **Robert Reichert**, a local architect well known for unconventional designs. This building's form, wrote Sally B. Woodbridge and Roger Montgomery in *A Guide to Architecture in Washington State*, "expresses its interior organization, in which levels, like graduated trays, diminish in size as they rise." It's a private residence. ♦ 1500 Lakeview Blvd E (between Belmont and Harvard Aves)

17 JOHN LEARY HOUSE

When completed around 1904, this stone and half-timbered manse was one of the largest and most lavish in the city. The architect was Seattle's **J. Alfred Bodley**. The owner, John Leary, arrived in Seattle in 1869 and founded the West Coast Improvement Company, which was primarily responsible for the development of Ballard. In 1882, Leary became principal owner of the *Seattle Post*, which he soon merged with the competing *Intelligencer* to create what is still the city's morning daily, the *Seattle Post-Intelligencer*. He also opened and operated a coal mine, was partly responsible for supplying Seattle with its first natural gas, and set up a waterworks system that brought in water from Lake Washington for the first time. Not content with his accomplishments, Leary was elected mayor of Seattle in 1884 and served two terms in office. It seemed John Leary could have anything he wanted. But he died at the age of 68 before he could move into his dream house. The mansion is now home to the Episcopal Diocesan offices. A stained-glass window designed for the house by New York's Tiffany & Company is now at UW's Burke Museum. ♦ 1551 10th Ave E (between Highland Dr and Blaine St)

18 LAKE VIEW CEMETERY

Before **Volunteer Park** could begin to grow in the 1890s, the city had to relocate one of its principal graveyards from what is now the park's north end. Regrettably, most of the dead residents had already been moved once before, in 1885, when the city turned its pioneer cemetery into **Denny Park**, south of Lake Union. Two years later, Leigh S.J. Hunt, owner and editor of the *Seattle Post-Intelligencer*, convinced the city council that the graves should be moved again, just a few hundred feet north. This final site is now the **Lake View Cemetery**, with perhaps the best views of any graveyard in the city. People come from as far away as China to visit the gravesites (near the summit) of kung fu star Bruce Lee, a former Seattleite who died in 1973, and his son Brandon, who was killed in a shooting accident during the making of the 1994 film *The Crow*. And there are some wonderful old tombstones here, dating back to the 1850s. Pioneer David Swinton "Doc"

Maynard, who perished in 1873, is buried here beside one of his two wives, Catherine, whose epitaph reads, "She did what she could." Nearby is a rugged headstone under which Princess Angeline, the daughter of Chief Sealth, the city's namesake, lies in a canoe-shaped coffin. ♦ 15th Ave E (between Highland Dr and Howe St). 322.1582

19 ST. MARK'S EPISCOPAL CATHEDRAL

This graceful but somewhat chilly Episcopal temple for the Diocese of Olympia was designed by **Bakewell and Brown**, a San Francisco architectural firm. Built between 1926 and 1930 in a neo-Byzantine style, the church has an interior that one critic described as "an immense masonry box." Inside is a world-renowned 3,744-pipe Flentrop organ, acquired in 1965, which draws musicians from all over the world to perform in the cathedral's annual recital series. A recent addition is a spectacular 57-foot-high steel-and-glass screen installed behind the main altar and in front of the new Great Window on the west wall. The effect of this contemporary sculptural construction in an austere, traditional space is breathtaking. ♦ 1245 10th Ave E (between Highland Dr and Blaine St). 323.0300. www.saintmarks.org

20 VOLUNTEER PARK

During the 1880s, this 43-acre plot was known simply as **City Park**. But in 1901, it was renamed to honor Seattle men who fought in the Spanish-American War of 1898. The same year, a 20 million–gallon reservoir was carved from the park's southern flanks, and around 1906, a 75-foot-tall water tower was put up to increase water pressure in the mansions sprouting nearby. The Olmsted Brothers engineered the final refinements. As part of their comprehensive plan, they decided that this should be one of several "neat and smooth" central parks (as opposed to such "wild" outlying greens as **Seward Park**). Second-growth fir trees were felled and replaced by a more ordered regiment of blue spruce, flowering cherry trees, and Port

---

Restaurants/Clubs: Red | Hotels: Purple | Shops: Orange | Outdoors/Parks: Green | Sights/Culture: Blue

FOWL PLAY

Northwesterners seem generally fascinated by the peregrinations of birds, and Seattle residents are no exception. On almost any weekend you'll see clutches of watchers bouncing high-tech binoculars on their chests or toting cameras mounted with lenses big enough to subdue a charging elk. Bird-watching is best here in winter, when migrating species make the long flap down from the north in pursuit of warmer climes. But early and late summer aren't without their viewing opportunities.

The local Audubon Society recommends that bird-watchers scope out **Lincoln Park** in **West Seattle**, **Magnolia**'s **Discovery Park** (where more than 150 bird species have been sighted, including red-tailed hawks, goldfinches, and ospreys), the **University of Washington** campus, and the **Washington Park Arboretum** (a stopping point—by last count—for some 200 species). Endangered peregrine falcons have been spotted in north **Ballard**, and members of another threatened species—purple martins—have been known to nest downtown, amazingly enough on the skybridge of the **Bon Marché** department store. **Green Lake**, in summer one of the best locations to espy the red-breasted Coppertone slatherer and the ogle-eyed people peeper, is most attractive for birders in the winter. Mergansers, mallards, and other ducks swoop down between November and January to grab bread crumbs, as do the visiting Canada geese on their migration southward. Bald eagles are also known to perch in trees above Green Lake, but they actually nest in **Discovery Park** and **Seward Park** on the west bank of **Lake Washington**. And, as is common with other port cities, seagulls are ubiquitous in Seattle. Their screeches are as memorable as the blast of a ferry horn, and their flight patterns as familiar as the march of rain clouds.

If you have time for a day trip, about an hour's drive to the south, amidst the docklands near **Tacoma**'s **Lincoln Avenue Bridge**, is the **Gogle-hi-te Wetland**, an artificial estuary inhabited by more than a hundred varieties of birds.

Orford cedar. A carriage concourse was laid, fountains and a giant bandstand were built, and a semicircular concert grove was pruned out of the undergrowth. With only a few exceptions, the park today looks much as it did when the Olmsteds completed their work.

Fine clear-weather views of the **Space Needle**, Puget Sound, and the Olympic Mountains are available from this 445-foot elevation. Climb to the top of the brick-faced water tower—a tricky ascent, given its steep stairs—for an even better perspective. The park fills with people during summer theater performances and weekend festivals. Two outdoor tennis courts are well maintained but underused. A popular children's playground and wading pool lie in the northeastern corner.

Despite the tranquility, a few cautions should be exercised here. Behind the concrete bandstand, situated just north of the reservoir, is a public rest room where various criminal activities have occurred despite frequent police patrols; it's best to avoid it after nightfall. It seems quite safe at all other hours, however. ◆ 1247 15th Ave E (at Highland Dr)

Within Volunteer Park:

CONSERVATORY

Constructed for $20,000 in 1912, this conservatory was patterned after London's spectacular Crystal Palace exhibition hall. It was a prefab building: Manufactured in New York, the components were shipped to Seattle and put together by parks department employees. Capitol Hill's landed gentry of the time readily embraced the conservatory, calling it the finest structure of its kind west of Chicago and contributing plant specimens to its collection. During the Depression, however, the conservatory fell on hard times, its humid environment rotting the Southern swamp cypress frames and rusting some of the iron supports. By the 1970s, the greenhouse was beginning to list to one side and visitors weren't allowed on the premises during windy weather because panes of glass tended to pop out of their frames. A $500,000 restoration program in the early 1980s re-created the building's graceful roof and sides using steel, cast iron, and Alaska cedar. During refurbishment, a colorful etched-glass canopy—*Homage in Green*—was installed over the entrance. Created by Richard Spaulding, a former artist-in-residence with the Seattle Arts Commission, *Homage* is enlivened with lilies, passion flowers, and morning glories, all of which are familiar from Victorian designs. Inside, more than a quarter-million visitors each year study an incredible array of orchids, cacti, and tropical species in three crowded wings. Sadly, the abundant foliage permits no room for wheelchairs. Admirers periodically lobby the city for expansion, but the park's neighbors, fearing more traffic, object. ◆ Daily. E Highland Dr (between 15th and Federal Aves). 684.4743

MONUMENT TO WILLIAM H. SEWARD

The weathered bronze statue is a likeness of the former US Secretary of State and real-estate tycoon who bought Alaska from the Russians in 1867 for 2 cents an acre. New York artist Richard Brooks created this piece for the **1909 Alaska-Yukon-Pacific Expo**. This statue, which was originally intended to be moved to **Seward Park** after the exposition was over, has been in its current "temporary" location for close to 90 years. ♦ E Highland Dr (between 15th and Federal Aves)

SEATTLE ASIAN ART MUSEUM

This beloved building (the old **Seattle Art Museum**) was given new life in 1994 as a showcase for the museum's extensive assembly of Asian art, which ranks in the top 10 collections outside of Asia; its Japanese collection is one of the top 5 in the US. The works here reflect a span of many ages and cultures in India, China, Japan, Korea, and Southeast Asia. The museum is also an education venue for scholarly exchange about Asian art and culture. Designed by **Carl Gould**, the building is a Moderne gem. It was completed in 1933 and was a gift to the city from Dr. Richard Fuller, philanthro-pist and president of the Seattle Fine Arts Society, and his mother, Mrs. Eugene Fuller. At the time of its construction, the museum was a fresh Protomodern design—with rounded corners, curved walls, and a foyer flowing gracefully toward side galleries and stairways. ♦ Admission; children under 12 admitted free; discount for seniors and students. Tu-Su. 1400 E Prospect St (between 15th and Federal Aves). 625.8900. www.seattleartmuseum.org.

Next to the Seattle Asian Art Museum:

BLACK SUN

One of the park's focal points is this massive black granite sculpture—9 feet in diameter—created in 1968 by artist Isamu Noguchi (who also did *Landscape of Time*, a collection of carved granite boulders at Second Avenue and Marion Street). Area residents call it either "The Doughnut" or "The Black Hole." Not to discourage anyone, but if you choose to frame a photograph of the **Space Needle** through the hole in the middle, you won't be the first to do so.

21 ISAAC STEVENS SCHOOL

Early school district architect **James Stephen**, whose institutional artistry is also on display at **Summit Grade School** on First

Hill and **Latona Elementary** and **Interlake School** in Wallingford, designed this huge wooden Colonial Revival edifice in 1906. ♦ 1242 18th Ave E (between Highland Dr and Galer St). 726.6710. www.seattleschools.org

22 HARVARD-BELMONT HISTORIC DISTRICT

Many of Seattle's top industrialists, financiers, and business leaders, including **Great Northern Railroad** heir Sam Hill, lived in this venerable Capitol Hill enclave. Horace C. Henry, another railroader, who'd moved to Seattle in 1890 from his native Vermont to build the original belt line around Lake Washington for the **Northern Pacific Railroad**, also lived here. Most of the mansions in the district were built between 1905 and 1910, with the predominant architectural styles being Tudor, Colonial, and Georgian Revival. In the 1920s, a second wave of building brought a number of elegant brick apartment complexes to the area, many of them designed by **Fred Anhalt**. Unlike most of the city's old neighborhoods—which have largely succumbed to modern development—this area has remained a gracious retreat of tree-lined streets, professionally tended gardens, and majestic residential and institutional buildings. It is on the National Register of Historic Places. ♦ Bounded by Broadway E and Belmont Ave E and by Roy St and Highland Dr

22 SAM HILL HOUSE

Designed by the Washington, DC, architectu-ral firm of **Hornblower & Marshall**, this mansion was built in 1909 for the son-in-law of **Great Northern Railroad** magnate James J. Hill. The five-story fortress is a concrete variation of an 18th-century manor house, resembling in many respects the Petit Trianon at Versailles. Hill supposedly built it to be able to properly receive Crown Prince Albert of Belgium, who, despite two planned trips to Seattle, canceled both times. It's still a private residence. ♦ 814 E Highland Dr (between 10th and Harvard Aves)

23 C. J. SMITH HOUSE

This beautiful brick mansion, with leaded-glass windows and an elegant low brick wall separating the front yard from the sidewalk, was built in 1907, though it's been renovated and altered recently. The design, by Spokane architect **Kirtland K. Cutter** and his frequent partner **Karl Malmgren**, was influenced by the work of English architect **Richard Norman Shaw**, who was much in favor in

America at the time. Born in 1854, Charles Jackson Smith, a native of Kentucky, was president of the Dexter Horton National Bank. The house remains a private residence. ♦ 1147 Harvard Ave E (between Prospect St and Highland Dr)

23 BROWNELL-BLOEDEL HOUSE

Architect **Carl Gould** departed from his usual style by sheathing this 1910 Georgian Revival residence in natural wood shingles. It's a private residence. ♦ 1137 Harvard Ave E (between Prospect St and Highland Dr)

24 CAPITOL HILL ADDITION

Many of the comparatively modest residences found just east of **Volunteer Park** were part of the **Capitol Hill Addition**, a residential development begun around 1905. Spearheading that project was James A. Moore, the real-estate promoter who later built the **Moore Theater** downtown and created the University Heights district. Moore already had an interest in this neighborhood; in 1901 he had acquired a good portion of it. Moore's wife, Eugenia, named the development after an exclusive section of Denver, her hometown. Before opening the area to occupants, Moore spent $150,000 on improvements (cement sidewalks, paved streets, sewers, and water), "a previously unheard-of procedure," wrote the *Seattle Times*. The subdivision attracted the construction of many Colonial Revival homes—a style now commonly referred to as the Classic Box—along a nearby streetcar line. The houses here still delight with intricate details, such as squared-off corner bay windows, leaded glass, and Moorish keyhole windows. It's worth walking these thoroughfares to observe Moore's early legacy. One of the finer examples of the Classic Box can be found at **747 16th Avenue E** and is identified by its shallow ground-floor bays. ♦ Bounded by 23rd and 15th Aves E and by Mercer and Galer Sts

25 BACON MANSION

$$ Built in 1909 by Cecil Bacon, this Edwardian-style mansion is now a bed-and-breakfast providing all modern comforts. The eight rooms and three suites—nicely decorated with antiques and reproductions—have telephones (with voice mail and data ports), color TV, and table fans; five have private baths, and a few have refrigerators. The **Carriage House**, a separate two-story building, is perfect for a small family or four people. The library with its leaded-glass windows, the grand piano in the lobby, and the patio with a fountain and garden create a charming mood. An expanded continental breakfast is included. ♦ Reservations 6 weeks in advance are recommended. 959 Broadway E (at Prospect St). 329.1864, 800/240.1864. &. www.baconmansion.com

26 PARKER HOUSE

A vast Colonial Revival mansion was built in 1909 for George H. Parker, the West Coast fiscal agent for the United Wireless Company. Parker's $150,000 home, supported by Corinthian columns, boasted 5 covered porches, 12 bedrooms and 16 other rooms, 7 fireplaces, 5 bathrooms, hardwood floors, muraled walls, and an adjoining coach house. Parker, however, was not to enjoy his mansion for long. In 1910, he was convicted of stock and mail fraud and given a 2-year sentence at the federal prison on McNeil Island in south Puget Sound. It's a private residence. ♦ 1409 E Prospect St (between 15th and 14th Aves)

27 ALEXANDER PANTAGES HOUSE

Lying south of Madison Street and north of where Lake Washington Boulevard dips down to the lake from the **Washington Park Arboretum** is a wooded and palatial residential canton called Washington Park. Although it only began to develop after the 19th century, the neighborhood has the classic weight of a much older subdivision. One of the most impressive architectural statements made here is the home of impresario Alexander Pantages, who owned vaudeville theaters all over the West. His half-timbered mansion was designed in 1909 by **Wilson & Loveless** and carries overtones of California Mission Revival style. It's a private residence. ♦ 1117 36th Ave E (between Ward and Madison Sts)

28 R.D. MERRILL HOUSE

Built in 1909, this modified Georgian mansion, complete with formal garden and carriage house, is the only West Coast structure designed by famed New York architect **Charles A. Platt**, who is best known for his Freer Gallery in Washington, DC. Merrill was born in Michigan in 1869 to a lumber family from Maine. Continuing in the family tradition, he moved to the Pacific Northwest in 1898 to manage the Washington and British Columbia properties of Merrill and Ring, a leading lumber firm of the era. ♦ 919 Harvard Ave E (between Aloha and Prospect Sts)

Alexander Pantages House

Matthew S. Morrow / North Market Street Graphics

29 COBB HOUSE

Built in 1910, this house—"a fusion of the spirit of the German Black Forest and the English Arts & Crafts movement," as *A Guide to Architecture in Washington State* so eloquently puts it—was designed by the prestigious early-20th-century firm of **Bebb & Mendel**. It has lovely leaded-glass windows and a sizable second-floor balcony secluded by a parapet. The first owner was C.H. Cobb, a native of Maine, who moved west to California in 1876, then headed north to Seattle, where by the 1890s he had incorporated four logging and timber companies and the Marysville and Arlington Railroad Company. ♦ 1409 E Aloha St (between 15th and 14th Aves)

30 SALISBURY HOUSE

$$ A Victorian charmer owned and operated by Mary Wiese and her daughter Catheryn, this bed-and-breakfast has five rooms—all with queen-size beds and private baths—and a lower-level suite with a private entrance, a fireplace in the living room, a small refrigerator, and a whirlpool tub. Family-style vegetarian breakfasts are served here, the library is comfy and well stocked, and **Volunteer Park** is two short blocks away. Off-street parking is not available, but there's rarely a problem finding parking on the street. ♦ 750 16th Ave E (at Aloha St). 328.8682. www.salisburyhouse.com

31 ST. JOSEPH'S CATHOLIC CHURCH

Pay close attention to the tall, tapering belfry of this stripped-down Gothic house of worship, for it's there that you can find some relationship between this 1932 building and a still more impressive structure also designed by architect **Joseph Wilson**: downtown's **Seattle Tower**. The facing of the church was apparently intended to be something grander than cast concrete, but the Depression forced Wilson to simplify his dreams. Don't miss the stained-glass window on the entrance face. ♦ 732 18th Ave E (between Roy and Aloha Sts). 324.2522

32 VIOS

★★★$$ A family-friendly restaurant with a big kids' play area. Chef-owner Thomas Soukakos infuses Mediterranean classics—

St. Joseph's Catholic Church

chicken souvlaki, grilled lamb, hummus, and tzatziki—with his distinctive flourishes. All in a warm and homey environment, where owner and staff are cheery and enthusiastic, and where dinner doesn't cost an arm and a leg. ♦ Mediterranean ♦ Tu–Sa, lunch and dinner; closed Su, M. 903 19th Ave E (at Aloha St). 329.3236. www.vioscafe.com

33 HOLY NAMES ACADEMY

Beaux Arts styling receives grand exposition in this domed Catholic girls' school, designed by **C. Alfred Breitung**, who also created the tiny **Triangle Hotel Building** in Pioneer Square and Wallingford's **Home of the Good Shepherd**. ♦ 728 21st Ave E (between Roy and Aloha Sts). 323.4272. www.holynames-sea.org

34 NISHINO

★★★★$$$ Chef Tatsu Nishino has been orchestrating his many busy sushi and sous chefs in the cramped open kitchen of this elegant beige-toned room since 1995. In a town where fresh fish well-prepared is expected by local restaurant patrons, Nishino scores high; sushi and sashimi are fresh and inventively presented. But this is more than a sushi bar. The menu features such surprising taste treats as albacore tuna tartare with ginger salsa, dynamite (baked geoduck, scallops, and mushrooms), and *nasu dengaku* (eggplant in sweet miso sauce). Or you could order the omakase dinner (Japanese for "leave it to me"), and the chef will prepare a unique and unforgettable prix-fixe meal. To say that reservations are recommended is an understatement; Nishino has a corps of regulars from around the area who turn up in droves every night the place is open. ♦ Japanese ♦ Daily, dinner. Reservations recommended. 3130 Madison St (between Lake Washington Blvd and 32nd Ave E). 322.5800

35 WALKER-AMES HOUSE

Architects **Charles Bebb** and **Leonard L. Mendel** designed this stately Colonial Revival manse in 1907. It is now the residence of the **University of Washington**'s president. ♦ 808 36th Ave E (between Valley and Ward Sts)

36 CORNISH COLLEGE OF THE ARTS

This "quietly elegant building of Mediterranean persuasion," as it is described in *A Guide to Architecture in Washington State*, was designed in 1921 by the Seattle architectural firm of **Albertson, Wilson & Richardson**. Nellie Cornish, the piano-playing daughter of a Tennessee sheep farmer who moved to Seattle in 1900, founded the school without any initial support from the city. But with programs in art, music, theater, and dance, the institute has since come to play an important part in Seattle's cultural life. Renowned choreographer Martha Graham and painter Mark Tobey were members of the faculty. Nellie Cornish lived in an apartment on the top floor of this terra-cotta–ornamented edifice. ♦ 710 E Roy St (between Harvard and Boylston Aves). 323.1400. www.cornish.edu

37 LOVELESS BUILDING

Designed in an English cottage vein by architect **Arthur B. Loveless**, this graceful block of first-floor shops and second-floor apartments arranged around a concealed courtyard was built in 1933. In his book *Seattle Past to Present*, Roger Sale refers to the "enchanting Loveless Block, stores and apartments of an elegance that Arthur Loveless alone among traditional Seattle architects seemed to have." Loveless was a master of well-sited period revival designs. His houses are dotted over Capitol Hill, and in 1930, he remodeled the **Colman Building** on First Avenue in an Art Deco style. ♦ 711 Broadway E (between Roy and Aloha Sts)

37 RAINIER CHAPTER HOUSE OF THE DAR

City architect **Daniel R. Huntington** designed the chapter house of the Daughters of the American Revolution in 1924 as a replica of George Washington's Mount Vernon estate. The building is rented out for parties, chamber-music concerts, and the like, and it is a favorite for wedding receptions. ♦ 800 E Roy St (at Harvard Ave). 323.0600. www.bravoseattle.com

38 MILLIONAIRES' ROW

This tree-lined cluster of Xanadus extends south from **Volunteer Park** along 14th Avenue to Roy Street. Seattle's most prominent families once found status and security here, as this mini-neighborhood was protected from mere mortals by a private gate. The gate is now gone, but the district retains much of its earlier elegance. As in other affluent Seattle neighborhoods, however, many of the mansions have been converted from single-family residences to apartments. ♦ 14th Ave E (between Roy and Prospect Sts)

Along Millionaires' Row:

THOMAS BORDEAUX HOUSE

The builder of this house was a Canadian who arrived here in 1852 and later ascended to the presidency of the Mason County Logging Company and the Mumby Lumber and Shingle Company. Thomas Bordeaux was also a director of the First National Bank of Seattle. His home, complete with a decorated tower, was built in 1903. Designed by Seattle architect **W.D. Kimball**, it reflects the half-timber style then in vogue. ♦ 806 14th Ave E (between Valley and Aloha Sts)

39 LAKE WASHINGTON BOULEVARD

Those landscaping Olmsted Brothers, and their father before them, were great believers in contouring human developments to the land. Their comprehensive plan for Seattle included this scenic and meandering boulevard along the west side of Lake Washington, running south from the Alaska-Yukon-Pacific Exposition grounds (now the **UW** campus) to **Seward Park**. Today, some parts of this 1910 contoured drive have been bypassed by straighter Lakeside Avenue S (especially the famous curves through **Colman Park**, just south of the Lacey V. Murrow Floating Bridge). But you can still follow the old route; watch closely for signs.

40 HARVARD EXIT

Seattle's first luxury art theater makes its home in a building that once held a women's club. From the crowded entryway, pass through what once must have been an elegant drawing room or living room but is now a very comfortable, old-fashioned space to meet your movie-going partners. Games of checkers are available for extended waits. The theater schedules some of the better flicks passing through town, and entries in the annual Seattle International Film Festival often play here. ♦ Box office opens 1 hour before show time. 807 E Roy St (between Broadway and Harvard Ave). 323.8986. www.landmarkstheatres.com

40 DELUXE 1 BAR AND GRILL

★$ Amidst the Broadway area's fervid grab for glitz and its increasing dependence on patrons from beyond Capitol Hill, this spot has managed to retain its down-home feeling—there are no bow ties behind the bar, no leather-skirted waitresses, no Art Deco menus. Warm a stool or pull up a chair and order a bacon, onion, and avocado burger that's guaranteed to put permanent frown lines in your doctor's forehead. Or try a pint of one of those 17 old-time microbrewed beers. In summer a retractable wall out front allows for maximum people watching with maximum comfort. ♦ American ♦ Daily, lunch and dinner. 625 Broadway E (at Roy St). 324.9697. &

40 DANCER'S SERIES: STEPS

Look down as you're strolling along either side of busy Broadway between Pine and Roy Streets. Periodically, you will spot arrangements of bronze footprints, accompanied by dance instructions, by Seattle artist Jack Mackie. Mackie, with assistance from artist Charles Greening, created these eight street-level artworks to be used, not just observed. He even mixed a few steps of his own creation (the Busstop, for instance, and the Obeebo) in with the classic rumba, waltz, and tango. Mackie gave special treatment to the heels, imbedding parking tokens in those footprints outside a parking lot and even offering a simplified view of the skyline in a set near a bus stop.

41 ANHALT APARTMENTS

Dating to the late 1920s, these units are fine representations of the stylish but practical sort of brick apartment houses designed and constructed by developer-builder **Fred Anhalt**. Some apartments here have nine rooms, two baths, and a fireplace. To ensure soundproofing, Anhalt used double floors and double interior walls. The lovely landscaped courtyard and picturesque round-stair tower (an interesting and space-saving alternative to stairways) are Anhalt trademarks. ♦ 1005 E Roy St (at 10th Ave)

42 BYZANTION

★$ You'll find Greek food (and lots of it) at this place that's renowned for the quality of its *spanakopita* (spinach pie) and lamb dishes. Try the feta-cheese omelette at breakfast. ♦ Greek ♦ Daily, breakfast, lunch, and dinner. 601 Broadway E (at Mercer St). 325.7580. &

Being a town of the Old West, Seattle was no stranger to mob justice. The first lynching here, on 18 January 1882, was of two men who had robbed and killed a store clerk. Unlike in many other Wild West communities, however, this event was a civic embarrassment in Seattle. To avoid portraying the city in an unfavorable, dangerous light, the coroner's office listed the men's cause of death as "irate citizens."

Funny thing about Seattle: Cartoonists Lynda Barry and Gary Larson have put the city on the map, and local outfit Fantagraphics is avant-garde cartoonist Robert Crumb's favorite publisher.

Restaurants/Clubs: Red | Hotels: Purple | Shops: Orange | Outdoors/Parks: Green | Sights/Culture: Blue

43 SIAM ON BROADWAY

★★$ Regulars don't even consider sticking around here to eat—there's generally a 10- to 20-minute wait for a table. Instead, they call ahead, then fly by to pick up steaming orders of garlicky orange beef, *pad thai* noodles, or pan-fried butterfish. Among the best choices is this place's version of *tom kah gai* (chicken soup with chiles, lemongrass, and coconut milk). *Be forewarned:* The spice heat ratings of the dishes should be taken seriously. ♦ Thai/ takeout ♦ M-F, lunch and dinner; Sa, Su, dinner. 616 Broadway E (between Mercer and Roy Sts). 324.0892. க

44 CANTERBURY ALE & EATS

★$ Good burgers, good fries, good food overall, fast and cheap—that's reason enough for the *Weekly* readers to vote this best bar food in town. Besides, where else can you chow down in the comfort of a pool hall or in a room with heavy wood furniture and a baronial stone fireplace? Or, for that matter, in a space dominated by a standing suit of armor holding a sign that says, "Seat thyself"? 534 15th E (at Mercer St) ♦ Pub food. ♦ Daily. 322.3130. க

45 THE KINGFISH CAFE

★★★$$ The Coaston sisters have run this place since 1996, and the lines still form outside just about every day except Tuesday, so they don't take reservations. But that's not the reason for the popularity of this contemporary, casual restaurant with blown-up sepia-tinted family photos on the walls. It's because chef Kenyetta Carter serves up lots of Southern comfort food. They've got buttermilk chicken. They've got pumpkin soup. They've got crab and catfish cakes with Dixie tartar. And the cumin lamb shanks and curried ginger rice! Lunch is great too—try the braised pulled pork sandwich, the meat simmered in tangy barbecue sauce and piled high. Sunday brunch features those crispy fried crab and catfish cakes again, this time topped with poached eggs and homespun hollandaise. And their strawberry shortcake—to die for. ♦ American/Southern ♦ No reservations accepted. M, W-F, lunch; M, W-Sa, dinner; Su, brunch. 602 19th Ave E (at Mercer St). 320.8757. க

mōnsoon

46 MONSOON

★★★$$ Even after almost a decade in operation, this small, sparsely decorated space (in tones of beech and graphite) still draws the crowds down to quiet 19th Avenue E. They come for tamarind soup, delicate curries, and wonderful spring rolls. Some of the best seafood in town is served up here: steamed halibut served on bamboo leaf (with lily buds and green onions plus tree ear and shiitake mushrooms); crusty sea bass flavored with chiles, coriander, and shallots; and sea scallops with yams. ♦ Vietnamese ♦ Tu-F, lunch; Tu-Su, dinner. Reservations recommended. 615 19th Ave E (between E Republican and E Mercer Sts). 325.2111

47 ROVER'S

★★★★$$$$ Chef Thierry Rautureau's small, semiformal, and exquisitely intimate establishment in its frame-house setting is a French restaurant par excellence. Perhaps it's because he gives familiar Northwestern fare a French accent, rather than simply producing Gallic classics. Rautureau specializes in generous servings of seafood, including Columbia River sturgeon and halibut, the latter served with an embarrassment-of-riches lobster sauce. Ellensburg lamb, rabbit, and game entrées also make appearances among the several five-course prix-fixe menus (there's one entirely vegetarian choice). If you're up for it, you might try the eight-course grand menu. Wines from the Northwest and France complement the meal. There's also a courtyard for warm-weather dining. ♦ Northwestern/French ♦ Tu-Sa, dinner. Reservations recommended. 2808 E Madison St (between 29th and 28th Aves). 325.7442. க. www.rovers-seattle.com

48 CAFE FLORA

★★★$$ Bright and airy, this vegetarian eatery has an energetic, lively atmosphere. Dishes are presented in a stylish fashion; highlights include Portobello Wellington (mushroom–pecan pâté and grilled Portobello mushrooms wrapped in pastry) and Oaxaca tacos (which come filled with spicy mashed potatoes and cheddar, mozzarella, and feta cheeses, served with black-bean stew and sautéed greens on the side). The menu also offers nondairy items for the strict vegan, as well as a good selection of beers and wines. For dessert, there's always fresh fruit and a number of pastries, such as cheesecake, nondairy fruit crisps, and cakes. The large "outdoor" dining area is wonderful to linger in during warm weather. ◆ Vegetarian ◆ Tu-F, lunch and dinner; Sa, Su, brunch and dinner. Reservations taken for parties of eight or more. 2901 E Madison St (at 29th Ave). 325.9100. ᕕ. www.cafeflora.com

49 PAGLIACCI

★$ Seattle boasts three branches of this popular pizzeria chain. Top choices include Pizza Centioli, which features an extra-thin crust coated with olive oil, fresh garlic, peppers, and mozzarella and fontina cheeses; the South Philly, a pizza topped with Italian sausage, mushrooms, and onions; calzones; and pasta dishes. By the way, if somebody here tries to sell you the Brooklyn Bridge, it's not a scam—they're talking about a pizza with pepperoni, Italian sausage, mushrooms, black olives, and green peppers. You can either eat here (though the surroundings are rather unprepossessing) or get an order to go; delivery service is also available to most neighborhoods after 5PM. ◆ Pizza/takeout ◆ Daily, lunch and dinner. 426 Broadway E (between Harrison and Republican Sts). 324.0730; delivery, 726.1717. ᕕ. Also at 4529 University Way NE (between 45th and 47th Sts). 632.0421. ᕕ; 550 Queen Anne Ave N (at Mercer St). 285.1232. ᕕ. www.pagliacci.com

50 BAILEY/COY BOOKS

Covering a lot of area in a fairly confined space means that this bookstore, for all its efforts, must be very selective. Look for current best-sellers, a wide selection in the gay and lesbian studies section, and respectable depth in the gardening and fiction categories. ◆ M-Th, until 10PM; F, Sa, until 11PM. 414 Broadway E (between Harrison and Republican Sts). 323.8842. ᕕ

50 DILETTANTE PATISSERIE & CAFE

★$ Dana Davenport, continuing a trade taught to his grandfather by the master candy maker to Czar Nicholas II, offers some of the most tempting truffles, butter crèmes, and dragées (nuts or dried fruits dredged through high-quality dipping chocolates) you will ever try to resist. There's a small menu offering such things as Romanian borscht and sandwiches. They also operate an imperfect-chocolates outlet store (2300 E Cherry St, at 23rd Ave; 328.1955). ◆ Café ◆ Daily. 416 Broadway E (between Harrison and Republican Sts). 329.6463. ᕕ. Also at The Inn at the Market, 86 Pine St (at First Ave). 728.9144. www.dilettante.com

51 JALISCO

★$ A small, family-run Mexican operation, this restaurant is patronized almost exclusively by Hill residents. The standard dishes—especially enchiladas and burritos—are well done, and servers will help you design a combination plate. Or you could just order the delicious quesadillas. There are great margaritas and a wide selection of Mexican beers, but entertainment is limited mostly to the clientele, who seem eager to practice their dubious Spanish on the patient and extraordinarily efficient staff. ◆ Mexican ◆ M-Sa, lunch and dinner. 1467 E Republican St (at 15th Ave). 325.9005. ᕕ. Also at numerous locations throughout the city. ᕕ

51 HORIZON BOOKS

An old house has been converted to a used-book cavern, where intrepid literati wander labyrinthine passageways in search of affordable reading. Your best bet is to ask for directions on entering the maze. The science-fiction section is out of this world. ◆ Daily. 425 15th Ave E (between Harrison and Republican Sts). 329.3586

52 CASITA

A wonderfully crowded shop that's a great place to shop for gifts. It has a lot of unusual items from Latin America, from folk art masks to ceramics to hand-woven carpets to jewelry and fabrics—even a saint or two. Special orders are available. ◆ Gift shop ◆ 513 Fifteenth Ave E (between E Harrison and E Republican Sts). 322.7800. ᕕ

53 ALL THE BEST

This upscale pet-supply store is typical of the stores now opening along a once slumlike stretch in the Madison Valley area that has undergone extraordinary gentrification in recent years. The pet foods sold here pack natural ingredients. Indulgent pet owners will appreciate the diversity of neat toys and books in stock here too. ◆ Daily. 2713 E Madison St (between Martin Luther King Jr. Way and 27th Ave). 329.8565. www.all-the-best.com

54 THE ONLINE INTERNET CAFE

$ If you need electronic refills even more than a snack, this is your place. The traditional menu has espresso drinks, herbal teas, fruit juices, soft drinks, and pastry. And for those other cravings, there are seven computer systems, a color scanner, and two printers waiting. ◆ Cybercafé ◆ Daily. No credit cards accepted. 219 Broadway E (between John and Thomas Sts), suite 22. 860.6858

Restaurants/Clubs: Red | Hotels: Purple | Shops: Orange | Outdoors/Parks: Green | Sights/Culture: Blue

55 CAFE SEPTIÈME

★$$ Some outdoor seating makes this a popular place to hang out, sip espresso, and definitely see and be seen. Lunch sandwiches are reasonably priced—try the Portobello mushroom version. Dinners are better than average, and desserts are deeply tempting. ♦ American ♦ Daily. 214 Broadway E (between John and Thomas Sts). 860.8858

55 STEVE'S BROADWAY NEWS

Steve Dunnington, formerly a mustachioed fixture at **First & Pike News** in **Pike Place Market**, has brought his love of magazines and other periodicals to hyperkinetic Broadway. The usual mix is available here, as are some oddball foreign papers. ♦ Daily; F, Sa, until midnight. 204 Broadway E (between John and Thomas Sts). 324.7323. ♿

56 HILL HOUSE

$$ Herman and Alea Foster own this lovingly restored 1903 Victorian home. The seven guest rooms (five with private baths) are individually decorated, and all have queen-size beds and down comforters. The location is excellent—close to Broadway and on bus routes to both downtown and the **University of Washington**. A full gourmet breakfast is included in the rate. ♦ 1113 E John St (between 12th and 11th Aves). 720.7161. www.seattlebnb.com

57 GROUP HEALTH COOPERATIVE OF PUGET SOUND

In their efforts to find affordable medical care, farmers, union members, secretaries, and a handful of professional people defied the medical establishment of the 1940s to establish this cooperative in 1947. Today **GHC** is the nation's largest consumer-governed health-care organization, serving more than a half-million residents of Washington and Idaho, and it's a model for accessible, cost-effective, quality health care. This central facility is Seattle's largest hospital and the neighborhood's major employment center, spawning an attendant flock of shops and restaurants on 15th Avenue. ♦ 200 15th Ave E (between Denny Way and Thomas St). 326.3000. www.ghc.org

58 CRUSH

★★★$$ This elegantly renovated 100-year-old house, decorated in ultramodern white on white, focuses on local organic ingredients stylishly presented. There are layered flavors and great mouthfuls galore—slow-braised ribs, duck confit, and warm potato salad with pickled chanterelles, for example. And the prices are as easy on your pocketbook as the food is easy on the eyes. ♦ 2319 E Madison St (between 23rd Ave and E John St). 302.7874. www.crushonmadison.com

59 DENNY-BLAINE PARK

🅿 Here is a tranquil little public beach on Lake Washington; note, however, that there's no bathhouse and no lifeguard on duty. ♦ 200 Lake Washington Blvd E (between Howell Pl and 39th Ave)

60 GASLIGHT INN

$$ This bed-and-breakfast is a good choice if you want easy access to downtown: The **No. 10** bus stops right out front and goes all the way to the Waterfront. Antique Mission-style furniture graces the dining room, parlor, living room, and library. During the summer, guests can enjoy the heated pool surrounded by beautiful plantings and container gardens. The 16 guest rooms, 12 of which have private baths, are all decorated in different styles—contemporary, Art Deco, antique, Mission. One guest room has a city-view deck, and another has a fireplace. The Howell Street suites next door include maid service and laundry facilities. A continental breakfast is served. No pets, no kids, no smoking. ♦ 1727 15th Ave (between E Olive and E Howell Sts). 325.3654. www.gaslight-inn.com

61 MOUNT ZION BAPTIST CHURCH

This over-a-century-old church is a prominent feature of the Central District community. It seats a thousand people and is packed to the rafters every Sunday. Its 100-member gospel choir has become nationally famous through several acclaimed gospel recordings. The church's more than 2,000 members include several of the city's major politicians, and its pastor—the Reverend Braxton—is an assertive voice for African-Americans in Seattle. ♦ 1634 19th Ave (at E Madison St). 322.6500

61 MADISON STREET

Seattle's only waterfront-to-waterfront thoroughfare, this street stretches from Elliott Bay through the Central District to Lake Washington. Look at it as a core sample of local history and economics, taking in affluent neighborhoods, poverty-stricken pockets, new condominiums (especially in the area known as Madison Valley, from 23rd Avenue to the lake), and old, single-family residences.

62 HUGO HOUSE

Named after the noted West Coast poet Richard Hugo, **Hugo House** is a 16,206-square-foot Victorian house built in 1902. It has been a mortuary, an apartment house, and a theater before its current incarnation. Dedicated to "keeping alive the vital connection between writing and community," Hugo House offers creative-writing classes, writing and reading groups, and a writer-in-residence program, as well as scheduled readings by local and visiting writers. Within the building there's a writers' room, a library, a conference room, a 150-seat theater, and a café with a cabaret stage. ♦ 1634 11th Ave (at Olive St). 322.7030. ♿

63 BROADWAY PERFORMANCE HALL

This stately old structure, standing back from the street in a landscaped, parklike setting, is what remains of Seattle's first high school, built in 1902. All but the auditorium was demolished in 1974 to make room for expanding the **Seattle Central Community College**. That renovated auditorium, dedicated in 1979, is now a theater where more than 200 events are scheduled yearly—highlighting dance, poetry readings, alternative theater, mime, and more. ♦ E Pine St and Broadway

64 JIMI HENDRIX

On the sidewalk directly across the street from Broadway Performance Hall, a nearly life-size bronze of the noted native-son guitarist and rock star Jimi Hendrix captures him in a typical pose—on his knees leaning back, his guitar held high, his head thrown back. Michael Malone (CEO of AEI Music Network) commissioned local sculptor Daryl Smith to do the piece, which was unveiled in early 1997. The bronze is popular with Japanese visitors to the city (including the

During the Klondike Gold Rush of 1897, Seattle's pawnshops took in as much as $1,000,000 per day.

Coincidence or karma? The electric guitar was invented in Seattle. Jimi Hendrix was born in Seattle. You be the judge.

many students at the college across the street) who pose with Jimi for pictures to send back home. The locals too are fond of the statue. Don't be surprised if you see small offerings on the base, in his hands, or around his neck; people have left flowers, snacks, beer bottles, even the occasional joint. ♦ 1600 Broadway (about 100 feet north of Pine St)

65 EGYPTIAN THEATER

One of the city's classiest movie houses is within an old Masonic temple that also serves as headquarters for the Seattle International Film Festival, held each May. Inside is **Cafe Cairo**, an espresso bar operated by Craig Donarum, who gave this city its first espresso cart. Cairo also serves the sidewalk trade through a window. The theater also houses studios, offices, and classrooms for **Seattle Central Community College**, which owns this and a number of other buildings in the neighborhood. ♦ Box office opens 1 hour before show time. Cash only. 801 E Pine St (at Harvard Ave). 323.4978. www.landmarktheatres.com

66 NEIGHBOURS

Opening at 9PM, this is your happening disco, catering mostly to a gay crowd. Very-late-night patrons may need extra strength to find their way around this truly cavernous space. ♦ Cover. Daily. 1509 Broadway (between E Pike and E Pine Sts); enter through the alley. 324.5358. ♿. www.neighboursonline.com

67 COMET TAVERN

This pub's clientele is a Whitmanesque sampler of politicians, aspiring artists, writers, and escapees from nearby **Seattle University**. There's plenty of graffiti but zero video games; it's just an honest drinking joint. Cash only. ♦ Daily, until 2AM. 922 E Pike St (at 10th Ave). 323.9853. ♿

68 1200 BISTRO & LOUNGE

★★★$$ This warmly lit restaurant presents an ever-changing bistro menu. The calamari with crème fraîche, roasted free-range chicken, and tangy, tender braised short ribs are customer favorites. In the heart of the Capitol Hill gay community, this place is hetero-friendly. Daily, dinner. 1200 E Pike St (at 12th Ave E). 320.1200. www.1200bistro.com

69 GLOBE CAFE & BAKERY

★$ Soy-milk *lattes* might seem too healthy for some, but the vegan tilt here is balanced by a relaxed atmosphere and outrageously

---

Restaurants/Clubs: Red | **Hotels: Purple** | **Shops: Orange** | **Outdoors/Parks: Green** | **Sights/Culture: Blue**

good gingerbread. Toys are on hand for the young ones. ♦ Coffeehouse ♦ Cash and local checks only. Daily, until 7:30PM. 1531 14th Ave (between E Pike and E Pine Sts). 324.8815. &

70 SUMMIT GRADE SCHOOL/ NORTHWEST SCHOOL

One of the finest among architect **James Stephen**'s many Seattle schools, this 1905 wood structure is a catalog of brick-and-stucco facing, stepped parapets, and decorative ironwork, with an octagonal bell tower. The local school district closed this building in 1965, but more than a decade later it was bought and rehabilitated by operators of the **Northwest School**, a private institution for grades 6 through 12. ♦ 1415 Summit Ave (between E Union and E Pike Sts). 682.7309. www.northwestschool.org

71 TEMPLE DE HIRSCH SINAI

Built in 1960 as a stylized mountain with exquisite stained glass, this Jewish sanctuary is a commanding presence on Capitol Hill. There is some disagreement about the architect, but the prevailing opinion is that it was **B. Marcus Priteca**. ♦ 1520 E Union St (at 16th Ave). 323.8486. www.tdhs-nw.org

72 CRÉMANT

★★★$$ Paris-trained chef Scott Emerick does a fine job here, turning out a bounty of classic French bar food—half a dozen homemade pâtés, steak tartare with real frites, onion soup—plus some special main dishes for two: roasted chicken (needs a one-hour notice), bouillabaisse, a grilled one-pound rib steak à la française, plus to-die-for cassoulet. And all of this at reasonable prices. There are lots of wines by the glass. Crémant is well worth the drive out to Madrona. ♦ 1423 34th Ave (between E union and E Pike Sts). 324.4600. www.cremantseattle.com

73 HI-SPOT CAFE

★$ This revitalized old-time coffeehouse is in a Madrona home where the meal of choice is breakfast (hearty omelettes and terrific cinnamon rolls). Lunch, however, brings sumptuous burgers, terrific BLTs, and

good vegetarian soups. The dinner menu, which changes monthly, includes pasta, seafood dishes, and salads. ♦ American ♦ Daily. 1410 34th Ave (between E Union and E Pike Sts). 325.7905. &. www.hispotcafe.com

74 MADRONA PARK BATHING BEACH

Change in the bathhouse and then hit the beach. The water is pristine here (thanks to a major civic cleanup of Lake Washington back in the 1960s), but it's painfully cold, even in summer. For a less Arctic experience, take a seat in one of the usually unoccupied lifeguard perches and watch the joggers, dog-walkers, and picnickers do their thing. In clear weather, there is no better place from which to view 14,410-foot Mount Rainier, which (although 50 miles away) dominates the southeastern horizon. Clear skies also reveal other snowy peaks in the Cascade mountain range to the east, and the sharp-eyed may spy 10,778-foot Mount Baker north of the lake. It would be easy to forget that you're in a city, were it not for the jagged profile of Bellevue across the lake. ♦ Madrona Dr and Lake Washington Blvd

75 STIMSON-GREEN MANSION

As Seattle began to establish itself in the mid-19th century, the city's captains of industry all competed furiously to build grander mansions than those of their rivals. The first such examples graced First Hill, just east of downtown. It became Seattle's earliest status neighborhood, but the reign was brief, lasting only a generation or two before developments more remote from the city were settled. This baronial house is a fine reminder of those times. Built between 1899 and 1901 from designs by architects **Kirtland K. Cutter** and **Karl Malmgren** (whose efforts were heavily influenced by the European Arts and Crafts movement), the house was occupied from its completion until 1914 by the family of Ballard mill owner Charles D. Stimson. From then until 1975, it was the property of the Joshua Green family (Green was a prominent early Seattle banker). Today the mansion is a full-service catering facility. ♦ Business office: M-F, 1204 Minor Ave (at Seneca St). 624.0474. www.stimsongreen.com

The lowest recorded temperature at Seattle-Tacoma International Airport was 0 degrees Fahrenheit, on 31 January 1950. That's a far cry from the usual winter temperatures here (in the mid-40s on average).

THE BEST

Bud Young

Owner, Bud's Jazz Records

Pioneer Square Area—preserved turn-of-the-19th-century downtown—nightlife, art galleries, bookstores.

Pike Place Market–Farmers' Market—seafood, craftspeople, street performers (big stretches, for four to five blocks).

Waterfall Garden—a humanmade waterfall with sculptures—a wonderful escape from the hustle and bustle in only a quarter block.

Waiting for the Interurban in **Fremont** neighborhood—outdoor sculpture, well loved by neighbors.

The Troll—a monstrous, whimsical ogre that is really amusing in a surprising site—Fremont.

Walker Rock Garden—a 30-year project in a middle-class home that is a spectacular array of structures. Private but available by appointment.

The music scene—symphony, ballet, opera, jazz, blues, chamber music, choral.

Theater—About nine Equity theaters.

Clouds—come to Seattle to see the beautiful cloud cover—fascinating. (Who wants to see monotonous blue skies?)

76 CHAPEL OF ST. IGNATIUS

Every year about 40,000 people, whatever their religious views, come to the campus of the Jesuit **Seattle University** to visit this chapel. An architectural gem, it is described by its Manhattan-based designer, **Steven Holl** (an area native), as "a stone box, containing seven bottles of light." From "billowing" cast-bronze door handles to the zinc-clad bell tower, from undulating ceilings to a rectangular reflecting pool, from the colored-glass lenses set in glazed light scoops to the fragrance of beeswax embedded in the walls, this chapel is serene and otherworldly, yet sensuous and earthy. Don't miss it. ◆ Daily, until 8PM; service daily at noon. Seattle University, 12th Ave (between E Cherry and E Spring Sts). 296.5587; information and group tours, 296.6075

77 LARK

★★★$$$ Chef John Sundstrom started the small-plate dinner craze in Seattle—and nobody does it better. (John received the James Beard award for Best Chef, Northwest in 2007.) You'll need at least three items per person to feel full when you're done, but the bites are fabulous: clams with sausage, rabbit leg confit, rotisserie chicken, smoky duck, a salad of blood oranges, endive, and hazelnuts with Roquefort vinaigrette, and yellowtail carpaccio. It is pricey, and Lark takes no

The Odd Fellows Hall once played host to comedian W.C. Fields. Novelist Tom Robbins lived in the building in the mid-1980s; he says he was once visited there by Timothy Leary, who declared the place haunted.

reservations. People line up at 5PM for the experience. ◆ Daily, dinner except Monday. 926 12th Ave (between Marion and Spring Sts). 323.5275. www.larkseattle.com

78 SORRENTO HOTEL

$$$ Built in 1908, this hotel boasted the city's first rooftop restaurant. (The architect was **Harlan Thomas**.) Restored to its original elegance, it's small by comparison with today's hotels; it does, however, have an unusual intimacy. Some of the 76 guest rooms are small (a few have only narrow views), but all are comfortably appointed and feature an Asian décor. Try to reserve a room with a view over Puget Sound. The lobby's **Fireside Lounge** has an appealing clublike atmosphere, and complimentary sedan service is available within the downtown area. There's also a fitness center. ◆ 900 Madison St (at Ninth Ave). 622.6400, 800/426.1265. & www.hotelsorrento.com

Within the Sorrento Hotel:

HUNT CLUB

★★★$$$ Chef Brian Scheehser prepares a variety of seasonal game and seafood dishes combined with a Northwestern flair in this elegant, intimate dining room. The menu changes daily, depending on what is in season and what can be found at the local markets. At lunchtime, try Dungeness crab cakes on a bed of baby field greens. For

---

Restaurants/Clubs: Red | Hotels: Purple | Shops: Orange | Outdoors/Parks: Green | Sights/Culture: Blue

dinner, breast of Sonoma duckling is a winner. ◆ Northwestern ◆ Daily. Reservations recommended. 343.6156. ♿.
www.sorrentohotel.com

79 ST. JAMES CATHEDRAL

Imagine what this astonishing neo-Baroque church, with its twin 175-foot-tall towers, would look like with a copper dome above its entrance. That was its appearance from 1907 until January 1916, when the canopy collapsed beneath the weight of 30,000 pounds of snow. "A roar like the boom of a heavy gun brought priest and layman to the cathedral," wrote the *Seattle Post-Intelligencer*. "They saw a huge jagged hole where the massive dome had soared and poured great clouds of mortar dust and flying snow." Months later, the church was reopened with a flat roof that lessened the building's visual impact (it was designed by **Heins & LaFarge** and **John Graham Sr.**) but actually improved interior acoustics. ◆ Ninth Ave and Marion St. 622.3559.
www.stjamescathedral.com

80 FRYE ART MUSEUM

Dominated by the 19th-century European salon paintings of patrons Charles and Emma Frye, this small museum also includes Wyeth works and some by non-native Alaskan artists. The International-style building was designed in 1952 by **Paul Thiry** and is similar to his **Museum of History and Industry** in Montlake. ◆ Free. Daily. 704 Terry Ave (at Cherry St). 622.9250.
www.fryeart.org

80 TRINITY PARISH EPISCOPAL CHURCH

This handsome, rough-cut stone landmark near **Harborview Hospital** and overlooking Pioneer Square is in the style of English country parish churches. **John Graham Sr.** restored the building and gave it a new rectory after a terrible fire in 1901. ◆ 609 Eighth Ave (between James and Cherry Sts). 624.5337.
www.olympia.anglican.org

81 CATFISH CORNER

★★$ Though this eatery does have other things on the menu, the breaded catfish is so superb that there's no reason to choose anything else. The potato salad is excellent. ◆ Soul food ◆ M-Sa, lunch and dinner. 2726 E Cherry St (at Martin Luther King Jr. Way). 323.4330. ♿

Trinity Parish Episcopal Church

THE BEST

Jane Wu, Ph.D.

Regional Business Manager, Children's Administration, Region 4

FOR GOOD FOOD, TRY:

El Puerco Lloran, 1501 Western Avenue (Pike Market Hillclimb). Authentic, delicious, inexpensive Mexican eats. Try the chili rellenos!

94 Stewart, 94 Stewart Street. A comfortable bistro, serving Mediterranean/Middle Eastern cuisine in the Pike Street Market. Sip your wine and savor the atmosphere!

Chelan Café, 3527 Chelan Avenue SW. A wonderful find in West Seattle—a real, honest-to-goodness diner with blue-plate specials!

Love our Seattle seafood? Ship some home from **Mutual Fish**, 2335 Rainier Avenue S. Everything is *very* fresh, the variety is extensive, and the service impeccable.

PLACES TO SEE:

Kubota Gardens, 9600 Renton Avenue S. The jewel of South Seattle, this 20-acre Japanese garden is a landscaped dream—native plants, waterfalls and ponds, set into the natural contours of the Rainier Valley. Complete with a red footbridge, it's a must-see.

Frye Museum, 704 Terry Avenue. A fantastic museum with changing exhibits and a great gift shop. Best of all, it's free!

Olympic Sculpture Park. Next to Myrtle Edwards Park, this 9-acre downtown park crosses Elliot Avenue and extends to the waterfront. The park displays 22 sculptures, a pavilion, a café, an amphitheater, and underground parking.

Seattle Public Library, 1000 Fourth Avenue Described as a "house of glass," the $165.5 million library designed by renowned Dutch architect Rem Koolhaas is an amazing combination of stunning interior design and efficiency surrounded by spectacular views of Seattle.

Discovery Park, 3891 W Government Way. On 534 acres overlooking Puget Sound, this park offers spectacular views of both the Cascade and Olympic mountain ranges. The park includes tidal beaches, open meadowlands, dramatic sea cliffs, forest groves, sand dunes, and hiking trails.

And don't forget to take a ferry . . . **Seattle to Bainbridge Island** is a short trip, with shops and restaurants to sustain and entertain at your destination. Ride inside or outside—the scenery is fantastic either way. Salt air, seagulls, seals . . . what could be better for an afternoon's jaunt?

82 EZELL'S FRIED CHICKEN

★★$ This is the take-out place that talk-show hostess Oprah Winfrey calls to have out-of-this-world fried chicken shipped to her overnight (no matter what the status of her weight- loss program). ♦ Southern ♦ Cash only. Daily, lunch and dinner. 501 23rd Ave (at E Jefferson St). 324.4141. &

83 DANIEL'S BROILER

★★★$$$ As the name suggests, the emphasis is on flame-broiled prime steaks and chops, but they also make a number of good seafood specialties. The restaurant offers a terrific perspective of Mount Rainier and Lake Washington to the east. There's a second, more chichi venue in Bellevue and one on Lake Union. ♦ American ♦ Daily, dinner. 200 Lake Washington Blvd (at E Alder St). 329.4191 W. Also at Bellevue Place, 10500 NE Eighth St (between 106th Ave and Bellevue Way), Seafirst Bldg, 21st floor, Bellevue. 425/462.4662; 809 Fairview Pl N (at Valley St). &. www.schwartzbros.com

84 R&L HOME OF GOOD BARBEQUE

★★$ A Central District culinary landmark since Robert and Louise Collins opened the pit in 1952, this is where daughter Mary continues to serve excellent alder-smoked pork ribs, hot links, and baked beans. ♦ Barbecue ♦ Tu-Sa, lunch and dinner. Cash only. 1816 E Yesler Way (between 19th and 18th Aves). 322.0271. &

85 LESCHI PARK

🅟 The name comes from an 1850s Nisqually tribal leader who liked to camp here and who was accused by Territorial Governor Isaac Stevens of leading attacks against Seattle's pioneers in the Battle of Seattle; it was a bloody uprising and resulted in death on both sides. Chief Leschi, the focus of so much hatred, was tried for the deaths of two federal peacekeeping volunteers and then shamefully hanged despite evidence of his innocence. At the turn of the 19th century, a trolley carried Seattleites here to an amusement park and opera house, both long gone; and a cross-lake ferry docked

Restaurants/Clubs: **Red** | Hotels: **Purple** | Shops: **Orange** | Outdoors/Parks: **Green** | Sights/Culture: **Blue**

THE ELEPHANT ON AURORA

Fremont, home to the Lenin statue, the Troll, and "Waiting for the Interurban," is also the birthplace of the Aurora elephant. In the 1920s and '30s, John Giovanni Braida, a mosaic craftsman, and his crew worked intermittently on this near-life-size gray concrete pachyderm, attaching howdah and saddle blanket, painting them vivid colors, and studding them with jewel-like tiles. This lovely creature graced the tile yard until 1946, when it was bought by a flower shop owner. He moved his purchase very slowly, on a flat-bed truck, to its installation atop the one-story business on Aurora Avenue North at 88th Street. And there it reigned for decades, slowly, and rather visibly, declining; there were fears that new owners would break the thing up and haul away the pieces to the dump.

Fortunately, in December of 2005, Ryan and Allison Gaylord bought the property and decided to restore the elephant to its former glory. It is now both the symbol and new name for their contracting business: The Elephant Among Us.

here before the Interstate 90 floating bridge was opened in 1940. The Olmsted-designed park across the street from the marina is styled as a classic English garden and includes an ancient stone bridge (over which the trolley once rumbled). Until the 1970s, the neighborhood was decidedly blue-collar and bohemian; it ascended to its present affluent status only since the 1980s—as indicated by the modern architecture of its homes and condos. Joggers and cyclists travel frequently over the 5 tree-lined and lightly trafficked miles between this greenbelt and **Seward Park** to the south. ♦ 100 Lake Washington Blvd S (between Leschi Pl and Lakeside Ave)

86 LESCHI LAKE CAFE

★★$$ A busy bar (with 18 beers on tap) and a kitchen that does its best work with fresh- and saltwater fish, particularly salmon, are the main attractions. The fish and chips are delicious. In warm weather, the outdoor tables are packed with the tanned and single. ♦ Seafood ♦ Daily, lunch and dinner. 102 Lakeside Ave S (between Leschi Pl and Superior St). 328.2233. &

87 TABERNACLE MISSIONARY BAPTIST CHURCH

Certainly one of the most exuberant African-American churches in Seattle, the congregation here is inspired by the Reverend Robert Manaway. The choir is loaded with energy and with talent. ♦ 2801 S Jackson St (at 28th Ave). 329.9794; prayer request line, 517.3790

88 REMO BORRACCHINI'S

A lot of Seattleites wouldn't go anywhere other than this landmark Italian bakery to get cakes for special occasions. The confections are outrageous: The chocolate Bavarian cream should really be listed as a controlled substance. The bakery also makes pasta and breads and sells Italian canned goods and wines. And, although not officially a restaurant, it has a few tables for snackers and serves sandwiches, a rich lasagna, pizza, and baked items. ♦ Daily, from 6AM. 2307 Rainier Ave S (between McClellan and College Sts). 325.1550. &

88 MUTUAL FISH COMPANY

Here's the best seafood store south of **Pike Place Market**, owned and operated by the Yoshimura family since about the beginning of time. They'll pack your purchases for the trip home. ♦ M-Sa. 2335 Rainier Ave S (between McClellan and College Sts). 322.4368. www.mutualfish.com

89 EVANS HOUSE

This is the compelling work of **Ellsworth Storey**, a Chicago native who arrived in Seattle in 1903 and set about building houses in the developing neighborhoods along the west bank of Lake Washington, especially Madrona and Mount Baker. Apparently not interested in a large-scale practice, Storey stuck with residential design, an eminent example of which is this wood home. Note the strong diagonal emphasis. ♦ 2306 34th Ave S (between McLellan St and Dose Terr)

90 STAN SAYRES MEMORIAL PARK

On the first weekend in August, this park becomes—in more ways than one—"The Pits," the staging area for the annual Seafair hydroplane extravaganza. The racecourse is a long oval just off the park, with straightaways paralleling the shoreline. The usually quiet park becomes a circus of noise, warm beer, exposed flesh, and confusion, with attendees angling for close-up looks at the monster boats and their frenzied crews. For years, young Seattleites anxiously awaited this weekend, packing the shoreline and engaging in a variety of creative behaviors, but that tradition seems to be on the wane as Seafair swings more toward the family-values crowd. Race-day attendance is noticeably slimmer, down from the half-million reported in the 1970s and 1980s. ♦ Lake Washington Blvd S and 46th Ave

91 MUSEUM OF FLIGHT

Biplanes, military jets, early mail planes, and a giant B-47 dangle from the ceiling of this museum's glass-and-steel **Great Gallery**. Children especially love to wander among these relics; they can study a reproduction of Boeing's first seaplane and a real DC-13, or trace the history of modern aviation in the adjacent **Red Barn**, which was the Boeing Company's original 1910 airplane factory. Although the museum is often called Boeing's Museum of Flight, it is, in fact, an independent operation adjacent to the **Boeing Development Center**. A gift shop is fully stocked with models, books, and leather bomber jackets. ♦ Admission; discounts for senior citizens and children. Daily, 10AM-5PM; first Th, until 9PM (free). 9404 E Marginal Way S (between Norfolk St and Ellis Ave). 764.5720. www.museumofflight.org

92 KUBOTA GARDENS

A Japanese immigrant to Seattle started this 20-acre garden in 1929 in the midst of a swamp that he transformed into a delight to the eye (not to mention the nose). A creek trickles through the lush greenery, feeding five ponds. Among the many rare plants are *tanysho* pines and weeping blue atlas cedars. ♦ Renton and 55th Aves S. 725.4400

93 SEWARD PARK

According to the Olmsteds' comprehensive plan, this was intended to be a "wild" park, contrasting with more manicured garden spots like **Volunteer Park**. The peninsula's 277 acres of mainly Douglas fir trees are true old-growth forest; a 2.5-mile paved roadway circles the park's outer shoreline, offering strollers, joggers, in-line skaters, and cyclists a quiet respite. Somehow, the park never seems crowded.

A variety of pathways—some marked, some obscure—lace the woodlands, and a public fishing pier and swimming beach provide recreation on the northern end. Boaters will find a public ramp and city docks. In addition to picnic tables, barbecue pits, and a small amphitheater atop the hill, there is a state trout hatchery out at the end of the point and Japanese gardens, which, while quite pleasant, are obviously outclassed by those at the **Washington Park Arboretum**.

A grouping of three traditional Japanese stone lanterns and an inscribed granite boulder stand sentinel at the park's entrance. These were placed here during the 1976 US bicentennial to commemorate the gift of 1,000 cherry trees given by the citizens of Japan to the American people. Though shaped from Washington State granite, the lanterns were carved in Japan; the granite boulder carries an inscribed duplication of calligraphy painted by Takeo Miki, then prime minister of Japan. Translated, it reads: "Congratulations on the bicentennial of the United States of America's independence."

Visitors may wish to avoid the parking lot along the southern shoreline, where local youths hang out and crank their cars' stereo equipment into the upper decibel ranges. ♦S Orcas St and Lake Washington Blvd

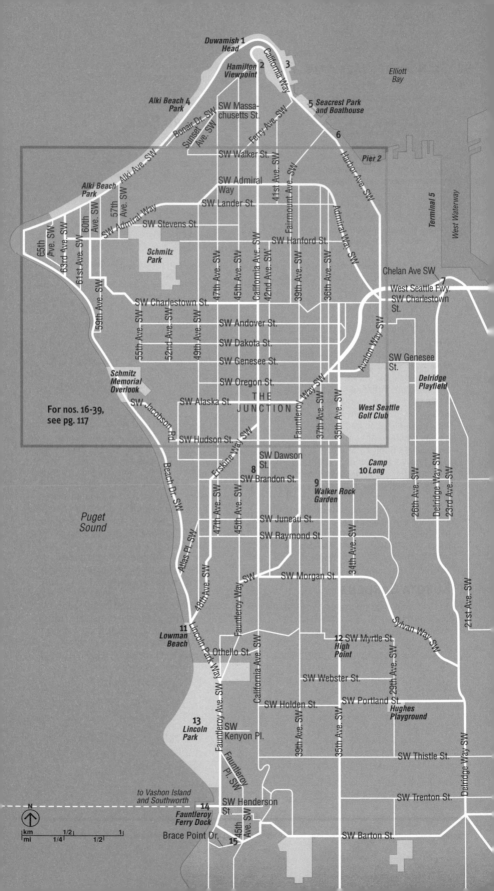

WEST SEATTLE

O n balmy summer afternoons, **Alki Beach** in West Seattle is a polychromatic amalgam of people and vehicles and noise, noise, noise. Sunbathers stroll along the sand, boom boxes blare, and skaters, cyclists, runners, strollers, and families with tethered German shepherds jockey for position along the bike path. On the other hand, if you go in the late evenings, on weeknights, or even in the off-season (between September and June), you might see herons and sea lions on the shore along with a few solitary, contemplative people. Along **Alki Avenue**, a variety of restaurants provide everything from elegant dinners to fast food. It's not exactly L.A.'s Venice Beach, but then again, it's not stereotypical Seattle either.

Today's scene is in marked contrast to that of November 1851, when a schooner dropped Arthur Denny's small cadre of pioneers at this very same spot. The settlers built their first cabins in the primitive Alki wilds and established relationships with the native Duwamish people before moving on to seek shelter on **Elliott Bay**.

Located southwest of downtown, across the **Duwamish River**, West Seattle is primarily a collection of residential areas distinguished by their views of downtown, **Harbor Island**, the **Cascade** and **Olympic Mountains**, and three **Puget Sound** islands: **Vashon**, **Blake**, and **Bainbridge**. Downtown West Seattle, as it is occasionally (if facetiously) called, is centered on the confluence of **California Avenue** and **Alaska Street** and is best known simply as The Junction. This central shopping area has had its ups and downs over the years; a number of businesses have made fleeting appearances, whereas others have stood almost unchanged for more than half a century. Although the growing number of high-rise condominiums on Alki Avenue attracts young urbanites, property values in many parts of West Seattle remain affordable, and the area retains some of its historic working-class spirit. But Alki Beach—which many residents claim is the only *real* beach in Seattle—is the area's principal attraction, boasting a wide expanse of sand, a long lane for cycling, jogging, and in-line skating, a boat launch, and grassy areas dotted with picnic tables.

1 DUWAMISH HEAD

Thanks to its views of Elliott Bay and downtown, this headland has long been a popular spot. In the late 19th and early 20th centuries, the broad shoulders of beach were frequented by summer revelers and campers. In 1901, a former Klondike gold miner built the **Coney Island Baths**, which offered "a good bath and swim and use of fresh running water." Six years later, it became the site of the largest and showiest amusement park ever built in Seattle: **Luna Park**. As with many other amusement parks of the early 20th century, this one sat on the water—actually and symbolically on the very edge of things. Created by Charles I.D. Looff, a German who had installed the first carousel at Coney Island, New York City, in 1876, Luna Park stretched over more than 10 acres, an imposing admixture of Atlantic City kitsch, Spanish Mission, and carnival Gothic. This fantasyland wanted to be all things to all people, and that's what finally got it in trouble. Along with the arcades and thrill rides, it also boasted "the longest bar on the bay," an easy target for reform-minded West Siders shocked by tales of drunkenness. The final straw came when Looff was implicated in a scandal involving the construction of a 500-room brothel on Seattle's Beacon Hill. When the park opened for the summer of 1913, Looff was gone. The park itself closed down three years later, but the natatorium (with its huge billboard exhorting. "Let's Swim!") remained until an arsonist set fire to the one-story frame

---

building in 1931. All that's here now is a popular beach and some apartment buildings. ♦ Harbor and Alki Aves SW

2 HAMILTON VIEWPOINT

Generations of West Seattle teenagers have come to this lookout to, uh, "watch the submarine races." They couldn't help noticing also that it offers one of the most outstanding views of downtown Seattle across Elliott Bay. Two coin-operated telescopes are available for a closer look. ♦ Donald St SW and California Ave

3 DON ARMENI PARK BOAT RAMP

A popular place for boaters to enter Puget Sound, this ramp was named after a deputy sheriff, active in fishing derbies, who was shot and killed in the line of duty in 1954. ♦ Harbor Ave SW (between California Way and Alki Ave)

4 ALKI BEACH PARK

For many years, this was the spot where teenagers showed off their cars and themselves. In the 1980s, laws were passed that prohibited both cruising and amplified sound on the beach, thus cutting down considerably on the summer noise and traffic that had plagued local residents but hardly decreasing the park's popularity. Today, the park is a two-mile stretch with a sandy strip that's the closest thing Seattle can claim to a southern California beach. Volleyball courts on the sand are usually filled with players and lined with spectators when the sun shows its face. A bike path is active with skaters and runners. Picnic tables and shelters are available, and this is one of the few city parks that allows beach fires, although only in designated concrete rings. There are no lifeguards on duty, so swim at your own risk. ♦ Alki Ave SW (between Harbor Ave and 64th Pl)

Within Alki Beach Park:

ALKI BATHHOUSE ART STUDIO

The old bathhouse on Alki Beach is now open to all local artists as a studio (for a small quarterly fee). It's staffed by volunteers and administered by the **Alki Community Center**: ♦ Call for hours. Alki and 60th Aves SW. 684.7430

STATUE OF LIBERTY

The Boy Scouts of America dedicated this 3-foot-high replica of New York City's harbor heroine to the City of Seattle in 1952. ♦ Alki and 61st Aves SW

MONUMENT TO THE BIRTHPLACE OF SEATTLE

A concrete pylon marks the spot where Arthur Denny's pioneering party landed in 1851. Presented to the city in 1905 by Denny's daughter, Lenora, the column was originally installed beside the old **Stockade Hotel**, just across the street. It was moved to the beachside in 1926 when a piece of Massachusetts's famed Plymouth Rock was embedded in the pylon's base and a plaque was added to commemorate the occasion. The hotel, by the way, folded in 1936; apartments now occupy its former site. ♦ Alki and 63rd Aves SW

5 SEACREST PARK AND BOATHOUSE

This clean park has watercraft for hire, a simple coffee shop, and a fishing pier. You can rent a wide variety of vessels. Even if you never get so much as a bite on your line, views from out on the water are spectacular. ♦ Call for hours and information. 1660 Harbor Ave SW (between Fairmount Ave and California Way). 938.0975

6 SALTY'S ON ALKI

★$$ Owner Gerald Kingen claims that no other place in the city commands as good a view as his upscale restaurant. That's debatable, but you do get a fine perspective on the downtown skyline and the ferries cruising across Puget Sound; it's especially beautiful at night. The food is a little pricier here than at most West Seattle restaurants, but it's served with more flair. Alder-smoked salmon stuffed with Dungeness crab and clams steamed with vegetables and white wine are two favorites. Noise, however, can be a problem. ♦ Seafood ♦ M-Sa, lunch and dinner; Su, brunch and dinner. Reservations recommended. 1936 Harbor Ave SW (between Florida St and Fairmount Ave). 937.1600. ᕕ. www.saltys.com

7 CHELAN CAFÉ

★$ Located just under the West Seattle Bridge, this is an old-time greasy spoon, without the grease. They even have the real thing, a diner's blue plate special. The service can be hit or miss, but that's because the waitress is pleasantly chatty with customers. ♦ 3527 Chelan Ave SW. 932.7383

8 WEST SEATTLE NURSERY

This is a wonderful place to find answers to your gardening dilemmas. The nursery carries a full line of seeds, bulbs, bedding plants, perennials, vines, shrubs, trees, landscaping paraphernalia, gardening videos, plus horticultural books for gardeners of all ages and stages, charming gifts, and botanical items. The staff is friendly and knowledgeable. ♦ Daily. 5275 California Ave SW (at Brandon St). 935.9276

CHIEF SEALTH

A pivotal figure in Seattle's early history was Chief Sealth, leader of the Suquamish and Duwamish people. Born around 1786 on **Black Island** in **Puget Sound**, Sealth is said to have witnessed the 1792 arrival in Puget Sound of Captain George Vancouver, the first European explorer of the area. The young boy's fascination with these foreign visitors marked the beginning of his lifelong relationship with the white newcomers.

At the age of 20, already proficient in the arts of warfare and persuasion, Sealth was named *tyee* (chief) of the Suquamish and Duwamish tribes. As more and more whites began to explore the area, Sealth, who ruled with a firm, benevolent hand, continually advocated a peaceful coexistence between his people and the settlers. (In fact, he went so far as to convert to Christianity in the 1830s, taking the baptismal name of Noah.)

In 1851, when settlers arrived in what is now **West Seattle**, the Suquamish and Duwamish people welcomed them warmly. Sealth soon befriended one of them, a young pioneer from Ohio named Dr. David Swinton "Doc" Maynard. He persuaded Maynard and his companions to move to the **Pioneer Square** area, where the forests were thicker and the land was better suited to development. He also encouraged his people to help the white men build houses and lay out streets. Maynard opened a shop here and quickly became prosperous; grateful for the chief's friendship and helpful advice, he suggested that the founding fathers call their new town *Seattle*, a more pronounceable version of Sealth's name. They agreed, preferring it to its original name, *Duwamps*.

As Seattle grew, tensions began to develop between the whites and many of the native groups in the region. In 1854, Congress proposed the Point Elliott Treaty, which stipulated that the US government would purchase two million acres of land in the region for $150,000, which would be paid over 20 years. The agreement also allotted 2,600 acres to be used as reservations and promised to provide services such as education and medical care to the natives. In January 1855, Chief Sealth addressed a crowd of natives and settlers, including Territorial Governor Isaac Stevens. Although he expressed a willingness to go along with the government's proposal, he also touched on several other themes, including sensitivity to nature, the sanctity of the landscape, the inevitable decline of the tribal peoples, and the danger that civilization could wreak havoc on the environment. He also warned the white men that they were not invincible—they were no less susceptible to conquest than the natives. The speech is still remembered today for its eloquence and wisdom.

Many of the tribes followed Sealth's lead in signing the treaty, but some refused, including the Muckleshoot, the Nisqually, and the Klickitat. Their attacks on the settlers ultimately led to the Indian War of 1855-1856. During this conflict, the natives fired on the settlers from the cover of the forest, and the settlers barricaded themselves in the stockade and returned fire, assisted by the battle sloop *Decatur*. At last, the settlers prevailed, and Governor Stevens ordered that the remaining natives be placed in the reservations that had been created by the treaty.

After the war, things were never the same for the Native Americans, even the peace-loving Sealth and his people. Despite the chief's history of friendly relations with the white settlers, many of them still distrusted and disliked him. And the government did not adhere to its part of the Point Elliott Treaty: Not only were services denied to the residents of the reservations, but the government did not even make the entire $150,000 payment for the land. As Seattle continued to grow and expand, the Suquamish, Duwamish, and other native groups grew smaller and poorer. Throughout, however, Maynard and Sealth remained fast friends.

Chief Sealth died in June 1866 and was buried in **Suquamish Village** on the **Port Madison Reservation** in **Kitsap County**. His funeral was attended by a large crowd of his native followers and a few older settlers (including Maynard) who remembered him fondly. Today, the towers of his namesake town are visible from his gravesite, and there are several monuments to his memory; the largest and most prominent is a statue of the chief at **Denny Way** and **Fifth Avenue**.

9 WALKER ROCK GARDEN

Ⓟ Local businessman Milton Walker designed and constructed this 100-square-foot space, which was built between 1959 and 1979. Fountains, bridges, towers, and small mountains have been fashioned from various rocks that Walker and his wife collected during their travels (including volcanic rock, pumice, colored stones, and even some semiprecious gems). The garden is still owned by the Walkers, who lead guided tours through it by appointment. ♦ Daily, by appointment; closed Sept-late Apr. 5407 37th Ave SW (between Juneau and Hudson Sts). 935.3036

10 CAMP LONG

Ⓟ One of the city's few parks to offer overnight facilities, this 68-acre patch is open to organized groups for camping and wilderness-skills programs. There are 10 cabins for rent (each sleeps 12), picnic

Restaurants/Clubs: Red | Hotels: Purple | Shops: Orange | Outdoors/Parks: Green | Sights/Culture: Blue

shelters, and a rustic lodge that is a popular spot for weddings. There's a rock wall for climbing practice and instruction (with a minimum class size of 15). Free nature walks are scheduled on Saturday, and there are educational programs for kids; call ahead for a rundown. ◆ Park ranger station: Tu-Sa. 5200 35th Ave SW (at Dawson St). 684.7434

11 LOWMAN BEACH

Ⓟ Named after a former Seattle parks commissioner, this tiny park offers access to the sand plus a swing set and one tennis court. In December, locals gather here to watch Seattle's ceremonial Christmas ships make their loop through Puget Sound. Walkers can take pleasant strolls down an access road into the lower portion of adjacent **Lincoln Park**. ◆ Beach Dr SW and 48th Ave

12 HIGH POINT

Ⓟ The highest point in Seattle, this intersection tops off at 518 feet above sea level, higher even than lofty Queen Anne Hill. The views, from Puget Sound to the Olympic Mountains, are expansive. ◆ SW Myrtle St and 35th Ave

13 LINCOLN PARK

Ⓟ Designed by Frederick Law Olmsted Jr. and John Charles Olmsted, who developed Seattle's 1903 comprehensive greenery plan, this park comprises 130 acres of wooded and waterfront trails, with picnic areas, tennis courts, softball fields, horseshoe pits, and children's playground equipment. Access is limited to foot traffic; park roads are open only to park vehicles or for emergencies. As with most beach parks on Puget Sound, no lifeguards are on duty even during summer months. A bit of historical trivia: The park was named at the request of the local Young Men's Republican Club, which promised to erect a statue of Honest Abe at the park entrance. The promise was never kept. ◆ Fauntleroy Ave SW and Kenyon Pl

Within Lincoln Park:

COLMAN POOL

This heated, outdoor, Olympic-size pool is filled with both chlorinated fresh water and salt water. One negative: It's open only during summer vacation for the Seattle School District. ◆ Admission; discount for senior citizens, disabled persons, and children 18 and younger. Daily, noon-7PM late June-Aug. 684.7494

14 FAUNTLEROY FERRY DOCK

Washington State Ferries leave this dock to take passengers to Vashon Island, a 28-minute ride that's packed with commuters

on weekday mornings and late afternoons. Vashon is a charming rural area; many residents work in town, but others have found work on the island itself in a variety of industries, such as ski manufacturing (K2 Corporation), orchid growing, or food processing. ◆ Fauntleroy Ave SW and Henderson St. 464.6400, 800/542.0810

15 THE ORIGINAL BAKERY

A working day bakery, specializing in gooey cinnamon rolls, birthday cakes, and bread, this place also has a small seating area and serves espresso. ◆ Tu-Su. 9253 45th Ave SW (between Brace Point Dr and Wildwood Pl). 938.5088

15 ENDOLYNE JOE'S

★★$$ Named after a ne'er-do-well conductor of old trolley #2, Endolyne Joe's is the right name for this lively place. The food: updated American classics, plus seasonal regional specials—Little Italy in winter, New Orleans French in spring . . . you get the picture. Located just south of scenic Lincoln Park and a short jaunt up the hill from the Fauntleroy ferry terminal, the "Eat at Joe's" neon beckons. ◆ Daily, breakfast, lunch, dinner, and cocktails. 9261 45th Ave SW (between Brace Point Dr and Wildwood Pl). 937.JOES. www.chowfoods.com

16 PAILIN THAI CUISINE

★★$ This comfortable restaurant is a neighborhood favorite. The food—especially the *pad thai* noodles—is good, and the prices can't be beat. ◆ Thai ◆ M-F, lunch and dinner; Sa, Su, dinner. 2223 California Ave SW (between College and Walker Sts). 937.8807

17 ADMIRAL THEATER

Originally built as the **Portola Theater** in 1919, this playhouse has had a remarkably long and colorful history. In the 1920s, the theater—along with the nearby **Olympus** and **Apollo** theaters—screened feature films, newsreels, and comedy shorts, all for a mere 20 cents per customer. An $18,000 pipe organ was added in 1924, talkies followed in 1929, and, in response to the realities of the Depression, in 1933 admission was dropped to 15 cents. In 1942, the movie house was expanded amid great fanfare. John Danz, the owner, held a contest for West Seattle residents to name the picture palace. The architect was **Marcus Priteca**, famed designer for Alexander Pantages's nationwide theater chain, whose local work may be remembered best in the **Coliseum** and **Paramount** theaters in downtown Seattle. Priteca used the winning moniker as a theme, adding nautical allusions to the façade (note

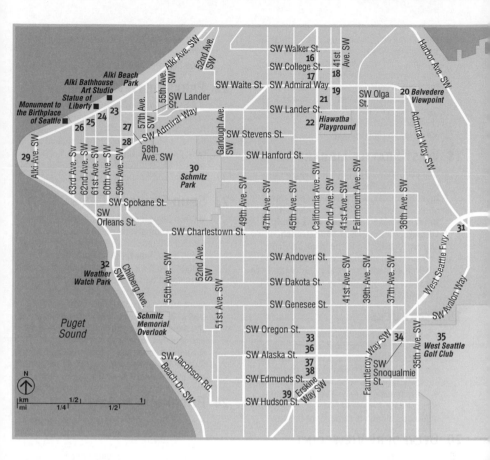

the portholes, anchors, and a giant mast with crow's nest on the "upper deck," as well as the seahorses riding exit signs). Usherettes sported naval uniforms. A gala opening in 1942 drew 3,000 people to a showing of *Weekend in Havana*, starring Alice Faye, Carmen Miranda, and John Payne. In 1953, the theater put in "the first panoramic wide screen installed in a sub-urban theater." Twenty years later, it was converted to a "twin" with two 430-seat viewing rooms. But the theater closed in 1989, after several years of false hopes that its Canadian owners would restore its original majesty. A campaign by the Southwest Seattle Historical Society finally led locals to purchase the theater in 1991 and open it as a second-run movie palace. There are now five to six shows per week at about $3 a seat, a bargain these days. ♦ 2343 California Ave SW (between Admiral Way and College St). 938.3456

17 ANGELINA'S TRATTORIA

★$ Here is yet another member of Dany Mitchell's group of Seattle trattorias. Like the others (including **Stella's** in the University District and Pioneer Square's **Trattoria Mitchelli**), this restaurant provides Italian fare at reasonable prices. Entrées range from simple pastas of the day with marinara sauce to the more elaborate *fettuccine con pollo e nocciole* (pasta in a velouté sauce with roasted hazelnuts and chicken). ♦ Italian ♦ M-F, lunch and dinner; Sa, Su, brunch, lunch, and dinner. No checks. 2311 California Ave SW (between Admiral Way and College St). 932.7311. &

17 BLACKBIRD BISTRO

★★$$ Brunch here is particularly pleasing, and vegetarian options abound. Many dishes feature Field Roast, a tasty animal-free

---

Restaurants/Clubs: Red | Hotels: Purple | Shops: Orange | Outdoors/Parks: Green | Sights/Culture: Blue

grain-meat product. Or go for the scrambled-egg sandwich (caramelized onion, organic spinach, spicy sauce, and sharp New York cheddar on a warmed-up potato baguette). And yes, you could order sausage with that. The staff is young, casual, and colorful. ♦ Daily, breakfast, lunch, and dinner. 2329 California Ave SW (between Admiral Way and College St). 937.2875. www.blackbirdbistro.com

18 WEST SEATTLE LIBRARY

This attractive 1910 brick building was created by **W. Marbury Somervell** and **Joseph C. Cote**, who also designed three other Carnegie libraries: the **University Branch Library**, the **Green Lake Public Library**, and the **Queen Anne Branch Library**. In addition to the usual services, free special programs are offered for children and adults. ♦ Daily. 2306 42nd Ave SW (between Admiral Way and College St). 684.7444

19 STARBUCKS

★$ No Seattle neighborhood seems complete anymore without its own branch of this coffee chain, selling pastries, espresso drinks, coffee by the pound, and all the equipment to brew your own beans at home. ♦ Coffeehouse ♦ Daily. 4101 SW Admiral Way (at 41st Ave). 937.5010. Also at numerous locations throughout the city

20 BELVEDERE VIEWPOINT

The totem pole here, carved by Boeing engineers Michael Morgan and Robert Fleishman and dedicated in 1966, is modeled after one that had been presented to the city in 1939 by J.E. "Daddy" Standley, owner of the Waterfront's **Ye Olde Curiosity Shop**. (Standley's original, crafted by the Bella Bella tribe of British Columbia's Queen Charlotte Islands, had decayed beyond repair.) There's an excellent view over Harbor Island to downtown. *Be forewarned:* There are only a few parking spaces in a tiny lot nearby. ♦ SW Olga St and Admiral Way

21 ALKI BIKE & BOARD

This store has been outfitting local cyclists for years. (Its name reflects the shop's original location on Alki Beach.) Besides peddling bikes and all manner of accessories, it also provides repair service and snowboarding equipment. ♦ Daily. 2606 California Ave SW (between Lander St and Admiral Way). 938.3322. www.alkibikeandboard.com

22 PARKSIDE NEWS CAFE

★$ Espresso, sandwiches, pastry, muffins, and croissants are the specialties at this friendly place. In keeping with the shop's name, a wide variety of magazines and newspapers are for sale. ♦ Café ♦ Daily, until 2PM. 2735 California Ave SW (between Stevens and Lander Sts). 932.2279. &

23 SPUD FISH AND CHIPS

★$ Two English guys, Jack and Frank Alger, opened a summer fish-and-chips stand here in 1935. Fish and chips were then 10 cents per order, to go. Today, Ivar's Seafood runs it, though now it's a year-round eatery that seats as many as 82 people inside. That's not the only change: These days, the food is a bit more expensive. Eating here, however, remains part of the quintessential Seattle experience. The menu includes prawns, oysters, clams, and scallops, as well as chicken strips. ♦ Seafood/takeout ♦ Daily, lunch and dinner. Cash only. 2666 Alki Ave SW (between 59th and 60th Aves). 938.0606. &

24 PHOENICIA AT ALKI

★★★$$ Since this eatery opened its doors in 1975, it has changed locations again and again, but its many loyal fans keep following it, lured by the fine cooking of owner-chef Hussein Khazal. In this casual beach setting, the restaurant's third locale, Khazal presents the ultimate pan-Mediterranean experience: Highlights include marinated lamb, pine-nut risotto with shellfish, and Moroccan eggplant. Even if you're not a beach person normally, it's worth the trip just to eat here. ♦ Mediterranean ♦ Tu-F, lunch and dinner; Sa, Su, dinner. 2716 Alki Ave SW (between 60th and 61st Aves). 935.6550. &

24 LIBERTY DELI

★★$ After 14 years of yearning for the deli food they were used to in Manhattan, the three Ansart brothers (Bob, Tom, and Nick) decided to open their own place here in 1995. To ensure authenticity, they import their cold cuts from New York, make their own soups (including chicken basil and Manhattan clam chowder), and feature quintessential deli staples, such as corned beef on rye and lox and bagels. But there's also a local flavor to the menu: The breads come from **The Essential Bakery**, and Thomas Kemper root beer and cream soda are available. ♦ Deli ♦ Daily, lunch and dinner. 2722 Alki Ave SW (between 60th and 61st Aves). 935.8420. &

In 1907, John McLean built the world's first gasoline service station at Holgate Street and Western Avenue in Seattle. Not all agree on this distinction. Nevertheless, a plaque honoring the world's first gas station is located at Seattle's Waterfront Park.

PAINTING THE TOWN

Historical murals have become increasingly familiar sights in West Seattle. Located primarily in the **Junction**, these paintings reflect a variety of artistic styles, ranging from a stylized folk-art look to trompe l'oeils, but most are lifelike images of West Seattle in the late 1800s and early 1900s. After admiring murals in southwestern Washington and in Chemainus, British Columbia, where more than 25 murals serve as that town's primary tourist draw, area resident Earl Cruzen decided that his neighborhood should adopt the popular public-art theme. Most of the 11 murals painted in West Seattle have been funded by local donations, city matching funds, and contributions from building owners. Brochures are available from the **West Seattle Chamber of Commerce** (4151 California Avenue SW, between Genesee and Dakota Streets, 932.5685). Here's a brief guide to the works of art:

1 Lany Little of Gresham, Oregon, depicted the *Wizard of Oz* float from a 1973 parade in a mural on the wall of the **West Seattle Post Office** (4412 California Avenue SW, between Oregon and Genesee Streets).

2 *Tuesday's Bank Day* is the subject of the mural on the north side of the **Washington Mutual Bank** building (SW Oregon Street and California Avenue). It commemorates a project begun in 1923 to teach schoolchildren about saving money; at the time, this was the only bank that was willing to take the pennies and nickels that kids wanted to deposit, and they even offered interest on accounts exceeding a few dollars. British Columbian Alan Wylie was the artist.

3 *The Old Mud Hole* by Mike Svob of Coquitlam, British Columbia, shows the swimming area that Laurence Colman created in what is now **Lincoln Park**. In 1940, the Colman family donated funds for a swimming pool to be built at the same site. The mural is on the side of an apartment building (44th Avenue SW, between Alaska and Oregon Streets).

4 Another artist from Nova Scotia, Susan Tooke Crichton, depicted a 1910 landing by the old steamships that hauled freight and passengers between **Puget Sound**'s ports. *Mosquito Boat Landing* is on the east wall of the **Campbell Building** (SW Alaska Street and California Avenue).

5 A deep-blue nighttime scene of a horse-drawn wagon dashing away from the 1913 Junction Fire Station brightens the south side of the **Don Swanson Insurance Building** (4711 44th Avenue SW, between Edmunds and Alaska Streets), across from where that fire station once stood. Seattleite Don Barrie painted the mural, titled *Midnight Call*, in 1990.

6 Part of the west side of **Morton's Drugs** (4707 California Avenue SW, at Alaska St) is covered with *West Seattle Ferries*, which includes images of onetime local attraction **Luna Park**, the old **West Seattle Cable Railway**, and turn-of-the-19th-century ferries. Artist William Garnett of Portland, Oregon, completed the mural in 1989.

7 The days of hot metal type are revived in *Press Day*, a mural illustrating putting the **West Seattle Herald** to bed. Painted by Alan Wylie of Fort Langley, British Columbia, the mural is on the **Seawest Building** (44th Ave SW, between Edmunds and Alaska Sts).

8 *The First Duwamish Bridge*, a panorama of the old swing bridge that crosses the **Duwamish River**, is the work of Louisiana artists Robert and Douglas Dafford. Located on the north wall of the **Jacobson Building** (SW Edmunds Street and 44th Avenue), it shows a trolley crossing the river, with the Cascade Mountains in the background.

9 **Huling's Chevrolet** dealership (4755 Fauntleroy Avenue SW, at Edmunds Street) is the site of a mural by Nova Scotian artist Bruce Rickett entitled *Alki in the Twenties*, a portrait of a 1919 Chevrolet and a woman painting. In the background are Alki residences, a streetcar line, and a ferry dock.

10 *The Junction* depicts the intersection during the 1920s, when the old streetcar lines converged here. The work of Eric Grohe, this trompe l'oeil looks so realistic that locals have suggested the city hang a traffic light in front of the painted tracks. It's framed by a mock concrete arch on the south wall of the **Junction Feed & Seed Store** (4747 California Avenue SW, between Edmunds and Alaska Streets).

11 A colorful 1937 view of the old *Morgan Street Market* was painted in 1990 by Bruce Rickett on the west wall of **Olsen's Drugs** (6501 California Avenue SW, at Fauntleroy Way). The original market stood across the street.

25 ALKI HOMESTEAD

★$$ Originally a log cabin and a roadhouse for people who made the long journey by automobile from Seattle, this restaurant features a romantic ambience with lace tablecloths and crystal lamps on the tables. The food is straight out of the 1940s—the specialty is pan-fried chicken with mashed potatoes, gravy, and green beans (which appear to be of the canned variety). The menu also includes steak, prime rib, and seafood. Cocktails are served in a spacious glassed-in porch. ♦ American ♦ W-Su, dinner. 2717 61st Ave SW (between Stevens St and Alki Ave). 935.5678. &

Restaurants/Clubs: **Red** | Hotels: **Purple** | Shops: **Orange** | Outdoors/Parks: **Green** | Sights/Culture: **Blue**

25 PEGASUS PIZZA AND PASTA ON ALKI

★$ The pizza here has become legendary. One of the best varieties is Tom's Special, with mushrooms, green peppers, onions, olives, feta and mozzarella cheeses, spinach, pepperoni, fresh garlic, diced tomatoes, and sunflower seeds. The Greek pizza, the feta bread, and the ravioli are also worth a taste. Expect a line on weekends. ♦ Italian ♦ Daily, lunch and dinner. 2758 Alki Ave SW (between 61st and 62nd Aves). 932.4849. www.pegasusonalki.com. &.

26 SUNFISH SEAFOOD

★★$ You can get regular fish and chips here, or for a little more (and the difference is worth paying), halibut and chips. The influence of the Greek brothers who own this place shows up in such menu offerings as halibut shish kebab and calamari. Indoor seating and outdoor seating are both available. ♦ Seafood/takeout ♦ Daily, lunch and dinner. 2800 Alki Ave SW (at 62nd Ave). 938.4112. &

27 ALKI PLAYGROUND

Facilities at this small playground a block from the beach include a softball field, a soccer field, children's play equipment, and two lighted tennis courts. An artistic touch is added by *Whale's Tale*, a huge sculpture shaped like a whale's tail that was created in 1982 by local artist Richard Beyer (who also did the popular *Waiting for the Interurban* sculpture in Fremont). ♦ SW Lander St and 58th Ave

28 ALKI COMMUNITY CENTER

Local families come here for yoga, billiards, or foosball, or for basketball, tai chi, or Ping-Pong games in the gym. Pottery classes also available. Call for information. ♦ Daily. 5817 SW Stevens St (at 59th Ave). 684.7430

29 ALKI POINT LIGHT STATION

Alki Point marks the southern entrance to Seattle's harbor, Elliott Bay. It's been the site of a warning beacon for ships since the mid-1870s, when Hans Martin Hanson, who bought the land from pioneer Doc Maynard, began lighting lanterns on the point every night. In the 1880s, the US Lighthouse Service erected a lens-lantern on a scaffold. The present 37-foot-high octagonal tower was completed in 1913. Its light was converted to electricity 5 years later, and in 1984, its operation became fully automatic. Today, the lighthouse stands surrounded by apartments and condominiums. The station is maintained by the US Coast Guard. ♦ Walk-in tours Sa, Su, and holidays, May-Aug; tours by appointment W, noon-4PM, May-Aug. 3201 Alki Ave SW (between Beach Dr and Point Pl). 217.6123

30 SCHMITZ PARK

Donated to the city by wealthy West Siders Ferdinand and Emma Schmitz in 1908 on the condition that the land be forever maintained as closely as possible to its natural state, this park is home to one of the last stands of old-growth forest—some of the trees are over 800 years old—within the city limits. It is also a 50-acre nature preserve where narrow trails through the thick woods can be hard to follow. There are no picnic areas or playgrounds. ♦ 5551 SW Admiral Way (between Stevens St and 57th Ave)

31 LUNA PARK CAFE

★$ Eat 1950s-style food beneath a black-velvet Elvis painting. A neon-lit Seeburg jukebox (the remote selectors at each table actually work) spins 200 eclectic selections, from Elvis to Frank Sinatra, Bob Marley, and Annette Funicello, and costs a quarter per play. A 1946 Wurlitzer 1015 Bubbler is a display jukebox only. Other kitschy décor includes an impressive collection of children's lunch boxes along with old business signs. The food here is basic but good. (Try the meat loaf on whole wheat or the Cobb salad—turkey, bacon, bleu cheese, egg, Swiss cheese, tomato, and olives.) The milk shakes (root beer, coffee, fresh fruit, and more) are much in demand on steamy days. Servings are enormous; if they say "jumbo," they mean it. The name is taken from the amusement park that once graced Duwamish Head (see page 113). ♦ American ♦ Daily, breakfast, lunch, and dinner. 2918 SW Avalon Way (between Charlestown and Spokane Sts). 935.7250

32 WEATHER WATCH PARK

Once a dock site for Puget Sound's ferry service from Seattle, this teeny lookout, on a small knoll between the apartments and cottages lining Beach Drive, was designed by local artist Lezlie Jane in 1991 and built with the help of many local residents. The centerpiece is an interpretive column—it's got a sundial, information on cloud formation

Arthur Denny of Seattle proposed an amendment in 1854 at the first session of the territorial legislature "to allow all white females over the age of 18 years to vote." It was defeated by a single vote.

Did you know that the first person to graduate from the University of Washington was a woman? In the summer of 1876, Clara McCarty (1858–1929) obtained her degree. Her graduation took place 15 years after the university opened. UW student dormitory McCarty Hall is named after her.

and weather prediction, and historical photographs, all topped off by a sculpture of ducks in flight. With its brick patio and benches, this makes a lovely spot from which to watch the weather over Puget Sound and the Olympic Mountains. ◆ SW Carroll St and Beach Dr

33 CAPERS

★$ The kitchen here whips up terrific scones, muffins, and cobblers, as well as an estimable seafood salad. It's a popular lunch spot for local office workers. Decorator items, seasonal gifts, and specialty foods are also sold. ◆ Café ◆ Daily, breakfast, lunch, and dinner until 8PM. 4521 California Ave SW (between Alaska and Oregon Sts). 932.0371. &

34 YMCA

The main branch of the West Seattle **Y** is also the most deluxe. There's a swimming pool, a weight room with free weights and exercise machines, basketball and volleyball courts, a running track, two racquetball courts, and a spa. All facilities, except regularly scheduled classes, are available on a drop-in basis for a fee. ◆ Daily. 4515 36th Ave SW (at SW Oregon St). 935.6000. www.ymca.com

35 WEST SEATTLE GOLF CLUB

Set on relatively hilly terrain, this public 18-hole course features tree-lined fairways and great views of the city skyline. ◆ Greens fees. Daily. Reservations required. 4470 35th Ave SW (between Snoqualmie St and Avalon Way). 935.5187. www.westseattlegolf.com

36 PEGASUS BOOK EXCHANGE

This bookshop buys, sells, and trades used books. Its principal stock is in paperback fiction, but the owner also has an interest in metaphysics and will help you find anything in that category that isn't already available here. ◆ Daily. 4553 California Ave SW (between Alaska and Oregon Sts). 937.5410. &

36 EASY STREETS RECORDS

Right in the middle of the Junction is a store selling new and used records and CDs in a wide range of styles, from rap and world music to classical and jazz. ◆ M-Sa, until 9PM; Su, until 7PM. 4559 California Ave SW (at Alaska St). 938.3279

37 HUSKY DELICATESSEN

A local institution since 1933, this family-owned establishment grew from an ice-cream parlor specializing in large chocolate-covered cones to a full-fledged deli. It attracts customers from all over Seattle with its homemade ice cream; also available are cold cuts, salads, beers and wines, and truffles. ◆ M-Su, until 9PM; Su until 7PM. 4721 California Ave SW (between Edmunds and Alaska Sts). 937.2810. &. www.huskycatering.com

37 ARTSWEST

This nonprofit organization has established a cultural center offering educational theater, music, dance, and other arts programs. There's also an art gallery that displays local talent. ◆ Tu-Sa. 4711 California Ave SW (between Edmunds and Alaska Sts). 938.0963. www.artswest.org

38 NORTHWEST ART & FRAME

One-stop shopping for graphics needs: calligraphy pens and paper, watercolors, oils, enamels, children's art supplies, stationery, gifts, and cards. Picture framing is also available—do it yourself or pay more and have it done for you. ◆ Daily. 4733 California Ave SW (between Edmunds and Alaska Sts). 937.5507. &

39 VILLA HEIDELBERG

$$$ A converted 1909 house (constructed and named by a German immigrant), this bed-and-breakfast inn has leaded-glass windows, beamed ceilings, a finely landscaped yard (from which the owners pick their decorative flowers), and a wraparound covered porch with a stunning view of the Olympic Mountains. Four guest rooms share two baths. One of the rooms offers an Olympic-view sundeck; another has a fireplace. Two new suites, on the first and third floors, also have magnificent views. Full gourmet breakfasts are available. ◆ 4845 45th Ave SW (between Hudson and Edmunds Sts). 938.3658, 800/671.2942. www.villaheidelberg.com

---

Restaurants/Clubs: Red | Hotels: Purple | Shops: Orange | Outdoors/Parks: Green | Sights/Culture: Blue

QUEEN ANNE/MAGNOLIA

To much of Seattle's old guard, Queen Anne and adjacent Magnolia *did* represent idyllic escapes from the burgeoning city. After First Hill and Capitol Hill were developed, it was to this area that the wealthy retreated, erecting their capitalist castles as the 20th century made its debut. "The Hill," as residents called it, looked down its nose—both literally and figuratively—at the city's center. The exclusive area adopted an air of elegance; so many of the homes on its south flank were designed in an Americanized spin on classic Queen Anne architectural style that by the 1880s the district had been dubbed **Queen Anne Town**. Unfortunately, most of

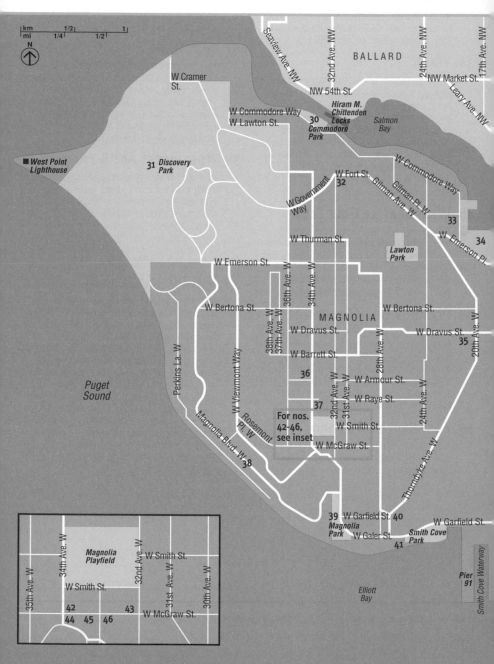

the towered villas that inspired this name a century ago are now gone. Many of the other older dwellings have been carved into duplexes and triplexes to make room for the neighborhood's growing population.

Bordered by the **Lake Washington Ship Canal** to the north, **Lake Union** to the east, and **Elliott Bay** and Magnolia to the west, for years Queen Anne managed to maintain the atmosphere of a place set apart. In time it was conquered by cable-car lines and then annexed to the city of Seattle in 1883.

Today hideous 500-foot-tall television towers—which, ironically, disturb TV and radio reception in the immediate neighborhood—have been thrust up against the sky here. But still, Queen Anne strives to rise above it all.

Magnolia is even more luxuriously isolated. Connected to Queen Anne and the rest of the city by only three streets, this hamlet—named in 1865 after a United States Coast Survey misidentified a stand of madrona trees as magnolias—used to be dominated by single-family houses. Along with the properties bordering **Magnolia Bluff** and the waterfront homes hugging **Perkins Lane** (those, that is, that haven't slid into the water), the area now has many apartment and condo complexes. A clear indication of Magnolia's shifting profile is the main shopping district along **McGraw Street** between **32nd** and **35th Avenues**. More than half the businesses in "The Village," as Magnolians call the area, have opened since the mid-1980s. Successful thirtysomething couples are moving in, drawn to Magnolia's manageable size, natural beauty, and relative calm.

QUEEN ANNE

1 PANDASIA

★★$ Like its much-praised older sibling in North Seattle, this restaurant is known for relatively inexpensive, high-quality food, and fast, friendly service. Soup noodles, dumplings, buns, and sauces are made fresh daily. The *moo shu* pork with home-made pancakes, the explosive General Tso's chicken, and Happy Family (stir-fried scallops, shrimp, and breast of chicken) specials are outstanding. Sit at the counter and observe firsthand the kitchen staff's skill. ♦ Chinese/takeout ♦ M-Sa, lunch and dinner; Su, dinner. 1625 W Dravus St (between 16th and 17th Aves). 283.9030. &. www.pandasia.com

2 PONTI SEAFOOD GRILL

★★$$ The location—right on the south lip of the Lake Washington Ship Canal, with a direct watch on the tiny blue-and-orange Fremont Bridge—cries out for a restaurant with big windows. And that's exactly what owners Richard and Sharon Malia created in this upscale establishment. Chef Josh Green offers wonderfully fresh seafood salads, and the dishes are often influenced by Mediterranean or Asian cooking styles. Signature dishes include Thai curry penne and gingerbrown butter scallops. The wine list is on the expensive side, and service can be slow when the house is packed. In summer ask for seating on the porch, where the views compensate for the restaurant's few deficiencies. ♦ Northwestern/seafood ♦ M-F, lunch and dinner; Sa, dinner; Su, brunch and dinner. Reservations recommended. 3014 Third Ave N (between Florentia and Etruria Sts). 284.3000. &. www.pontiseafoodgrill.com

CANLIS

3 CANLIS

★★★$$$$ Since 1950, Peter Canlis's restaurant—now in the capable hands of his son and daughter-in-law, Chris and Alice—has occupied a commanding position high above Lake Union at the south end of the Aurora Bridge. And the service is impeccable—from the moment you walk in, you'll be pampered by waitresses in up-to-date garb (the **Canlis** tradition of kimonos is a thing of the past), a modern—albeit dubious—result of a $2 million renovation that updated the place and menu for Northwest sensibilities. The dining spaces now feature wood ceiling beams, 20-foot granite columns, and a muted palette that echoes the gray and blue-green of the stone—it's described by some as the quintessential Northwest ambience. For an appetizer, try the Dungeness crab legs with mustard sauce or the Canlis chowder. The place made its rep as a steak house, and many people think the cuts of beef here are the very best in town. The mahimahi broiled over Kiawe wood and Kōbe-style Washington beef, naturally raised from Japanese sires and Angus cows, a Canlis exclusive, are other highly recommended main courses. And the ever-popular Canlis salad ("with no apologies to Caesar," as the menu says) is prepared at your table; pick up the recipe at the reception desk on your way out. ♦ Steak house ♦ M-Sa, dinner. 2576 Aurora Ave N (north of Halladay St). 283.3313. www.canlis.com

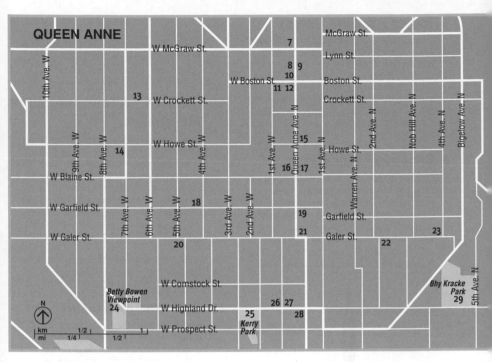

4 TURRET HOUSE

This arresting residence is a multigabled, cedar-shake structure, complete with solarium, turret, and a widow's walk. In the 1970s, this was the home of the commune of the controversial Love Israel Family. It's since been carved up into apartments.
♦ W Halladay St and Sixth Ave

5 KINNEAR PARK

This 14-acre park of majestic trees, sloping lawns, and mountain and Puget Sound views was donated to the city by Midwesterner George Kinnear, who visited Seattle in 1874 and invested his money in local real estate. Unfortunately, in addition to natural views, the park also looks down on the Port of Seattle grain terminal, which is one of Seattle's few real eyesores. ♦ 700 W Olympic Pl (between Third and Ninth Aves)

6 QUEEN ANNE COUNTERBALANCE

The name for the steep ascent on Queen Anne Avenue north of Roy Street dates back to the late 1800s and early streetcar technology. Although other Seattle cable-car lines employed conventional underground mechanical power until 1940, the car that ran through these parts was converted in 1900 to draw electricity from overhead wires. But to scale the 18% incline of Queen Anne Hill, the streetcar needed assistance from a pair of special counterweight arrangements. Here's how it worked: One streetcar could go up the hill and one could go down, each linked via cable to a 16-ton "truck," which ran on tracks through a tunnel beneath the street. As the truck went downhill, it helped pull the heavier streetcar uphill. Going the other direction, the ascending truck restrained the descending streetcar. At 8 miles per hour, it was slow going. In a race up the Counterbalance on 5 March 1937, a more modern trackless trolley loaded with 92 passengers "embarrassed the Queen Anne streetcar, making the 2,150-foot hill in less than half the time required by the streetcar," reported the *Seattle Times* the next morning. The Counterbalance's last two cable cars were retired in 1943, but the pair of tunnels remains in place under Queen Anne Avenue. ♦ Queen Anne Ave N (between Roy and Galer Sts)

7 A&J MEATS

In addition to the usual meat market offerings, this shop purveys convenient prepared specialties: Bavarian rouladen (rolled beefsteak stuffed with onion, bacon, mustard, dill pickles, and sliced carrots), chicken cordon bleu, chicken puff pastries, and more. There's a variety of fine sausages too. ♦ Tu-Su. 2401 Queen Anne Ave N (at W McGraw St). 284.3885

Restaurants/Clubs: Red | Hotels: Purple | Shops: Orange | Outdoors/Parks: Green | Sights/Culture: Blue

8 NANCY'S SEWING BASKET

Amateur and professional tailors alike will enjoy all the exotic silks, imported cottons, and designer fabrics for sale. There's even a separate **Ribbon Room**, with a sumptuous selection of brocade, embroidered, silk, cotton, and rayon ribbons from whisper-thin to 6 inches wide. ♦ Daily. 2221 Queen Anne Ave N (between W Boston and W McGraw Sts). 282.9112

9 BROADWAY CLOCK SHOP

Certified master clockmaker Roger Hewat moved his business from Capitol Hill some years ago but kept the original store's name. Browsing among the antique wall clocks and wonderful grandfather timepieces is like stepping back in, well, time. ♦ Hours vary; call ahead. 2214 Queen Anne Ave N (between W Boston and W McGraw Sts). 285.3130

Caffe Ladro
ESPRESSO BAR & BAKERY

10 CAFFE LADRO

★$ This comfortable, laid-back coffee shop (one of a growing local chain—they were up to 10 at press time) is artistically decorated, from giant metal ceiling fans to a collection of assorted window frames pieced together above the counter. In Italian, *caffè ladro* means "coffee thief"; the joke, of course, is that this neighborhood Queen Anne coffeehouse has made off with a number of caffeine fans from the nearby chains (there are several within a rock's throw of this spot). The *lattes* here are very good, as is the lovely pastry from their own bakery. ♦ Coffeehouse ♦ 2205 Queen Anne Ave (between W Boston and W McGraw Sts). 282.5313. & www.caffeladro.com

10 TEACUP

Order a cup of tea from the counter at Elizabeth Knottingham's charming shop, then place your bulk-tea order from a list of more than 130 selections. She sells fine English marmalades and has a wide variety of teapots as well. ♦ Daily. 2207 Queen Anne Ave N (between W Boston and W McGraw Sts). 283.5931

10 MCCARTHY & SCHIERING WINE MERCHANTS

This is the second location for the friendly and knowledgeable team (the original shop is in Ravenna), who are as attentive to your request for a $10 Chardonnay as they are to someone else's interest in a case of Bâtard-Montrachet. The owners have built a state-of-the-art wine-cooling room, so you can order a case of Taittinger Blanc de blancs in the morning and pick it up chilled for the evening's dinner party. ♦ Tu-Sa. 2209 Queen Anne Ave N (between W Boston and W McGraw Sts). 282.8500. Also at 6500 Ravenna Ave NE (at 65th St). 524.0999

11 ORRAPIN THAI CUISINE

★★$$ This isn't the typical undecorated Thai restaurant; the owners have taken as much care with ambience—exotic décor, art on the walls, a friendly staff, and the gentle pace—as with the food. Try an inspired salad—like *yum talay* (prawn, scallops, squid, mussels, lime juice, and peppermint) or be adventurous and order hot basil beef (and they mean hot!). They've even given a new twist to an old favorite, *shoo shee pla* (salmon cooked in red curry with coconut milk and Thai basil). But come early; it fills up quickly at lunch and dinner with local fans of excellent Thai food. ♦ Daily, lunch and dinner. 10 Boston St (between Queen Anne Ave N and First Ave N). 283.7118. &

12 PARAGON

★★$$ Talented chef **Christopher Cunio** does the honors at this elegant place, putting a Northwest perspective on bistro cooking from around the world. Feast on savory chicken with garlic fried rice or the mouthwatering seared ahi tuna, which is accompanied by local greens with toasted sesame seeds and cucumber mint coulis. The lively dining room gets crowded early, so come before 6:30PM if you can. There's live music Sunday through Wednesday. ♦ Northwestern ♦ Daily, dinner. 2125 Queen Anne Ave N (between W Crockett and W Boston Sts). 283.4548. &

13 RHINESTONE ROSIE

In this out-of-the-way little store, find a world of fabulous sparkle and dazzle. In business for over 23 years, Rosie, with the help of her daughter, specializes in buying, selling, and repairing vintage and estate costume jewelry.

Once you've been in this shop, you'll never think of rhinestones the same way again. She's even got vintage eyeglasses and bags. A must stop for any fashionista. ◆ Tu, W, 11AM–5PM; Th–Sa, 10AM–6PM. 606 W Crockett St (between Sixth and Seventh Aves W). 283.4605. www.rhinestonerosie.com

14 QUEEN ANNE HILL BED & BREAKFAST

$$ Mary and Chuck McGrew own this charming bed-and-breakfast situated at the top west side of Queen Anne Hill. There are three guest rooms upstairs, including one with a private deck that affords glorious views of the Olympic Mountains and the sunsets, and another that boasts a private bath. (The shared bath, however, is big and airy and has a claw-foot tub.) Downstairs is a bright and cheerful two-bedroom suite with its own bath as well. Common areas include a deck facing west, a cozy living room, and a small sun porch. The lovely English garden is a good place to relax. The full breakfast often includes croissants and quiche. The house is decorated with attractive artwork—from original works to posters. ◆ 1835 Seventh Ave W (at W Howe St). 284.9779

15 METROPOLITAN MARKET ON QUEEN ANNE

Seattle's first—and many would say its best—upscale supermarket boasts everything from an exceptionally good wine department, with depth in European, California, and Northwest labels, to an organic gourmet salad bar. The bakery section features French breads, croissants, and other fresh comestibles from the justly celebrated **Boulangerie** in Wallingford. The seafood department is likewise estimable, and the staff is helpful and friendly, even at 3AM. ◆ Daily, 24 hours. 1908 Queen Anne Ave N (between Howe and Crockett Sts). 284.2530. www.metropolitan-market.com

16 EL DIABLO COFFEE CO.

Even in Seattle, it is possible to have an unusual coffee experience. Stopping at this vibrant café is like stepping into the fiery Cuban dwelling of *el diablo*, where murals of devils tempt you into exotic culinary treats. The specialty here is Cuban-style coffee (espresso with carmelized sugar); have it with the authentic Cuban sandwich or the tropical fruit salad. On your way to the partially covered patio, stop in the Love Grotto and sneak a kiss from your partner.

And if the fire is too hot for you below, climb the spiral staircase into a peaceful heaven where cleverly disguised cherubs and inspirational quotes adorn the cloud-painted walls. Live music some nights. Check web site for details. ◆ Su–Th, 6:30AM–11PM; F, Sa, 6:30AM–midnight. 1811 Queen Anne Ave N (between W Blaine and W Howe Sts). 285.0693. www.eldiablocoffee.com

16 QUEEN ANNE AVENUE BOOKS

This fine, small bookstore is especially strong on fiction, with a good selection of travel books, magazines, and children's literature as well. ◆ Daily. 1811 Queen Anne Ave N (between W Howe and W Blaine Sts). 283.5624. www.queenannebooks.com

17 BETHANY PRESBYTERIAN CHURCH

Completed in 1930, this beautiful example of English Gothic architecture is a definite standout against the ever-changing neighborhood of upper Queen Anne Avenue. This is not the first home to the First Presbyterian Church congregation (the original being on the site of the Seattle Center fountain). Designed by James Hay, the L-shaped building includes a tower and spire rising to over 80 feet. A beautiful stained-glass window depicting the Good

Seattle is truly a cyclist's city. Some Seattle bicycle statistics from recent years:

- Number of times cyclists put their bikes on Metro buses every year: 300,000+
- Number of times cyclists forgot to take their bicycles off the bus: 353
- Number of free Seattle bike route maps requested in a 2-year period: 50,000+
- Percentage of downtown bike commuters who are female: 25
- Ratio of streets to bike trails in Seattle: 45:1
- Miles of bike trails in Seattle: 28
- Miles of striped bike lanes in Seattle: 15
- Time to drive from University District to Pike Place Market in light traffic: 15 minutes
- Driving time during rush hour: 35 minutes
- Cycling time, moderate pace: 30 minutes
- Number of racks for bicycle parking in Seattle: 1,800

THE WORD OUT WEST

Seattle is a bibliophilic town. Nationally, the average per-household expenditure for books is $50 a year. Here, it's about double that. Meanwhile, Seattle public libraries lend more volumes per capita than any other system in the country. Noteworthy authors—including the likes of Norman Mailer, Terry McMillan, Carlos Fuentes, Philip Roth, Jill Eisenstadt, and Robert B. Parker—cycle through town for readings or book signings, and the **Seattle Arts and Lectures Series** schedules about half a dozen famous writers annually for lectures and special events (call 621.2230 for schedule and registration). In addition, a number of nationally recognized authors—including Jonathan Raban and Pete Dexter—have relocated to **Puget Sound** country.

Is Seattle's bookwormish tendency attributable to high standards in local education? Or can it be traced simply to the number of inclement days that send waterlogged residents inside to the comfort of their reading lamps? Whatever the reason, the publishing industry has benefited. Counting the number of bookstores per person, Seattle ranks seventh in the nation (San Francisco tops the list).

A number of useful guidebooks and historical studies have evolved with Seattle's increasing popularity. The city has also become a popular setting for detective novels. However, there is still nothing that can be pointed to as the quintessential Seattle novel—nothing that acutely captures the spirit and essence of the city. The local literati await. For the time being, however, here are some must-reads on the city of Seattle.

Nonfiction

Bertha Knight Landes of Seattle: Big City Mayor, by Sandra Haarsagen (University of Oklahoma Press, 1994): A biography of Seattle's—and America's—first female mayor, elected in the 1920s.

Calabash: A Guide to the History, Culture, and Art of African-Americans in Seattle and King County, Washington, by Esther Hall Mumford (Ananse Press, 1993): Informative and well-written, this book offers a perspective on the African-American community in this area.

Five Days that Shook the World: the Battle for Seattle and Beyond, by Alexander Cockburn, Jeffrey St. Clair, and Allan Sekula, photographer (Verso, 2001): The 1999 WTO protests will be forever associated with violence

when Seattle streets were transformed from festival to a police state in a matter of hours.

The Good Rain: Across Time and Terrain in the Pacific Northwest, by Timothy Egan (Alfred A. Knopf, 1990): Prepare to enjoy an eminently readable and not-too-egregiously romanticized take on the Northwest's beauty and blemishes by the *New York Times* local bureau chief.

Impressions of Imagination: Terra-Cotta Seattle, edited by Lydia S. Aldredge (Allied Arts of Seattle, 1986): Spend a few hours flipping through this handsome, essay-filled encomium to Seattle's days as a white city on the **Sound**. It offers a wonderful architectural history.

Jackson Street After Hours: The Roots of Jazz in Seattle, by Paul De Barros (Sasquatch Books, 1993): A fascinating, often humorous take on the rise of jazz music in the city, with plenty of photographs.

Jimi Hendrix, Musician, by Keith Shadwick (Hi Marketing, 2003): Perfect for any devotee of Hendrix. It is a well-researched account of the career and personal history of Jimi Hendrix.

Meet Me at the Center, by Don Duncan (Seattle Center Foundation, 1992): An entertaining former *Seattle Times* writer looks back at the 1962 World's Fair and forward to the future of the site that has become the **Seattle Center**.

The National Trust Guide, Seattle: America's Guide for Architecture and History Travelers, by Walt Crowley (John Wiley & Sons, 1998): A well-known local provides a knowledgeable perspective for those who like to take the historical and architectural view.

The Natural History of Puget Sound Country, by Arthur Kruckeberg (University of Washington Press, 1995): Beginning with the shaping of the land by glacial activity in the Ice Age and volcanic eruptions later on, this book discusses the natural attributes of the region, including flora and fauna, climate, and the current ecosystem.

Out Here, by Andrew Ward (Penguin, 1991): A Bainbridge Islander and lighthearted commentator with National Public Radio draws his sights on beggars, road-kill dogs, and other local exotica.

Seattle and the Demons of Ambition: from Boom to Bust in the Number One City of the Future, by Fred Moody (St. Martin's Press, 2003): A first-hand look at Seattle's changes through the years, from Starbucks,

Microsoft, Amazon, and other dot.commers to the new architecture of the city.

Seattle in the Twentieth Century, Volumes I and II, by Richard C. Berner (Charles Press, 1991, 1992): If you want to find out the city's population in any year between 1990 and 1940 or brush up on political machinations in early Seattle, these are the pages to start scanning. Volume I, *From Boomtown, Urban Turbulence, to Restoration*, covers 1900 to 1920; Volume II, *From Boom to Bust*, dissects 1921 to 1940.

Skid Road, by Murray Morgan (Comstock, 1978): Morgan's book is an irreverent, insightful, often embarrassingly candid parsing of Seattle history. No one who wants to know about this area's past should be without this book.

The Great Northwest Nature Factbook: A Guide to the Region's Remarkable Animals, Plants & Natural Features, by Ann Saling (Graphic Arts Center Publishing, 1999): An entertaining take-along guide to the natural wonders of Washington, Oregon, and Idaho, from the rivers and volcanoes, to the wildlife, both on the land and in the water.

1001 Curious Things: Ye Olde Curiosity Shop and Native American Art, by Kate C. Duncan (University of Washington Press, 2001): This is a fond look at a famous Seattle store, one that has been in business since 1899 and now offers a huge and bewildering jumble of souvenirs and trinkets (shrunken heads, Seattle T-shirts) intermingled with authentic Northwest Coast and Alaska Eskimo carvings, baskets, blankets, and other artworks. The remarkably complete archives maintained by the family since the time the store was opened provides a fascinating chapter in the history of Seattle, especially in its early days.

Fiction

Final Bearing, by George Wallace and Don Keith (Tom Doherty Associates, 2004): Novelist Keith and retired submariner Wallace join forces to create this thriller about a submariner/drug lord, Juan de Santiago.

Fish Story, by Richard Hoyt (Viking, 1985): Private eye John Denson, connoisseur of screw-top wine and raw cauliflower, gets mixed up in a Native American fishing rights case that leads to the disappearance of a federal judge and the grisly discovery of various human body parts in **Pioneer Place Park**.

Good Night Seattle, by Adam Gamble and Jo Veno (Independent Publisher's Group, 2006): A children's book that takes the reader to the area's attractions, designed to instill an early appreciation for natural and cultural wonders.

Half Asleep in Frog Pajamas, by Tom Robbins (Bantam Books, 1994): Frog gods from Sirius and thieving monkeys travel from the rainy climes of Seattle to Timbuktu, taking in the **Queen Anne Thriftway** and a **Ballard** bowling alley.

Indian Killer, by Sherman Alexie (Atlantic Monthly Press, 1996): A serial killer is stalking Seattle, taking the scalps of white males. As retaliatory crimes against Indians escalate, Native American John Smith must confront the violence in the streets—and in his own heart.

Never Mind Nirvana, by Mark Lindquist (Villard Books, 2000): This is a kind of coming-of-age novel where the hero, almost 40, yearns to be an adult and to do adult things. But he is trapped in his rock-and-roll–grunge band past. Will he mature? Will he commit to an adult relationship? Even if the answers to these questions don't much interest you, the book, with its hip dialogue, pop-culture references, and setting in the venues of the '80s and '90s alternative rock scene in Seattle, gives you a terrific tour of that side of things.

Picture Postcard, by Fredrick D. Huebner (Random House, 1990): Lawyer Matt Riordan's efforts to locate a famous but long-missing Northwest painter take him back 50 years to a fateful houseboat party on **Portage Bay** and embroil him with more than a sufficient share of dangerous characters.

Snow Falling on Cedars, by David Guterson (Vintage, 1995): The murder trial of a Japanese-American fisherman kindles a haunting fugue of memory, including a childhood romance between a white boy and a Japanese girl, a land dispute, and wartime internment.

Without Due Process, by Judith A. Jance (Morrow, 1993): Homicide detective J.P. Beaumont trails a killer through Seattle to protect a dead friend's good name and his scared little boy.

Ulterior Motive, by Daniel Oran (Kensington Publishers, 1998): This high-tech thriller involves computer programs, conspiracies, and generally mysterious goings-on at Megasoft. Our hero is an ambitious young Megasoft project manager. The author, formerly at Microsoft, invented the Start Button and Taskbar for Windows 95, so he knows whereof he writes.

Restaurants/Clubs: Red | Hotels: Purple | Shops: Orange | Outdoors/Parks: Green | Sights/Culture: Blue

Shepherd welcomes everyone into the sanctuary. In the later 1960s, **Durham, Anderson and Fried** designed a compatible addition. ♦ 1818 Queen Anne Ave N (between W Blaine and W Howe Sts). 284.2222. www.bethanypc.org

18 QUEEN ANNE BRANCH LIBRARY

On New Year's Day 1914, this library was opened in a festive celebration attended by more than a thousand people. *Seattle Times* owner Alden J. Blethen had contributed $500 to help buy the land, and the city kicked in the remaining $6,500. Pennsylvania steel-and-iron magnate Andrew Carnegie had donated the money for the building: $32,667. And a couple of prominent architects had been brought out to develop the handsome library in a style that might best be labeled English Scholastic Gothic: **W. Marbury Somervell**, who, along with partner **Joseph C. Cote**, already had the **Providence Hospital** in the Central District and the **West Seattle Public Library** on his curriculum vitae; and **Harlan Thomas**, best remembered for downtown's 1924 **Chamber of Commerce** building on Columbia Street. During the library's first year, it circulated 71,623 books and became an active community center. Interior highlights include small-pane, leaded-glass windows, oak-panel doors with bronze mortise handles and locks, and stained-glass entry windows. *Quintet in D*, a vividly colored art-glass mural created by Seattle artist Richard Spaulding in 1978, hangs on the north wall. ♦ M-Sa. 400 W Garfield St (at Fourth Ave). 386.4227

19 PASTA BELLA

★$$ Owner David Rasti has created a cozy décor in this restaurant, where deep, rich green predominates. A very pleasant deck enhances warm-weather meals (try to ignore the monstrous TV tower next door). *Linguine amatriciana* (with tomatoes, pancetta, chili, garlic, and wine), *pollo agrodolce* (bitter-sweet chicken), and chicken in savory mango chutney tomato–wine sauce topped with sweet glazed pecans are highly recommended. The selective wine list is 80% Italian. ♦ Italian ♦ Daily, lunch and dinner. Reservations recommended. 1530 Queen Anne Ave N (at Garfield St). 284.9827; fax 284. 9774. www.pastabellaseattle.com. Also at 5909 15th Ave NW (between 59th and 60th Sts). 789.4933

20 WEST QUEEN ANNE ELEMENTARY SCHOOL

This historic brick structure, with its whimsical medieval hints, was created in 1896 by the Seattle architectural firm of **Skillings and Corner** (responsible also for

the **Old Main Building** at Bellingham's **Western Washington University**). It was used as a school until the 1980s, when it was converted into condominiums by local architect **Val Thomas** (who reserved the former gymnasium for himself). The building rests on lovely landscaped grounds in a neighborhood of residential grandeur. ♦ 515 W Galer St (between Fifth and Sixth Aves)

21 OLYMPIA PIZZA & SPAGHETTI HOUSE

★$ Perched at the top of the **Counterbalance**, this eatery offers 30 varieties of pizza, including the three house specialties: the Spiro (pepperoni, Canadian bacon, shrimp, mushrooms, olives, green peppers, cheese, and tomato sauce); the Olympia (sausage, Canadian bacon, fresh garlic, mushrooms, olives, onions, and fresh or cooked tomatoes); and the House Special (salami, pepperoni, sausage, Canadian bacon, green peppers, olives, cheese, mushrooms, and tomato sauce). Delivery is available, of course. ♦ Pizza/takeout ♦ Daily, lunch and dinner. 1500 Queen Anne Ave N (between Galer and Garfield Sts). 285.5550. ♿ Also at other locations around town

21 THE 5-SPOT

★★$$ Local restaurateur Peter Levy has stretched himself here, developing a menu strong on regional American cooking, with regular 3-month changes of theme. Some representative dishes: salmon cakes from the Northwest; shrimp enchiladas *con queso* (with cheese) from the Southwest; brisket and corn chowder à la New England; and, from the heart of Dixie, honey-stung fried chicken. There's also a dynamite red-flannel hash for breakfast and a different dinner special every day, dished up from 5PM "till it's gone." Portions are plentiful, and the **Counterbalance Room** bar, set off near the kitchen, is a surprisingly peaceful place, rarely crowded. Weekend mornings, there's a line out the door for the dining room. ♦ American ♦ Daily, breakfast, lunch, and dinner. 1502 Queen Anne Ave N (between Galer and Garfield Sts). 285.7768. ♿ www.chowfoods.com

22 QUEEN ANNE HIGH SCHOOL APARTMENTS

A successful conversion from institution to residence, this school closed its doors in 1981 and now has 139 apartments on five floors. Many of the units have expansive views; from a top-floor apartment, for instance, you can see almost all the way to Canada. The school was designed in 1909 by **James Stephen**, the accomplished son of a Scottish cabinetmaker, who received his architectural training through a Chicago correspondence course and served as the Seattle School District's resident architect between 1899 and 1908. (He also created **Summit Grade School** on First Hill, **Latona Elementary** and **Interlake School**—now **Wallingford Center**—in Wallingford, and many other educational facilities needed to service the city's growing population during its early boom years.) The building was converted by **Bumgardner Architects** in 1988 and is still the most visible landmark on the hill, especially at night, when the windows are lit up. ♦ 201 Galer St (at Second Ave N). 285.8800

23 WILLIAMS HOUSE

$ Doug and Sue Williams are the owners of this charming bed-and-breakfast located in a quiet residential neighborhood on the east side of the hill. Built in 1905, the small, beautifully restored Edwardian mansion has five spacious guest rooms with private baths; most offer commanding views south and west. A winning sun porch on the first floor also faces south. ♦ 1505 Fourth Ave N (between Galer and Garfield Sts). 285.0810

24 BETTY BOWEN VIEWPOINT

Tony Bennett would be the ideal musical accompaniment on a visit to this romantic spot at the end of Highland Drive. From here the views of Puget Sound, the Olympic Mountains, and the dying blaze of sunsets are unrivaled. The overlook was designed in 1977 by **Victor Steinbrueck**, the architect and preservationist who brought the **Space Needle** to concrete reality and fought successfully to save **Pike Place Market**. ♦ Seventh Ave W and Eighth Pl

25 KERRY PARK

From this small, rectangular park, views of the **Space Needle**, downtown office spires, and Elliott Bay are stunning, day or night; the sight of Mount Rainier will take your breath away. Also worth appreciating: *Changing Form*, a steel sculpture of framed holes created by local artist Doris Chase in 1969, and a seemingly out-of-place totem pole across from the park. ♦ 211 W Highland Dr (between Queen Anne Ave N and Fifth Ave W)

26 VICTORIA APARTMENTS

Built in 1921, this large, Tudor-style brick apartment building, enclosing a lovely courtyard, was designed by prolific architect **John Graham Sr.** It was later refurbished as Seattle's first condominium complex. ♦ 100 W Highland Dr (at First Ave)

27 BALLARD-HOWE MANSION

This stately white house, built in 1906, was designed in the Colonial Revival style by **August Heide**, whose larger-scale work can be seen in the **Lowman Building** at Pioneer Place. It now contains apartments. ♦ 22 W Highland Dr (between Queen Anne Ave N and First Ave W)

28 HIGHLAND DRIVE

Heading west from Queen Anne Avenue and about halfway up the hill, this elegant residential street reflects a variety of architectural styles in its mix of mansions and lovely brick apartment houses. For many years, beginning at the turn of the 19th century, Highland Drive was *the* finest address in Seattle. One of the most prominent residents there was Alden J. Blethen, a bombastic former lawyer from Maine who'd entered journalism in the Midwest and lost a fortune there before moving to Seattle in 1896 to found the *Seattle Times*. So proud was Blethen of his pillared manse and the neighborhood in which it sat that for years he paid out of his own pocket to have Highland Drive gaslit every night. Leisurely strolls are highly recommended along this route; at the end of Highland Drive, notice the brick-in-concrete retaining walls at Seventh and Eighth Avenues, designed by W.R.B. Wilcox in 1913. The steps, railings, and lights are all part of the design. ♦ W Highland Dr (between Queen Anne Ave N and Seventh Ave W and Eighth and Ninth Aves W)

28 GABLE HOUSE

This house of 14 gables was completed in 1905 by Harry Whitney Treat, an investment banker who came to Seattle in 1904. His first act—a confirmation of his wealth and stature—was to commission the firm of **Bebb & Mendel** (responsible for downtown's **Hoge Building** and the vast **University Heights Elementary School**) to design a Queen Anne residence that would accommodate his family of four, plus a domestic staff of 14, and would cost $101,000. Treat kept coaches and horses and a tallyho pulled by blooded steeds purchased from the New York Vanderbilts. Not content with his existing fortune, he bought hundreds of acres just north of Ballard, creating Loyal Heights (named after one of his two daughters) and establishing **Golden Gardens Park**. An acquaintance of Colonel William F. "Buffalo Bill" Cody, Treat had Cody's entire Wild West troupe come to Queen Anne Hill to entertain his daughter on her ninth birthday. It was also in this house

---

Restaurants/Clubs: Red | Hotels: Purple | Shops: Orange | Outdoors/Parks: Green | Sights/Culture: Blue

that Treat and Cody planned the acclaimed Whitney Gallery of Western Art in Cody, Wyoming. Originally, 61 rooms occupied the 18,000 square feet of living space; it now has 15 private residential suites. ♦ 1 W Highland Dr (at Queen Anne Ave N)

29 BHY KRACKE PARK

Werner "Bhy" Kracke, a wealthy bank auditor, world traveler, and gardener, donated 1.5 acres of his property to the city, along with $20,000 to develop the land as a park, but he died before the deal could be closed. (Kracke got his nickname from "By cracky," one of his favorite expressions.) His heirs completed the transaction, and the city created the park and named it in Kracke's memory. Visit here for the views, sweeping from Lake Union and the Cascade Mountains to the **Space Needle**. The park is constructed on several levels; follow the winding paved path. You'll feel you've discovered a little gem that most locals don't know exists—and you'll be right. For parking, look for the street sign signaling Comstock Place and Bigelow Avenue, ignore the "Dead End" sign, and head east to the three-car parking area just ahead. ♦ Comstock Pl (just southeast of Bigelow Ave N)

MAGNOLIA

30 COMMODORE PARK

Across from the **Hiram M. Chittenden Locks** (see page 140), this aptly named park is a secluded spot for picnicking underneath the trees while watching boats cruise by. ♦ 3330 W Commodore Way

Adjacent to Commodore Park:

FISH LADDER

In 1976, this $2.3 million, 21-level fish ladder—connected by walkways to the **Hiram M. Chittenden Locks**—was opened on the south shore of the Lake Washington Ship Canal. More than a half-million salmon, steelhead, and trout scale the ladder annually, bound for spawning areas in the Cascade range. You can watch (and even cheer on) their progress from an interior viewing port. In the mid-1980s, sea lions, recognizing a feast when they smelled one, caused quite a stir with their extended stay near the fish ladder. Officials were determined to send them packing, and locals were equally determined that the creatures—known collectively as Herschel—not be harmed. After defeating a number of human (and humane) efforts to discourage them, Herschel was sent to California; undaunted, some of the sea lions turned right around and swam back home to Seattle.

31 DISCOVERY PARK

When Captain George Vancouver was exploring Puget Sound in 1792, he reportedly anchored nearby; the park is named after his ship, the *Discovery*. This is the largest park in Seattle, comprising 527 acres of richly varied terrain—woods, bluffs, beach, meadows, and trails. The farthest link in the 20-mile string of Frederick L. Olmsted's planned parklands built north and west from **Seward Park** on Lake Washington during the early 20th century, it is a haven for Seattleites desperate to escape urban forests of concrete and steel. Walking or jogging along the 2.5-mile-loop trail will take you through a quiet forest, across colorful meadows, and up to windy bluffs with panoramic views west to the sound and mountains. Follow signs for trails to the beach and to the **West Point Lighthouse**, a still-functioning lighthouse built in 1881. Bald eagles are a common sight here (you'll know where they are by the crowds of people milling about with their faces craned to the sky). In 1982, a cougar also turned up in the park; mercifully, restraint and sensitivity prevailed, and the creature was captured without harm. Picnic possibilities are endless and playing fields abound. ♦ 3801 W Government Way (west of 36th Ave). 386.4236

Within Discovery Park:

DAYBREAK STAR INDIAN CULTURAL CENTER

Built in 1977 on a piece of parkland leased for 99 years to the United Indians of All Tribes Foundation, this dramatic timbered building was designed by **Arai Jackson** in collaboration with **Lawney Reyes**. The place is filled with interesting works of art by Native American artists, including John J. Hoover's carved polychromed cedar panel, *Ancestor Spirit Boards*; *Buffalo Hunt*, a ceramic-tile mural by Glenn LaFontaine; and Marvin Oliver's painted and carved fir tree, *Bear and Raven*. There's also a small gallery of rotating Native American art, and the center sponsors a variety of Native American activities. Energetic children will delight in the well-equipped playground, and everyone will enjoy relaxing at the picnic tables and savoring the spectacular view. ♦ W-Su. 285.4425. www.unitedindians.com

32 FLORA & FAUNA BOOKS

Had Charles Darwin discovered this cloistered basement establishment, he might never have left. The packed stacks are filled with new, used, and rare natural history and life sciences books—approximately 25,000 titles in all. ♦ M-Sa. 3121 W Government Way (at W Fort St). 623.4727. www.ffbooks.net

33 VERTICAL WORLD

Practice your mountaineering technique on this gym's 14,000 feet of indoor climbing walls. Established in 1987, the facility, which is regarded by knowledgeable locals as the top indoor rock gym in America, gives participants the opportunity to lead, top rope, and boulder via 200 different routes on the 35-foot-high walls. Day passes and instruction are available. A complete line of climbing gear is also sold here. ♦ M,W,F, 10AM-10PM; Tu-Th, 6AM-10PM; Sa, Su, 10AM-7PM. 2123 W Elmore St (between 21st and 23rd Aves). 283.4497. www.verticalworld.com

34 FISHERMEN'S TERMINAL

Owned and operated by the Port of Seattle since 1913, this terminal, located on the south side of Salmon Bay, is home base to more than 700 commercial fishing vessels, ranging in length from 30 to 300 feet. Here are the trollers, gill-netters, seiners, long-liners, crabbers, and trawlers that make up the North Pacific fleet, one of the largest commercial fishing fleets in the world. Every year, Washington fishers harvest 2.3 billion pounds of fish and other seafood, more than half the total edible catch in the United States. The huge factory trawlers that moor at the terminal—some as long as a football field—catch 85% of the bottom fish taken in US waters. The moorage provides not only a good location for sightseers and photographers but opportunities to buy whole fish right off the boat. Take a peek at the bulletin board inside, advertising everything from Puget Sound seine permits to all manner of ships for sale, for a glimpse into the world of commercial fishing. Guest mooring available; call for rates. ♦ 3919 18th Ave W (just north of Emerson Pl). 728.3395

At Fishermen's Terminal:

CHINOOK'S

★★$$ As you might expect, fresh Northwest seafood is featured—as is a wall-to-wall view of the fishing boats—at this popular addition to the **Anthony's Homeport** restaurant fleet. The grilled Copper River salmon (seasonal) is superb, and the mussels are fresh and flavorful. Right next door is **Little Chinook's**, an informal and inexpensive fish-and-chips bar under the same ownership. ♦ Seafood ♦ M-F, lunch and dinner; Sa, Su, breakfast, lunch, and dinner. 283.4665. &

WILD SALMON SEAFOOD MARKET

From Alaskan king salmon to Dungeness crab, the catch is always the freshest at Paul Cassidy's superb seafood market. One of the best in Seattle, this place will also ship anywhere in the US. The canned tuna here will make you forget all about the stuff you buy in the supermarket. ♦ Daily. 283.3366

E.F. KIRSTEN TOBACCONIST

Get a world-renowned Kirsten pipe and choose from a broad selection of pipe tobaccos, including the unusual Mariner's Mixture and Dutch Harbor Blend. The cigar humidor is as big as a walk-in closet. You'll also find a serious selection of knives, card decks, and flasks. ♦ Daily. 286.0851

SEATTLE FISHERMEN'S MEMORIAL

The gathering point for the ceremonial blessing of the fleet, held annually in May, this memorial was created by Seattle sculptor Ron Petty in honor of the 500 Seattle fishers lost at sea during the 20th century; their names are inscribed on a plaque at the base. Dedicated 8 October 1988, the memorial is a bronze-and-concrete sculpture, with a variety of North Pacific marine life sculpted at the base and a lone bronze fisherman perched at the top. www.seattlefishermensmemorial.org

35 ROMIO'S PIZZA

★$$ One of this chain's many Seattle locations, this joint is just west of **Burlington Northern**'s main railroad yard. It's a popular, busy stop, with a constant stream of deliveries going out the door. Although all the pizzas are good, the Zorba (onions, tomatoes, Greek feta cheese, olives, and gyro meat with a house-made yogurt-cucumber sauce) and the GASP (an acronym for *garlic, artichoke hearts, sun-dried tomatoes, and pesto*) are the most memorable. ♦ Pizza/takeout ♦ M-Th, Su, until 11PM; F, Sa, until midnight. 2001 W Dravus St (at 20th Ave). 284.5420. www.romiospizza.com. Also at numerous locations throughout the city

36 MAGNOLIA LIBRARY

Designed by Seattle architect **Paul Kirk**, this handsome modern institution occupies three lots that were acquired from the Catholic diocese. Kirk used weathered

---

cedar shingles and large plate-glass windows that would "bring the beauty of the outside inside." Clerestory windows face north to admit the best light for reading. Even the furniture is noteworthy: hand-crafted solid walnut chairs and tables that were made by Pennsylvania artist George Nakashima. Outside, a bronze sculpture by Glen Alps graces the courtyard wall; inside, you'll find a fused-glass screen by Steven Fuller and two ceramic sculptures by Ebba Rapp MacLauchlan. The building was dedicated in 1964 and, 2 years later, won awards from the American Institute of Architecture, the National Book Committee, and the American Library Association. Despite those laurels, the library has not won unanimous neighborhood approval; occasional complaints about the "raw shingles" and "big, bare windows" can still be heard. ◆ M-Th, Sa. 2801 34th Ave W (at Armour St). 386.4225

37 CATHERINE BLAINE ELEMENTARY SCHOOL AND COMMUNITY CENTER

Built in 1952, this school was designed by Seattle architects **J. Lister Holmes and Associates**, with **Robert Dietz** and **Charles MacDonald**. "An outstanding example of the large public school in the full-fledged post-war Modern idiom," enthuses *A Guide to Architecture in Washington State*, "with natural lighting through sawtooth skylights, antiglare ceiling baffles, window walls, and modular construction." ◆ 2550 34th Ave W (between Smith and Raye Sts)

38 MAGNOLIA BOULEVARD

This scenic route west of **Magnolia Park** is noteworthy for its distinctive madrona trees and views of Puget Sound and the Olympic Mountains. Heading west on the boulevard leads you to Seattle's largest park, **Discovery Park**. ◆ Between Howe and Emerson Sts

39 MAGNOLIA PARK

Take a break, enjoy the breeze and the quiet, and gaze up at the trees or out to the water— this is one of the most spectacular viewpoints in the city. It's also a great picnic site. Look for a small parking area on the boulevard's west side. ◆ 1461 Magnolia Blvd W (between Galer and Howe Sts)

40 SMITH COVE PARK

On the Elliott Bay waterfront between **Pier 91** and the **Elliott Bay Marina**, this small spot of greenery is a fine place to catch sea-level views of the harbor and watch the car-carrying ships docked at **Pier 91**. Two men played key roles in establishing this place, the more powerful being James J. Hill, of the **Great Northern Railroad**. After Hill muscled his tracks to Seattle in 1893, he constructed giant double docks at Smith Cove to service the steamers *Minnesota* and *Dakota*, which carried silk from the Orient to be loaded onto trains in Seattle and shipped to East Coast markets. It was a lucrative trade until about 1940, when nylon replaced the demand for silk. Smith Cove was taken over for a time by the US Navy, but the Port of Seattle bought it back in the 1970s and created this park, named for Dr. Henry A. Smith, who arrived from Ohio and built a log cabin here in 1853. A well-liked gentleman farmer, poet, and surgeon, known for anesthetizing patients through hypnotism and promoting the therapeutic use of dream analysis, Smith was King County's first school superintendent and a territorial legislator. He also supposedly translated Duwamish Indian Chief Sealth's famous 1854 caution to invading white men that their day of decline would come as surely as had the Native Americans'—a translation that became controversial in the early 1990s when questions were raised about its authenticity. The argument has not yet been resolved. ◆ W Garfield St (east of Galer St)

41 ELLIOTT BAY MARINA

This privately owned state-of-the-art marina, located at the base of Magnolia Bluff, can accommodate 1,200 boats. An interesting mix of graceful old boats and sleek new yachts is moored here, some of them 100 feet long. This is a select sightseeing spot for all recreational sailors. ◆ W Galer St (between Garfield St and 28th Ave). 285.4817

At the Elliott Bay Marina:

PALISADE

★★★$$$ Rich Komen, the man behind Restaurants Unlimited (**Triples, Palomino, Cutters Bayhouse**) never does anything without a splash. And this huge, high-concept, $4 million Polynesian restaurant is no exception. The main dining room, designed by interior architect **Gary Dethlefs**, is a soaring space, complete with an elevated piano trellis and player piano. To get to it, you cross a 60-foot-long bridge over a 1,000-square-foot pool of seawater filled with Pacific Northwest finfish and shellfish. The 180-degree view spans the Port of Seattle grain terminal, past downtown, across Elliott Bay to West Seattle and Alki Point, and out to Puget Sound and the Olympic Mountains. Fish, poultry, and meat dishes are prepared here in a variety of ways: from the wood-fired oven, searing grill, wood-fired rotisserie, or apple-wood broiler. Menu highlights include a shellfish chowder, Dungeness crab cakes, wood-oven roasted black tiger prawns, apple-wood-grilled salmon (king or silver), and guava-wood rotisserie prime rib au jus and fresh horseradish. ♦ Northwestern ♦ Daily, lunch and dinner. Reservations recommended. 285.1000. &. www.palisaderestaurant.com

Maggie Bluffs Marina Grill

$ This cafeteria-style restaurant below **Palisade** specializes in grilled seafood, burgers, and breakfasts. Unfortunately, it is almost impossible to escape the TVs, but those who want to catch the latest sports scores with their burgers will do well here. ♦American ♦M-F, lunch and dinner; Sa, Su, breakfast, lunch, and dinner. 283.8322. &

Elliott Bay Yachting Center

If you've always wanted to lease a yacht—sail or power, 27 feet to 50 feet—you've come to the right place. Various options are available, and expert instruction is provided when you sign up. ♦Daily. 285.9499; 800/422.2019 in Washington and Oregon. www.ebyc.com

42 Hot Cha Cha

Interactive art reaches a boisterous high in this kinetic sculpture, created in 1987 by artist Kenny Schneider and located beside Fire Station No. 41. Seventy-seven identical stainless-steel firefighters, arranged in 11 rows, dance at a speed determined by turning a wheel on the sculpture's side, a peculiar ode to hand-cranked motion pictures of the early 20th century. The piece's name is a humorous allusion both to the movement of the figures and to the working environment of firefighters everywhere. ♦ W McGraw St and 34th Ave

43 Magnolia's Bookstore

Thanks to owner Georgiana Bloomburg, this neighborhood has a bookstore to call its own. There's a good selection of general fiction and mysteries, along with travel, self-help, cooking, reference, and other categories. A surprising variety of alternative magazines greets you up front, and more conventional magazines are found in the back of the store.

♦ Daily. 3206 W McGraw St (between 32nd and 33rd Aves). 283.1062

44 Szmania's

★★★$$$ Thanks to owners Ludger and Julie Szmania, Magnolia finally has a restaurant of the first order. Chef Ludger uses regional ingredients but reveals his German roots in the signature sauerkraut "à la Szmania," with smoked pork loin and homemade sausages. There's a large outside deck for balmy evenings. ♦German/Northwestern ♦Tu-Su, dinner. Reservations recommended. 3321 W McGraw St (at 34th Ave). 284.7305. &. www.szmanias.com

45 Bleu Papillon

Crammed into this tiny shop is everything you might expect to find wandering through a Paris flea market. Gorgeous antiquities, glowing chandeliers, linens for your parlor, candles for your senses, silver, glassware—too much to list. Make sure you look from floor to ceiling so as not to miss a single thing. ♦ M-F, 11AM–6PM; Sa, 10AM–6PM. 3315 W McGraw St (between 33rd and 34th Aves W). 284.3526. www.bleupapillonseattle.com

46 Caffè Appassionato

★$ At this unusually handsome coffeehouse, the *caffè latte* is consistently tasty, and the pastries, made off-premises by a "cottage-industry" baker, are also delicious. Lightly grilled panini (sandwiches)—including a variety with prosciutto, provolone, tomato, and fresh basil served on *schiaciatta* (Tuscany's version of focaccia)—make a satisfying lunch. ♦ Coffeehouse ♦ Daily; F-Sa, until 11PM. 3217 W McGraw St (between 32nd and 33rd Aves W). 281.8040. www.cafeappassionato.com

46 Village Pub

★$ Popular for lunch, this friendly public house draws all segments of the Magnolia community: long- and short-termers, old and young, well-to-do and just barely squeaking by. Though it is known for its juicy hamburgers and "snowshoe fries" (huge, wide, and flat), the kitchen also turns out good fish and chips. Sixteen microbrews can be found here as well. ♦American ♦Daily, lunch and dinner; bar until midnight. 3221 W McGraw St (between 32nd and 33rd Aves W). 285.9756. &

BALLARD

ocated north of the **Lake Washington Ship Canal** and extending west to **Puget Sound**, Ballard was once home to a settlement of Shilshole Indians. (*Shilshole*, meaning "tuck away a bit" in the Salish dialect, aptly describes old Ballard's protected position on **Salmon Bay**.) Concealed from raiding parties, the village's location served the natives well, and their population grew to about 1,000. But Ballard was eventually discovered and repeatedly attacked by northern tribes. By the beginning of the 19th century, the population of the village had dwindled to a mere dozen families. Enter Ira Wilcox Utter, who in 1852 filed a claim to become the first

white settler at Salmon Bay, then an area of pristine beauty, with a virgin forest of giant thousand-year-old cedars. By 1870, 50 to 100 white settlers had staked claims in the area; before the decade was over, the logging of the bay's shore—which was to change this place forever—had begun.

In 1890, with a population of 1,636, Ballard was the first community to incorporate as a city after Washington became the 42nd state. It started out as an industrial city with a predominantly Scandinavian population, boasting five shingle mills, three sawmills, a sash-and-door factory, a steel- and ironworks, a boiler works, three shipyards, a blacksmith shop, and a booming saloon district to service all of the workers. The sawmills provided much of the wood used to rebuild Seattle after the fire of 1889. The mills clouded the skies with a blizzard of "Ballard snow"—air pollution dense enough to produce a "vast-wall of smoke which makes an impenetrable barrier between the city and Salmon Bay," in the words of one frustrated photographer.

The waterfront was equally bustling: Salmon Bay had become a harbor for log shipping; the commercial fishing fleet brought in tons of halibut, salmon, and cod; and oceangoing ships docked at nearby shipyards for hull repairs. (Today it's still home to one of the largest fishing fleets in the world.)

By 1906, Ballard had more than 10,000 residents and was the seventh-largest town in the state. Such rapid growth brought inevitable problems, none more urgent than finding an adequate water supply. Annexation to the city of Seattle, which was eager to expand northward, became a hot topic. After a bitter, divisive battle, the citizens of Ballard approved the merger.

Separated geographically from the main body of Seattle, Ballard continues to exist very much as a small town within larger metropolitan boundaries. The community had managed to preserve its historic character while gentrifying its older sections. Young professionals are moving in, attracted to the abbreviated skyline, classic main street, unpretentious style, and reasonably priced housing. They describe their neighbors in the most generous of terms. "A typical native Ballardite," says one, "is a down-to-earth sort of person, careful with money but generous with friendship."

1 GOLDEN GARDENS

Harry Whitney Treat, a New York investments mogul and real-estate mover, established this park soon after he moved to Seattle in 1904. Treat even built a special trolley line (the fare: 3 cents) from downtown Ballard, which was later incorporated into the Seattle transit system. Much of this 95-acre reserve is covered in woods and crisscrossed with trails, but it is always the expanse of beach north of the marina—where Ballard families used to camp for weeks at a time during the summer—that receives the most attention. It's perfect for beachcombing, walking, or just looking out to Puget Sound and breathing in what is arguably this city's freshest air. Windsurfers test their mettle nearby, in part because the sound is warmer than Lake Washington during the wintertime (though the water here is still only for the hardy). Lawrence Beck's enamel and welded-steel sculpture *Atala Kivlicktwok Okitun Dukik* (*The Golden Money Moon*) is at the park's south end. ◆ 8498 Seaview Pl NW (at Golden Gardens Dr)

2 SUNSET HILL PARK

From here, high above **Golden Gardens**, the unobstructed view is, in a word, spectacular. ◆ NW 77th St and 34th Ave

3 SHILSHOLE BAY MARINA

In 1950, the waterfront at Shilshole was not a pretty sight, what with its derelict ferry dock, scattered boathouses, vacant, untended land, a shipyard in decline, and what one writer derisively described as an "expanse of beach with a perimeter road that kept slipping off into the water." Today, after a 30-year effort to build a breakwater (completed in the early 1980s), the marina is the preferred moorage of Seattle's sailboat fleet; the waiting list to win berth space there is a mile long. The boat ramp is a terrific place to waste an afternoon watching boat owners curse their craft onto or off of trailers. ◆ 7001 Seaview Ave NW (at 70th St). 728.3385. www.portseattle.org

Within the Shilshole Bay Marina:

WIND WORKS

Take a basic sailing course or (if you've passed the official qualifying course) rent a sailboat from this enterprise, one of Seattle's leading big-boat sailing schools. The friendly and helpful instructors, all US Coast Guard–licensed captains, teach on 28- to 40-foot crafts. Navigation instruction is included. ◆ Daily, but hours vary; call ahead. 784.9386. www.sail1.com

4 NORDIC HERITAGE MUSEUM

Founded in 1979, this is the only museum in the United States that covers all five Scandinavian countries: Denmark, Finland, Iceland, Norway, and Sweden. Its emphasis is on the Nordic people who settled in the Pacific Northwest. Permanent exhibits include *Promise of the Northwest*, which describes life in early Washington, and *Ballard Story*, a richly detailed history of the community. The museum also offers Scandinavian-language classes, lectures, and films and sponsors ethnic festivals. ◆ Free for children younger than 6 and on the first Tu of the month. Tu-Su. 3014 NW 67th St (between 30th and 32nd Aves). 789.5707. www.nordicmuseum.org

5 CENTER ON CONTEMPORARY ART (COCA)

Featuring works by local, national, and international artists, this organization features "risk-oriented" programs with controversial exhibits. *Modern Primitives*, COCA's most famous show to date, made national news and is credited with starting the recent tattooing and body-piercing craze among young Americans. ◆ In Shilshole Bay Beach Club, 6412 Seaview Ave NW. Call or check web site for more information. 728.1980. www.cocaseattle.org

6 RAY'S BOATHOUSE

★★★$$$ Begun in 1946 as a coffee shop at a charter-fishing boat dock, this place has passed through several incarnations on its way to becoming one of Seattle's best seafood restaurants—and some say it's *the* best. The kitchen, run by executive chef Charles Ramseyer, makes good use of fresh regional ingredients, and both the steamed clams and the pasta with smoked salmon have won raves from food critics. Ask for the daily fish sheet to check for specials, and call early if you want to reserve a window seat. So popular is the main-floor restaurant that you may want to head upstairs to the blond wood–and-glass café, which offers a similar, but smaller, menu. Both floors have views of the water, the Olympic Mountains, and spectacular sunsets. ◆ Seafood ◆ Daily, lunch and dinner. Reservations recommended at the restaurant; no reservations at the café. 6049 Seaview Ave NW (just west of 38th Ave). 789.3770. & www.rays.com

6 ANTHONY'S HOMEPORT

★★$$ With its waterfront location and plentiful outdoor seating, this restaurant is a great place for views of Puget Sound and the Olympic Mountains, especially at sunset. Fresh seafood is the order of the day, with cioppino a particular palate-pleaser. ◆ Seafood ◆ M-Sa, lunch and dinner; Su, brunch and dinner. Reservations recommended. 6135 Seaview Ave NW (between 38th Ave and 67th St). 783.0780. & www.anthonys.com. Also at numerous locations throughout the city

7 CAFE BESALU

★★$ This is an utterly pleasant place to linger. The barista and co-owner, Meg Hagele, is completely understanding when customers request *lots* of whipped cream on their orange-currant brioche; James Miller, pastry chef and co-owner, adds a wonderful quiche Lorraine to the many mouthwatering treats on the menu. Sit a while on this beautiful tree-lined street in Ballard enjoying a perfect mocha (homemade chocolate recipe) and a ginger biscuit (like a cream scone with chunks of crystallized ginger). Tu-Su, breakfast and lunch. ◆ American. ◆ 5909 24th Ave NW. 789.1463

8 SALMON BAY BRIDGE

Built in 1914 by the Great Northern Railroad (now Burlington Northern) to limit congestion along the Ballard waterfront and to handle the boat traffic from the locks, this imposing bascule bridge can be raised quickly to allow passage for big ships (and high-masted sailboats). Normally suspended, the bridge is lowered only for approaching trains. ◆ Seaview Ave NW (just west of 34th Ave)

9 TOTEM HOUSE

$ Originally opened in 1937 as an Indian artifact shop, the building that houses this restaurant is a replica of an Indian *haiat* house (resting place). It became a fish-and-chips place during World War II, and that dish is still a specialty here, as is the homemade clam chowder. ◆ Seafood ◆ Daily, lunch and dinner. No credit cards accepted. 3058 NW 54th St (at 32nd Ave). 784.2300

10 ARCHIE McPHEE

This is the place in Seattle to purchase wacky widgets and doodads—rubber slugs, chattering teeth, rubber chickens, plastic pink flamingos, wind-up fire-breathing nuns, punching Amish puppets, and on and on. All visitors to Seattle, if they get out as far as Ballard, must drop in for a browse and a laugh at this huge collection of oddments and gimmicks. The store's hilarious and peculiar free catalog is mailed to McPhee fans all over the world. Daily ◆ 2428 NW Market St, between 24th Ave NW and 28th Ave NW, 297.0240. & www.mcphee.com

11 STONE GARDENS

This rather startling building, which looks like a warehouse with a three-part industrial-tech sculpture attached, is not, despite what its name suggests, a Zen meditation center. It's a climbing gym, featuring a 40-foot-tall outdoor wall and indoors, textured walls, natural features, and a 65-foot lead roof. If you don't know what that last item is, then you aren't an indoor rock climber. ◆ Daily. 2839 NW Market St (between 28th and 29th Aves NW, next to the Ballard Locks). 781.9828. www.stonegardens.com

12 LOCKSPOT CAFE & TAVERN

★$ You can't miss this place, sitting on the northern side of the **Chittenden Locks**, with its sign boasting the "World's Best Fish and Chips." The claim is open to debate, but the restaurant does have a long history here; it opened in the early 1930s to take advantage of traffic at the locks and along Seaview Avenue. There's a convenient take-out window. ◆ Seafood/takeout ◆ Daily 3005 NW 54th St (between Market St and 32nd Ave). 789.4865. &

Restaurants/Clubs: Red | Hotels: Purple | Shops: Orange | Outdoors/Parks: Green | Sights/Culture: Blue

13 HIRAM M. CHITTENDEN LOCKS

Completed in 1917, after decades of indecisiveness, legal delays, and government red tape, the 8-mile-long Lake Washington Ship Canal—winding through the Ballard, Magnolia, Fremont, Queen Anne, Wallingford, University, and Montlake districts—is a protected route connecting the saltwater of Puget Sound and Shilshole Bay with the higher-elevation fresh water of Salmon Bay, Lake Union, and Lake Washington. Attended by much fanfare, the locks were officially opened 2 months after completion of the canal, on 4 July, when the *Roosevelt*, flagship of Admiral Robert Edwin Peary's North Pole expedition, led a procession of ships through the canal. In 1956, the locks were named for Major Hiram M. Chittenden, who, as Seattle's district engineer of the Army Corps of Engineers from 1906 to 1908, had chosen and designed the site for this project; locals also call them the **Ballard Locks**. The buildings were created by renowned Seattle architect **Carl Gould**. In an average year, 100,000 commercial and pleasure craft and two million tons of cargo and logs pass through the locks. People line up on weekend afternoons to watch the regatta rise and fall. The shorter of the two locks—150 feet long and 28 feet wide, with a wall 42 feet high—is used for small pleasure boats; larger vessels are "locked" through the bigger portal: 825 feet by 80 feet, with a 55-foot-high wall. Depending on tides and lake levels, the lift varies from 6 feet to 26 feet. ♦ Visitors' Center: daily; guided tours: daily; free concerts during the summer. 3015 NW 54th St (between Market St and 32nd Ave). 783.7059.

At the Hiram M. Chittenden Locks:

CARL S. ENGLISH JR. ORNAMENTAL GARDENS

These lovely seven acres of lawn, trees, shrubs, and flowers—a thousand plant species in all, including palm trees—were developed from a handful of plantings in 1916. A fine spot for picnicking, the gardens are named for the man who, as head of the Corps of Engineers' gardening staff, spent 34 years cultivating them.

14 BARDAHL MANUFACTURING CORP.

Manufacturers of the best-selling motor-oil additive Bardahl, this company was founded in 1939 by Ole Bardahl, a native of Norway. By 1952, the company was an industry leader in automotive and industrial additives. Today, it produces more than 100 oil and fuel additives, which are sold in 80 countries. The company's hydroplane, *Miss Bardahl*, has won five gold cups and six national championships and has set numerous world records. A gigantic sign—"ADD BARDAHL OIL"—is clearly visible from the Ballard Bridge and announces the company's location (and stature). ♦ 1400 NW 52nd St (at 14th Ave). 783.4851. www.bardahl.com

Hiram M. Chittenden Locks

SEATTLE: THE PLAY'S THE THING

Seattle is known for its lively and often provocative artistic community, and local theater here is often interesting and multifaceted. Productions range from revivals of classic Chekhov and Shakespeare, recent Broadway hits on tour, and cabarets to new works by up-and-coming local playwrights and avant-garde shows. And the settings are equally varied: plush modern theaters, dimly lit church basements, and funky warehouse spaces. In any given week, there's bound to be something worth checking out.

Several mainstream theaters are clustered inside the **Seattle Center** (Fifth Avenue N, between Broad and Mercer Streets). Among the best are the **Bagley Wright Theater** (443.2222), home of the renowned **Seattle Repertory Theatre**, nicknamed The Rep (www.seattlerep.org); the **Intiman** (269.1900; www.intiman.org), recipient of the 2006 Tony Award for Outstanding Regional Theatre; and the **Charlotte Martin Theater** (441.3322; www.sct.org), which hosts productions by the popular **Seattle Children's Theatre**.

In the downtown area are two beautifully restored showpieces: the **Paramount** (901 Pine Street, at Ninth Avenue; 682.1414; www.theparamount.com), designed in 1929 by **B. Marcus Priteca**, and the **Fifth Avenue Theatre** (1326 Fifth Avenue between University and Union Streets; 625.1900; www.5thavenue.org), a former vaudeville house whose interior resembles the imperial throne room in the Forbidden City. Both of these venues host touring productions of blockbuster shows such as *Titanic* and *The Phantom of the Opera*.

New works are featured at **A Contemporary Theatre (ACT)**, in the renovated **Eagles Auditorium** (1416 Seventh Avenue, between Union and Pike Streets; 292.7676; www.acttheatre.org) in the **Business District**. Multicultural themes are presented at the

Langston Hughes Cultural Arts Center (104 17th Avenue S at Yesler Street; 684.4757; www.ci.seattle.wa.us/langstonhughes) and the **Northwest Asian American Theater** (409 Seventh Avenue S, between King and Jackson Streets; 340.1445; www.theatreoffjackson.org) in the **International District**.

And theatergoers with a sense of adventure should check out Seattle's abundant fringe theaters, featuring offbeat and colorful offerings. Although some productions are less successful than others, there's something for every taste, and ticket prices are much lower than at mainstream venues.

The **Annex** (728.0933; www.annextheatre.com) puts on musicals by local playwrights at various locations; **Cabaret de Paris** (1333 Fifth Avenue, in Rainier Square; 623.4111; fax 623.4114) and **Theater Schmeater** (1500 Summit Avenue between Pike and Pine Streets; 324.5801; www.schmeater.org) are famous for such delights as *Boogie Oogie Fever* and *Zombie Temps from Outer Space*. A less well-known local treasure is the **Northwest Puppet Center** (9123 15th Avenue NE, at the corner of NE 92nd Street and 15th Avenue NE; 523.2579; www.nwpuppet.org).

The **Velvet Elvis Art Lounge Theater** (107 Occidental Avenue S, between Washington Street and Yesler Way; 624.8477) in **Pioneer Square** performs wacky original works and hosts small touring productions.

Inexpensive (or even half-price) tickets at Seattle's major venues are often available on the day of the performance; check with **Ticket/Ticket** (324.2744; cash only) or **Ticketmaster** (628.0888). Smaller and fringe theaters may feature low-cost previews, rush tickets, senior discounts, free for under-18, and pay-what-you-can performances.

15 LE GOURMAND

★★★$$$ One of the city's finest French restaurants, this intimate dining spot is located in a nondescript building at the eastern edge of Ballard. Ingredients are fresh, and the menu is limited so owner-chef Bruce Naftaly's kitchen can concentrate on—and unfailingly deliver—excellence. Roast duckling with black currant sauce and sautéed rabbit with chanterelles are two examples of excellence. The menu changes twice a year. The wine list is as selective as the menu items—and just as good. ◆ French ◆ W-Sa, dinner. Reservations recommended. 425 NW Market St

(near 6th Ave NW). 784.3463. ♿. www.restaurantlegourmand.com

16 MIKE'S CHILI PARLOR

★$ This little redbrick place looks like a diner you'd see somewhere along Route 66. Mike Semandaris started out here in 1933 with a sidewalk stand, and the popular tavern is still owned by his family. The chili—beans on the side for nonpurists—is still good. The eatery was a featured location in filmmaker Bud Yorkin's 1985 movie *Twice in a Lifetime*. ◆ American ◆ M-Sa, lunch and dinner. 1447 NW Ballard Way (at 15th Ave). 782.2808

Restaurants/Clubs: Red | Hotels: Purple | Shops: Orange | Outdoors/Parks: Green | Sights/Culture: Blue

17 OLSEN'S SCANDINAVIAN FOODS

Everything from *rullepolse* (lamb sandwich meat) to *kransekake* (marzipan cake) can be found here. Anita and Reidun Endresen bought the shop from the Olsen family in 1996. After working with the Olsens for many years, the Endresens continue a line of homemade specialties, including outstanding lamb sausage, fish cakes, fish loaf, and smoked salmon. There are also imported foods, such as dry soups from Norway, Swedish peas, and cloudberries. ◆ Daily. 2248 NW Market St (between 22nd and 24th Aves). 783.8288

18 SECRET GARDEN BOOKSHOP

Named for the well-known story by Frances Hodgson Burnett, the oldest and best children's bookstore in the Seattle area carries hundreds of titles, many at bargain prices. It's also a general bookstore with a decent selection—the helpful staff is happy to place a special order for your convenience. ◆ M-W, 10AM-8PM; Sa, 10AM-6PM; Su, 1-5PM. 2214 NW Market (between 22nd and 24th Aves). 789.5006; fax 789.2816

19 BALLARD BUILDING

This four-story Second Renaissance Revival edifice—representing the only large-scale use of terra-cotta in Ballard—was erected in the early 1920s by the Fraternal Order of Eagles. Ballard's community hospital occupied the second floor from 1928 to 1954, with doctors' offices on the third floor. The second level now contains offices of the *Ballard News-Tribune*. ◆ 2208 NW Market St (between 22nd and 24th Aves)

19 LOMBARDI'S CUCINA

★$$ This place serves such honest Italian cuisine as *gamberoni di scampi* (shrimp sautéed with garlic, capers, red pepper, white wine, and lemon juice). There's a select list of good Italian wines, moderately priced, and pleasant outdoor seating in warm weather. ◆ Italian ◆ M-Sa, lunch and dinner; Su, brunch, lunch, and dinner. 2200 NW Market St (at 22nd Ave). 783.0055. ᕈ. www.lombardiscucina.com

20 LA TIENDA

★ Begun in the early 1960s by an anthropology aficionado who brought back a carload of trinkets from Tijuana, this small shop has flowered into a folk-art treasure trove. Gift-hunters can choose items from 80 countries, including Chilean rain sticks, Guatemalan ceremonial *huipils* (woven ponchos), Balinese masks, and Indonesian shadow puppets. ◆ M-Sa; Th, until 7:30PM. NE 2050 NW Market St (between 20th and 22nd Aves NW). 632.1796, 297.3605. www.latienda-folkart.com

21 MAJESTIC BAY THEATRE

Elttaes Theatres, LLC purchased the shuttered old **Bay Theatre** property in 1998 and has since done a major rebuild. Chairman Kenny Alhadeff wanted an intimate state-of-the-art theater that recalls the grace of the past but offers the innovations and luxuries that modern audiences expect. An elegant modern neon marquee invites patrons into the Majestic Bay with a signature neon treatment on the third-floor windows facing Market Street. The "Bay" letters from the old marquee were refurbished and incorporated into additional signs for the side and rear of the new building. (The corporate name is a local native word when you spell *Elttaes* backwards.) ◆ 2044 NW Market St (between 20th and 22nd Aves). 781.2229. Buy tickets on-line at www.majesticbay.com

22 CARNEGIE LIBRARY

Built in 1904 with a $15,000 grant from the Andrew Carnegie Foundation, this was the first Carnegie library in King County. (A total of 10 were eventually erected in the Seattle area.) It served bookish Ballardites for nearly 60 years, until it was replaced by a much less interesting facility in 1963. Today, it hosts a nondescript mall filled with antiques vendors and a law firm. ◆ 2026 NW Market St (between 20th and 22nd Aves)

23 THE OLD PEQULIAR ALE HOUSE

The only thing peculiar about this place is the spelling of its moniker. Before it went *veddy, veddy* British, it was known as the **Valhalla Tavern**—a tad more in keeping with Ballard's Scandinavian heritage. There is a good selection of Northwest brews on tap. ◆ Daily. 1722 NW Market St (between 17th and 20th Aves). 782.8886

24 BALLARD SMOKE SHOP

★$ It's not a smoke shop at all (although it is smoky inside) but a simple, old-fashioned restaurant (with a separate entrance to the bar) where you can still get a T-bone or top sirloin steak for under $15. Built in 1903, this is one of the last frame structures left from Ballard's early days. Remodeled in the 1920s, it is now Spanish-style white stucco with a red-tile roof. ◆ American ◆ Daily. 5443 Ballard Ave NW (between 22nd Ave and Market St). 784.6611

25 BALLARD FIREHOUSE

Built in 1908, **Firehouse No. 18** was designed by the successful Seattle architectural firm of **Bebb & Mendel**. It served Ballard for more than 60 years before

MUSIC IN THE AIR

Whether you're making a pilgrimage to the Northwest to see the birthplace of grunge, looking to tip back a few pints of local brew to the tune of Irish music, or want to make your romantic weekend getaway even more romantic, you'll find what you're looking for in one of Seattle's many nightclubs. The region's long history of rock 'n' roll is memorialized at the **Experience Music Project (EMP)**, a museum that was initially conceived by Microsoft co-founder Paul Allen to honor hometown guitar god Jimi Hendrix but has since grown to encompass much more. Since Jimi—and The Kingsmen before him—the region has spawned a number of bands with styles ranging from grunge to "emo-core." Nirvana, Mudhoney, Alice in Chains, Soundgarden, and Pearl Jam put Seattle on the map in the early '90s as the "grunge capital." Women have held their own here with riot grrl and all-female bands Sleater-Kinney, 7 Year Bitch, Bikini Kill, and Babes in Toyland. Sir Mix-a-Lot paid homage to Capitol Hill's main drag and local burger joint Dick's Drive-in his 1989 release "My Posse's on Broadway," and paved the way for other local hip-hop acts Source of Labor and Blue Scholars. The Northwest continues to produce bands that carry on the region's legacy while carving out their own niches: Modest Mouse, Death Cab for Cutie, The Blood Brothers, The Postal Service, and The Long Winters, to name a few. Pick up local free publications in the *Stranger* or *Seattle Weekly* for weekly listings of live bands, DJs, and events. It's still a good bet that on any given night at whatever club you choose, an unknown act could be the next big thing.

Crocodile Café (2200 Second Ave; 441.5611), **Chop Suey** (1325 E Madison St; 324.8000), **El Corazón** (109 Eastlake Ave E; 262.0482), and **Neumo's** (925 E Pike St; 709.9442) all book the best up-and-coming and established indie bands of the sort you might hear on local independent radio station KEXP 90.3 FM. **The Funhouse** (206 Fifth Ave N; 374.8400), **Sunset Tavern** (5433 Ballard Ave NW; 784.4880), and **Lobo Saloon** (433 Eastlake Ave E; 223.9204) are packed with patrons prone to sweaty, drunken mosh pits. **Tractor Tavern** (5213 Ballard Ave NW; 789.3599) and **Little Red Hen** (7115 Woodlawn Ave NE; 522.1168) are for those who like their music served on the country side,

while the **Jewel Box Theater** at the **Rendezvous** (2320 Second Ave; 441.5823) holds an intimate amount of people for an array of eclectic events.

Bands at **Blue Moon Tavern** (712 NE 45th St; 675.9116) cater to free thinkers and their brethren. **Kells** (1916 Post Alley; 728.1916) remains the most popular Irish pub. **Jazz Alley** (2033 Sixth Ave; 441.9729) and **Patti Summers** (94 Pike St; 621.8555) are your best bets for live jazz, while **New Orleans Café** (114 First Ave S; 622.2563) is for a Fat Tuesday kind of crowd. The irreverent nightly (except Mondays) cabaret at the **Pink Door** (1919 Post Alley; 443.3241) is free with dinner or drinks; **Triple Door** is pricey but elegant dinner theater (216 Union St; 838.4333). Whatever your taste in music, the **Showbox** (1426 First Ave; 628.3151) is the place for mid-career bands that don't quite have the same draw as the **Paramount** (911 Pine St; 467.5510 or **Moore Theater** (1932 Second Ave; 467.5510), but are well on their way.

Dance to down tempo, drum and bass, hip hop, and more at the typically crowded **Baltic Room** (1207 Pine St; 625.4444) or **Mirabeau Room** (529 Queen Anne Ave N; 217.0654). If you're of the male persuasion and prefer your dance partners to be the same, **Neighbours** (1509 Broadway; 324.5358), **R Place** (619 E Pine St; 322.8828), and **Manray** (514 E Pine St; 568.0750) are where to go to and shake your thang. Get your goth on at **Club Noc Noc** (1516 Second Ave; 223.1333) and your queer disco happening at the **Re-bar** (1114 Howell St; 233.9873). Yo Son! at **War Room** (722 E Pike St; 328.7666) on Saturday nights is *the* place for hip-hop with appearances by break-dancing troupe Circle of Fire. The Hawaiian-inspired **Lava Lounge** (2226 Second Ave; 441.5660) and sexy **Viceroy** (2332 Second Ave; 956.VICE) host guest DJs with eclectic record collections.

For karaoke, try loungey **Bush Garden** (614 Maynard Ave S; 682.6830) or seedy **Baranof** (8545 Greenwood N; 782.9260), or cap off the weekend at hipster hot spots **Bus Stop** (508 E Pine St; 322.9123) or **Twilight Exit** (2020 E Madison St; 324.7462), with karaoke every Sunday night..

being replaced in the 1970s by a new station a few blocks away. Now a hot spot on the Ballard nightclub scene, this is a big space, with lots of room for dancing to the blues, country, reggae, and rock bands that play here nightly. You can also grab lunch or dinner; the kitchen features Italian fare.
♦ Cover. Daily, until midnight.
5429 Russell Ave NW (at Market St).
784.3516

26 BALLARD CENTENNIAL BELL TOWER

Ballard City Hall, built in 1899, stood proudly on this corner for more than 60 years. The three-story structure, one of the first on Ballard Avenue, included the usual administrative warrens and a jail, community meeting rooms, and, on the top floor, a dance hall. There was also a bell tower,

Restaurants/Clubs: Red | Hotels: Purple | Shops: Orange | Outdoors/Parks: Green | Sights/Culture: Blue

whose occupant—a 1,000-pound brass noisemaker—was saved when the building was torn down in 1965 after extensive earthquake damage. Thanks to efforts by former state senator Ted Peterson, who grew up hearing the bell, it has been returned to its original site and is now housed in a copper-capped cylindrical obelisk designed by architect **Thom Graham**. ♦ 22nd and Ballard Aves NW

27 PORTLAND BUILDING

Erected in 1901, this two-story brick pile was home to various well-established businesses—**Cascade Drug** and **JCPenney** among them—before Ballard's commercial district moved to Market Street. Taverns anchored the corner storefront for 40 years until its renovation in 1985. Now, a seafood trading company, picture frame shop, and hair salon occupy the ground floor; there are studio apartments upstairs. ♦ 5403 Ballard Ave NW (at 22nd Ave)

28 JAY WHITE LAW OFFICES

This wood-frame structure is a combination of two pre-1890 houses, looking much like those that lined Ballard Avenue around 1900. In 1976, the Historic Seattle Society rescued the buildings from development in the International District and moved them to their present location. The law offices had an interesting past: A bordello reportedly occupied them in their first lives. ♦ 5341 Ballard Ave NW (between Vernon Pl and 22nd Ave)

28 GUITAR EMPORIUM

Owner Robb Eagle's merchandise ranges from fine, inexpensive imported instruments to handmade acoustic masterpieces. He'll also recommend instructors—and offer encouragement—to would-be Segovias. ♦ Tu-Sa. 5349 Ballard Ave NW (at 22nd Ave). 783.7607. www.guitaremporium.com

29 C.D. STIMSON COMPANY

Charles D. Stimson, the one-armed scion of a wealthy Michigan lumber family, arrived in Seattle just in time to help fight the Great Fire of 1889. When the nascent milling industry moved from what's now Pioneer Square north to Lake Union and Ballard, Stimson went with it and founded the huge Stimson Mill Company. This surprisingly modest single-story dark brick building was designed in 1913 in a modern English style by noted Spokane architect **Kirtland K. Cutter** (who also created the **Rainier Club** in downtown). It still houses the Stimson offices, although that company is no longer in the lumber business. The combination of declining markets and escalating tariffs sent Ballard's shinglemaking industry into a tailspin in the early 20th century and eventually forced the mill to close. The Stimson operation now leases commercial real estate in the Seattle metropolitan area and operates a pleasure-boat marina on Salmon Bay. ♦ 2116 NW Vernon Pl (at Shilshole Ave)

30 HATTIE'S HAT

★★$ The staff is a hoot, and this Ballard diner has earned its reputation for stiff drinks and good pub grub. **Hattie's** menu reads like a diner bible—lots of fryin' and lots of griddlin'. The fried chicken, soaked in buttermilk before frying, then drenched in country gravy after, is terrific, as is the Hat Burger. Weekend brunch attracts the hungry and hung-over for standard breakfast fare: cheesy eggs, griddle pancakes, thick-sliced bacon, and homemade shredded hash browns. Check out the amazing sweet-potato fries. ♦ American ♦ Daily; open late. 5231 Ballard Ave NW (at NW Vernon Pl). 784.0175. ♿ www.hattieshat.com

31 THE JUNCTION BLOCK

Built in the late 1890s, this was once a three-story structure (now it's two), complete with elaborate turret, and one of the largest brick buildings on Ballard Avenue. It was a gathering place for locals, who held meetings and dances here. Today, the edifice is home to a community arts center that offers classes in printmaking, painting, and watercolor. ♦ 5202-10 Ballard Ave NW (at 20th Ave)

32 CORS AND WEGENER BUILDING

Once the grandest edifice in town, it had an elegant wine room on the ground floor in the 1890s and early 1900s, and the *Ballard News* occupied the second floor for years. One of the first of the city's old buildings to be renovated, it now has apartments on the top floor and offices on the street level. ♦ 5000-04 20th Ave NW (at Ballard Ave)

32 BALLARD AVENUE

Named a Historic Landmark District in 1976, this seven-block stretch—slanting southeast from Market Street—represents the heart, if not also the soul, of Ballard. It contains many of the community's oldest buildings (and newest businesses). The majority went up between 1890 and 1930: brick, stone, and stucco constructions of no more than two or three stories in height. Thanks to a shift of commercial development north to Market Street in the 1930s, these buildings were still sitting here, just waiting to be revitalized, in the 1970s. Pick up a "Historic Ballard Avenue Walking Tour" brochure, available from most avenue merchants. The **Ballard Historical Society** (706.9236; www.ballardhistory.org) also conducts guided excursions, sometimes with docents in 1890s attire; call for schedules and reservations. Donation requested

32 CONOR BYRNE'S PUBLIC HOUSE

This traditional Irish pub features the requisite dark-wood bar, stained-glass lamps, and brick walls. It is proud to offer 15 beers on tap, including imports and micros that span all tastes, from lager to stout. The Northwest is well represented, and there's a fine selection from England and Ireland. The house special, a 20-ounce pint of Guinness, is deemed by all the experts to be truly spectacular. There is live music four nights a week beginning at 9PM and an open mike one night a week beginning at 8PM. ♦ Cover. Daily, until 2AM. 5140 Ballard Ave NW (between Ione Pl and 20th Ave). 784.3640. www.conorbyrnepub.com

33 THE TRACTOR

This is the central gathering place for Seattle's alternative-country scene, as well as a venue for all kinds of roots, folk, and traditional musical styles, from acoustic singer-songwriters to rockabilly rave-ups to Cajun-flavored zydeco to traditional Irish music. There's nothing slick or trendy about this place; tractor-related items and other rural paraphernalia hanging from the walls make sure of that. Live shows 5 to 7 nights a week. **The Tractor** purveys a fine assortment of liquor, beer and wine, and good BBQ, plus a wide variety of local microbrews, as well as lots of nonalcoholic beverages. The bar opens and food service begins at 6PM. ♦ Cover. 5213 Ballard Ave NW (between 20th Ave NW and NW Vernon Pl). 789.3599. ♿. www.tractortavern.com

34 SALMON BAY CAFE

★$ Hearty breakfasts draw a devoted clientele every morning and a lined-up-out-the-door crowd on weekends. Among the many egg dishes, the Ballard omelette—with bacon, cream cheese, green onion, and tomato—and the crab, shrimp, and green onion omelette topped with hollandaise stand out. You can also get eggs with steak or with Polish or Italian sausage. A side order of the huge french fries makes a satisfying meal in itself. ♦American ♦Daily, breakfast and lunch. 5109 Shilshole Ave NW (at 20th Ave). 782.5539. ♿

35 ST. CHARLES HOTEL

When it was built in 1902, this place, with its projecting bays and 100 feet of building frontage, was an imposing presence in early Ballard. Now painted an appalling lavender, the building is home to Ballard Mini Storage. ♦ 4714 Ballard Ave NW (between Ballard Way and 48th St)

FREMONT/WALLINGFORD

The two neighborhoods to the north of **Lake Union** were once suburban, but to-day Fremont and Wallingford are about as citified as they can get without actu-ally having high-rises in their midst. In fact, Fremont is home to one of the city's most popular public works of art, *Waiting for the Interurban*, a sculpture reflecting that ultimate urban experience—public transportation. Both areas are filled with funky shops, friendly taverns, and inexpensive restaurants and teem with traffic. (In a tizzy over parking congestion caused by Wallingford's popularity, residents have won restrictions that make it near impossible to park within a quarter-mile of a given destination on a Friday or Saturday night.)

Fremont was originally a mill town, plotted first as the **Denny-Hoyt Addition** in 1888, where sawmills operated until 1932. Wallingford was stitched together from the rural communities of **Latona** and **Edgewater**—an area that once supported dairies, a furrier, and a candy store that made Easter eggs to order. In 1907, the Seattle Gas Com-pany plant opened on Lake Union and transformed Wallingford into a working-class district showered with sparks and soot from the burning of coal. The gasworks shut down in 1956 and 25 years later was transformed into the high-tech **Gas Works Park**.

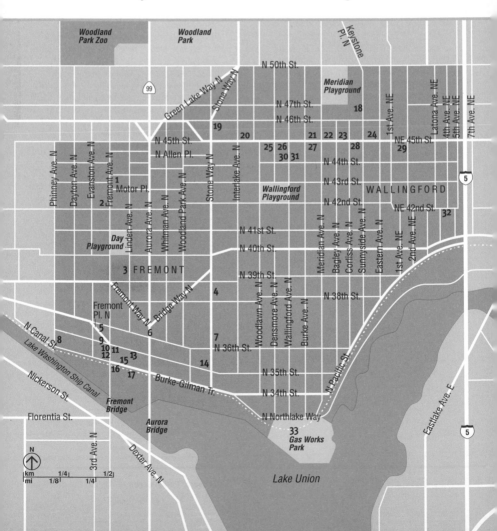

Today both neighborhoods come across as confident and cool, with a long history of protest and civic activism, although Fremont is by far the more radical of the two. In the late 1970s, Fremont declared itself one of the city's earliest nuclear-free zones—no nuclear waste or power plants here. More recently, on 18 June 1994, it also "seceded" from Seattle, Washington State, and the rest of the country, calling itself the Republic of Fremont Center of the Known Universe. Wallingford, which plays the civil, quiet sibling to the rebellious republic, has defended itself successfully against urban blight and low-flying seaplanes, in addition to blocking the assembly of an enormous set of golden arches on the local **McDonald's**. It's clear that both districts have a strong sense of their own identities and are determined to protect themselves from the ravages of unnecessary progress.

FREMONT

1 SWINGSIDE CAFE

★★$ The small, divided, and low-ceilinged dining room, fielded with baseball paraphernalia, is best enjoyed with one close friend (who isn't averse to shouting or repeating sentences several times to be heard above the din). Lunch features barbecued chicken and sandwiches. Dinners focus on traditional pastas and dishes with unpredictable North African, Creole, and nouvelle-American accents. The *Seattle Weekly* recently wrote that the Louisiana gumbo here "positively sings with Northwest seafood treasures." Expect a line at the door, but the wait is worth it. ◆ Mediterranean ◆ Tu-F, lunch and dinner; Sa, dinner. No reservations for fewer than six. 4262 Fremont Ave N (between Motor Pl and 43rd St). 633.4057. &

2 BUCKAROO TAVERN

Most of the motorcycles have disappeared from out front, and there are more young white-collar businesspeople in the crowd, but the "Fabulous Buckaroo" has hardly lapsed into respectability. Billiard balls still crack against one another, and voices still rise in cursing contraltos. It is still possible to disappear here, to sink your elbows into the bar and drink beer for hours without anyone disturbing you. Founded in 1938, the establishment has so far warded off the forces of civil gentrification that prey so merrily on Fremont. The food—burgers, thick potato wedges, steaming bowls of chili with cheddar and onions—hasn't yet become cuisine. Hot dogs go for 25 cents apiece on Monday nights from 6PM until they run out. Twenty-nine tap beers, most of them microbrews, can be had too. ◆ Daily, until 2AM. No credit cards accepted. 4201 Fremont Ave N (at 42nd St). 634.3161. www.buckarootavern.com

3 B.F. DAY ELEMENTARY SCHOOL

Although other classic Seattle schools have been torn down or closed, this brick structure was restored to return to the grandeur it enjoyed at its 1892 dedication. Designed by **John Parkinson**, this is the city's oldest school in continuous operation. Its history predates the building: Classes were held in private homes for some years before this edifice was built. ◆ 3921 Linden Ave N (between 39th and 41st Sts)

FUSION BEADS

4 FUSION BEADS

Everything imaginable for hand beading is here: Swararovski crystal beads, pearls, seed beads, cubic Zirconia, silver and sterling silver, charms, plus findings in gold, silver, and brass. The shop offers beading classes and special events. Check out their exceptionally well-detailed web site. ♦ 3830 Stone Way N (between N 38th and N 39th Sts). 782.4595. www.fusionbeads.com

5 DELUXE JUNK

A stock of mid-20th-century clothing (which rotates seasonally), furniture, housewares, and stacks of kitschy doodads are all on display in a onetime funeral parlor. ♦ Daily. 3518 Fremont Pl N (between 35th and 36th Sts). 634.2733

6 AURORA BRIDGE

Nobody uses its proper name—**George Washington Memorial Bridge**—and most don't even know it. (The bridge's 1932 dedication to the first US president can be found only on a plaque at its south end, not on regular city maps.) And sometimes this span is referred to as Suicide Bridge because of the number of people (an average of three per year) who leap from its 135-foot height into Lake Union below. The sidewalk across is narrow; walk at your own risk and never on rainy days, when taking a bath in your clothes would leave you less soaked than the speeding traffic does.

Beneath the Aurora Bridge:

FREMONT TROLL

Come face-to-face with a Brothers Grimm nightmare: the crook-nosed, long-haired, malevolent-looking troll that hides beneath the north end of the **Aurora Bridge** (waiting for the three Billy Goats Gruff?). Constructed in 1990 of ferroconcrete, with a real Volkswagen Bug squeezed in its left hand, the 18-foot-high sculpture was a whimsical community project from the Fremont Arts Council, built with money from the Seattle Neighborhood Matching Funds Program. Adults and children seem equally ready to climb all over it. ♦ N 36th St (between Whitman and Linden Aves)

7 STONEWAY CAFE

★$ Don't expect any "heart smart" entrées at this restaurant. Do, however, anticipate outstanding plates of biscuits and gravy or corned-beef hash, not to mention weighty, onion-slathered hamburgers and omelettes stuffed shamelessly with meats and cheeses. Owner Charlene Iverson usually has a few healthful soups cooking (don't miss the vegetable and navy-bean varieties), and there are always muffins on hand. Expect to wait in line on weekends. ♦ American ♦ Daily, breakfast and lunch. No credit cards accepted. 3620 Stone Way N (between 36th and 38th Sts). 547.9958

8 REDHOOK ALE BREWERY

Seattle's first microbrewery has an unusual setting: Fremont's 1905 Seattle Electric Company streetcar barn. Trolleys used to roll out of this building on their various routes, but when the city converted to trackless trolleys in 1940, the barn went first to the US Army for use as a wartime warehouse and later to a garbage company. Paul Shipman and Gordon Bowker, owners of the Redhook beer company, ultimately bought the barn and commissioned architect **Skip Satterwhite** to turn it into a brewery, which opened in 1988. ♦ Fee. One-hour tours daily, 1-5PM. 3400 Phinney Ave N (at 34th St). 548.8000

9 TRIANGLE LOUNGE

★★$ This longtime establishment, which used to be a classic tavern (called the **Classic**) before it was the **Triangle Tavern**, has been transformed into a lounge—more sophisticated, somewhat more elegant, but with a funky edge you'd expect in this neighborhood. There's lots of bar-style grub on the menu, including fresh fish, spinach lasagna, and a Middle Eastern plate. There are many regional beers on tap, plus a full bar. ♦ American ♦ Restaurant: daily, lunch and dinner; bar: until 2AM. 3507 Fremont Pl N (between 35th St and Evanston Ave). 632.0880

10 FREMONT ANTIQUE MALL

The entrance is at street level, but the goods—collectible toys and appliances, along with some larger antique furniture—are in the basement of this mall, built in 1901. Take a nostalgic browse. ♦ Daily. 3419 Fremont Pl N (between Fremont Ave and 35th St). 548.9140

10 SIMPLY DESSERTS

Some of the baked delights you've enjoyed at several of the more upscale movie theaters around town can now be savored with a cup of espresso from this dinky outlet

Seattle gets 16 hours of daylight in summer, but only 9 in winter.

IT'S ABOUT TIME

Seattle is laid back by reputation, a major city with the easygoing attitude of a small town. Its residents are hardly clock watchers, and many people visit (for short and long stays alike) precisely because the city is so free of the stress and pressures of other large metropolises. So why are there so many street clocks here? Seattle proper boasts 13 of them—more than any other city in the country. These cast-iron timepieces weigh an average of 1 ton apiece, and some of them are as tall as 20 feet. People bump into them, lean against them to tie their shoes, use them as handy meeting spots, and sometimes even check their watches by them.

Originally these clocks were to jewelers what red-and-white-striped poles were to barbershops. Most of them were made by **Mayer and Co.**, whose factory was on **Dexter Avenue N**. They became popular in 1913, when **Carroll's Fine Jewelry** set one up on the sidewalk outside its shop on **Fourth Avenue** (where it still stands today). Other jewelers followed suit, and eventually shopping plazas, bookstores, and restaurants got into the act as well.

Though Seattleites are now passionately fond of their street clocks, they have not always felt that way. In 1953, convinced that the 28 clocks in the downtown area were a nuisance and a public hazard, the Board of Public Works proposed a measure to abolish them. Clock lovers and historians fought back, and finally a compromise was reached: The clocks could remain, provided they were kept to the proper time. The task of checking the clocks' time each morning fell to the jewelers, who were less than

pleased with this new responsibility. Many of the clocks ended up being moved to the backyards of private homes or banished to scrap heaps. Their number dwindled to 11 by 1980, when the city council suddenly woke up to the historical value of the clocks and began the process of registering them as official landmarks. Ten of them eventually were so designated, and in the ensuing years two new ones were built and a third was moved to downtown Seattle from the nearby suburb of **Kirkland**.

The designs range from whimsical to kitschy to elegant. The **Hickory Dickory Clock** in front of **1201 Third Avenue** (at Seneca Street) has two small mice running up a column that leans crazily to one side. The modern clock that stands in front of **Jay Jacobs** (1530 Fifth Avenue, at Pine Street) looks as if its face is being yanked around by the giant crescent wrench that makes up its column. The clock on the northeast corner of Dexter Avenue N and Harrison Street, near **Seattle Center**, is painted a rather garish red, and the clock in front of Carroll's Fine Jewelry (1427 Fourth Avenue, at Pike Street) sports lamp fixtures that look like antlers.

Other noteworthy timepieces in the downtown area are at **Ben Bridge Jewelers** (Fourth Avenue and Pike Street) and the **Century Square Building** (1529 Fourth Avenue, between Pike and Pine Streets). In **Pioneer Square**, there are clocks at **F.X. McRory's** (419 Occidental Avenue S, at King Street) and the **Elliott Bay Book Company** (101 S Main Street, at First Avenue). Other examples in the area include clocks outside **Colette's Vintage Time Shoppe** (129 N 85th Street, between Greenwood Avenue N and First Avenue NW), the **Lake Union Cafe** (3119 Eastlake Avenue E, between Allison Street and Fuhrman Avenue), and **Menashe & Sons Jewelers** (4532 California Avenue SW, between Alaska and Oregon Streets).

store. The white-chocolate strawberry cake is outstanding. ◆ Daily; F, Sa, until 11:30PM. 3421 Fremont Ave N (between 34th and 35th Sts). 633.2671

10 FREMONT PLACE BOOK COMPANY

For a small shop, this general bookstore carries a lot of feminist and ecological titles, as well as a good selection of regional literature. ◆ Daily. 621 N 35th St (at Fremont Pl). 547.5970. &.
www.fremontplacebooks.com

11 FRANK AND DUNYA

Here's the place to shop for colorful and sometimes outrageous home furnishings and accessories made by local artists. Canines are popular motifs in the statuary, jewelry, and hangings, but so are other members of the wild kingdom—a two-legged drinking cup painted like a cow, or a huge green frog perfect for mounting on your

Restaurants/Clubs: Red | Hotels: Purple | Shops: Orange | Outdoors/Parks: Green | Sights/Culture: Blue

dining room wall. ♦ Daily. 3418 Fremont Ave N (between 34th and 35th Sts). 547.6760

11 THE 35TH STREET BISTRO

★$ This unpretentious coffeehouse once epitomized the hippie attitude of Fremont. Well, the 1960s may be long gone, but this anachronism continues to serve some of the better café grub in town: Pasta specials are usually terrific, soups are chunky, and sandwiches are thick and savory. The sidewalk seating is pleasant—much better than enduring the interior stagnation in summer. And it's a quiet spot for coffee drinking. ♦ Vegetarian ♦ Daily, breakfast, lunch, and dinner. 709 N 35th St (between Aurora and Fremont Aves). 547.9850. ♿ www.335bistro.com

12 RED DOOR ALE HOUSE

One of several upscale groggeries in Fremont, this is the neighborhood's best-known and most crowded after-work hangout. (Don't even *try* to get in on a Friday night.) The least claustrophobic seating can be found on a small back deck. Inside, try for a bar seat—no easy task. Eighteen beers are on tap, and there's a small menu, which is strongest on steamed mussels, burgers, and french fries. ♦ Daily, until 2AM. 3401 Fremont Ave N (at 34th St). 547.7521. ♿

12 FREMONT SUNDAY MARKET

On Sunday, a parking lot behind the **Red Door Ale House** fills up with vendors of jewelry, pottery, produce, and hot dogs. In classically lowbrow Fremont fashion, there are also people here selling recycled castoffs—old radios and books, used videotapes, clothes, shoes, and lamps. Musicians provide entertainment, as do the shoppers themselves, a cross section of hippie holdouts and slumming stockbrokers. ♦ Su, May-Dec. 670 N 34th St (between Fremont and Evanston Aves)

At 1.4 miles long, Evergreen Point Floating Bridge is the longest floating bridge in the world.

13 FREMONT PUBLIC LIBRARY

This was the last of 10 Carnegie-financed libraries raised in the Seattle area during the early 20th century. Money for construction—$35,000—had been promised from the Carnegie Corporation in 1917, but work didn't get under way until after World War I, and the library didn't open until 1921. **Daniel R. Huntington**, for many years Seattle's city architect, designed this excellent neighborhood library in an echo of California Mission style. ♦ M-Sa. 731 N 35th St (between Aurora and Fremont Aves). 684.4084

14 PACIFIC INN

Although this pub is pocket size, it has disproportionately large windows; it also serves assertively spiced fish and chips. Wash it down with one of the 10 microbrews on tap; espresso drinks are served as well. ♦ Daily, until 2AM. 3501 Stone Way N (at 35th St). 547.2967. ♿

15 FRITZI RITZ

A Marlene Dietrich fantasy of a vintage store where you'll find feather boas and sequinned dresses on display. Well-preserved wing-tip shoes and fedoras wait for Fred Astaire to waltz through the door. ♦ Daily. 750N 34th St (between Aurora and Fremont Aves N). 633.0929

16 *WAITING FOR THE INTERURBAN*

The first work created by local artist Richard Beyer, this sculpture portrays a motley clutch of people awaiting a bus or train. Installed in 1978, the popular cast-aluminum tableau is decorated appreciatively through the seasons, making it one of the most interactive pieces of art in the country. Beyer, who has lived in Seattle since 1957, is also responsible for other works around town, including the wooden *Sasquatch* at **Pike Place Market**; *The Itinerant*, which portrays a newspaper-draped man sleeping on a bench in Capitol Hill's Broadway district; and the *Kingstones*, a takeoff on the cartoon Flintstone family, with a mom, dad, and kids sitting around the television set in front of the **KING-TV** studios on Dexter Avenue N. ♦ Fremont Ave N and 34th St

17 ADOBE SYSTEMS

In 1998 Adobe Systems, a software developer, moved into a 20-acre site along the Lake Washington Ship Canal, beside the Aurora bridge and in the heart of alternative downtown Fremont. The architecture is unobtrusive and this airy, park-like setting includes a lovely wide stairway down to the Burke-Gilman bicycle trail (see page 178),

THE BEST

Craig R. Jonov, DMD, MD
Facial Surgery Center of Seattle

The international flavor of this city, with all the different cultures and traditions that people bring to Seattle. Every day you can hear a different perspective, taste a new flavor, or hear music like you've never heard before.

Yet there is still a small-town feel in quaint neighborhoods like **Belltown, West Seattle, Queen**

Anne, **Greenlake, Ravenna**, and **University District**, to name a few. Each neighborhood has created its own community where people gather to shop, eat, and talk.

The variety of sports is phenomenal, from the major sports teams to sailing, skiing, bicycling, soccer, Ultimate Frisbee, dodge ball . . .

The pure beauty that we all share. We have the best of all worlds with the mountains, the sound, lakes, ocean, and islands. Why would you want to be anywhere else?

---

as well as plantings and seating along the trail beside the canal. The design opens up the area to walkers and increases public access from Fremont down to the canal and under the **Aurora Bridge**. ♦ 801 N 34th St (between Aurora Ave and Fremont Bridge)

WALLINGFORD

18 GOOD SHEPHERD CENTER

Built in 1906 from a plan by architect **C. Alfred Breitung** (who designed other Seattle edifices such as the **Triangle Hotel Building** in the International District), this was originally a Catholic convent and residence for unwed mothers called the **Home of the Good Shepherd**. In more recent years, it has become something of a political football, fought over by historic restoration forces and Wallingforders, who can't agree on its appropriate use. Presently, Greenpeace, private art and elementary schools, and the Seattle Tilth Association all occupy some portion of the building and grounds. The grounds and the Tilth gardens are a good place for a stroll. ♦ 4649 Sunnyside Ave N (between 46th and 50th Sts). 547.8127

19 BIZZARRO ITALIAN CAFE

★★$$ With its funky, outrageous, and frequently changed décor (brightly painted cellos, a grand piano hanging from the ceiling, a dinosaur motif, and surprising food combinations, this neighborhood café offers a truly unusual dining experience at a reasonable price. Included among the more creative entrées are risotto specials, chicken piccata, prosciutto and squash served with walnut–marsala cream, and "sordid" (a pun on *assorted*) marinated vegetables. There's sometimes a wait, but take the trouble anyway. ♦ Italian ♦ Daily, dinner. Reservations accepted. 1307 N 46th St (between Interlake Ave and Stone Way). 632.7277. ♿

20 MUSASHI'S

★$ This place has lots of fans, and they may all be trying to get one of the few tables on the night you visit. (Luckily, takeout is available.) A wide variety of excellent sushi is offered, and there are a few other choices— try the teriyaki chicken. *Bento* box meals, including rice, a crab cake, sashimi, and a teriyaki chicken skewer, are available at lunchtime. Cooks tend to throw extra items in for regular customers. ♦ Japanese/takeout ♦ Tu-F, lunch and dinner; Sa, dinner. 1400 N 45th St (at Interlake Ave). 633.0212

21 TWEEDY & POPP/ACE HARDWARE

Very organized, very well stocked, and very old-fashioned, this is the sort of small store your parents knew as kids. ♦ Daily. 1916 N 45th St (between Meridian and Burke Aves). 632.2290

21 MURPHY'S PUB

This Irish pub has a façade with Old World charm and dark furnishings that give the interior the almost reverential atmosphere common to so many historical taverns. Fifteen tap beers (primarily substantive microbrews and imports) and a trio of alcoholic ciders are on hand, accompanied by a limited menu that makes its biggest splashes with the enormous nacho platter and the cider stew. There are the requisite dartboards to one side of the bar. Wednesdays are open-mike entertainment nights; live Irish music is played (usually too loudly) on Fridays and Saturdays. ♦ Cover. Daily, until 2AM. 1928 N 45th St (at Meridian Ave). 634.2110. ♿ www.murphyseattle.com

---

Restaurants/Clubs: Red | Hotels: Purple | Shops: Orange | Outdoors/Parks: Green | Sights/Culture: Blue

THE BEST

Phillip Levine

Sculptor

Seattle and Washington were among the initiators of public funding for the arts, and there is a lot of it to be seen around the city. The private sector was prodded into commissioning and buying sculpture, painting, and other art forms.

The **Frye** has a permanent collection along with changing exhibits, often focusing on Northwest artists.

The **Nordic Heritage** in Ballard has a permanent historical collection with ongoing exhibits by Scandinavian and local artists.

The **Wing Luke Museum** features changing exhibits of Asian art and history.

And you can look at the sculpture to be found at most Seattle and King County libraries.

The Best: Phillip Levine

The Wing Luke Museum, the Nordic Heritage Museum, and the **Seattle Art Museum (SAM)** have or will have new buildings in the immediate future. The new SAM waterfront sculpture garden opened in January 2007.

The **4Art Galleries** of the Public Art Program has its own gallery space, and there are many new galleries in and around the Pioneer Square section of town.

22 STARBUCKS

★$ Local resentment ran high when this ubiquitous chain took over the old premises of **Murphy's Pub**. People worried about the coffeehouse's close commercial proximity to the much-loved **Boulangerie** bakery. But, so far, this venue—large, compared with some of its brethren around town—has had no negative effects on the neighborhood. In fact, it's a pleasant hangout before and after films at the **Guild 45th Movie Theater** across the street. ♦ Coffeehouse ♦ Daily; F, Sa, until 11PM. 2110 N 45th St (between Bagley and Meridian Aves). 548.9507. &. Also at numerous locations throughout the city

23 BOULANGERIE

Repeatedly chosen by Seattleites as their favorite bakery, this place specializes in crusty baguettes and other French loaves, as well as such memorable sweets as the Tarte Normande, made of Granny Smith apple slices arranged within a nutty pastry. It's also a very popular take-out coffee and pastry stop. Try the *pain au chocolat* (croissant filled with chocolate). ♦ Daily. 2200 N 45th St (at Bagley Ave). 634.2211

OPEN BOOKS:
A Poem Emporium

24 OPEN BOOKS

One of only two bookstores in the US dedicated strictly to poetry (the other is in Boston), this "poem emporium" features an extensive collection of new, used, and out-of-print poetry and texts on poetic theory in a clean, bright, orderly space. ♦ Tu-Th, Sa; F, 11AM-8PM. 2414 N 45th St (between Eastern and Sunnyside Aves). 633.0811. &. www.openpoetrybooks.com

25 FIREHOUSE NO. 11

Erected in 1913, this building is surprisingly unimposing, even given its tower (where they dry out the hoses), which was long ago blocked on the skyline behind taller structures. Architect **Daniel R. Huntington** covered the building with cedar shakes, shutters, and trellises surrounding the accordion-style doors through which horse-drawn fire wagons once charged. The design was meant to blend in with Wallingford's growing predominance of bungalow homes. At one time both police and firefighters occupied this building, but since 1984 it has been home to a community health clinic. The Wallingford-Wilmot branch of the **Seattle Public Library** shares part of the ground floor as well. ♦ Densmore Ave N and 45th St

26 GUADALAJARA

★$ This unassuming Mexican outpost can be easily (and unjustly) overlooked amid the proliferation of chic restaurants. Although service can be curt, the kitchen turns out fine and filling burritos and enchiladas. The tacos are so-so, but the Guadalajara nachos (chicken or beef), topped with guacamole and sour cream, are excellent. A chunky salsa of veggies marinated in pepper juice is some of the hottest around. And the bartenders usually have a heavy hand on the tequila bottle when mixing margaritas. ♦ Mexican

Sam Spade may be San Francisco's most famous fictional private eye, but he got his start elsewhere. In Dashiell Hammett's renowned novel *The Maltese Falcon*, Spade explains that in 1927 "I was with one of the big detective agencies in Seattle."

QUITE A ROAD SHOW: THE CAMPY FLAIR OF AURORA AVENUE

Aurora Avenue **(Route 99)** used to be the main north-south highway running through Seattle. Today, it's a comparatively minor thoroughfare. At the city's heart, Route 99 is an elevated highway (the **Alaskan Way Viaduct**) running along the **Waterfront**; south of the city, it's known as **Pacific Highway**. But north of Seattle, rolling out into the suburban hinterlands of **Lynnwood**, now, that's a different kettle of kitsch. There, this road becomes the car culture equivalent of a Marrakech bazaar, bordered by blinding neon, strip malls and strip joints, questionable motels, taverns, used-car lots, and assorted other businesses—alternately cheerful and new or grim and shopworn, but always unique. Aurora Avenue's style evokes three essential aspects of American life: fast cars, quick bucks, and a high tolerance for personal weirdness.

"Aurora is the homely and affordable face of American capitalism" writes Jonathan Raban, a British author expatriated to Seattle. "Driving Aurora is like riffling at speed through the text of an eccentric illustrated encyclopedia. The entries rush past too rapidly to follow, and they couple promiscuously with each other: Something about pest control gets tangled up with something about foam rubber and chiroprac- tors and The Love Pantry."

For example, the **Twin Teepees**

Restaurant is a loony tribute to Native American culture. Built in 1937, it cheerfully mixes Northwest Coast and Plains Indian clichés with no particular regard for accuracy; a case in point are the paintings that flank the entrance to the "teepees"—they look like bears (or is it whales?).

Another classic is an extremely ratty-looking life-size elephant that advertises the **Aurora Flower Shop** (8808 Aurora Ave N, between 88th and 90th Sts). It was also built during the Depression, as were so many of these highway come-ons. Legend has it that a florist who once owned this shop kept the paunchy proboscidean in his backyard for years before hoisting it onto a pole above busy Route 99. **Seal's Motel** (12035 Aurora Ave N, between 109th and 125th Sts) displays a seal balancing a ball on its nose.

And all along the way the signs reel by, each more outlandish than the last until you reach some true showstopppers such as "Do bugs, not drugs," which promotes an exterminator.

Patti Kahler / North Market Street Graphics

♦ M-Sa, lunch and dinner; Su, dinner. 1715 N 45th St (between Wallingford and Densmore Aves). 632.7858. ♿

27 BOTTLEWORKS

Walking into this dimly lit shop, you get the sneaking suspicion that you are surrounded by "beer nerds." It's dim—because they are experts and store their beer properly, at the proper lighting and temperature, so you receive the flavor the brewers want you to taste. Opened in 1999 by owner Matt

Vandenburgue, there are now over 600 beers in this little shop, specializing in Northwest micros and Belgian beers. You can also find a good selection of Northwest barley wines. The staff is disturbingly knowledgeable and can also recommend one of their fresh, imported Belgian chocolates from their chilled case, which they import weekly. Try some De Dolle ("the mad brewers") with a Manon Café truffle. Weekly tastings; call for info. ♦ Daily. 1710 N 45th St, suite 3 (between Wallingford and Densmore Aves). 633.2437. www.bottleworks.com

Restaurants/Clubs: Red | Hotels: Purple | Shops: Orange | Outdoors/Parks: Green | Sights/Culture: Blue

27 TEAHOUSE KUAN YIN

★$ Running distinctly against the grain in a coffee-lover's town is this quiet teahouse owned by Jim Labe, who traveled throughout Asia tasting teas before selecting the blacks, oolongs, and greens served here. Quiche, pot stickers, and other light edibles provide nice supplements to the tea. An educated staff is always willing to explain the characteristics of the different teas. ◆ Teahouse ◆ Daily. 1911 N 45th St (between Meridian and Burke Aves). 632.2055. www.teahousechoice.com

28 KABUL

★★$$ Chef Wali Khairzada has introduced the rich pleasures of Afghan cuisine into Wallingford's culinary melting pot. Kebabs are a good introduction, especially the tender fillets of chicken marinated in turmeric, garlic, and cayenne. A hands-down favorite is the *qorma-i tarkari* (fresh vegetables and lamb tossed with dill, saffron, turmeric, and cumin). The *ashak* (flat dumplings stuffed with scallions, leeks, and cilantro and covered in a sauce of yogurt, garlic, and ground beef) is also popular. For an appetizer, try the *burta* (crushed eggplant blended with yogurt, sour cream, garlic, cilantro, and mint); it's served with a somewhat dry but satisfying lavash bread. The room is filled with small tables and pleasant sconce lighting. Service is friendly and efficient. ◆ Afghan ◆ Daily, dinner. 2301 N 45th St (at Corliss Ave). 545.9000. www.kabulrestaurant.com

28 EROTIC BAKERY

As you might expect, this bakery specializes in creating party cakes designed to look like male or female sex organs. It's all done with good humor and not really as ribald as it sounds. ◆ Daily. 2323 N 45th St (at Sunnyside Ave). 545.6969. ⅍. www.theeroticbakery.com

On 7 July 1946, the Roman Catholic church declared Mother Frances Xavier Cabrini (1850–1917), founder of Cabrini Hospital in Seattle, a saint. She was the first American to be declared a saint by the Roman Catholic Church.

29 DICK'S DRIVE-IN

★$ The long, pencil-thin fries here are best consumed from the grease-spotted bag in great gangly handfuls. Complete your feast with a thick chocolate milk shake. You might be able to find better fast food in this town, but there are few more interesting human-study environments than the parking lot here. The scene is especially entertaining just before closing time on Friday and Saturday nights. ◆ Fast food ◆ Daily, lunch and dinner until 2AM. 111 NE 45th St (between Second and First Aves). 632.5125. Also at 115 Broadway E (between E Denny Way and E John St). 323.1300; 9208 Holman Rd NW (between 92nd St and 12th Ave). 783.5233. www.ddir.com

30 WIDE WORLD BOOKS & MAPS

Here are shelf upon shelf of guidebooks and travel literature, plus staff members who have probably already been where you want to go and can help you make the most of your visit. The shop also features maps, some luggage, and a passport-photo service. ◆ Daily. 4411A Wallingford Ave N (between 44th and 45th Sts). 634.3453. ⅍. www.travelbooksandmaps.com

31 WALLINGFORD CENTER

There were plans in the 1950s to condemn or relocate this three-story, neoclassical wooden behemoth that was then the **Interlake Public School**. The neighborhood's population of children was in decline, and business leaders argued that soon there would simply not be enough of them left to justify continued operation. It was finally closed in 1981, but before commercial interests could even aim a

CHILD'S PLAY

After the requisite trip on the **Monorail**, what's a parent to do on those restless-kid days? Here are 10 tips for keeping them entertained:

1. Visit the **Tropical Rain Forest** at the **Woodland Park Zoo** and check out the poison-dart frogs.
2. Prick up your ears for Saturday-morning story time at the **Elliott Bay Book Company**.
3. Rent a paddleboat and churn up the waters of **Green Lake**.
4. Climb into a space capsule at the **Pacific Science Center**.
5. Walk under the sea at the **Seattle Aquarium**.
6. Attend a performance of the **Seattle Children's Theater**.
7. Take a guided nature walk with the park rangers at **Discovery Park**.
8. Build a miniature sailboat at the **Center for Wooden Boats**.
9. Browse among the shrunken heads (and peek at Sylvester the Mummy) at **Ye Olde Curiosity Shop**.
10. Check out the model ships at the **Museum of History and Industry**.

wrecking ball at the building, preservationists joined forces with community officials to gentrify the structure. The edifice became a warren of stores and restaurants. Outside, on the corner of N 45th Street and Wallingford Avenue, look for *Wallingford Animal Storm*, a 1984 bronze and aluminum totem created by local resident Ronald W. Petty. A tribute to local wildlife, the installation features raccoons, Canada geese, cats, pigeons, and even slugs. ◆ 4400 Wallingford Ave N (at 44th St). 632.2781

Within the Wallingford Center:

CRACKERJACK

This craft store offers a wide diversity of contemporary items—ceramics, dolls, jewelry, creations made of fiber, glass, leather, and wood, as well as Tintin comic books from Belgium and work by more than 250 artists from the Northwest and around the country. ◆ Daily. Main level. 547.4983. &. www.crackerjackcrafts.com

ZANADIA

ZANADIA

Among the many nicely designed accessories for the kitchen and home are a wide array of glassware and some intriguing candlesticks. ◆ M-F, 10AM-8PM; Sa,

10AM-6PM; Su, 11AM-5PM. Second level. 547.0884. &. www.zanadia.com

32 LATONA ELEMENTARY SCHOOL

You may see this great wooden building from I-5, just south of the NE 45th Street overpass. If you have a chance, get closer for a better view. Dating back to 1906, this is the only one of architect **James Stephen**'s many Seattle schools to feature Queen Anne-style towers. ◆ 401 NE 42nd St (at Fourth Ave)

33 GAS WORKS PARK

Ⓟ Twenty-five years after the Seattle Gas Company plant belched its last coal dust in 1956, the gasworks at the north end of Lake Union reopened as a park for picnickers and kite fliers, its industrial towers retained as totems of the industrial age. It's like that scene from *Planet of the Apes* in which Charlton Heston rides his horse past the submerged Statue of Liberty and realizes just how much the world has changed. Children now scamper over ground that was once so polluted it demanded intensive purifying before it was safe to walk on. Landscape architect Richard Haag (who had earlier remodeled the Century 21 fairgrounds into **Seattle Center**) was responsible for seeing aesthetic value in this industrial wasteland and saving the plant as a bizarre relic. His modifications were relatively minor—bright primary colors in some covered areas, a huge symbolic sundial (created by artist Charles Greening in 1979) that's mounted atop a knoll to the west, and outdoor dining tables on the beautified grounds. Visitors have an unobstructed view of boats chopping over the lake. ◆ N Northlake Pl (southeast of Northlake Way)

GREEN LAKE/ GREENWOOD/ NORTH SEATTLE

A quiet residential district, the Green Lake–Greenwood area is bordered by Ballard to the west, Wallingford and Fremont to the south, and Ravenna and the University District to the east. Its houses range from modest bungalows to some of the most desirable homes in Seattle—the large turn-of-the-19th-century residences and modern dream houses atop **Phinney Ridge**, for instance, command views of both the **Olympic** and the **Cascade Mountains**.

The centerpiece of the area is **Woodland Park**, located at the south end of Phinney Ridge, where the **Woodland Park Zoo**, playgrounds, tennis courts, a rose garden, and acres of wooded trails and picnic areas can be found. Bisecting the park is **Aurora Avenue (Route 99)**, which in the early 1930s—following bitter public debate—was extended north from downtown Seattle. The benefits of this bit of progress are dubious: The highway created what Washington writer Ivan Doig called "a concrete gorge" in the park—the western half contains the zoo, whereas most of the rest of its attractions, including Green Lake, are in the eastern half.

Green Lake, with two paths circling it, is "Jogging Central" and *the* center of summertime fun in Seattle. Aside from running, there's plenty of kayaking, bicycling, inline skating, windsurfing, pram pushing, golfing, baseball playing, fishing, and just plain people watching here. A couple of small commercial areas on the east and north sides of the lake service the area year-round, and seasonal businesses (such as inline skate and Windsurfer rentals) pop up in the summer. And, of course, this is Seattle, so you won't need to travel far before encountering an espresso stand.

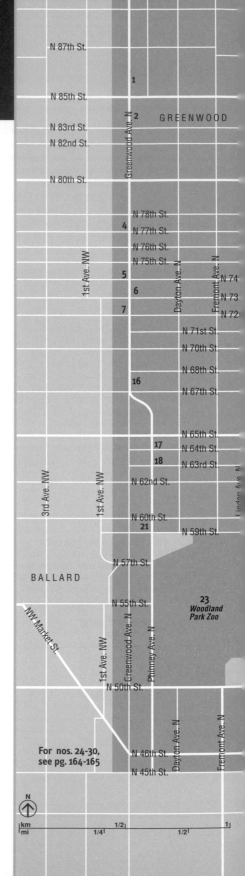

For nos. 24-30, see pg. 164-165

Parallel to Aurora Avenue on the park's western edge—along the spine of Phinney Ridge—runs **Phinney Avenue,** which becomes **Greenwood Avenue** farther north. With its secondhand stores spanning the gamut from junky to sublime, the avenue is ripe territory for antiques lovers. The Greenwood district, centered at the intersection of **N 85th Street** and **Greenwood Avenue,** retains a funky charm that has endured nobly against encroaching gentrification.

A little farther afield is North Seattle. The city limits used to end at N 85th Street, but as Seattle has grown (the line now stands at **145th Street**), the various smaller communities embraced by the *North Seattle* rubric—**Lake Forest Park, Northgate, Broadview, Maple Leaf,** and **Wedgewood** among them—have developed. North Seattle is primarily home to auto dealerships, budget motels, strip malls, modest housing, and the world's first shopping mall, the **Northgate Shopping Center.**

GREEN LAKE/ GREENWOOD

1 PHAD THAI

★$ There's been an explosion of Thai restaurants in Seattle over the past several years. This eatery is informal in décor and cheerful in service; employees have been known to take fussy children in hand for a kitchen tour, giving parents a chance to eat. The food is fresh, well presented, and cooked without MSG. Try the vegetable curry or the chicken in peanut sauce. ◆ Thai ◆ M-Tu, Th, F, lunch; daily, dinner. 8530 Greenwood Ave N (between 85th and 87th Sts). 784.1830

2 GREENWOOD SPACE TRAVEL SUPPLY COMPANY

A fantastic little space oddity located in the heart of Greenwood, this store has everything, from cherry-scented smoke-ring guns and stylish space wear to pop-culture literature. All proceeds go to 826 Seattle, a nonprofit writing and tutoring center dedicated to helping youth ages 6 to 18. ◆ M-Sa, until 6PM. 8414 Greenwood Ave N (between 83rd and 85th Sts). 725.2625. www.greenwoodspacetravelsupply.com

3 URBAN BAKERY

★$ A convenient spot for runners and walkers to pick up an espresso or iced *latte.* Hearty sandwiches, soups, fresh pastries, and a full line of juices are also on hand. ◆ Café ◆ Daily. 7850 E Green Lake Dr N (at Stroud Ave). 524.7951

4 PETE'S EGGNEST

★$ It's all about comfort foods like Denver omelettes, blueberry pancakes, liver and onions, and gyros. The walls are covered with posters of the Greek islands, the owners' home turf. The breakfast menu is served all day. ◆ American/Greek ◆ Daily, 7AM-3PM, breakfast and lunch. 7717 Greenwood Ave N (between 77th and 78th Sts). 784.5384. &

5 74TH STREET ALE HOUSE

★★$ This former hard-drinker's dive has been reincarnated as an airy neighborhood tavern serving an excellent array of Northwest microbrews and standard-issue beer (16 taps in all), along with wine. The brains behind this operation are Jeff Eagan, formerly of **Roanoke Park Place Tavern** on Capitol Hill and the **Mark Tobey** restaurant in downtown, and Jeff Reich, who runs the kitchen. The menu is brief but thoughtful. Try the big burgers (decked with grilled onions and peppers) or the Reuben. Many claim this alehouse serves Seattle's best chicken sandwich, and the daily homemade soup is a constant crowd-pleaser. ◆ American ◆ Daily, lunch and dinner. 7401 Greenwood Ave N (at 74th St). 784.2955

YOU WANNA BET?

Unlike Reno or Vegas, Seattle is not a gambling destination per se. In town, there's not much legal gambling aside from the state lottery and the occasional bingo game for charity. But not far outside the city limits are several Vegas-style casinos, all operated by local Indian reservations as a way to earn revenue. Exempt from local and state laws prohibiting casino gambling, these establishments have become very popular in recent years. The standard table games are featured—poker, blackjack, baccarat, craps, and roulette—as are bingo and keno, and of course, the ever-popular slot machines. In most cases, the minimum bet is $3. Most casinos are open 24 hours a day, Friday through Monday, and closed for a few hours beginning in the early morning (4AM or 5AM) the other days of the week. All have gift shops, plus multiple restaurants and bars. Some offer major entertainment as well. An added attraction: in keeping with their Native American heritage, almost all of them also have a museumlike area displaying cultural artifacts (so you can enrich your mind, if not your wallet). You must be 21 or older to enter a casino.

The gaming place closest to Seattle, and by far the state's largest at 227,000 square feet, is the **Tulalip Casino** (whose name is pronounced "Too-*lay*-lup"; 360/651.1111, 888/272.1111; www.tulalipcasino.com &) in **Marysville**, about 35 miles north on I-5, off exit 202. Recent entertainers have included Bruce Springsteen, Gordon Lightfoot, and B.B. King.

The **Muckleshoot Casino** (253/804.4444, 800/804.4944; www.muckleshootcasino.com &), 25 miles south on Route 164 in Auburn, offers 2,000 machines and 20 table games. **The Emerald Queen** (888/831.7655; www.emeraldqueen.com &), a riverboat casino operated by the Puyallup ("Pew-al-lup") tribe, is 32 miles south of Seattle off I-5 at Exit 135 in Tacoma. This casino offers 2,000 video slot machines and 56 table games. Recent shows have included Air Supply, Chubby Checker, and Foreigner.

In the **Skagit Valley**, about an hour's drive north of Seattle, there are two gambling options. **Northern Lights Casino** (360/293.2691, 800/877.PLAY; www.swinomishcasino.com &) is located a few miles off I-5, near Anacortes on Highway 20 W. Among other amenities, this casino offers 35 full-service RV sites. And on the north side of the valley is the **Skagit Valley Casino** (I-5, exit 236; 360/724.7777; www.theskagit.com &), which offers nightly live entertainment (recently, Joan Rivers, Glen Campbell, and Rich Little), three restaurants, interactive video games, valet parking, and a hotel with 74 rooms plus 29 suites.

There are a number of other tribal casinos across the state. If you plan to drive anywhere in Washington and want to make a bet, check out www.500nations.com for maps and details.

5 YANNI'S LAKESIDE CAFE

★★$ Huge portions of good Greek cooking are offered at this congenial neighborhood hangout (which, despite its name, is about five blocks from Green Lake). Try the gyro platter, any of the lamb dishes, roasted chicken, or moussaka. The appetizer plate of calamari can make a whole meal. Desserts are less interesting. There's a simple, no-nonsense wine list. ♦ Greek ♦ M-Sa, dinner. 7419 Greenwood Ave N (between 74th and 75th Sts). 783.6945. &

6 CARMELITA

★★$$ Disappointed with eating-out choices when they became vegetarians, Chicago artists Kathryn Neumann and Michael Hughes opened their own restaurant. The menu here changes seasonally to incorporate fresh regional veggies and fruits. ♦ Vegetarian ♦ Tu-Su, dinner. 7314 Greenwood Ave N (between 73rd and 74th Sts). 706.7703. www.carmelita.net

7 2ND HAND HUBE

Furniture and kitschy stuff from the 1930s to the 1950s, some of it high-quality collectibles and some of it near junk, are featured in this browser's delight of a shop. Seventeen dealers display their wares here. ♦ Daily, noon-5:30PM. 7217 Greenwood Ave N (between 72nd and 73rd Sts). 782.1335

7 THE COUTH BUZZARD

This dusty bookstore with the peculiar moniker contains a treasure trove of unlikely and sometimes unheard-of finds in used hardcovers and paperbacks. Mainstream fiction is the strongest section here, but with 100,000 books, anything is possible. When the mood strikes you, you can sit and play

Green Lake, which has an average depth of only 15 feet, is what's left of a huge Ice Age lake that once stretched between the present cities of Everett and Olympia. Haller and Bitter Lakes, in North Seattle, are also remnants of that ancient body of water.

Restaurants/Clubs: Red | Hotels: Purple | Shops: Orange | Outdoors/Parks: Green | Sights/Culture: Blue

I LOVE THE JAVA JIVE

Over the last 35 years, Seattle has grown to be the undisputed espresso capital of America, where the popular drink is dispensed in coffee shops and cafés, from sidewalk carts, drive-through stands, and handy windows. You can get espresso in laundries and drycleaners, at bookstores and supermarkets—even at gas stations.

There are over 300 espresso carts in town, in addition to the more than 200 shops and stands. That works out to five espresso sources per square mile! And surprisingly, they are all busy, especially first thing in the morning, as folks on their way to work or school stop to stoke their engines with caffeine.

There are many places in Seattle where, if you stand on a street corner and gaze out in all four directions, you can see, within a block or two, several coffee shops and a couple of stands or carts. The rarest sight is a downtown street corner not occupied by an espresso cart.

Starbucks is without question the biggest presence in the scene; there are some 70 Starbucks outlets in Seattle. **Tully's**, another big player, has 30. Running a distant third, are **SBC**, **Caffé Ladro**, and **Petes**. In addition, there are the many independent stores, stands, and carts, which range from grungy to funky to artsy to chic to almost indescribable.

The people who frequent these various caffeine venues are often quite passionate about their particular favorite and quite scathing about all the others. They'll tell you that so-and-so's coffee is too bitter or too bland, that the foam is overheated or too thin, that the crema design (brown coffee foam) in the white milk foam is derivative or sloppy, that the baristas (those who "draw"—never "pour"—the espresso) are rude or poorly trained, that the customers are too Eddie Bauer or too gothic. So it is very hard to get an unbiased opinion about where to go for a good cup of espresso.

The word *espresso* comes from the brewing method—hot water *pressed* by piston or pump through finely ground, firmly packed coffee. The main point of espresso is strong coffee flavor, so a purist might order an undiluted single shot, which will have a very intense flavor, or a cappuccino, which is a shot of espresso plus a little steamed milk and foam. There's also *americano*, a shot of espresso somewhat diluted with hot water. However, by far the most popular drink is *latte* and consists of a shot of espresso (or two shots, which is called a double) in a cup filled with steamed milk and capped with foam. *Lattes* come in short (8 ounces), tall (12 ounces), and grande (16 ounces). If you're new at the game, you might order a single short. For stronger coffee flavor, go for a double tall. You can get chocolate added (mocha), and if you're worried about caffeine but still want intense flavor, ask for a split double tall—one shot of caffeinated espresso plus one shot of decaf in a 12-ounce cup filled with steamed milk and capped with milk foam.

By the way, that whole concept of jangled caffeine nerves due to espresso consumption is a myth. Espresso is made from *Arabica* beans, as opposed to the *Robusta* beans used to make regular brewed java, which means that a single shot of espresso carries half the caffeine of an 8-ounce cup of brewed coffee. So join the aficionados, double up, and worry not.

---

the piano. Look for sidewalk sales. ♦ Daily. 7221 Greenwood Ave N (between 72nd and 73rd Sts). 789.8965

7 GREENWOOD BAKERY

The excellent pastries, breads, cookies, and other delectables made here are complemented by the good espresso drinks.
♦ Daily. 7227 Greenwood Ave N (between 72nd and 73rd Sts). 783.7181

7 KEN'S MARKET

This better-than-average grocery store caters to an upscale crowd, with its wealth of coffee beans, delicious deli sandwiches (try the meat loaf), and fresh pasta. The espresso drinks served here are just as good as those sold next door at **Greenwood Bakery**, and the service is faster.
♦ Daily, 6AM-11PM. 7231 Greenwood Ave N (between 72nd and 73rd Sts). 784.3470

8 BETH'S CAFE

★$ This greasiest of spoons attracts plenty of college students who finish up their all-nighters with a stop here to wolf down inexpensive 12-egg omelettes (be prepared to share!), layered over a 2-inch bed of hash browns with toast on the side. Half orders can be had by the less gluttonous. Breakfast is served all day. Burgers and enormous french fries carry on the stomach-busting tradition. It's a real scene. You might find yourself sitting next to one of Seattle's great new artists or musicians. ♦ American ♦ Daily, 24 hours. 7311 Aurora Ave N (at Winona Ave). 782.5588. www.bethscafe.com

9 GREEN LAKE BOAT RENTALS

Rent a canoe, small boat, or paddle-wheel craft at this Parks Department concession. Windsurfing equipment and lessons are also available. ♦ Daily, April-Sept, weather permitting. 7351 E Green Lake Dr N (at Fourth Ave NE). 527.0171

10 GREEN LAKE PUBLIC LIBRARY

Perched on a grassy knoll, this well-maintained building shows Mediterranean and Chicago School influences. Opened in 1910, it is one of eight libraries still standing in the Seattle area (two were lost to wrecking balls) that were built thanks to the largesse of iron-and-steel magnate Andrew Carnegie. Designers were **W. Marbury Somervell** and **Joseph C. Cote**, who in the year of its opening would also see two of their other library projects inaugurated: the **University Branch Library** on Roosevelt Way NE and the **West Seattle Public Library** on 42nd Avenue SW. Not surprisingly, these three structures bear some resemblance to one another. ♦ Daily. 7364 E Green Lake Dr N (between Fourth and Latona Aves NE). 684.7547

11 ROSITA'S

★$ Just a couple blocks off the lake, this unpretentious place is commonly crowded and uncommonly efficient. Try any of the combination plates or the *chiles rellenos*. The super nachos platter is a winning appetizer. ♦ Mexican ♦ M-Sa, lunch and dinner; Su, dinner. 7210 Woodlawn Ave NE (between 72nd and 73rd Sts). 523.3031. &. www.rositasrestaurant.com

12 MY FRIENDS CAFE

★$ Fresh fruit and other healthy ingredients whipped up into good (and good-for-you) breakfasts, and tasty sandwiches at lunch are the offerings here. ♦ American ♦ Daily, breakfast and lunch. 310 NE 72nd St (between Woodlawn Ave NE and E Green Lake Dr N). 523.8929. &

13 THE LITTLE RED HEN

Feel like doing a two-step? You won't believe you're still in Seattle when you step into this longtime country venue. There's live music every night, but on Wednesday you can hear everything from good ol' bluegrass to boot-kickin' line dancing (with free dance lessons). ♦ Su-Th. 7115 Woodlawn Ave NE (at NE 71st St). 522.1168. www.littleredhen.com

Gregg's Greenlake Cycle

14 GREGG'S GREENLAKE CYCLE

This is the biggest and busiest of several shops around Green Lake that rent bicycles, in-line skates, and skateboards for a nominal fee. All these types of wheeled conveyances are also for sale here, and there's a helpful service department for when things go bewilderingly wrong. ♦ Daily. 7007 Woodlawn Ave NE (between Ravenna Blvd and 71st St). 523.1822. www.greggscycles.com

15 SPUD FISH AND CHIPS

★$ Yes, the ambience is a big zero, but this is a choice spot on sunny days when all you want is to grab a quick lunch and burn off a few skin cells beside the lake. The fish is remarkably flaky and the fries are filling and salty, though everything's a bit greasy. ♦ Seafood/takeout ♦ Daily, lunch and dinner. 6860 E Green Lake Way N (at Fourth Ave NE). 524.0565. &. Also at 2666 Alki Ave SW (between 59th and 60th Aves). 938.0606. &

16 STUMBLING GOAT BISTRO

★★★$$ This place is up north in an area called Phinney Ridge, but you'll be glad you made the trip. Once there, you'll enjoy the vaguely Bohemian feel of the décor, and the brief menu, which tends toward such seasonal innovations as squash soup topped with herbed croutons and smoked sturgeon

---

Restaurants/Clubs: Red | Hotels: Purple | Shops: Orange | Outdoors/Parks: Green | Sights/Culture: Blue

with an egg-celeriac salad and caramelized leeks. The crisp-skinned roast chicken with roasted garlic cloves has a huge following, and it's always on the menu. There's a well-priced wine list, great cocktails, and friendly staff. What more do you want? ♦ Tu-Su, dinner, 5PM–10PM; closed M. 6722 Greenwood Ave N (between 67th and 68th Sts). 784.3535. www.stumblinggoatbistro.com

GRAZE AWAY!

17 MAE'S PHINNEY RIDGE CAFE

★★$ Mae is the shared *nom de cuisine* of three women who have created this congenial nook for breakfast, served all day, and lunch. The sandwiches, burgers, and cinnamon rolls are all wonderful. Omelettes are the top pick at breakfast; for the truly famished, a cheese-covered mountain of hash browns is served as a main course. This is one of the few breakfast joints in town where you can get a good bowl of grits! The **Moo Room** features a soda fountain, great milk shakes, a jukebox, and more cow-related art than you can shake a hoof at. Service can be slow, and the lines form quickly on weekends, but the wait isn't usually too long. ♦ American ♦ Daily, 7AM–3PM. No reservations accepted. 6412 Phinney Ave N (between 64th and 65th Sts). 782.1222. ᕒ. www.maescafe.com

18 12-STEP BOOKSTORE AND GIFT SHOP

For books on a multiplicity of dysfunctions, lists of various meetings, gifts for fellow 12-steppers, bumper stickers for those who want to be less than anonymous, and notices of upcoming workshops and speakers, check out this store. ♦ Tu-Sa, 10AM–6PM. 6300 Phinney Ave N (at 63rd St). 789.6300

19 LATONA BY GREEN LAKE

This funky, friendly neighborhood tavern offers a good selection of wines and a frequently changing assortment of microbrews, including products from the Rogue Brewery in Newport, Oregon, and the Maritime Pacific Brewing Company in Seattle. Bartenders will give recommendations. The menu is limited but does include homemade soups and a tasty cheese plate to nosh on. Sit at the bar; avoid the balcony overlooking the main floor, where you'll feel cut off from the action. A variety of local musicians, usually of the folk or jazz persuasion, play Friday. And Monday is open-mic night. ♦ M-Sa, until 12:30AM; Su, until midnight. 6423 Latona Ave NE (at 65th St). 525.2238

20 MONA'S

★★$$ The owner-artists, Tito Class and Annette Serrano, devised the lush art on the walls and the royal color scheme. But if food is what you care about, don't miss the tapas served in the lounge. On a romantic night out, be sure to order a piece of Mona's luscious chocolate cake to share. ♦ European ♦ Daily, dinner. 6421 Latona Ave NE (between NE 64th and NE 65th Sts). 526.1188

21 SANTA FE CAFE

★★★$$ Sparse but elegant décor combines with consistently high-quality, innovative cuisine to create Phinney Ridge's classiest restaurant. A couple of the appetizers alone—an order of garlic custard, say, and a luscious artichoke ramekin—could make a meal. And the green-chili stew, enchiladas, and green-chili burritos made with blue-corn tortillas are all delicious entrées. The owners, both from Albuquerque, New Mexico, import tons of red and green chilies from their home state. If your server warns you that something like the red-chili burrito may be too hot for most palates, take his or her word for it. There's another branch in Ravenna. ♦ Southwestern ♦ Daily, lunch and dinner. Reservations recommended. 5901 Phinney Ave N (at 59th St). 783.9755

22 GREEN LAKE SMALL CRAFT CENTER

Located at the southwest corner of the lake, this concession offers year-round canoe and kayak instruction plus rowing and sailing lessons. The lake is active on weekday mornings when rowers embark on their journeys. ♦ Daily. 5900 W Green Lake Way N (N of N 55 St). 684.4074. www.greenlakekrew.org

23 WOODLAND PARK ZOO

Origins of this zoo and the surrounding park go back to Guy Phinney, a flamboyant Englishman who made his fortune in Canadian real estate before moving to Seattle at the end of the 19th century. Phinney built a private park on his estate, at the southern end of the ridge that bears his name. He included—among other amenities—a trolley line, flower garden, conservatory, picnic grounds, zoo, bathing beach, and music pavilion. The city bought the park from him in 1900 for the then-extravagant sum of $100,000.

Today, Seattle's zoo is one of the nation's best. Attractions include a nearby rose garden with over 280 varieties and a historic, hand-carved wooden carousel; a rejuvenated version of the popular family farm petting zoo; *Northern Trail*, an exhibit that replicates the cold, rugged regions of Alaska, with brown bears, bald eagles, mountain goats, and wolves; and *Trail of Vines*, which leads visitors on a boardwalk past tufted deer, tapirs, pythons, and tropical primates.

In many of the exhibits animals are free to wander in near-natural settings: There's a new Willawong Station in **Australasia**, where zoo-goers are introduced to a variety of native Australian plants and parrots as they walk through and interact with surroundings. For a dollar, you can feed the birds; and the elephant forest in tropical **Asia** includes a replica of a Thai logging camp.

The zoo offers lectures, summer musical performances, and educational series for youngsters; stop by the **Discovery Barn** for unsupervised educational fun, as well as the occasional wine-tasting event for adults. Older children will love the **Bug World** and the **Day and Night** exhibits that include creatures of the night. ♦ Admission; children under 2 admitted free; discount for senior citizens, disabled persons, and children ages 3 to 5. Daily. 5500 Phinney Ave N (between 50th and 59th Sts). 684.4800. www.zoo.org

NORTH SEATTLE

24 PARKER'S

Parker's, a legendary North Seattle teen hangout of the 1950s and 1960s, and later a more sophisticated music venue, has reinvented itself as a casino offering such gaming favorites as blackjack, *paigow* (poker), and Caribbean stud. There are dartboards, pool and foosball tables, and 30—that's right, 30—color monitors and three giant screens for watching televised sports. ♦ Daily, until 2AM. 17001 Aurora Ave N (at 170th St). 542.9491

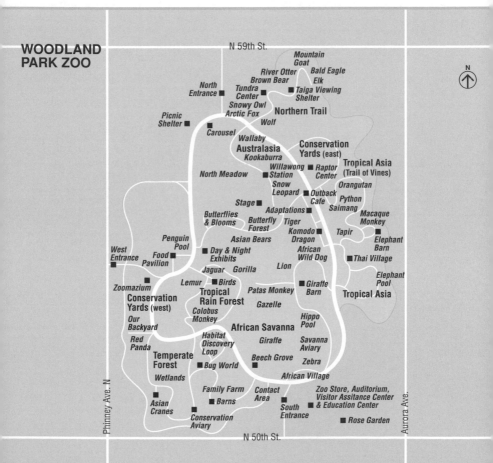

25 CARKEEK PARK

This 198-acre greensward bordering Puget Sound has been left mostly to wilderness. Here you can follow pathways winding through dense woodlands and gaze on streams rushing down forested hillsides. View the Olympic Mountains from a high bluff or cross the overpass to explore 23 acres of tidelands along Puget Sound. There are a number of picnic areas for nature lovers. Crews of Camp Fire Girls conduct weeklong summer camps out here, and folks run their dogs or enjoy lunch by the water. The newly built **Environmental Learning Center** is the first of its kind in Seattle. Constructed of 80% recycled materials, the center features such energy-efficient details as solar-electric panels, rooftop rainwater harvest for flushing the toilets, and an architectural design that fits it into its surrounding landscape. ◆ N W Carkeek Park Rd and 116th St

26 NORTHGATE SHOPPING CENTER

This, the world's first shopping mall, was designed in the 1950s by architect **John Graham Sr.**, who also invented the revolving restaurant and helped develop the **Space Needle** for the 1962 World's Fair. Oddly enough, considering Seattle's prevailing weather, it was originally uncovered; only later was a roof added. The mall is currently undergoing a massive remodel and expansion to add 100,000 square feet of retail and restaurant space. **Nordstrom**, **Macy's**, and **JCPenney** are the main anchors. ◆ Daily. NE Northgate Way (between Fifth and First Aves). 362.4777. www.northgateshoppingctr.com

27 LARRY'S MARKET

Welcome to Grocery Land USA, a pop-culture spin on the classic American supermarket. Larry McKinney was a grocer's son who inherited his first store in the 1960s and has since expanded the family business into a chain of fine food emporiums in the suburbs. The stores have a faux-industrial appearance—exposed ventilation pipes and rafters and metal racks supporting boxes of unpacked supplies. But interior design is theater, so enjoy the show. The sheer quantity and quality—of everything from fresh flowers to fresh sushi—is mind-boggling, and the especially long hours the shop keeps are convenient. ◆ Daily, 6AM-1AM. 10008 Aurora Ave N (at 100th St). 527.5333. Also at 100 Mercer St (at First Ave N). 213.0778. www.larrysmarkets.com

28 DOONG KONG LAU

★★★$ Hot and spicy Hakka regional cuisine is served in this usually busy Chinese restaurant. The hot pots—the name is quite literal—are prepared in an assortment of styles (vegetarian, seafood, pork, etc.), and the garlic eggplant should not be missed. ◆ Chinese ◆ Daily, lunch and dinner. 9710 Aurora Ave N (between 97th and 98th Sts). 526.8828

29 MAPLE LEAF GRILL

★★$ Here's a true neighborhood hangout, serving an excellent assortment of beers and wines. The décor has lots of old wood and open space. Lunch and dinner choices include not just one of the most succulent burgers in town but a changing array of imaginative specials featuring fish, chicken, and pasta. There's live music Thursday, usually blues. ◆ American ◆ M-F, lunch and dinner; Sa, Su, dinner. 8909 Roosevelt Way NE (between 89th and 90th Sts). 523.8449. www.mapleleafgrill.com

30 COOPER'S NORTHWEST ALEHOUSE

It's technically not a brewpub (no beers are prepared on the premises), but this crowded and cheery tavern is a mecca for Northwest microbrews: 22 tap brews mostly West Coast specialties. The staff is knowledgeable about the subtle distinctions of each type, and sipping samples of new brews are accompanied by enthusiastic debate over their relative merits and flaws. Wine and some bar food (like fish and chips) is served, but beer is the draw. Shoot pool free on Sundays. ◆ M-Sa, until 2AM; Su, until midnight. 8065 Lake City Way NE (between 16th and 15th Aves). 522.2923. ♿. www.coopersalehouse.com

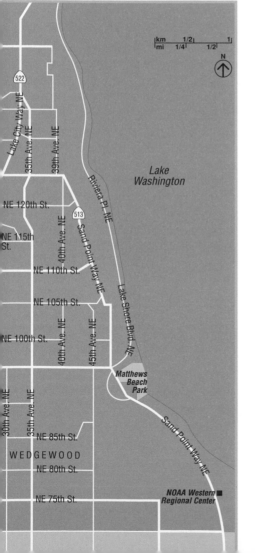

UNIVERSITY DISTRICT/RAVENNA

Centered around the **University of Washington** (UW, which is pronounced "U Dub" by locals), the University District has grown with the institution, which opened its doors downtown in 1861, then relocated to this area just north of **Lake Union** in 1895. Around the beginning of the 20th century, the "U District" was sparsely populated, without paved streets, sewers, lights, or sidewalks. It could take half a day to journey downtown by streetcar. Residents called it Brooklyn back then, trusting that this neighborhood, like its namesake in New York, would thrive because it was adjacent to a big city.

In 1909, their faith was rewarded when Seattle held the Alaska-Yukon-Pacific Exposition on the UW campus. This, the city's first world's fair, was heavily promoted by business burghers who wished to attract East Coast attention and stimulate regional growth. University officials eagerly volunteered their land for the fair's site, hoping to reap a legacy of buildings and development for what was then a backwoods campus.

The exposition was a stunning success. It took two years to build, cost $10 million, drew 3.7 million visitors, turned a small profit ($62,676) despite the fact that liquor was banned in the district at the time, and stamped Seattle as a young city on the rise. Exhibits showcased 26 countries and featured dozens of classical-style buildings set amid stately grounds laid out by the Olmsted Brothers of Massachusetts, the nation's foremost landscape architecture firm and principal players in Seattle's early planning. The exposition opened when President William Howard Taft pressed

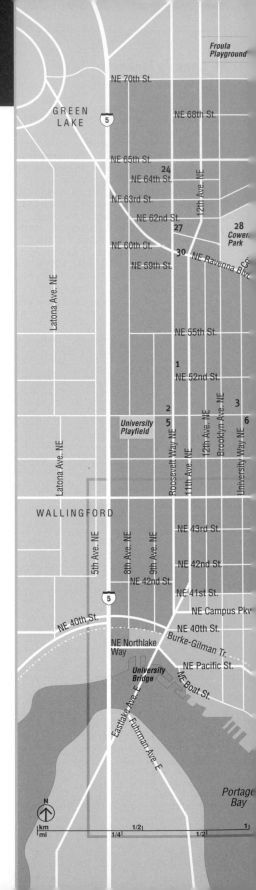

View Ridge
Playfield

20th Ave. NE
21st Ave. NE
Ravenna Ave. NE
23rd Ave. NE

NE 70th St.

NE 68th St.

NE 65th St.

25
26

Bryant
Playground

22nd
Ave. NE

27th Ave. NE
29th Ave. NE
30th Ave. NE

NE 60th St.

29
Ravenna
Park

NE 58th St.

31
Lower
Ravenna
Park

32

NE 55th St.

Burke-Gilman Tr.

AVENNA

16th Ave. NE
17th Ave. NE

50th St.

4

22nd Ave. NE

Burke-Gilman Tr.

NE Blakeley St.

30th Ave. NE

35th Ave. NE

NE 52nd St.

40th Ave. NE

45th Ave. NE

NE 50th St.

7

20th Ave. NE

21st Pl.
NE

25th Ave. NE

NE 47th St.

Sand Point Way NE

47th St.

39th Ave. NE

45th St.

513

Union Bay Pl. NE

NE 45th St.

36th Ave. NE

42nd Ave. NE

**Burke
morial
seum**

Stevens Way

Pend Oreille Rd.

Clark Rd.

NE 41st St.

NE Surber Dr.

NE 38th St.

For nos. 8-23,
see pgs. 170-171

**University of
Washington**

Montlake Blvd. NE

513

Walla Walla Rd.

Stevens Way

**Edmundson
Pavilion**

NE Pacific Pl.

**Husky
Stadium**

Union
Bay

Walla Walla Rd.

**University of
Washington
Hospital**

bia Rd.

an Rd.

**Waterfront
Activities
Center**

**Montlake
Bridge**

a golden telegraph key in Washington, DC, and switched on the fair's opening lights. (That same key would be used by President John F. Kennedy 53 years later to kick off the 1962 Century 21 Exposition.) The exposition lasted more than four months, drawing visitors to hundreds of industrial, educational, and carnival exhibits. When the exposition was over, the neighborhood was left with sewers, water mains, and other modern amenities, and the university had been given a parklike campus and about 20 buildings. With the Olmsteds' help, the fairgrounds were adapted to university use.

Today UW is one of the largest single-campus universities on the West Coast. Its 694-acre tract, hosting about 40,000 students in 16 schools and colleges, occupies nearly half the neighborhood. It is the number-one federal public research institution, and several of its component schools—including health sciences, engineering, and computer science—are counted among the nation's top 10. The neighborhood mirrors the school's diversity and energy. Streets are filled with bookstores, clothing shops, coffeehouses, and informal, inexpensive cafés. This area is a big reason why Seattle consistently ranks so high in per-capita movie attendance, book purchases, and espresso consumption. The district's spine, as well as its heart, is represented by University Way (better known as "The Ave"), which hosts the annual University Street Fair. Held in May, this popular arts and crafts fest brings long-haired vendors, street musicians, and the scent of patchouli oil back to these streets.

Colorful as it is, the U District isn't as interesting as it could be. Outside of the campus, it's dominated by dull, modern apartment buildings and loaded with bargain-filled restaurants, few of which are among the city's finest. And there is a dearth of places that have good music or dancing. More seriously, the Ave is frequently besieged by panhandlers and drug dealers. In general, however, this and other streets are safe to stroll after dark, which is a relief, because the district's flat topography invites walking.

Named for the large, lovely park that graces its center, Ravenna lies just north of the University District. It is a safe, well-tended, middle-class enclave where many UW professors and other staff members reside in 1920s and 1930s "bungaloids"—remodeled two-bedroom houses that have retained the neighborhood's original character. Only a few decades ago, mainly middle-aged and older people dwelled here, but many families with young children have moved in and the playgrounds are full again. Nightlife in this neighborhood is practically nonexistent, but several good restaurants have popped up.

UNIVERSITY DISTRICT

1 GIGGLES COMEDY NITE CLUB

Stand-up comics with national reputations (including Jerry Seinfeld and Ellen DeGeneres) have appeared here. Music acts are sometimes featured as well. ♦ Cover. Shows: Th-Sa, 8:30PM and 10:30PM; Su, 8:30PM. Reservations recommended. 5220 Roosevelt Way NE (between 52nd and 55th Sts). 526.5653. www.gigglescomedyclub.com

2 UNIVERSITY BRANCH LIBRARY

Architects **W. Marbury Somervell** and **Joseph C. Cote** were busy in the year 1910. Not only were they putting the final touches on this building but they were also working on two other Seattle libraries that opened that same year: the **Green Lake Public Library** and the **West Seattle Public Library**. All three structures look eerily similar, all showing Mediterranean touches, as perhaps was the architects' intention. In any case, this building, like its brethren, is a handsome legacy of an ambitious project. It is one of eight libraries still standing in the Seattle area that were built thanks to the largesse of iron-and-steel magnate Andrew Carnegie. ◆ M, W-Sa. 5009 Roosevelt Way NE (at 50th St). 684.4063

3 UNIVERSITY HEIGHTS ELEMENTARY SCHOOL

Established in 1902, the district's first primary school grew in the 1920s to become the largest in Seattle. Contending that major repairs were needed, the school district closed the school down several years ago, despite widespread community protest. The wooden-framed structure, designed by **Bebb & Mendel** (who would later create the **Ballard Firehouse**), is now used by nonprofit organizations and community groups. ◆ 5031 University Way NE (between 50th and 52nd Sts). 527.4278

4 THE CHAMBERED NAUTILUS

$$ Innkeepers Joyce Schulte and Steve Pool operate this charming bed-and-breakfast named after a type of seashell. Built in 1915, the historic Georgian Colonial was originally the home of Dr. Herbert Gowan, a British missionary who founded the Asian Studies department at the university. It features six antique-filled guest rooms with private baths, a living room with a fireplace, a formal dining room with a spectacular view of the Cascades to the east, and a large enclosed sun porch overlooking the garden. It's conveniently located close to the university, **Ravenna Park**, Green Lake, and downtown Seattle. A full breakfast is included in the room rate, and complimentary tea and cookies are served each afternoon. ◆ 5005 22nd Ave NE (between 21st Pl and 54th St). 522.2536. www.chamberednautilus.com

5 MAMMA MELINA RISTORANTE

★★★$$ Excellent Neapolitan cuisine is served in an open, elegant room decorated with bright frescoes. The sounds of Puccini (sometimes too loud) flow through the air, and Mamma herself may be in the kitchen. You can't really go wrong with any of the dishes. The appetizers, along with the spinach cannelloni, veal dishes, scampi, and chicken cacciatore, all deserve stars. Singers perform arias from Italian operas on Tuesday, Friday, and Saturday evenings. ◆ Italian ◆ Tu-Su, dinner. 4759 Roosevelt Way NE (at 50th St). 632.2271. &

5 CINEMA BOOKS

A major find for film buffs, this specialty shop sells movie picture books, celebrity bios, screenplays, guidebooks to shows, technical and analytical treatises, and some film memorabilia (posters, stills, a hundred different Marilyn Monroe postcards). ◆ M-Sa. 4753 Roosevelt Way NE (between 47th and 50th Sts). 547.7667. www.cinemabooks.net

5 SEVEN GABLES THEATER

Once upon a time there was a single theater in Seattle that showed high-quality films. Called Seven Gables, it grew into a chain and then sold out to a California operator. Now with nine theaters and 28 screens in town, it operates on the premise that if given the chance, people will support literary and/ or noncommercial movies. Often used as a test market for independent productions, this chain has saved several small, noteworthy films (among them *The Black Stallion*, *The Stunt Man*, and *Never Cry Wolf*) that Hollywood had written off. This theater is the chain's flagship and specializes in fine foreign films. Its viewing room is small, but the antique-decorated lobby is beautiful. ◆ 911 NE 50th St (between Roosevelt Way and Ninth Ave). 632.8820. www.landmarktheatres.com

🎬 GRAND ILLUSION CINEMA

6 GRAND ILLUSION

This independently owned theater regularly books experimental or political films. The screen is small and the viewing room is claustrophobic, but a blue velvet couch in the back row gets a thumbs-up for romance. There is also a comfy little café. ◆ Box office opens a half hour before show time. 1403 NE 50th St (at University Way). 523.3935. www.grandillusiontheater.org

7 GREEK ROW

Blocks of stately, traditional, brick-faced fraternity and sorority houses set amid a long archway of tall trees will make you want to get out your college letter sweater and

The Seattle band Soundgarden took its name from *Sound Garden*, a 1983 sculpture by California artist Douglas Hollis. The work, which stands outside the National Oceanic and Atmospheric Administration's Western Regional Center on the shores of Lake Washington, consists of 12 steel towers topped with structures resembling weather vanes. On one end of each tower is a vertical organ pipe; on the other is a wind vane that rotates the pipe. When the wind blows, a musical sound is created.

Restaurants/Clubs: Red | Hotels: Purple | Shops: Orange | Outdoors/Parks: Green | Sights/Culture: Blue

UNIVERSITY DISTRICT

yell, "Sis boom bah!" Of the 31 frat houses and 18 sororities, the most interesting include the **Sigma Nu House** (1616 NE 47th St), built in 1926 and designed by architect **Ellsworth Storey** with Wrightian overtones; the **Alpha Tau Omega House** (1800 NE 47th St), completed in 1929 and designed by **Lionel Pries**, a former professor at **UW**'s Department of Architecture; and the **Phi Gamma Delta House** (5404 17th Ave NE), a Tudor Revival edifice built in 1927 and designed by **Mellor, Meigs & Howe** with **J. Lister Holmes**. Sadly, this Ivy League atmosphere was also the setting for the

1975 disappearance of Georgann Hawkins, an 18-year-old coed living at a nearby sorority house. She was among the victims of serial killer Ted Bundy, a good-looking, smooth-talking former UW psychology student who terrorized Seattle during the 1970s before he was caught and finally executed in Florida in 1989. Bundy confessed to committing more than a dozen murders in Washington, Oregon, and Utah, but detectives suspect he actually committed somewhere between three dozen and 100. ♦ Bounded by 22nd and 16th Aves NE and by 45th and 55th Sts

in generous portions. ♦ Greek ♦ Daily, breakfast, lunch, and dinner. 4549 University Way NE (between 45th and 47th Sts). 632.4700

8 UNIVERSITY SEAFOOD & POULTRY

Very fresh, high-quality gifts from the sea—Dungeness crabs, local oysters, salmon, halibut, caviar—are sold at this third-generation, family-owned business. The shop will pack and ship your fish by overnight courier or put it in an airline-approved, odorless, leak-proof carton good for 48 hours. ♦ M-Sa. 1317 NE 47th St (at University Way). 632.3900

9 NEW SEATTLE MASSAGE

A longtime district fave for relaxing, hands-on treatments, this salon offers a variety of techniques, including Swedish, shiatsu, and sports styles by 44 licensed massage therapists. ♦ Daily, until 9PM. Call for an appointment. 4519 University Way NE (between 45th and 47th Sts). 632.5074. www.newseattlemassage.com

10 UNIVERSITY VILLAGE

Several large chain stores (including **Eddie Bauer**, **Barnes & Noble**, **Abercrombie & Fitch**, and **Pottery Barn**) anchor this shopping center, and more than 80 independent shops sell clothes, gifts, and home furnishings. Brick walkways, fountains, ample seating, a large children's play area, and a casual pace suited to browsing help reduce the stress that so often accompanies mall shopping. **Caldwell's** (522.7531) carries ethnic home accessories such as New England crafts, Mexican folk art, and African pots, as well as wicker tables, baskets, and boxes; **VIVA** (525.8482) and **Marlee** (522.6526) are popular for their exclusive women's apparel; **Paint the Town** (527.8554) sells plain ceramics for you to decorate as you wish; **Teri's Toybox** (729.0750) sells kids' playthings and games; and **Pasta and Co.** (523.8594) offers tempting appetizers and salads (try the marinated chicken breasts or Chinese vermicelli). Recent additions include jewelry and home accessories; a gigantic **Starbucks**; and a **Ben & Jerry's Scoop Shop** and **Burrito Loco**, a source of authentic

8 THE CONTINENTAL RESTAURANT & PASTRY SHOP

★$ Old-timers play backgammon, the post-grad crowd sips retsina in an unhurried atmosphere, and parents of young children return time and again because owner Demetre Lagos works magic with unruly tots. The souvlaki sandwiches, Greek fries, and feta cheese omelets are all good—and served

---

Restaurants/Clubs: Red | Hotels: Purple | Shops: Orange | Outdoors/Parks: Green | Sights/Culture: Blue

Mexican food. ♦ NE 45th St (between Union Bay Pl and 22nd Ave). 523.0622. www.uvillage.com

11 BLUE MOON TAVERN

Poet Carolyn Kizer once described this tavern as "a grubby oasis just outside the university's one-mile-limit Sahara. Here, the jukebox roars, Audrey the waitress slaps down schooners of beer, and poets, pedants, painters, and other assorted wildlife make overtures to each other." She wrote that in 1956, but not much has changed. This fabled bar, supposedly frequented by Ginsberg, Kerouac, Roethke, and Tom Robbins, still attracts free spirits and loosely wrapped crazies. In 1990, it was scheduled to be razed, but an 11th-hour campaign to save the bar prevailed. Sunday nights, the tape deck plays only Grateful Dead music; Mondays are Opera Nights. ♦ Daily, noon-2AM. 712 NE 45th St (between Eighth and Seventh Aves). No phone

12 METRO CINEMAS

With 10 screens, Dolby sound, and a mix of good-quality, first-run commercial and independent films, this theater is a sanctuary on a rainy afternoon. There's even a soundproof room for those with infants. ♦ 4500 Ninth Ave NE (at 45th St). 633.0055. &. www.landmarktheatres.com

12 STELLA'S TRATTORIA

★$$ This lively, bistro-like establishment is ideal for grabbing a quick bite before or after a movie at the adjacent **Metro Cinemas**. Nighthawks, rejoice: One of Seattle's rare all-night eating spots, this joint is still jumping at 3AM. Pastas, fish, and breakfast are served after 11PM, when the full menu isn't available. This is one of a small chain of restaurants that also includes **Trattoria Mitchelli** in Pioneer Square and **Angelina's** in West Seattle. ♦ Italian ♦ Daily, 24 hours. 4500 Ninth Ave NE (at 45th St). 633.1100

Longtime Seattleites seem surprisingly undaunted by the precipitation here. Many don't carry umbrellas on wet days, and chances are they don't even *own* one, preferring for some reason to make mad dashes from the car to the office and back. And is it wishful thinking or downright denial that leads locals to buy more sunglasses per capita than residents of any other city in the United States? Probably neither. More likely they stash their old pairs away during rainstorms and, after a while, forget where they put them.

13 BEST WESTERN UNIVERSITY TOWER HOTEL

$$ The district's first luxury hostelry, this 14-story building opened to great fanfare in 1931. The architect was **Robert C. Reamer**, who also designed those oversize mountain cabins known as the Old Faithful Inn and the Canyon Hotel in Yellowstone National Park (a far cry from the Art Deco column here). Today, it's one of the neighborhood's nicer hotels—not as luxurious as some of the downtown spots, but much more economical. Reamer (whose other credits include the **Skinner Building** and the **1411 Fourth Avenue Building** downtown) shaped the hotel so that each of the 155 guest rooms provides a broad corner view. (Ask for a room facing either south to the city or east across Lake Washington.) On the first floor, the **District Lounge** serves steaks and seafood in an Art Deco setting. ♦ 4507 Brooklyn Ave NE (at 45th St). 634.2000, 800/899.0251. www.meany.com

14 NEPTUNE THEATER

One of Seattle's first-run movie houses, this elaborate palace was built in 1921 to showcase silent movies. It was renovated in 1993, when plastic "stained glass" was covered up and the original plasterwork featuring renditions of Neptune's head was restored. Grillwork over the organ pipes features tridents and starfish. ♦ 1303 NE 45th St (between University Way and Brooklyn Ave). 633.5545. &. www.landmarktheatres.com

15 SAFECO BUILDING

At 23 stories in height, the tallest—and some would say the ugliest—building in the district is corporate headquarters for an insurance company. More interesting, the company has assembled a $1 million, 600-piece collection of modern Northwest art and makes some of it accessible to the public. Go into the lobby or up to the mezzanine to see rotating exhibitions of Pilchuck School glass and abstract paintings. The bronze fountain outside was created by famed local sculptor George Tsutakawa. ♦ M-F. 4333 Brooklyn Ave NE (at 45th St)

16 UNIVERSITY BOOK STORE

Banished from campus in 1925 when its location was deemed a fire hazard, the business landed here, the former site of a pool hall that was closed by state authorities to protect students from "distractions." The present store, now the largest bookstore in Seattle and one of the largest college bookstores in the nation, offers an extensive selection of general fiction, mysteries, science fiction, and travel books. The children's department is estimable, and textbooks and academic press offerings can be found in almost overwhelming proportions. There's free gift wrapping on the second floor and frequent sales on general-interest books. ♦ Daily; Th, until 9PM. 4326 University Way NE (between 43rd and 45th Sts). 634.3400. www.bookstore.washington.edu. Also at 990 102nd Ave NE (at 10th St), Bellevue. 632.9500

17 BULLDOG NEWS

The largest, most eclectic newsstand in the Northwest carries everything from the *New Yorker* and *National Review* to *Spin*, *Story*, *British Esquire*, *The Hockey News*, and *British Columbia Report*. Hundreds of alternative weeklies, out-of-town papers, and foreign periodicals are also on hand. Service can sometimes be indifferent to your requests. An espresso counter dispenses drinks to sidewalk patrons; watch out, the lines here can get long. ♦ Daily, 8AM-9PM. 4208 University Way NE (between 42nd and 43rd Sts). 632.6397. Also at Broadway Market, 401 Broadway E (at Harrison St). 322.6397. ♿

17 CAFE ALLEGRO

★$ Reputed to have introduced Seattle to espresso during the 1960s and still a funkier, more traditional coffeehouse than most in the city, this small, brick-lined café enjoys a remarkably loyal clientele. There's great coffee, ordinary pastries, and, best of all, a staff that will let you curl up in a corner to read *War and Peace* in its entirety, if you so desire. ♦ Coffeehouse ♦ Daily, until 11PM. 4214 University Way NE (between 42nd and 43rd Sts). 633.3030

18 MAGUS BOOKSTORE

Unswept floors, books stacked precariously high, and an erudite, helpful staff—this is your quintessential college used-book seller. Don't expect to find Judith Krantz among the piles of literature, philosophy, history, and art books. ♦ Daily, until 10PM. 1408 NE 42nd St (between 15th Ave and University Way). 633.1800. www.magusbks.com

19 UNIVERSITY INN

$$ A $2.5 million wing (erected in 1992) has added a sleek touch to this small, friendly, modern hotel. There are 102 comfortable rooms—none with a view worth mentioning, however—a small heated outdoor pool, a coffee shop, and complimentary continental breakfast. ♦ 4140 Roosevelt Way NE (between 41st and 42nd Sts). 632.5055, 800/733.3855. ♿

20 BIG TIME BREWERY AND ALEHOUSE

This tavern-turned–brewpub offers 12 kinds of beer made on the premises, all flavorful, unpasteurized, and heavier than your standard-issue Bud. An 80-year-old back bar, hardwood floors, vintage signs, and a jukebox create a traditional American alehouse atmosphere. Large front windows allow for a maximum of people watching. The small kitchen produces hefty sandwiches, pizza, and very acceptable nachos. ♦ M-Th, Su, until 12:30AM; F, Sa, until 1AM. 4133 University Way NE (between 41st and 42nd Sts). 545.4509. www.bigtimebrewery.com

21 SHULTZY'S SAUSAGE

★$ The homemade sausages served at this hole in the wall are ground and stuffed with Uncle Norm's recipe. Lines form out the door for the spicy-hot Ragin' Cajun and milder andouille choices. ♦ Deli ♦ Daily, lunch and dinner. 4114 University Way NE (between 41st and 42nd Sts). 548.9461. www.shultzys.com

21 EUROPEAN RESTAURANT & PASTRY SHOP

★$ German-style food (Hungarian goulash, stuffed cabbage rolls, sausage sandwiches) is served in an Old World atmosphere. Most people, though, come here for the pastries, especially the Black Forest cake. ♦ German ♦ M-Sa, breakfast, lunch, and dinner; Su, lunch. 4108 University Way NE (between 41st and 42nd Sts). 632.7893. ♿

22 UNIVERSITY OF WASHINGTON

The upper campus is the classic evocation of academia: ivy-covered Gothic buildings grouped around formal, brick-paved quadrangles; majestic sycamores, maples, and oaks; and curved walkways leading through nicely landscaped grounds. There's no denying that this is a lovely place to stroll, whether you're dazzled by the architecture, the cherry trees in bloom, or the million-dollar views of Lake Washington and the Cascade peaks from the student dorms. The lower campus, marked by newer, 1950s concrete edifices, also deserves attention for its beautiful gardens of medicinal herbs and its striking architecture (particularly the Drumheller Fountain, the four freestanding columns in a small grove on the southern part of campus, and even the parking garage, crowned with a small forest of evergreens

---

Restaurants/Clubs: Red | Hotels: Purple | Shops: Orange | Outdoors/Parks: Green | Sights/Culture: Blue

and ivies). Today, the university has an enrollment of about 34,000; its most popular graduate schools are arts and sciences, engineering, medicine, law, and dentistry. The main entrance is at the intersection of NE 45th Street and 17th Avenue, from which you travel along Memorial Way beneath a dramatic archway of sycamores to arrive on campus. At NE 41st Street, a pedestrian overpass crosses 15th Avenue to reach the university via Central Plaza. The entrance to the large parking garage (located below the plaza) is here too. A third point of entry is on the eastern backside of campus, at 25th Avenue NE, about three quarters of a mile north of **Husky Stadium**.

On the University of Washington campus:

VISITORS' INFORMATION CENTER

An ideal starting point for a tour of the neighborhood, the center offers campus maps; restaurant, lodging, and bus info; and local events schedules. ◆ M-F. 4014 University Way NE (at Campus Pkwy). 543.9198. www.washington.edu

CENTRAL PLAZA

Commonly referred to as Red Square (attributable to its expanse of red bricks, not to any Bolshevik incidents), this campus crossroads was designed in 1972. The vast, almost treeless plaza is surrounded by stark, hard-surfaced buildings constructed in a mishmash arrangement of architectural styles. It's overpowering and strikes many people as depressing and inhuman, but on sunny days, this spot resembles an Italian piazza, alive with students strumming guitars, throwing Frisbees, and enjoying brown-bag lunches.

Around Central Plaza:

HENRY ART GALLERY

The original redbrick Tudor-Gothic structure designed by **Carl Gould** features striking decorative brickwork and handsome skylit exhibition galleries. Opened in 1927, its construction was funded by Horace C. Henry, a local real estate and railroad magnate, who also donated his sizable collection of late 19th- and early 20th-century European and American paintings. The spectacular recent addition/expansion, designed by **Charles Gwathmey**, is an architectural collage of glass, textured stainless steel, and cast stone. The museum now encompasses 46,000 square feet of intimate exhibition spaces, balconies, bridged walkways, and spacious belowground galleries. You are as likely to see a contemporary video installation as modern Chinese prints or early 20th-century American paintings. ◆ Admission $5; free Th, 5-8PM. Tu-Su; Th, until 8PM. 543.2280. www.henryart.org

MEANY HALL

Named in honor of a popular and longtime history professor, Edmond S. Meany, this performing arts center contains a 1,200-seat theater, a 200-seat studio, and dance facilities. Excellent acoustics and intimate seating make it one of the city's premier venues for chamber music series, dance recitals, and concerts. ◆ 543.4880

SUZZALLO/ALLEN LIBRARY

Certainly the most impressive building on campus, this ornate Tudor Gothic library was designed by **Carl Gould** and dates from about 1926. Founder of the university's architecture department, Gould laid out plans for 18 campus buildings (as well as **Volunteer Park**'s old **Seattle Art Museum** and, with partner **Charles Bebb**, the **Times Square Building** downtown).

The library was the crowning achievement—and, ironically, the downfall—of Henry Suzzallo, former university president (1915-1926), who is often recalled as **UW**'s "modern father." Suzzallo wanted an ambitious, cathedral-like building, believing that "the library is the soul of the university." Washington Governor Roland Hartley didn't agree: He looked at the $900,000 invoice, dubbed it "Suzzallo's extravagance," and fired the respected educator, who went on to head the philanthropic Carnegie Foundation.

Outside, observe three sculptures perched over the entrance: *Thought, Inspiration,* and *Mastery,* created by Tacoma artist Allan Clark (see *Art,* below). Inside, follow the curved staircase from the building's entrance to the mezzanine-level **Graduate Reading Room,** where vaulting and 36-foot-high stained-glass windows tower above. ◆ Daily; M-Th, Su, until midnight (hours are more restricted during school breaks)

Ken Jennings, the man who won *Jeopardy* 74 times in a row, recently moved back to the Seattle area where he grew up. With more than $3 million in winnings, he's not resting on his laurels. No, he's been promoting his first book: *Brainiac: Adventures in the Curious, Competitive, Compulsive World of Trivia Buffs.* Rumor has it he's working on a book about his *Jeopardy* experiences. What is a tell-all, Alex?

ART

The west façade of the **Suzzallo/Allen Library** hosts 18 terra-cotta figures of famous people, including Shakespeare, Beethoven, and Plato. The original design for Darwin featured a small ape thumbing its nose at the humans below, but the university president vetoed that concept. (Look closely at Darwin, and you'll see a hole at the bottom of the figure where the ape was supposed to be.) Hidden behind oak trees, the Gothic **Administration Building** on the south side of the plaza is ringed by 24 gargoyles and other figures, each one representing an academic discipline. The square contains *Broken Obelisk*, a 2-ton, 26-foot steel work that resembles an upside-down pencil and is a rare sculpture by Barnett Newman, a New York painter known mostly for abstract color fields. The three faux-campaniles that soar into the sky are visually striking but have a more quotidian purpose as well: They are vents to disperse car exhaust fumes from the underground garage. A bronze statue of George Washington on the square's west side was sculpted in 1909 by Lorado Taft and unveiled for the Alaska-Yukon-Pacific Exposition.

SMITH HALL

Twenty-eight gargoyles decorate the exterior of this 1940 building, which houses the history and geography departments. Designed by faculty member Dudley Pratt, each gargoyle symbolizes something different. Six figures at the east entrance signify human-kind's primitive needs, whereas those on the southeast corner depict concepts of weather.

Married couples are still the majority of US and Washington households, but in Seattle, people living alone and unrelated roommates predominate.

Those on the northeast corner stand for the power and war of Europe, the magic of Africa, and the knowledge of the Orient. A book-laden egghead in the grouping stands for the intelligent democracy of America. Groups on the north side depict Seattle's history.
♦ Quadrangle

DENNY HALL

Built circa 1895, this turreted French Renaissance structure was the first—and for some time the only—building on campus. Given the hall's original importance, its very ordinary location (with no expansive view over Lake Union) seems curious. But campus legend has it that officials argued for so long over the building's proper site that one exasperated regent finally stuck his umbrella into a fallen fir tree and said, "You fellows can put the building where you want it; I'm going to put it here." And there it's been ever since.
♦ Memorial Way

THOMAS BURKE MEMORIAL WASHINGTON STATE MUSEUM

Exhibits in natural history, anthropology, and geology from Pacific Rim cultures span many epochs in this museum. High on the list of must-sees is the collection of Northwest Coast Indian artifacts. An Alaskan Arctic collection of basketry, ivory, beadwork, and masks wins accolades. Children will enjoy the dinosaur skeletons, fossils, and totem poles. Take a look at the stained-glass window portraying a peacock in the **Burke Room**: It's by master Louis Comfort Tiffany himself. The museum was designed in 1962 by **James J. Chiarelli** in honor of Judge Thomas Burke, an attorney who negotiated early Seattle land acquisitions for **Great Northern Railroad** builder James J. Hill.
♦ Daily; Th, until 8PM. NE 45th St (between

Restaurants/Clubs: Red **|** Hotels: Purple **|** Shops: Orange **|** Outdoors/Parks: Green **|** Sights/Culture: Blue

LIGHTS, CAMERA, ACTION: SEATTLE ON FILM

New York and Los Angeles are both overused (and increasingly expensive) backdrops for films, so many directors have chosen to set their stories in the Northwest instead. And Seattle—with its unusual combination of gritty urban and beautiful natural settings—has been cashing in on this trend. In recent years, the city's multifaceted character has been highlighted in movies ranging from romantic (*Sleepless in Seattle*) to suspenseful (*Disclosure*) to family-oriented (*Free Willy*). Here are a few of the better-known flicks shot in the Seattle area:

Agent Cody Banks (2003) Cody Banks, played by Frankie Muniz, is a shy, common teenager, living with his mother, father, and little brother in a suburban house. But he is also a very efficient undercover CIA agent. Filmed in Seattle.

American Heart (1993) Ex-con Jeff Bridges's life changes irrevocably when his son comes to live with him. The two of them try to make a life together on Seattle's rough **Waterfront**.

Black Widow (1987) Determined investigator Debra Winger is pitted against seductress Theresa Russell, who has murdered two previous husbands and is now in hot pursuit of a rich Seattle businessman. The **Elliot Bay Book Company** and the **Olympic Hotel** can be seen, and the **P-I Building** stands in for FBI headquarters in Washington, DC.

The Changeling (1980) In this atmospheric film, a man (George C. Scott), whose family has been killed in a car accident, moves to a lonely Seattle mansion that is haunted by a dead child.

Cinderella Liberty (1973) A shabby Seattle provides a perfect backdrop for the troubled relationship between sailor James Caan and hooker Marsha Mason.

Disclosure (1994) In this film adaptation of the best-selling novel by Michael Crichton, a ruthless executive (Demi Moore) falsely accuses a colleague (Michael Douglas) of sexual harassment. Some scenes take place in **Pioneer Square**, the **Four Seasons Hotel**, and the **Washington Park Arboretum**.

The Fabulous Baker Boys (1989) A jazzy Seattle is home to two piano-tickling brothers (Jeff and Beau Bridges) and a singer (Michelle Pfeiffer) who joins their act and changes their lives. It's definitely worth seeing.

Fear (1996) Stars hunky Mark Wahlberg as a stalker laying siege to a frightened family in an isolated location without a phone. According to critic S. Damien Segal, "The Seattle scene, from the city's striking architecture to its grunge-rock subculture, provides a slick, spirited backdrop that keeps the film moving at a brisk pace."

Firewall (2006) Jack Stanfield, played by Harrison Ford, is an executive responsible for the security of the computer system of a small bank. When the gang led by the criminal played by Paul Bettany invades his house, they force Jack to transfer a hundred million dollars to a bank account in the Cayman Islands as a ransom for his family. When his family is not release, Jack tries to save them on his own.

Frances (1983) This is a haunting portrayal of 1930s film star and Seattle native Frances Farmer (Jessica Lange).

Free Willy (1994) This heartwarming hit is about a young boy who befriends a killer whale in an aquarium and helps him to escape and return to his family.

From Dusk Till Dawn (1995) George Clooney teams up with Quentin Tarantino, Harvey Keitel, and Cheech Marin in a movie about escaped cons, hostage-taking, and a biker bar run by vampires.

The Hand That Rocks the Cradle (1992) An embittered childless widow (Rebecca DeMornay) seeks revenge against the woman who she thinks ruined her life (Annabella Sciorra).

The Heart of the Game (2005) This film captures the passion and energy of a Seattle high school girls' basketball team, the eccentricity of the unorthodox coach, and the incredible story of one player's fight to play the game she loves.

Highway (2001) A story about two friends, wannabe grunge rockers, who travel across the country to the Northwest to attend a vigil for Kurt Cobain, a Seattle native who died by suicide.

Memorial Way and 15th Ave). 543.5590, 543.7907. www.washington.edu

Within the Thomas Burke Memorial Washington State Museum:

THE BURKE MUSEUM CAFE

★★$ The museum's basement contains the toniest and one of the most pleasant coffeehouses in Seattle. The high-ceilinged room features 18th-century French pine panels and artwork, antique wooden tables, classical music, and very tasty pastries. It's a favorite spot for students between classes, and a rest stop for campus cops. Desserts are plentiful and delicious. The tree-shaded patio is ideal for lounging on warm days. ◆ Coffeehouse ◆ Daily; M-F, until 8PM. 543.9854. ⑤

PENTHOUSE THEATER

Built in about 1940 as the nation's first theater in the round (the frescoes and seats

House of Games (1987) Playwright David Mamet's directorial debut stars Joe Mantegna as a gambler who fears he'll be murdered over a bad debt.

Hype! (1996) This documentary chronicles the rise of grunge rock in Seattle and its growing national popularity. It includes live performances by Pearl Jam and Nirvana, among others.

It Happened at the World's Fair (1963) Shows Elvis Presley eating dinner at the **Space Needle** and singing on the **Monorail**.

Life or Something Like It (2002) Or, as one reviewer called it, "Rubbish or Something Like It," this finds Oscar-winner Angelina Jolie playing a smart but shallow Seattle reporter who, when told she has only 1 week left to live, promptly sets about rediscovering the joy of living.

McQ (1974) John Wayne stars in this chase-fest about a Dirty Harry–like cop who lives on a boat at the docks in **Fremont**. The seamier side of the downtown area is featured, as well as some lovely Washington Coast scenery.

The Night Strangler (1973) This made-for-TV film features Darren McGavin as a rumpled reporter hot on the trail of a murderous member of the "living dead" beneath the streets of Pioneer Square.

An Officer and a Gentleman (1982) Richard Gere plays a loner and aspiring navy pilot who tries not to fall in love with local factory worker Debra Winger. This film was shot in Seattle and **Port Townsend**.

The Parallax View (1974) Tells the twisted tale of a senator's assassination. Warren Beatty portrays a local reporter determined to get to the truth in Alan Pakula's **Space Needle**–hanger.

The Ring (2002) A remake of the Japanese horror flick "Ringu." Rachel Keller, played by Naomi Watts, is a young journalist with a divorced husband and a son. Filmed in the Seattle area, one of the most memorable scenes takes place on a Washington State ferry.

Rock Star (2001) Chris Cole, played by Mark Wahlberg, has been picked to replace Bobby Beers as the lead singer of Steel Dragon, his favorite band. The movie is fast and heavy-metal earsplitting, some of it filmed in Seattle.

Say Anything (1989) Often voted one of the best modern screen romances, this is a touching coming-of-age story about a beautiful straight-A student (Ione Skye) caught in an uncertain world.

Singles (1992) Campbell Scott, Bridget Fonda, and Matt Dillon star in director Cameron Crowe's second film. Dillon's character works at the **OK Hotel Cafe/Gallery**.

Sleepless in Seattle (1993) A paean to the classic weeper An Affair to Remember, this mega-hit romance (written and directed by Nora Ephron) features Tom Hanks as a lonely man who moves to Seattle.

The Slender Thread (1965) A **University of Washington** psychology student (Sidney Poitier) working at a suicide hotline fields a call from a desperate woman (Anne Bancroft). Director Sydney Pollack's first movie, it was filmed at the university, **Capitol Hill**, **Ballard**, and the downtown area.

Trouble in Mind (1985) In this not-quite-futuristic yarn, ex-cop and ex-con Kris Kristofferson tries to remake his life in "Rain City," a Seattle of the imagination, in which the **Seattle Art Museum** building on Capitol Hill is the mansion of an arch-gangster. Much of the action is set in the **Kingdome**.

Tugboat Annie (1933) Starring Marie Dressler and Wallace Beery, this film was inspired by Norman Reilly Raine's popular "Tugboat Annie" stories of the 1930s, which were in turn inspired by the tale of Thea Foss, who, operating from **Tacoma** in the late 19th century, began one of the country's largest tugboat empires.

Twice in a Lifetime (1985) is one of the few movies to accurately portray Seattle's blue-collar community. Gene Hackman plays a middle-aged husband who causes a family crisis when he falls in love with a young barmaid. **Mike's Chili Parlor** in Ballard is prominently featured.

---

have been restored to their original state), this is the stage for the **School of Drama's** productions. Tickets are available here at the box office or at the **UW Ticket Office** (4001 University Way NE, at 40th St; 543.4880), which is open Monday through Friday between 10:30AM and 6PM. ♦ Box office opens 1 hour before show time. NE 45th St (east of Memorial Way). 543.4880. www.ascc.artsci.washington.edu

SYLVAN THEATER

The grassy glade, site of an annual summer Shakespeare series, is easily missed. Tucked away within a grove of trees, it contains a

---

Restaurants/Clubs: Red | Hotels: Purple | Shops: Orange | Outdoors/Parks: Green | Sights/Culture: Blue

cool, shady amphitheater and four white columns standing by themselves with nothing to support. These columns, shaped of cedar poles, were transported—at the insistence of Professor Edmond Meany—from their positions at the entrance to the original downtown **Territorial University** building when that old edifice was finally being torn down in 1908. Each of the four columns has a name—Loyalty, Industry, Faith, and Efficiency—the first letters of each spelling *life*. ♦ Stevens Way

BURKE-GILMAN TRAIL

This beloved, 14-mile recreational route runs along an abandoned **Burlington Northern** railbed. More than a million people bike, jog, or walk here each year. The scenic trail, which starts in Ballard on Eighth Avenue NW just south of Leary Way, hugs the Lake Washington Ship Canal and Lake Union and then crawls east and north, virtually through the backyards of lakefront homes, until it reaches Kenmore's **Tracy Owen Station Park** at the northern tip of Lake Washington. *One caveat*: 70% of trail users are bicyclists, so walkers should take extra care.

HUSKY STADIUM

Football-crazed fans watch the **Huskies** (often called "the Dawgs" but never "Dogs") here in the Northwest's largest stadium, which seats 72,500 people. It's said that the wave cheer was invented here in 1981 by the marching band's director and cheerleader, Robb Weller. The south section of the cantilevered steel balcony and roof was finally erected in 1987, after a calamitous construction accident in which steel support beams weakened and the entire section crumpled into a massive pile of twisted metal. No one was hurt, but the scene was immortalized when a photographer, John Stamets, riding by on his bicycle, snapped a frame-by-frame account of the collapse and published it in a local newspaper. ♦ 3800 Montlake Blvd NE (between Pacific St and Walla Walla Rd). 543.2200

WATERFRONT ACTIVITIES CENTER

Rent canoes or rowboats to cross Union Bay and then wander through the soft, lily-

padded backwaters near the **Washington Park Arboretum** (see the "Capitol Hill to Seward Park" chapter) for a Monet-like experience. Bird-watchers might want to go north from the center, creeping along the shore to see blue herons, eagles, and other wild creatures in a protected reserve. ♦ M-F, Feb-Oct. Walla Walla Rd (south of Montlake Blvd NE). 543.9433

FROSH POND, RAINIER VISTA

During the Alaska-Yukon-Pacific Exposition, this body of water was a geyser basin. Afterward, it became a spot where first-year students received honorary dunkings from sophomores (hence the name). And today it's a decorative pool with a fountain—officially called the Drumheller Fountain—that's especially appealing when the surrounding roses are in bloom. Proud moms and dads snap photos of students here. The walkway down to Pacific Place was designed by the Olmsted Brothers in 1909 as a culminating viewpoint from which fairgoers could eyeball Mount Rainier.

ARCHITECTURE HALL

This is the only major structure built for the Alaska-Yukon-Pacific Expo that is left standing. San Francisco's **John Galen Howard**, who in 1909 was campus architect for the University of California, Berkeley, created the eclectic classical-style design. Today, the building houses the **Department of Urban Planning**. ♦ Stevens Way

COLLEGE INN GUEST HOUSE

$ Popular with visiting professors and other university types on a budget, this nonsmoking bed-and-breakfast was built as a hotel for the 1909 Alaska-Yukon-Pacific Expo and is on the National Register of Historic Places. The 25 rooms are very plain and spare (no TV, no telephones, no private baths), but they are clean and generally pleasant. ♦ 4000 University Way NE (at 40th St). 633.4441

23 NORTHLAKE TAVERN & PIZZA HOUSE

★★$ The principal wall decorations here are cartoons from the *Seattle Post-Intelligencer*'s David Horsey, but there's nothing comic about the pizza. Crusts (including a respectable whole-wheat variety) are chewy without threatening to yank out your wisdom teeth, and the cooks have nothing against piling on the toppings. Build your own pie from a 14-ingredient list, or just order the Italian Special (salami, Italian beef sausage, mushrooms, onions, and tomatoes). You can even buy an uncooked pizza to pop in the

On the first Wednesday evening of each month, the Vintage Motorcycle Enthusiasts (VME) meet at Teddy's Tavern (NE 65th St and Roosevelt Way). The event also attracts hordes of people who aren't part of the club—but come to stand outside and look at the rows of gorgeous, impeccably preserved cycles parked in front of the building.

oven later on. ♦ Pizza/takeout ♦ Daily, lunch and dinner. 660 NE Northlake Way (At Northlake Pl). 633.5317. ♿ www.northlaketavern.com

RAVENNA

24 SUNLIGHT CAFE

★★$ This vegetarian restaurant serves a full menu, including nutburgers, tofu scrambles, and various stir-fry concoctions. Whole-wheat waffles, blueberry pancakes, and nutritious muffins draw healthy crowds on weekends. ♦ Vegetarian ♦ M-F, breakfast, lunch, and dinner; Sa, Su, brunch and dinner. 6403 Roosevelt Way NE (at 64th St). 522.9060. ♿

25 BAGEL OASIS

★★$ Some of the best bagels in town are available here: big, soft, chewy, and often sold hot right out of the oven. Nosh on any of these with cream-cheese spreads and Port Chatham lox, or order them as part of a sandwich. Also served are soups, salads, and filling breakfast omelettes. ♦ Deli ♦ Daily, breakfast and lunch. 2112 NE 65th St (between Ravenna and 21st Aves). 526.0525

26 TREE OF LIFE

This shop has an eclectic mix of Jewish and spiritual books and a helpful, knowledge-able staff. It also offers fine Judaica, with an inventory that includes music, art, videos, software, jewelry, accessories, and toys. You can schmooze with artists and visiting writers, such as Rodger Kamenetz and Amos Oz, when they appear here. ♦ M-Th, Su, 10AM-7PM; F, 10AM-3PM. 2201 NE 65th St (at 22nd Ave). 527.1130. ♿ www.treeoflifejudaica.com

27 SALVATORE RISTORANTE ITALIANO

★★★$$ Specializing in Southern Italian cuisine, including veal so tender you could cut it with a plastic fork, this dining spot serves a varied selection of delicious pastas and features an extensive wine list with gentle prices to complement your meal. ♦ Italian ♦ M-Sa, dinner. 6100 Roosevelt Way NE (at 61st St). 527.9301

28 COWEN PARK

Donated in 1907 by Charles Cowen, an Englishman reared in South Africa, this area was undeveloped until the city filled and flattened it with dirt from freeway construction in 1961. The result is an 8-acre patch of picnic grounds with a playfield used for softball. The park is used heavily by the neighborhood despite periodic incursions by transients. ♦ NE Ravenna Blvd and Brooklyn Ave

29 RAVENNA PARK

Clarence Bagley, a Seattle pioneer and local historian, complained in the early 20th century that this 52-acre park was "a dark,

Upper Quad, University of Washington

Restaurants/Clubs: **Red** | Hotels: **Purple** | Shops: **Orange** | Outdoors/Parks: **Green** | Sights/Culture: **Blue**

CHARITY BEGINS AWAY FROM HOME: HELPING SEATTLE'S HOMELESS

Despite its explosive growth in recent years, Seattle has not been able to escape the problem of homelessness. By conservative estimates, the number of homeless people on the streets of the city each day ranges from 3,000 to 5,000 (and workers in the field will tell you that it's more like 7,000). But like many of America's major cities, Seattle has developed several innovative programs to help people make the transition from life on the streets to the life that most of us take for granted. Two of these are of particular interest to the visitor: *Real Change Magazine* and FareStart.

Real Change Magazine is a monthly newspaper run, written, and distributed by homeless or formerly homeless members of the community. Started in 1994, its circulation has grown to nearly 25,000. The paper offers interesting articles, fiction, and poetry, as well as the occasional investigative piece or interview. The $1 "suggested donation" is well worth it, as 75 cents of it goes directly to the vendor. A much more viable alternative to panhandling, selling *Real Change* has allowed many of Seattle's homeless to work their way off the streets.

FareStart operates the **FairStart Cafe** (1902 Second Avenue, at Stewart Street; 443.1233; www.farestart.org), which opened in 1992 and is run completely by the homeless and disadvantaged community. All of the staff behind the scenes are formerly homeless people receiving job training that may well allow them to make a living for themselves. The atmosphere is informal, the décor catch-as-catch-can (the plates and furnishings don't match, etc.), but the food is very good. The place is open Monday through Friday for lunch (with a menu of burgers, fries, and other basic American fare), but the best time to visit is on Thursday nights. That's when there's a special prix-fixe dinner menu planned and prepared with the students by one of the city's top chefs; the culinary talents who have donated their time and expertise here include Charles Ramseyer of **Ray's Boathouse** and Tim Kelly of **The Painted Table**. The schedule of chefs is planned several weeks in advance; for information and reservations, call 443.1233. Enjoy a gourmet meal worthy of Seattle's finest restaurants for much less money—and support a good cause at the same time.

It's a rare charity that benefits both the giver and the receiver, but *Real Change* and FareStart are two of them.

damp, dismal hole in the ground for which the city paid an outrageous price." Bagley must have been quite a sourpuss, because in our opinion this is an urban gem.

A creek once ran from Green Lake through this heavily wooded ravine and drained into Lake Washington. History buffs say the area was home to an invigorating mineral springs and a magnificent stand of trees—giant evergreens 30 to 60 feet in diameter. It so impressed a realtor named William W. Beck, who bought it as part of a 300-acre tract, that he named it after the parklike Italian town of Ravenna. Beck also named the largest trees after famous people—Teddy Roosevelt and Robert E. Lee among them—and charged visitors 25 cents a head to enter his sanctuary. The city coveted his land and eventually acquired it through condemnation in 1911. But it promptly destroyed much of the park's grandeur by lowering Green Lake and cutting off the creek, then constructing an underground drainage system and toppling the great trees Beck had so admired, to be sold as cordwood.

Today, the park is minus its virgin timber, but it still feels like a small piece of wilderness within city limits. It boasts two large playgrounds on either end (in **Lower Ravenna Park** and in **Cowen Park**), joined together by a natural ravine and small creek. Quiet and unsculpted, this ravine sometimes seems imbued with magic (one writer called it a hobbit's realm) as it follows Ravenna Creek through steeply sloped brush- and fern-covered forest land. A wide trail here provides a 20-minute walk for strollers and a shorter but still soothing escape for runners during the daytime. Come night, however, transients sometimes hang out in the park, so be cautious. ◆ NE 58th St and 20th Ave

30 RAVENNA BOULEVARD

Designed by the Olmsted Brothers to be part of their chain of Seattle parks linked by boulevards, this once marked the Ravenna neighborhood's northern boundary. Now, the wide, grassy, tree-lined strip is a favorite for runners.

Elliott Bay

31 LOWER RAVENNA PARK

East of the main park, the ravine empties into a broad field and baseball diamond. Above it, you'll come across a small playfield, playground, and tennis courts with full sun exposure. Keep walking up the hill and wind through a series of small, serene meadows where you can picnic at tables, read in solitude, or just listen to the many songbirds. Go farther, and you'll come to a dead end at a larger meadow that has a covered barbecue pit area. ♦ NE Ravenna Blvd and Ravenna Ave

32 QUEEN MARY

★★$$$ This could very well be the site of the Mad Hatter's Tea Party—from the shards of lovely crockery embedded in the sidewalk outside to the flowered chintz inside. Owner Mary Greengo has created a perfect spot for a leisurely afternoon tea of tomato-and-basil sandwiches and lemon curd tart. And, if you're late for a very important date, pick up a sweet morsel from the pastry case. ♦ American ♦ Daily, breakfast, lunch, and tea. 2912 NE 55th St (between 30th and 29th Aves). 527.2770. www.queenmarytearoom.com

---

Restaurants/Clubs: Red | Hotels: Purple | Shops: Orange | Outdoors/Parks: Green | Sights/Culture: Blue

EASTSIDE

Places separated from others by water—Venice, Valhalla, the New World—have traditionally held a certain allure. So it's not surprising that the suburban communities nestled on the near-east side of **Lake Washington**—principally **Mercer Island**, **Bellevue**, and **Kirkland**—always have been and probably always will be a dreamland for somebody.

Pioneer Peter Kirk set out in the 1880s to build the "Pittsburgh of the West" on the forested slopes above **Moss Bay**. But this industrial capital of belching steel- and ironworks never materialized. And in 1928, before the first bridge was built across the lake, real-estate baron James Ditty laid out a plan for an Eastside utopia that included blimps traveling to and from downtown Seattle and huge observation towers in the midst of Mercer Island; this dream also was unrealized. An advertisement from the 1940s solicited interest from Seattleites with the slogan "15 Minutes to Your Home in the Country." It seems a cruel joke now, when even a slug might outpace the heavy rush-hour traffic across the lake.

But thousands of new residents continue to be drawn here by the quality of life (including the fairly safe schools) and by booming high-tech industries (computer giant Microsoft and cellular phone purveyor McCaw Communications among them). Neighborhood strip malls and well-groomed suburban lawns characterize the Eastside of today. It's the fourth-largest urban area in Washington State, and very much ruled by the automobile. Only a few enclaves, such as **Beaux Arts Village**, southwest of downtown Bellevue, have escaped the rule of the road. Founded in 1908 as a rustic commune for artists (and for a while, it was a nudist colony), this lovely residential hideaway is still woven with streets barely wide enough for two cars to pass.

The look and attitude of the Eastside varies greatly from one district to the next. Mercer Island is primarily residential, crossed at its north end by Interstate 90 (I-90). It boasts only a small commercial zone and is a leisurely ride for bicyclists. Kirkland has several art galleries, antiques shops, and good restaurants. Bellevue, the most urban of the three areas, is characterized by businesses set back from the street in retail and office valleys—the legacy of one of the Eastside's most successful dreamers, Kemper Freeman Sr., who believed businesses that provided parking in front of their buildings would flourish. A rare Bellevue exception is **Main Street** in Old Bellevue, an area just off the downtown core that resembles compact Kirkland.

Aside from some obvious sites in Kirkland, historic buildings are in short supply throughout the Eastside, partly because of the area's relatively recent settlement and partly because the value of its first structures was not recognized in the furor of slapdash post–World War II development. Much of the architecture of the past 45 years has failed to consider the Eastside's potential; many of the structures raised were clearly second-class. But that's changing. Several award-winning multiuse projects, such as **Carillon Point** and **Bellevue Place**, have taken great steps in making huge complexes accessible to the public and compatible with the environment. As everywhere else, developers are, for better or worse, changing the face of the area in an effort to accommodate growth, whereas preservation-minded citizens strive to save what they can for future generations.

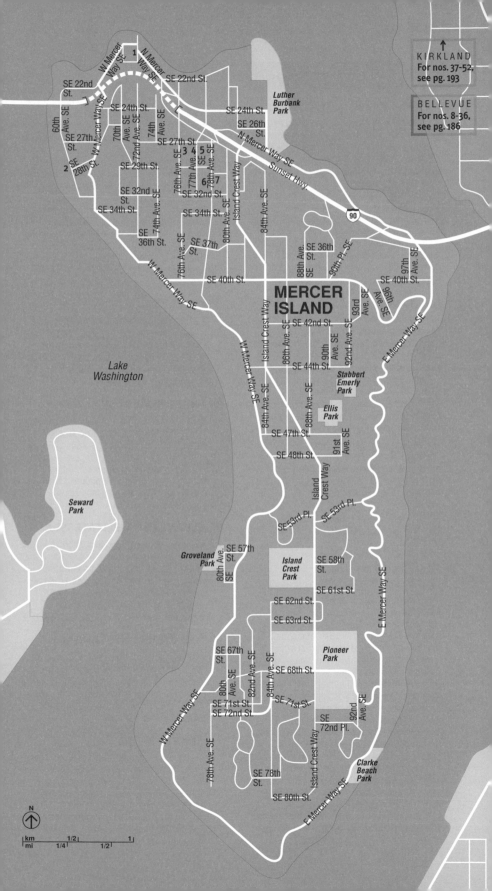

KIRKLAND
For nos. 37-52,
see pg. 193

BELLEVUE
For nos. 8-36,
see pg. 186

MERCER ISLAND

Lake Washington

Seward Park

Luther Burbank Park

Groveland Park

Island Crest Park

Stabbert Emerly Park

Ellis Park

Pioneer Park

Clarke Beach Park

N Mercer Way SE
W Mercer Way SE
W Mercer Way SE
E Mercer Way SE
Sunset Hwy
Island Crest Way

SE 22nd St.
SE 22nd St.
SE 24th St.
SE 24th St.
SE 26th St.
SE 27th St.
SE 27th St.
SE 28th St.
SE 29th St.
SE 32nd St.
SE 32nd St.
SE 34th St.
SE 34th St.
SE 36th St.
SE 36th St.
SE 37th St.
SE 40th St.
SE 40th St.
SE 42nd St.
SE 44th St.
SE 47th St.
SE 48th St.
SE 53rd Pl.
SE 55th Pl.
SE 57th St.
SE 58th St.
SE 61st St.
SE 62nd St.
SE 63rd St.
SE 67th St.
SE 68th St.
SE 71st St.
SE 72nd St.
SE 72nd Pl.
SE 78th St.
SE 80th St.

60th Ave. SE
70th Ave. SE
72nd Ave. SE
74th Ave.
74th Ave. SE
76th Ave. SE
76th Ave. SE
77th Ave. SE
78th Ave. SE
78th Ave. SE
80th Ave. SE
80th Ave. SE
80th Ave. SE
82nd Ave. SE
84th Ave. SE
84th Ave. SE
84th Ave. SE
86th Ave. SE
88th Ave. SE
88th Ave. SE
90th Ave. SE
90th Pl. SE
91st Ave. SE
92nd Ave. SE
92nd Ave. SE
93rd Ave. SE
96th Ave. SE
97th Ave. SE

I-90

1
2
3 4 5
6 7

N
km   1/2   1
mi   1/4   1/2

MERCER ISLAND

1 ROANOKE INN

Bartenders here are generally versed in the colorful history of Mercer Island's longest-operating business. They'll explain how this place was a general store when it opened in 1916, how there was once a pinball machine here that would pay off in quarters, and how it used to be a popular drinking spot for city swells. Those were the good old days, back when a ferry still connected the north end of Mercer Island with Seattle, before I-90 took all of the **Roanoke**'s drive-by business away and left it baby-sitting a dead-end route to a dark pier. Late owner Hal Reeck's stepfather was known to pack pistols into this place and fire them at inconvenient times, blowing holes in various walls and pieces of furniture.

Today, most of the action takes place on the TV screen, but much of the tavern's classic atmosphere endures. A giant fireplace sits opposite the front door, gold trophies elbowing each other for room on its mantel. Beer paraphernalia crowds the walls, and during warm months, the place to be is on the long front porch, swapping tall tales and watching Lake Washington capture moonbeams, or in the backyard, playing a game of croquet.

The bar stocks a few craft beers like Guinness, Red Hook, and Widmer, and one of four local beers is always on tap. Food selections run to burgers, soups and salads, and taco salads. Spaghetti dinners are served on Thursday nights. ♦ Daily. 1825 72nd Ave SE (between SE 20th St and N Mercer Way). 232.0800. &. www.roanokeinn.com

2 CALKINS'S LANDING

Charles Cicero Calkins was a lawyer from Illinois who abandoned the bar to become an entrepreneur, real-estate gambler, and Mercer Island's best-remembered dreamer. He arrived in Seattle in 1887 and soon determined that Lake Washington's only island should shed its pioneer image. He raised a three-story hotel just up the hill from the present-day landing, which must have been a magical sight—it was an architectural amalgam of an American railroad station and a Swiss chalet, with dormers, turrets, and chimneys punctuating its tile roof and broad elegant porches skirting its lower levels. The grounds boasted mazes, promenades, a huge greenhouse with 635 varieties of roses and 25 fountains, one with a 60-foot-wide bowl. A bathhouse held 100 boats and 28 dressing rooms, as well as a complete system of Turkish baths. The **Hotel Calkins** was designed to be the centerpiece of a new, nonindustrial

community called East Seattle—Puget Sound's version of Newport, Rhode Island. Hoping to start a trend, the developer built a lavish home for himself on the north tip of what is now **Luther Burbank Park**. But an evil turn of fate put an end to Calkins's schemes. Within the span of a few years, his daughter died, his wife divorced him, and the depression of 1893 depleted his fortune. Calkins's mansion and later his hotel burned to their foundations. He set out in despair for southern California, where he again tried (and failed) to make his fortune in gold mining before he died in 1948 at the age of 98. It's sad that the only thing remaining of the elegance Calkins brought to Mercer Island is a mispunctuated sign on this tiny wedge of lawn and sand, where his hotel once had a dock. ♦ SE 28th St and 60th Ave

3 FINDERS

A small store, chockablock with gift ideas: toys, handmade crafts, quilts, children's books, journals, stationery, and a wide selection of cards. ♦ Daily. 7607 SE 27th St (between 77th and 76th Aves). 236.1110. &. www.findersgifts.com

4 THAI ON MERCER

★★$$ Roast lamb and halibut with tamarind sauce are two of the favorites at this consistently excellent restaurant. Sit back and enjoy the restful, inviting ambience and the well-prepared, well-presented food. ♦ Thai ♦ M-F, lunch and dinner; Sa, Su, dinner. 7691 SE 27th St (at 77th Ave). 236.9990. &

5 ALPENLAND DELICATESSEN

★$ First look for **Walgreens**; then you can spot this tiny place above it. Behind a small storefront is a well-stocked deli offering sandwiches and other treats for eat-in or take-out lunches and picnics. ♦ Deli/takeout ♦ M-Sa. 2707 78th Ave SE (between 29th and 27th Sts). 232.4780. &

6 PON PROEM RESTAURANT

★$ Colorful, cool décor and well-prepared Thai food are the offerings here. Try the chicken with cashews or fresh ginger. ♦ Thai ♦ M-F, lunch and dinner; Sa, Su, dinner. 3039 78th Ave SE (between 32nd and 29th Sts). 236.8424. &

7 ISLAND BOOKS

This excellent general bookstore has a large stock and a friendly staff made up of genuine bibliophiles. The spacious back room is devoted to kids' lit; there's also a huge playhouse and enough toys to keep any number of small-size nonreaders occupied. ♦ M-Sa; Th, until 8PM. 3014 78th Ave SE (between 32nd and 30th Sts). 232.6920

7 HANDS OF THE HILLS

In the same shopping center as **Island Books**, this shop sells more beads than you'll ever be able to twirl around your neck, wrists, *and* ankles. Restringing services are also available. ♦ 3016 78th Ave SE (between 32nd and 30th Sts). 232.8121. ♿ www.hohbead.com

BELLEVUE

8 ROSALIE WHYEL MUSEUM OF DOLL ART

This Victorian-style museum was built slightly oversize to make visitors feel a little . . . well . . . doll-like. The exhibits showcase antiques and collectibles—not reproductions—from ivory Eskimo dolls to Barbie gift sets. ♦ Free for children age 4 and younger. Daily. 1116 108th Ave NE (between Eighth and 12th Sts). 425/455.1116. www.dollart.com

9 UNIVERSITY BOOK STORE

The University District original is so successful that branching out seemed inevitable, but the selections here of specialty literature, such as mysteries or science fiction, pale against those at the older main store. This outlet, however, contains two aisles of volumes about cooking, nutrition, and international cuisines. Browse to your heart's content. ♦ Daily. 990 102nd Ave NE (at 10th St). 888/335.7323; fax 425/462.4500. Also at 4326 University Way NE (between 43rd and 45th Sts). 634.3400. ♿ www.bookstore.washington.edu

10 MR. "J" KITCHEN GOURMET

Everything you need to operate your professional-level kitchen is available here. Hanging baskets, skillets, and giant utensils form a junglelike upper canopy. Bins full of citrus peelers, honey dippers, butter spreaders, and poultry lifters are constantly restocked so that no peg or shelf space is empty. An electric pepper grinder with a light (for poorly lit romantic dinners?), a crumb box with a removable trivet, a tripod-mounted solid-brass cork extractor, and a marble rolling pin can be found near Waterford crystal and Henckel's cutlery. ♦ Daily. 10116 NE Eighth St (between 102nd and 100th Aves). 425/455.2270. ♿

11 STARBUCKS

★$ Along with some of the best espresso made in the Seattle area, this coffeeteria sells everything for the home *latte* junkie.

♦ Coffeehouse ♦ Daily. 10214 NE Eighth St (between 103rd and 102nd Aves). 425/454.0191. Also at numerous locations throughout the Seattle area. www.starbucks.com

11 SILBERMAN/BROWN STATIONERS

Owner Sue Silberman sums up the selection of new and antique pens, inkwells, and letter openers with a quip: "There's nothing in here you *need*." But there may be things you *want*—like a Lorenzo de' Medici sterling-silver fountain pen ($1,500)—making this a gift shop for the executive who has almost everything. ♦ M-Sa. 10220 NE Eighth St (between 103rd and 102nd Aves). 425/455.3665. www.silbermanbrown.com

12 BELLEVUE PLACE

This high-rise complex was the first multiuse project of such magnitude in the Northwest, but as architecture, it is only mediocre. The complex includes the **Bank of America Building**, the **Bellevue Place Building**, and the glass-domed **Wintergarten**, linking the towers. ♦ 10500 NE Eighth St (between 106th Ave and Bellevue Way). 425/453.5634

Within Bellevue Place:

TULLY'S

★$ This espresso shop, wedged into an awkward space on the first floor of the **Bank of America Building**, has captured the workforce's coffee-break market, offering panini sandwiches, salads, and pastry, in addition to the usual espresso drinks, beans, and coffeemaking equipment. ♦ M-Sa. 1st floor. 425/453.9456. ♿ www.tullys.com

DANIEL'S BROILER

★★★$$$$ Simultaneously chic in appearance (dark woods, onyx tabletops) and simple in its meal preparations, this is an ideal spot for entertaining. Its 21st-floor setting in the **Bank of America Building** provides Bellevue's best dining views. A specialty is USDA prime corn-fed beef. And in both the 1987 and 1990 Puget Sound Chowder Off competitions, this eatery served up the prize-winning bowl. There's live piano music Tuesday through Saturday nights. The **Oyster Bar Lounge** is frequented by designer-suited people. ♦ American ♦ M-F, lunch and dinner; Sa, Su, dinner. Bank of America Building, 21st floor. 425/462.4662. www.schwartzbrothers.com. Also at 200 Lake Washington Blvd (at E Alder St); and 809 Fairview Place N (on the corner of Valley St and Fairview Ave). 329.4191. ♿

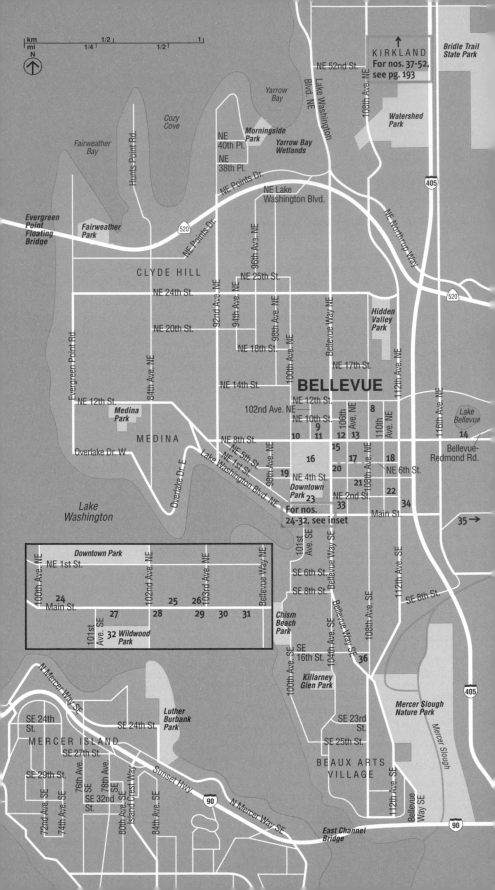

CUCINA! CUCINA!

★★$$ Bicycles hanging from the ceiling reflect the offbeat spirit of the after-work crowd that keeps this hot spot going. Try the focaccia as an appetizer. Dinner choices range from pizzas and pastas to seafood, soups, salads, and more. The veal scallopini sautéed with fresh sage, prosciutto, pine nuts, and garlic is a specialty. ♦ Italian ♦ Daily, lunch and dinner; bar; until 1AM. MGM Bldg, 1st floor. 425/637.1177. &. www.cucinacucina.com

12 HYATT REGENCY AT BELLEVUE PLACE

$$$ The 382 rooms here are the most centrally located in Bellevue. Appointments are classy, without being ostentatious, decorated in neutral and pastel hues with cherry trim. Best choices are those rooms located high up on the south side, which feature views of Mount Rainier and Lake Washington. The **Regency Club** on the 23rd and 24th floors is a luxury hotel within a hotel, offering complimentary concierge and executive business services. All the usual Hyatt amenities apply. ♦ 900 Bellevue Way NE (between Eighth and 10th Sts). 425/462.1234, 800/233.1234. &. www.hyatt.com

Within the Hyatt Regency at Bellevue Place:

EQUES

★★$$$ Northwestern cuisine—especially seafood—is served in an elegant venue among paintings and stone sculptures of horses. Natural-wood floors and private alcoves make this a great place to relax. Popular entrées are applewood-smoked salmon with seared lemon polenta, crab cakes with cracked mustard remoulade, and braised lamb shank with rosemary Cabernet au jus. ♦ Northwestern ♦ Daily. Reservations recommended. 425/451.3012. www.hyatt.com

13 THINKER TOYS

A large, imaginatively decorated shop full of toys, games, and puzzles designed to entertain and challenge. Besides the popular construction sets by Brio, Erector, and Playmobile, you'll find fingerprint kits, chemistry sets, and other intriguing toys from around the world. The shop is frequently listed as "Best Toy Store" by *Eastside Parent* magazine. ♦ Daily. 10610 NE Eighth St (between 108th and 106th Aves). 425/453.0051

14 THE PUMPHOUSE

★$ In such a car-oriented place, "neighborhood joint" has more to do with camaraderie than location. Aggressively nonglitzy, this tavern is Bellevue's version of Cheers. Burgers are large and juicy (order the bacon-and-cheese version), and potato skins are stuffed with green onions, melted cheese, and sour cream. ♦ American ♦ M-Sa, lunch and dinner; bar: until midnight. 11802 NE Eighth St (between Bellevue-Redmond Rd and 116th Ave). 425/455.4110, 425/455.4665

14 I LOVE SUSHI

★★$ Chef Tadashi Sato creates delectable raw-fish delicacies at this very popular restaurant. Specialties include tuna sashimi in the shape of a rose, an excellent *futumaki* roll of pink fish cake and mushrooms, and even Dungeness crab sushi. ♦ Sushi ♦ M-Sa, lunch and dinner; Su, dinner. 11818 NE Eighth St (between Bellevue-Redmond Rd and 116th Ave). 425/454.5706. Also at 1001 Fairview Ave N (at Ward St). 625.9602. &

15 LINCOLN SQUARE

Lincoln Square is big and busy and very much like other upscale malls that feature hotels, theaters, and huge amounts of (discreetly hidden) parking.

Within Lincoln Square:

THE NORSEMEN

This Scandinavian gift shop is loaded with such things as wooden plaques declaring "It's a Blessing To Be Finnish," but what it lacks in class is made up for in variety. Sweatshirts, books, crackers, dolls, Swedish crystal, and even sandwiches are all for sale. It's the ultimate in niche marketing. ♦ 425/822.8715. www.lincoln-square.com

THE BOMBAY COMPANY

The home of a retired English colonel could not be more stuffed with fox-hunt paintings, cricket tables, Italian leather decanters, and solid-brass lamps. Queen Anne and other reproductions are mostly of cherry or birch with mahogany finish, many adapted to the modern function of housing files, VCRs, or tapes. ♦ Daily. 425/455.8544. www.bombaycompany.com

HENREDON

In addition to offering the excellent Henredon line of furniture, this shop also features luxury accessories, including Ralph

PINING FOR NATURE: SEATTLE'S LUSH EVERGREENS

Nature lovers who visit Seattle don't have to drive out to the nearby **Olympic Peninsula** or the foothills of the **Cascade Mountains** when they want to get their fill of forests; trees can be found all over the city. They fill the parks, line streets and freeways, and decorate the yards of private homes. And because most of them are of the evergreen variety, they can be enjoyed throughout the year. Below are several of the more common evergreens you'll see in and around Seattle.

Western Red Cedar

This tree has fibrous reddish gray bark, scaly leaves, and drooping branches that overlap each other. The Salish carved the trees into totem poles, used the inner bark to weave clothing, and hollowed out the trunks to make seafaring canoes. Because the heartwood is rot resistant, the western red cedar is used to make roofing material, fence posts, house siding, and outdoor furniture and decks.

Western Hemlock

Designated the state tree in 1947, the western hemlock has short, rounded needles and small cones. The graceful, lacy branches and drooping top make it easy to identify. Because it requires little maintenance, is drought resistant, and grows well in the shade, the tree is a popular choice to plant on parkland, and it's also used for lumber and pulp.

Douglas Fir

The cones of this tree, which range from 3 to 4 inches long, feature distinctive, leaflike bracts (protrusions).

The needles are a little over 1 inch long. The Douglas fir's strong, durable wood is a mainstay of the region's timber industry, and the tree itself is frequently planted alongside freeways. It's also used as a Christmas tree.

Lodgepole Pine

Another popular choice for Christmas trees, the lodgepole pine sports 1- to 3-inch needles that grow in bunches of two. In this coastal area, the tree can grow as tall as 25 to 30 feet. As its name suggests, it has been used for poles; it's also good for lumber and pulp.

Western Larch

Unlike most evergreens, the western larch has clustered needles that turn golden as they get old and drop off in the fall. It is easily identifiable in the spring because of its bright green color, in contrast to the darker green of other conifers (cone bearers) around it.

Pacific Madrona

Even though it has neither cones nor needles, the Pacific madrona qualifies as an evergreen because its dark green, leathery leaves do not change color in autumn or fall off in winter. Technically, it belongs to the "broadleaf evergreen" category. The tree's unusual, smooth, reddish bark curls and peels periodically to reveal an avocado green underskin. Madronas often can be seen clinging to rocky outcroppings along **Puget Sound**, growing twisted and contorted like giant bonsai.

Lauren and Barbara Barry products for the home. ♦ 425/454.9000. www.henredon.com

KOOTS GREEN TEA

This purveyor of premium green tea and related beverages also sells elegant and wholesome cookies and desserts to accompany your tea. For a calming experience, take a break here from your shopping. ♦ 425/455.2949. www.kootsgreentea.com

PAPER SOURCE

Here you'll find distinctive paper products, stationery, gift wrap and ribbons, hand-made photo albums, creative tools, and keen gifts. ♦ 425/646.0100. www.paper-source.com

THE WESTIN BELLEVUE

$$ This hotel is an integral component of Lincoln Square—a mixed-use hotel, condo-minium, and retail complex. The 337 luxury guest rooms and suites, all with high-speed Internet access, offer views of the surrounding city or of Lake Washington. The hotel has a heated indoor lap pool and a restaurant, **The Manzana Rotisserie Grill**, which prepares Northwestern specialties. ♦ 600 Bellevue Way NE. 425/638.1000. www.westin.com

16 BELLEVUE SQUARE MALL

When people in this area say they're going to Bellevue, they're usually referring to **Bellevue Square**, an upscale shopping center with over 200 shops and restaurants. Here shoppers can find just about anything imaginable, from **J. Crew** to **Godiva Chocolates** and **Seattle's Best Coffee** to **Nordstrom**, **JCPenney**, **Fireworks**, and **Macy's**. About one third of Bellevue's retail business is conducted under this roof, which has skylights along its entire length to lend the mall below an ambiance that architects **Cober-Slater** hoped would suggest a narrow European street. Real ficus trees planted here support this effect, as do the indoor clock tower (with a late-19th-century bell and movement salvaged from Mississippi's Winona County Courthouse) and the bow-window storefronts and blade signs protruding into the mall. Though the mall is large, shops are spread out on several levels, so it's never overwhelming. Located in and around the six-story parking garage in the northeast corner of the Bellevue Square are five fine restaurants—**Ruth's Chris Steakhouse**, **Z'Tejas Southwestern Grill**, **Pagliacci Pizza** (fabulous!), **PF Chang's**, and **Ristorante Luciano**—and a huge multistory **Crate and Barrel**. The parking area is connected by sky bridge across Bellevue Way to **Lincoln Square**. The free covered parking, two children's play areas, stroller rentals, complimentary electric carts and wheelchairs, family rest rooms, and an information and services booth make it one of the most attractive shopping malls in the region. ◆ NE Eighth St (between Bellevue Way and 100th Ave). 425/454.8096. www.bellevuesquare.com

Within Bellevue Square Mall:

OIL & VINEGAR

This is where you can experience a world of taste. Choose from an exclusive international collection of 28 oils and vinegars "on tap," or discover that unique culinary gift idea for the gourmet on your list who has it all.

HELLY HANSEN

Since 1877, Helly Hansen products have been working the outdoors under all conditions. That tradition remains unbroken. They guarantee each garment is free from defects in material and workmanship and ready to give exceptional service. If there is any problem with anything that they make, the item will either be repaired or replaced at no charge. ◆ 425/467.6643. www.hellyhansengear.com

FIREWORKS GALLERY

This gallery, celebrating art in life, has another location here, showing wonderful art and artsy items for all kinds of gifts—to yourself and others. ◆ 425/688.0933. www.fireworksgallery.net

KENNETH BEHM ART GALLERY

Dali and Matisse prints vie for wall space with limited editions by Michel Delacroix and Jiang. The leaning is toward big, busy, and bright, but the gallery has presented a collection of small monochrome sketches and engravings by Rembrandt, two of which are part of the inventory. ◆ Daily. 425/454.0222

THE BODY SHOP

This international chain of soap and lotion shops is known for its politically active business policies. In the "Trade, Not Aid" program, founder Anita Roddick buys nature-friendly products from Third World countries. Items include paper from Nepal, acacia footsie rollers from southern India, and Brazil-nut oil from the Kayapo Indians of South America. High prices separate the dedicated from the curious. ◆ Daily. 425/637.9535. www.thebodyshop.com

MADE IN WASHINGTON

Here's the place to get just the souvenir gift to send or take to someone back home. Everything in this store is, as the name says, made locally. Choose from among jewelry, glass artwork, pottery, wall art, T-shirts and other clothing, a wide selection of smoked salmon, mussels, and oysters, and more. ◆ Daily. 425/454.6907. www.madeinwashington.com

EXCALIBUR

The quantity of sharp edges alone makes this shop an intrigue: kitchen cutlery by such household names as Henckel, Mundial, and Forschner; reproduction Viking and Samurai swords by Marta of Spain; Buck and Victorinox pocket and hunting knives. There are even battle-axes, just in case you've been looking for one. ◆ Daily. 425/451.2514. www.excaliburcutlery.com

---

Restaurants/Clubs: Red | Hotels: Purple | Shops: Orange | Outdoors/Parks: Green | Sights/Culture: Blue

MRS. FIELD'S CHOCOLATE CHIPPERY

Treat yourself after an afternoon's mall walking. Pick any semisweet chocolate variety. ♦ Daily. 425/454.1790

THE LODGE

A new building connected next door to Bellevue Square has **Ruth's Chris Steakhouse**, **Z'Tejas Southwestern Grill**, **Pagliacci Pizza**, **Crate and Barrell**, **PF Changs**, and **Ristorante Luciano**.

17 BARNES & NOBLE BOOKSTORE

The green arches of a former bowling alley shoulder this chain's superstore. Largest departments are general fiction, business, and computer books. ♦ Daily, until 11PM. 626 106th Ave NE (between Fourth and Eighth Sts). 425/451.8463. &. www.barnesandnoble.com

18 MEYDENBAUER CENTER

This facility, named for William Meydenbauer, who founded Bellevue in 1869, is this city's premier convention center, a facility that handles intimate gatherings of 300 and capacity crowds of 3,000. In the same building is the **Theatre at Meydenbauer Center**. For over a decade, this state-of-the-art, 410-seat venue has hosted productions by local, regional, and national performing arts groups. ♦ 11100 NE Sixth St (between 112th and 110th Aves). 425/637.1020. www.meydenbauer.com

19 LA RESIDENCE SUITE HOTEL

$$ This 24-unit inn caters to the corporate traveler but is also a good choice for families on a budget: All apartments have full kitchens. The views, unfortunately, are mostly a parking garage, but elegant rosewood and leather furnishings, a friendly and hard-working staff, and complimentary fax service make it an attractive choice right on the edge of the Bellevue business district. There is no restaurant. ♦ 475 100th Ave NE (at Fifth St). 425/455.1475, 800/800.1993. www.lopezislander.com

20 BELLEVUE ART MUSEUM

After some 25 years "in the attic" of Bellevue Square shopping mall, **Bellevue Art Museum** moved across the street and down the block early in 2001 into a splendid new building designed by **Steven Holl** (who also designed the exquisite **Chapel of St. Ignatius**). With its heavy, irregular mass of rough, red-painted concrete punctuated by glass and aluminum, it's a massive piece of

sculpture all on its own. Unfortunately, it is almost impossible to find a vantage point from which to view the building in its entirety, hemmed in as it is by taller buildings. The curved and angled interior walls and the dramatic "circulation device" (gently sloping stair) are well worth a look. The museum does not display a permanent collection but offers rotating exhibits, usually four or five at a time. Here's another name to join the recent architectural works of interest in the Northwest: Venturi, Gehry, Koolhaas, and Holl. ♦ Admission; free on the 3rd Thursday. Tu-Su. 510 Bellevue Way NE (between Fourth and Eighth Sts). 425/519.0770. www.bellevueart.org

21 SPAZZO

★★$$ *Spazzo* is Italian slang for "a good time," and that's exactly what you'll have in this bright restaurant atop the **Key Bank Building**. Diners are surrounded by murals on one side and views of the skyline and Lake Washington on the other. The food is from the cuisines of Italy, Greece, Turkey, and North Africa: lamb with vegetables, olives, and artichokes over saffron couscous, for example. Best of all is the tapas bar, where the chefs whip up tasty appetizers; there's also a children's menu. ♦ Mediterranean ♦ Daily, lunch and dinner. Reservations recommended. 10655 NE Fourth St (between 108th and 106th Aves). 425/454.8255. &

22 CHRISTMAS HOUSE

This year-round ornament and gift shop comprises three buildings (two are in the back alley) carrying a large selection of knickknacks, bric-a-brac, baubles, bangles, and gewgaws to stuff every stocking. Don't miss the traditional linden-wood carvings from the German Erzgebirge and several sizes of the hand-painted Fontanini nativity figures. ♦ Daily, Nov-Dec; call for times the rest of the year. 11024 NE Second St (between 111th and 108th Aves). 425/455.4225

23 BELLEVUE DOWNTOWN PARK

At a total cost of $20 million, the City of Bellevue purchased eight blocks of prime downtown real estate in the early 1980s and set it aside (ostensibly forever) as sacred, idle space, dedicated to daydreams and dawdling. From the park, a proper study can be made of downtown Bellevue's skyscraper growth during the late 20th century. The two blue ones most in evidence to the east, **Security Pacific Plaza** (10620 NE Eighth St) and **One Bellevue Center** (411 108th Ave NE), were built during the 1980s as bookends to anticipated heavy development along 108th Avenue NE. Depending on the sky, they can become beacons of fire or disappear altogether. The copper-toned **Koll Center** (500 108th Ave NE), at 27 stories Bellevue's tallest building, incorporates multiple angles and sides on a common center to suggest one building exploding out of another. All three reflective glass structures were designed by Seattle architect **Gerald Geron**. The most active area is the west side of the park, where kids play on a colorful, turreted Jungle Gym and swings. Elsewhere, workers and shoppers can enjoy a low waterfall and a hypnotic canal crossed by charming little bridges. Perhaps the leveling of two of Bellevue's oldest grade schools for this park will prove forgivable (the foundation of one remains as a topographic attraction), as people take refuge not far from the madding crowd. A stone marker and four elms planted in 1926 in memory of three World War I soldiers were left undisturbed. ♦ 102nd Ave NE (between First and Fourth Sts)

24 GILBERT'S ON MAIN

★★$ The owner, Steven Gilbert, points out that it has the largest breakfast menu in town. And sandwiches at this sunny café overflow with pastrami, corned beef, salami, and other goodies. But that doesn't mean you shouldn't make room for the enormous bowls of matzo ball soup served here. He prides himself on the broth, simmered with parsnips and a ton of garlic. The light, tasty, baseball-size matzo balls are equally worthy of praise. Definitely try the cheesecake: Gilbert, who buys it from a small producer, swears it's the best he's ever tasted. ♦ Jewish ♦ Daily, breakfast and lunch; Sa, Su, live jazz. 10024 Main St (between 100th Ave NE and 101st Ave SE), Bellevue. 425/455.5650

25 ROSS AND CO.

Ross Bendixen has been bending metal in this neighborhood for more than 25 years, specializing in custom-designed iron-and-steel furniture. His dynamic wall sculptures have become a hallmark of Old Bellevue. ♦ M-Sa. 10220 Main St (between 103rd and 102nd Aves NE). 425/455.4111. &. www.rossbendixen.com

26 LA COCINA DEL PUERCO

★$ In this cafeteria-style restaurant, you pay for the food—handmade tortillas and generous helpings—not for the overhead of fancy furnishings. Décor is upscale functional, but there are enough piñatas, posters, and other paraphernalia on the walls and ceiling to make you feel you've gotten tangled up in a Cinco de Mayo parade. Try the *chiles rellenos*. ♦ Mexican ♦ Daily, lunch

and dinner. 10246 Main St (between 103rd and 102nd Aves NE). 425/455.1151

27 NEWPORT HOUSE

An upscale ladies boutique featuring, among others, clothes from Painted Pony and Silverado. The shop also carries Pencel fabric. ♦ Daily. 10133 Main St (between 102nd and 101st Aves SE). 425/451.2880

28 BIS ON MAIN

★★★$$$ This is a classy room hung with huge oil paintings and serving up the usual: fish du jour, rack of lamb, crab cakes, New York steak. But oh! the preparation and the "accessories"—from gnocchi in a lemony pea sauce to duck slices fanned over truffled mashed potatoes in foie gras sauce. Lovely food, prepared exactly right and presented beautifully. ♦ 10213 Main St (at 102nd Ave). 425/455.2033. www.bisonmain.com

29 BELLEVUE BARBER SHOP

Nothing has changed since the days when your dad was a kid and your grandfather brought him into a place just like this to get his ears lowered. The Russel family has been giving no-frills haircuts here for almost 50 years. Their collection of **Bellevue High School** yearbooks, which you're welcome to peruse, predates the shop's 1926 building by 2 years. Opinions are plentiful and free, and haircuts are $15, which includes being finished up with a straight razor. ♦ Tu-Sa. 10251 Main St (between Bellevue Way SE and 102nd Ave SE). 425/455.0980

30 TOY'S CAFE

★$ Good Chinese food at irresistible prices has made this a neighborhood institution for decades. It's not fancy, but the service is quick and courteous. Combos are the way to go; sample three or four foods for less than each would cost separately. ♦ Chinese/ takeout. ♦ Tu-F, lunch and dinner; Sa, Su, dinner. 10311 Main St (between Bellevue Way SE and 102nd Ave SE). 425/454.8815

31 STAMP GALLERY

Proprietor John Kardos's philatelic shop specializes in European issues but also has one of Seattle's largest collections of international stamps. ♦ Tu-Sa. 10335 Main St (between Bellevue Way SE and 102nd Ave SE). 425/455.3781

32 WILDWOOD PARK

This little lawn that is surrounded by trees is all that's left of a park that once reached west to what is now the **Meydenbauer Yacht Club**. In the first years of the 20th century,

---

Restaurants/Clubs: **Red** | Hotels: **Purple** | Shops: **Orange** | Outdoors/Parks: **Green** | Sights/Culture: **Blue**

Seattleites crossed Lake Washington on a ferry to picnic on the grass here, dance in a pavilion, and mess about in canoes. ♦ 260 101st Ave SE (at Third St)

33 POGACHA

★★$ Named for the distinctive Yugoslavian bread crust that makes pizzas served here so unusual, this affordable restaurant is an Eastside favorite. The crunchy-yet-soft bread is made fresh daily and served in three forms: dinner rolls, sandwich bread, and the hefty pizza disks. The best pizza is topped with goat cheese, sun-dried tomatoes, and spinach. Owners Lisa and Brad Cassidy also serve chicken and lamb dishes and have a wine list containing about 30 selections. Catering is available. ♦ Pizza ♦ Daily. 119 106th Ave NE (between Main and Second Sts). 425/455.5670. www.pogacha.com

34 BELLEVUE HILTON

$$$ The 180 comfortable rooms here are all decorated in soft color tones, with cable TV and movies available. But it's the other amenities that win this place most of its plaudits. Hotel vans take guests around at no charge within a five-mile radius, which easily encompasses Bellevue's main attractions. Indoor activities include an indoor pool, sauna, and Jacuzzi. And security is great; on request, solo guests are walked to their cars. ♦ 100 112th Ave NE (between Main and Fourth Sts). 425/455.3330, 800/235.4458. www.hilton.com

Within the Bellevue Hilton:

BASIL'S KITCHEN

★$$ Northwestern and continental cuisine are served in a low-key stucco and tile-roofed setting just across the breezeway from the hotel's main entrance. Specialties include soups, salads, and sandwiches, along with steak and seafood entrées. ♦ Northwestern/continental ♦ Daily. 425/458.1717, 425/451.2473

35 BELLEVUE BOTANICAL GARDENS

In 1947, Calhoun and Harriet Shorts bought a seven-acre cherry orchard on Wilburton Hill, where they built a home and created a rhododendron glen. Today, that property is the center of a 36-acre public botanical garden. Some of the rhododendrons are 20 feet tall, and the garden contains a special collection of native and exotic trees, as well as rare shrubs and groundcovers. Near the entrance of the **Shorts Visitors' Center** (which includes a botanical library, gift shop, and meeting rooms), a miniature waterfall

cascades from a granite boulder through the courtyard; bricks appear to float in the small stream of water on its way to a small pond that contains water plants. Beyond the visitors' center are trails to the 17,000-square-foot botanical border on a hill high above downtown Bellevue. There's also a wheelchair-accessible garden loop trail about a half-mile long, as well as individual gardens devoted to ground covers, dahlias, herbs, fuchsias, the **Yao Garden** (a sister-cities project with Yao, Japan), and a rock garden. ♦ Daily. 12001 Main St (between 124th Ave NE and 118th Ave SE). 425/462.2749. &. www.bellevuebotanical.org

36 CHACE'S PANCAKE CORRAL

★$ If you like a hearty stack o'cakes served with a smile at the crack of dawn, this friendly flapjack and coffee stop is for you. It's the only place of its kind left in Bellevue. Owner Bill Chace quit counting birthdays at age 82 and still takes time to sit down with the customers, whether he knows them or not. A favorite is banana pancakes with coconut syrup, but if you want to play the field, try the Joe Adams assortment: Joe was a customer who could never make up his mind whether to have buttermilk, buck-wheat, potato, or strawberry pancakes, so Chace came up with this satisfying sampler. ♦ American ♦ Daily, breakfast and lunch. 1606 Bellevue Way SE (between 16th St and 108th Ave). 425/454.8888

KIRKLAND

37 CAFE JUANITA

★★★$$$ This converted house is small and unpretentious. People come here for the food, not the setting. New owner Holly Smith revamped the menu, and her appreciation of ingredients shows. Some examples are the combination of foie gras and ripe nectarines, the saddle of lamb (with taggiesche olives, Jerusalum artichokes, and bagna cauda sauce), and the sea scallops (with celeriac arugula salad, house-made bacon, lentils, and black truffle oil). ♦ North Italian ♦ Tu-Su, dinner. Reservations recommended. 9702 NE 120th Pl (between 100th Ave and 120th St). 425/823.1505. www.cafejuanita.com

38 THE BUCKLIN HOME

The Kirkland Land and Improvement Company built this wood-frame house in 1889, and in 1904, it was bought by Harry Thompkins, who started a successful shipyard at what is now **Carillon Point**. This house was nearly condemned after a

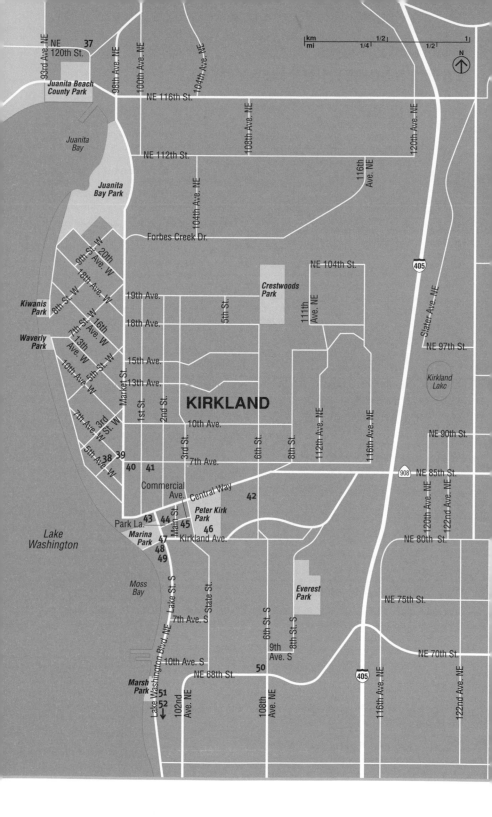

93rd Ave. NE — NE **37** — 120th St.

Juanita Beach County Park

98th Ave. NE

100th Ave. NE

104th Ave. NE

NE 116th St.

Juanita Bay

NE 112th St.

108th Ave. NE

120th Ave. NE

Juanita Bay Park

104th Ave. NE

116th Ave. NE

405

Forbes Creek Dr.

W. 20th St. Ave.

9th Ave. W

18th Ave. W

NE 104th St.

Crestwoods Park

Slater Ave. NE

NE 97th St.

8th St. W

19th Ave.

5th St.

111th Ave. NE

Kiwanis Park

W. 16th St. Ave. W

18th Ave.

Waverly Park

7th Ave. W

13th St. W

15th Ave.

Kirkland Lake

Ave. W

5th St. W

13th Ave.

10th Ave. W

Market St.

KIRKLAND

NE 90th St.

7th Ave. W

3rd St. W

1st St.

2nd St.

10th Ave.

6th St.

8th St.

112th Ave. NE

116th Ave. NE

5th Ave. W

38 39

3rd St.

7th Ave.

NE 90th St.

40 41

Commercial Ave.

Central Way

42

908

NE 85th St.

120th Ave. NE

122nd Ave. NE

Park La.

43 — **44**

Main St.

Peter Kirk Park

NE 80th St.

Marina Park

45

46

47

Kirkland Ave.

NE 80th St.

48

49

Lake Washington

Moss Bay

Everest Park

NE 75th St.

Lake St. S

State St.

7th Ave. S

6th St. S

8th St. S

NE 70th St.

Lake Washington Blvd. NE

10th Ave. S

9th Ave. S

50

NE 68th St.

108th Ave. NE

116th Ave. NE

122nd Ave. NE

Marsh Park

51

52

102nd Ave. NE

Restaurants/Clubs: Red | Hotels: Purple | Shops: Orange | Outdoors/Parks: Green | Sights/Culture: Blue

THERE'S SOMETHING FISHY HERE

Turn over a rock at **Golden Gardens** park in **Ballard** and you have a good chance of encountering *Pachygrapsus crassipes* (the lined shore crab). You may only have a moment or two before this inch-long green creature scurries off sideways in search of a new hideout. Don't bother giving chase. Plenty of other charming, if equally reclusive, animals can be found along this sandy stretch of land.

Puget Sound is inhabited by several thousand marine species. Most are small-bodied invertebrates (oysters, clams, urchins, crabs, anemones, and squids), but some are certifiable giants, thriving on this briny soup's ample food supply and fairly mild oceanic climate. Less than a hundred feet off the **Golden Gardens** shore, for instance, lurks *Octopus dofleini*, the world's largest octopus, a mottled red Schwarzenegger of a cephalopod with an arm span extending 25 feet. A bit farther out, on the sound's silty bottom, rests the 10-pound geoduck (pronounced "goo-ee-duck"), a megamollusk that qualifies as the world's largest burrowing clam.

Like the secretive *P. crassipes*, many local invertebrates are beach dwellers, occupying cozy niches in the intertidal zone—that thin strip of earth bathed by ocean waves as the tides move in and out. To survive under such transitional conditions, many animals have unusual appearances and behaviors. For example, the small colonial sea anemone, *Anthopleura*, resembles a plant more than an animal, whereas the limpet (a tiny, rock-hugging cousin of the snail) could pass for a smooth stone.

On the rocky beaches (such as in **Mukilteo**, 27 miles north of Seattle), fish and invertebrates hide in the cracks and crevices between boulders or among the kelp and other seaweeds that grow abundantly at the water's edge. Sandy shores (like those at **Golden Gardens** or the city of **Edmonds**, another short excursion 18 miles north of Seattle) are usually featureless plains that merge into eelgrass beds—underwater meadows that offer food and shelter to anything that lives on or near the bottom. Both beach types make fine destinations for intertidal explorers.

To get better acquainted with this curious, often colorful, community of the sea, visit the **Seattle Aquarium** (Waterfront Park, Pier 59; 386.4320), where you'll meet all local beach dwellers face-to-face. Afterward, you can pick up a good field guide to intertidal life, either Gloria Snively's revised edition of *Exploring the Seashore in British Columbia, Washington, and Oregon* (The Writing Works, 1991) or *Seashore Life of the Northern Pacific Coast*, by Eugene Kozloff (University of Washington Press, 1983). And finally, procure a local tide table, available from larger bookstores in the city.

Tidepooling requires taking advantage of two brief windows of opportunity, periods of approximately 4 to 6 hours each day, when the tides ebb and the intertidal zone is most accessible to exploration. Exactly how long and how wide these windows swing varies daily. But in the summer the lowest tides generally occur around midday. As winter approaches, they fall between 9PM and midnight, making tidepooling a more difficult enterprise but no less rewarding, as long as you have a flashlight in hand.

Don't presume, however, that only cold-blooded creatures will be joining you at the beach. A vast array of waterfowl and shorebirds also visits Seattle's coastline. Several of these, including the diminutive Bonaparte's gull, travel thousands of miles from central Alaska to winter in the Emerald City. Others, such as the western and glaucous-winged gull, prefer the year-round comfort of urban beaches, piers, and marinas over life on the road. Regardless of their summer plans, all arrive at these seashores with one thing in mind: the seafood smorgasbord that's uncovered with every outgoing tide.

Binoculars might help you espy some warm-blooded mammals—particularly harbor seals and California sea lions. Still farther from shore swim the area's sleek black-and-white killer whales, highly intelligent and surprisingly swift hunters of salmon, cod, halibut, and hake. Killer whales (or orcas) are actually more closely related to dolphins than to whales, and they spend their entire lives in extended family groupings called pods. For an excellent background on these mammals, read *Field Guide to the Orca*, by David G. Gordon and Chuck Flaherty (Sasquatch Books, 1990).

---

fire in 1975, but the Bucklin family was allowed to buy it with the promise that they would restore it. Renovations began with beams and other lumber salvaged from—of all places—the old shipyard. It is now a private residence. ◆ 202 Fifth Ave W (between Second and Third Sts W)

39 JOSHUA SEARS BUILDING

In 1891, Boston millionaire Joshua M. Sears built this two-story brick triangle in what was then the center of town to be the official bank of the Great Western Iron and Steel Works. The steel mill never produced so much as an ingot, and the bank failed without ever opening. The beautiful brick arches inside were covered up when the building's interior was divided into apartments in the 1940s. They were rediscovered by developer Lloyd Powell and his wife when they bought the place in 1982 and went at it with $800,000 and a trowel. The restoration won the Powells numerous awards, including *Metropolitan Home* magazine's "Home of the Year," and was featured on the *This Old House* TV show. ♦ 701 Market St (at Seventh Ave W)

40 PETER KIRK BUILDING

Kirk's urban dream began to materialize with the construction of this handsome 1891 brick edifice. Refurbished by the Creative Arts League, it now houses the **Kirkland Arts Center**, which holds classes and presents shows in all media. ♦ Arts Center: Tu-Sa. 620 Market St (at Seventh Ave). 425/822.7161

41 DR. TRUEBLOOD/CREGER HOME

In 1907, this slender wood-frame house was bought by Kirkland's first physician, Dr. Barclay Trueblood. The now-quiet street in front of the house was once the busiest avenue in town. It's a private residence. ♦ 127 Seventh Ave (between Second and First Sts)

42 PARKPLACE

Unlike a typical mall, this blissfully uncovered shopping center seems more like a collection of creative and accessible shops. The complex also includes a five-story office tower with a clock on the top. Nestled among the 45 shops and restaurants are the **Parkplace Theater** (with six screens), a health club, and, needless to say, a **Starbucks**. ♦ Sixth St (between Kirkland and Central Ways)

Within Parkplace:

CITY THAI

★$ Visit this small, quiet, and surprisingly elegant restaurant where owner Joe Suwanvichit takes much care with the presentation of food. For beginners, the *pad thai* noodles (with shrimp, egg, vegetables, and tofu in a peanut sauce) make a great introduction to an often daunting cuisine. Also tasty is the house special beef dish, cooked with carrots, potatoes, and roasted peanuts and served in a spicy curry with coconut milk. They'll be happy to turn down the temperature in any dish. ♦ Thai ♦ M-Sa, lunch and dinner; Su, dinner. 425/827.2875. &

43 KIRKLAND ROASTER & ALE HOUSE

★$$ This dazzling place has lots of glass and brass and a 9-foot-high vertical spit. Roasted meats, including lamb and ham, are the specialty, though they also serve a hearty bowl of clam chowder. And there are 25 draft beers on tap. It's generally crowded and noisy on Friday and Saturday nights. ♦ American ♦ Daily, lunch and dinner. 111 Central Way (between Lake St S and Market St). 425/827.4400. &

43 TRIPLE J CAFE

★$ You'll have trouble getting your mouth around one of the huge sandwiches at this tiny lunch joint owned by brothers Jim, Jeff, and Jason Harnasch. Split the meat loaf, the veggie, or the turkey and cranberry with a friend. Or enjoy an espresso and homemade muffins while you ponder the local artists' paintings featured on the walls. ♦ American ♦ Daily. 101 Central Way (at Market St). 425/822.7319. &

44 PARKLANE GALLERY

A cooperative effort, this gallery is owned and operated by professional Northwestern artists. Every month, the work of two featured artists is exhibited. In June, a miniature show presents some 60 items selected by an international jury, and from these the winners are eventually chosen. ♦ Daily. 130 Park Lane (between Main St and Lake St S). 425/827.1462. &

44 RISTORANTE PARADISO

★★$$ Sardinian Fabrizio Loi's Mediterranean café has a terrific location on Kirkland's most charming street, and in good weather, several tables materialize on the sidewalk outside. Inside or out, the cioppino—mussels, scallops, shrimp, clams, and the fish of the day served in a marinara sauce with homemade croutons—is a house specialty, as is the *vitello scampi* (veal pounded thin and wrapped around tender sage shrimp with butter, garlic, and a white-wine-and-lemon sauce). The wonderful, soft bread is made fresh at least twice daily. ♦ Mediterranean ♦ M-F, lunch and dinner; Sa, Su, dinner. 120 Park Lane (between Main St and Lake St S). 425/889.8601. &. www.ristoranteparadiso.com

45 KIRKLAND ANTIQUE GALLERY

More than 90 dealers are represented under this one roof (formerly **Old Heritage Place)**, each occupying a small space jammed with relics from yesteryear. The rub is that the dealers are not present, so there's no one to answer your questions about the old banjo or set of fine china that catches your eye. You're on your own—great if you know what you're looking for and don't like being pressured by salespeople. ♦ Daily. 151 Third St (between Kirkland Ave and Park La). 425/828.4993. &

46 KIRKLAND PERFORMANCE CENTER

This striking new facility, with its distinctive banding of beige and wine-colored custom-made masonry bricks, was designed by **Becker Architects**, a Kirkland firm. The center, which is adjacent to and part of the civic complex (which includes a swimming pool, a library, playing fields, and a large municipal parking garage with *4 hours of free parking*) is intended to provide an Eastside venue for many professional regional performing arts groups, including the **Pacific Northwest Ballet**, the **Village Theatre** (from Issaquah), **Seattle Children's Theatre**, **Cabaret Productions**, the **Northwest Chamber Orchestra**, **Spectrum Dance Theatre**, and many others. Call for a schedule of performances. ◆ Peter Kirk Park, 350 Kirkland Ave (between Kirkland Way and Third St). 425/893.9900. ら. www.kpcenter.org

47 KIRKLAND CLOCK

Captain John Anderson, who ran ferries and steamboats on Lake Washington for more than 40 years, gave this handsome pedestaled timepiece to the City of Kirkland in 1935. ◆ Kirkland Ave and Lake St S

47 PUBLIC ART

A friendly and accessible small town, Kirkland boasts a fascinating display of public sculpture, in addition to its numerous art galleries; many of the open-air pieces were gifts from families and the artists themselves. Made of bronze, marble, aluminum, and concrete, these sculptures of people and animals can be seen in an undemanding walk of several blocks; maps to guide you are available at virtually every business in Kirkland. Seventeen in all, the sculptures were made by such acclaimed artists as Rich Beyer, Glenna Goodacre, Katie Hiddleston, James FitzGerald, Prince Monyo Mihailescu-Nasturel, Peter Skinner, Lisa Sheets, and Brad Rude. ◆ Area bounded by Third St and Lake St S, Peter Kirk and Kirkland Ave and Central Way. Also at Carillon Point

48 ANTHONY'S HOMEPORT

★★$$ Some people come here for the sunset view over Lake Washington, but even if this first of many branches were located in an underground parking garage, people would visit for the sautéed scallops, grilled salmon, and oysters. For views, the next best **Anthony's** choice is on Shilshole Bay, in Ballard. ◆ Seafood ◆ M-Sa, dinner; Su, brunch and dinner. Reservations recommended. Moss Bay Marina, 135 Lake St S (between Second and Kirkland Aves).

425/822.0225. ら. Also at numerous locations throughout the Seattle area. www.anthonys.com

48 GUNNAR NORDSTROM GALLERY

Contemporary original prints and paintings by international and local abstract expressionists are found at this charming and friendly gallery. A real treat for aficionados, there's a fine collection available here, with 12 exhibits a year of national and regional artists. ◆ Tu-Su. 127 Lake St S (between Second and Kirkland Aves). 425/827.2822. ら. www.gunnarnordstrom.com

49 THIRD FLOOR FISH CAFE

★★★$$ Just yards from the famous **Anthony's** is this classy upbeat upstart. The views are as good as any on Moss Bay, and such thoughtful entrées as seared Alaskan sea scallops, pan-seared mahimahi, and seafood paella by chef Greg Campbell are complemented by some of the best appetizers and desserts around. Service here is consistently efficient. ◆ Seafood ◆ M-Sa, dinner. Reservations recommended. 205 Lake St S (at Second Ave). 425/822.3553. ら. www.fishcafe.com

50 SHAMIANA

★★★$$ The kitchen at this popular eatery (it's best to come on weeknights, when the crowds are smaller) prepares a westernized version of traditional Indian fare, mixing in Northwest ingredients and toning down spices somewhat for tender American palates; the results are pleasing and provide a slightly exotic gustatory experience. A lunchtime buffet offers the opportunity to sample many dishes, including variously flavored lamb curries, cumin-scented chicken in a tomato and cream sauce, potatoes studded with crushed peanuts, and a smooth *dal* of pureed lentils. At dinner, try the intensely flavored beef *vindaloo*, marinated in vinegar, ginger, and chili. The restaurant's moniker is taken from the name used for the colorful tents that hang, bannerlike, from the dining-room ceiling. ◆ Indian ◆ M-Sa, lunch and dinner. 10724 NE 68th St (at Sixth St S). 425/827.4902. ら

51 MARSH ESTATE

In the exclusive residential park called **Marsh Commons** sits an elegant 1929 Tudor-style home that is anything but common. It was erected by Louis Schuster Marsh, born in Wisconsin in 1892, who moved his family to the Seattle area in 1904. Marsh studied engineering at the **University of Washington**; in 1916, he went to work for William

Dance legends Mark Morris, Merce Cunningham, and Robert Joffrey all lived and worked in Seattle, as did famous stripper Gypsy Rose Lee.

Boeing's airplane company, becoming that outfit's chief metallurgist. Marsh was the engineer who invented all-metal fuselages, and Boeing stock made a small fortune for him. Just over 10 years after joining the company, Marsh commissioned the architectural firm of **Edwin J. Ivey** to build a home reflecting his success. It's been said that much if not most of the design work was done by Ivey's partner at the time, **Elizabeth Ayer**, the first female graduate of UW's architecture program and the first female architect licensed in Washington State. The finished estate included a series of waterfalls, tremendous hand-carved beams in the living and dining rooms, a darkroom in the basement, a pistol range, and an extensive wine cellar. A weather vane on the rooftop features the likeness of Marsh, an avid golfer, dressed in his sporting knickers. It remains a private residence. ♦ 6604 Lake Washington Blvd NE (S of 10th Ave S)

52 CARILLON POINT

The six bells or carillons in the center of this office and hotel complex, forged in France, chime every half hour, giving it the atmosphere of a small European plaza. The public dock, ample parking, and waterfront paths make the place accessible by boat, car, and foot, and the low-rise buildings don't jar against the wooded hillside to the east. This bulge in the shoreline started out as the **Lake Washington Shipyards** and later became the training grounds for the **Seattle Seahawks** football team for a time; the new buildings are the world headquarters of such firms as McCav Cellular Communications and Univar, and the street level offers a healthy handful of retail shops and restaurants, including the inevitable **Starbucks**. Lots of parking is available, mostly underground. ♦ 102nd Ave NE and Lake Washington Blvd NE. 425/822.1700

At Carillon Point:

TOPPERS

This florist specializes in English floral design, using Northwest natives such as salad and huckleberry as a base and flowers from all over the world as accompaniments. The shop doubles as an art gallery,

presenting shining creations by 40 glass artists. ♦ M-Sa; irregularly extended summer hours. No. 1260. 425/899.9311. &

HANNIGAN/ADAMS

Goldsmith Frank Hannigan is an avowed constructivist, but he will make whatever you can dream up. Partner Beth Adams's more organic, sculpted pieces complement Hannigan's Bauhaus designs, and if you like the classic Tiffany look, they can do that in their workshop too. The prices are realistic for handcrafted gold jewelry. ♦ Tu-Sa, 11AM-6PM. No. 1230. 425/889.9450. &. www.hanniganadams.com

YARROW BAY GRILL AND BEACH CAFE

★★$$$ One small kitchen creates sophisticated dishes for both the restaurant upstairs and the **Beach Cafe**, a lower outdoor deck where yuppies chill after work. Chef Vicky McCaffree offers at least three fresh seafood entrées daily, beautifully prepared and presented, but if you're not fond of fish, you can sink your teeth into an 11-ounce New York steak topped with a green peppercorn-and-brandy sauce. And that's not all; for a further change of pace, rack of lamb is also available. In the Beach Cafe, order a gin and tonic and one of the appetizers (like the zesty New Mexico artichoke dip served with bread, veggies, or crackers) and sit back comfortably on the deck to watch the sun set on Seattle. ♦ Northwestern ♦ Grill: M-F, lunch and dinner; Sa, Su, dinner. Beach Cafe: daily, lunch and dinner. Reservations recommended for the Grill. No. 1270. Grill: 425/889.9052; Beach Cafe: 425/889.0303. &

WOODMARK HOTEL

$$$ A bright atrium flanked by a curved staircase and filled with piano music welcomes you to the only hotel on the shores of Lake Washington. All 100 rooms and suites have TVs, and most boast balconies with views westward. For the insomniac with an appetite, a "Raid the Pantry" program offers complimentary late-night snacks. To really live it up, stay in the **Woodmark Suite**, a 1,456-square-foot suite with two balconies and a fireplace enjoyed by the likes of Paul McCartney, Arnold Palmer, and Harry Connick Jr. Satisfying meals are available at the **Waters Bistro** (425/803.5595), where casual, down-home fare means New American cuisine. ♦ No. 1200. 425/822.3700, 800/822.3700. &. www.thewoodmarkhotel.com

Restaurants/Clubs: Red | Hotels: Purple | Shops: Orange | Outdoors/Parks: Green | Sights/Culture: Blue

GAY SEATTLE

Dubbed the Emerald City, this lush and sparkling jewel in the shadow of the Olympic and Cascade Mountains has grown since the late 1980s into one of the nation's most inviting urban centers, especially for lesbians and gays. Drawn by its spectacular setting, progressive politics, vibrant music and theater scene, and less frenetic pace, and despite the rain, all sorts—techies, club kids, gay families, California dreamers, and those with an urge to start over again—have flocked here. And just about no one seems to be leaving the city, which now has a population of 579,000.

Fun-loving as well as politically active, Seattle's gay community appreciates the city as much for its quality of life as for its tolerance. Though nearly every section—from the Belltown nightspots to genteel Queen Anne, from funky Fremont to the forested Madison Valley—bustles with gay life and visibility, the Capitol Hill neighborhood remains the epicenter of gay business and social life. (All listings in this chapter are located there unless otherwise noted.)

As in other American cities, Seattle's early same-sex settlement took root in the "undesirable" part of town—Pioneer Square, whose seedy Yesler Way gave rise to the term *skid row*. The first gay bars appeared here in the 1930s, with proprietors paying off the police to ease up on harassment of their patrons. An FBI investigation ended this practice in the 1970s, by which time the earliest Gay Pride marches were being held in Pioneer Square, and several nascent gay rights organizations had opened offices in the neighborhood. But by then, many gays and lesbians had already begun leaving the confines of the "ghetto" and moving to areas throughout the city.

Of these, Capitol Hill soared in popularity, giving rise to its affectionate nickname, the Swish Alps. In the post-Stonewell years, it turned into a hotbed of liberalism and progressivism, and newspapers, bars, bookstores, and service organizations began sprouting like mushrooms. Broadway evolved from an isolated strip with a few random businesses into a commercial center offering almost anything shoppers could want. Today it's the heart of gay business in Seattle. Most bars and baths are located several blocks south near Pike and Pine Streets; with its hip cafés, dance clubs, alternative shops, and the city's premier lesbian nightspot, this part of Capitol Hill attracts a younger and trendier set. On warm days, Broadway comes alive, and gay boys take to the sand at Madison Beach on the shores of Lake Washington.

As in any urban area, there are antigay incidents, but Seattle is a relatively safe city, with homicide and gay bashing rates far lower than in most metropolises. Indeed, isolated bashings still cause headlines here; their rarity is due in part to the city's liberal atmosphere and politics. An antidiscrimination ordinance was passed back in the mid-1970s, and a bias-crimes ordinance has resulted in better tracking and prosecution of such offenses. The police department has earned praise from community leaders for making antigay harassment a major target, both on the streets and in the squad room, and there's a lot of gay support at city hall.

Some visitors have noted that while Seattle residents are nice, they are not necessarily friendly the way, for example, folks down South are friendly. It may be that gay Seattelites, like their straight siblings, are a bit reserved—but visitors willing to make the first move usually find the effort pays off. Just don't tell them you want to move here; more often than not, the locals would just as soon keep the place to themselves.

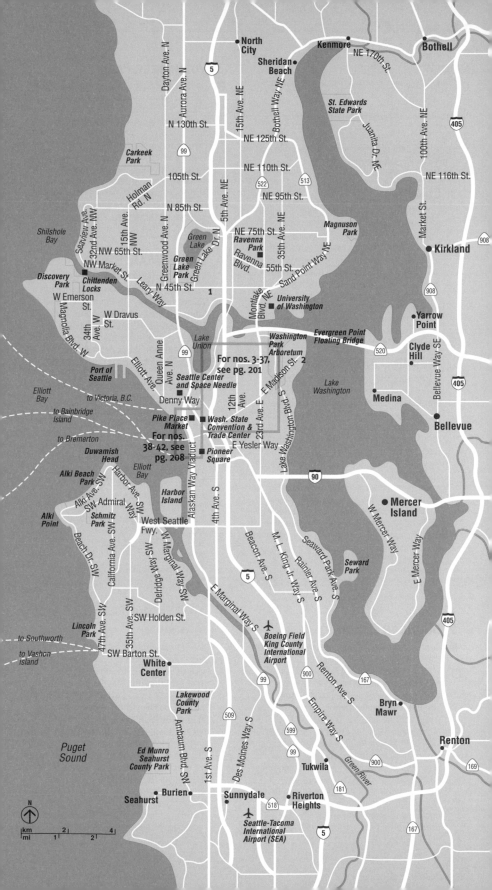

Symbols

♂ predominantly/exclusively gay-male–oriented

♀ predominantly/exclusively lesbian-oriented

♂♀ predominantly/exclusively gay-oriented, with a male and female clientele

1 CHANGES

♂ Popular with older guys, this neighborhood bar in Wallingford screens rock and pop videos nonstop and also hosts the occasional Sunday barbecue. It also has what may be the most unusual feature of any gay spot in Seattle: air conditioning. ♦ Daily, noon–2AM. 2103 N 45th St (between Bagley Ave N and Meridian Ave N). 545.8363. ♿

1 JULIA'S IN WALLINGFORD

★★$$ Upscale yet casual, this eatery has won numerous awards for its vegetarian breakfasts, though its delicious lunches and dinners merit a medal as well. As the day progresses, pancakes and a superb tofu scramble give way to creative pastas, tasty nutburgers (made of cashews, peanuts, and eggs), and other specials. The dining room has lots of windows, blond wood, and plants, and the work of local artists adorns the off-white walls. The outdoor seating and the fresh approach to meat-free cooking have made this one of the neighborhood's jewels—but success can sometimes spell a long wait for a table, especially for brunch. ♦ Vegetarian ♦ M-F, breakfast, lunch, and dinner; Sa, Su, brunch and dinner. 4401 Wallingford Ave N (at N 44th St). 633.1175. ♿

2 MADISON BEACH

♿ ♂ South Beach it's not, but this pretty setting on the west side of Lake Washington attracts buff local gay boys like nowhere else in Seattle. The mostly male crowd near the showers includes a few poseurs, but the atmosphere is generally friendly. Some hearty souls venture into the frigid lake, but mostly this beach is about tanning and views—of Mount Rainier and the Cascade Mountains, and the pretty things all around. *Après* beach, the nearby neighborhood of Madison Valley offers great shopping and eating along Madison Street. The beach is about five miles from downtown; take Madison Street east down Capitol Hill right up to the lake. ♦ E Madison St and 43rd Ave E

3 VOLUNTEER PARK

♿ ♂ Dedicated in 1901 to local veterans of the Spanish-American War, this cruisy park not far from the Broadway business district is home to the **Seattle Asian Art Museum**. Some men, however, come for the festivities that take place after dark. Vice squad officers engage in an ongoing game of cat-and-mouse with these fellows, and allegations of entrapment are not uncommon, so visitors cruise at their own risk. ♦ Bounded by 15th Ave E and Federal Ave E and by E Prospect St and Lake View Cemetery

4 BACON MANSION

$$ Built in 1909, this Edwardian Tudor mansion is part of the historic district near **Volunteer Park**, but the renovated interior offers all the standard modern comforts. The seven rooms and three suites are individually and tastefully decorated and furnished with a mix of antiques and antique-looking newer pieces. All are equipped with telephones, color TV, and table fans; most have private baths and a few have refrigerators. The library, with its stained-glass windows; the grand piano in the lobby; and the charming patio with a fountain and garden create a gracious ambiance that attracts a mixed clientele ranging from gay couples to business travelers to parents visiting their gay Capitol Hill offspring. Nonregistered overnight visitors are allowed (though not encouraged), breakfast is included, and reservations are recommended 6 weeks in advance. ♦ 959 Broadway E (between E Aloha and E Prospect Sts). 329.1864, 800/240.1864. ♿. www.baconmansion.com

5 SHAFER-BAILEY MANSION

$$ Stepping into the mammoth lobby of this huge brick Tudor calls to mind a time when people with fortunes were expected to show them off. Standing proudly on Millionaire's Row, a street of mansions and century-old chestnut trees a block from **Volunteer Park**, the grandfather of Seattle bed-and-breakfasts offers 11 rooms and grand suites in the main house, and two phoneless guest rooms in a garden cottage for romantic seclusion. Historically accurate right down to the bathroom fixtures, and with plenty of museum-quality antiques throughout, the place is popular with discerning homosexuals. Breakfast is included in the room rate, but there's no restaurant. ♦ 907 14th Ave E (between

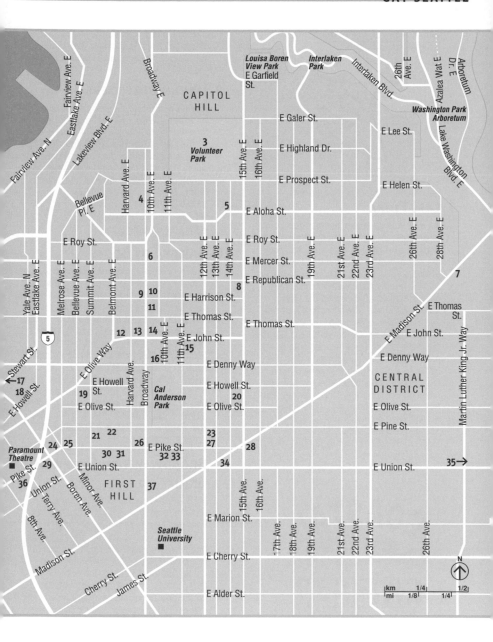

E Aloha and E Prospect Sts). 322.4654,
800/922.4654

6 JADE PAGODA

♂ ★$ An anomaly on Broadway among the
espresso bars and chichi boutiques, this
basic, old-fashioned Chinese cocktail lounge

and restaurant is quite popular with mature
gay men who like their drinks stiff and their
egg foo yong gloppy. The old-style
Cantonese cuisine will disappoint those who
like it hot and spicy, but the "chicken black
bean garlic sauce" is certainly edible.
♦ Chinese ♦ M-W, Sa, Su, dinner; Th, F,
lunch and dinner. Bar: daily, 5PM-2AM.

Restaurants/Clubs: Red | Hotels: Purple | Shops: Orange | Outdoors/Parks: Green | Sights/Culture: Blue

606 Broadway E (between E Mercer and E Roy Sts). 322.5900

7 CAFÉ FLORA

★★★$$ With its atrium, marble floors, and proximity to the gardens of the **Washington Park Arboretum**, this vegetarian café feels like an oasis even amid the tree-lined streets of Madison Valley. The location may explain why the heavily gay clientele tends to be older and more affluent than the typical Capitol Hill crowd. The bill of fare includes Portobello Wellington (in pastry stuffed with a scrumptious mushroom pâté) and Oaxaca tacos (filled with spicy mashed potatoes baked with cheese and served with a black-bean stew). The strictest vegans come for the family platter, which includes soy sausage made on the premises, tofu, potatoes, grits, and, for dessert, nondairy coffee cake. ◆ Vegetarian ◆ Tu-F, lunch and dinner; Sa, Su, breakfast and dinner. 2901 E Madison St (at 29th Ave E). 325.9100. ♿ www.cafeflora.com

8 COASTAL KITCHEN

★★$$ The two mainstays at this sunny, gay-popular eatery are the Mediterranean spinach salad and the Barbados grill (prawns and fish served with sweet-potato cakes and black beans). Otherwise, the cuisine changes monthly from Greek to French to South American, and so do the art, music, wine, and even the ridiculous language-lesson tapes that play continuously in the bathrooms. The kitchen opens onto the split-level dining room, which has Tabasco-red walls and wood wainscoting. There's a deck out back. *Warning*: the wait for a table at weekend brunch can be interminable. ◆ International ◆ Daily, breakfast, lunch, and dinner. 429 15th Ave E (between E Harrison and E Republican Sts). 322.1145. ♿

9 URBAN OUTFITTERS

Purists scoffed when grungewear became an expensive sartorial commodity, but that didn't stop people from buying it by the binful. This two-level, industrial-style store is chock-full of the proper attire, but it also offers a classy array of rugs, candles, ashtrays, and other household items. ◆ M-Sa, 10AM-10PM; Su, 11AM-7PM. 401 Broadway E (at E Harrison St). 322.1800. ♿ www.urbanoutfitters.com

10 BAILEY/COY BOOKS

The thinking homosexual's favorite stop on Broadway often has a line snaking out the front door and around the block, as all the big names come here to sign their latest: Harry Hay, Greg Louganis, and Col. Grethe Cammermeyer, to name but a few. The well-read staff writes helpful (and accurate) recommendations on notecards scattered throughout the store, which offers an impressive array of contemporary lit, gay and lesbian titles, and nearly every free rag in Seattle. ◆ M-Th, Su, 10AM-10PM; F, Sa, 10AM-11PM. 414 Broadway E (between E Harrison and E Republican Sts). 323.8842. ♿

11 BROADWAY NEW AMERICAN GRILL

★★$$ Known as much for its fun gay ambience as for the menu, the **Grill** has emerged as one of the most popular restaurants on Capitol Hill. The mile-high burgers, soup-and-sandwich combos, and vegetarian pastas get raves, but many come just for the mixed drinks and the party atmosphere at the back bar. Loud dance and pop tunes keep the mostly gay crowd on the younger side. ◆ Daily, breakfast, lunch, and dinner. Bar: M-F, 9AM-2AM; Sa, Su, 8AM-2AM. 314 Broadway E (between E Thomas and E Harrison Sts). 328.7000. ♿

12 B&O ESPRESSO

★★$ Mirrors, art, and antiques galore made this one of the fanciest dessert-coffeehouses in town—and then they started serving up delicious meals too. Now the young and the hip can preface their mountainous chocolate tortes and sublime fruit pies with soups, salads, and light healthy entrées on the order of chicken breast stuffed with spinach and feta or smoked salmon linguine.

♦ International ♦ Daily, breakfast, lunch, and dinner. 204 Belmont Ave E (at E Olive Way). 322.5028. ⅃

13 RETRO VIVA

Everything old really is new again. Come here to snatch up funky (and sometimes scary) 1970s hats and accessories. Where else could you find a T-shirt emblazoned with Erik Estrada? Or Superfly? A recent back-to-school promo said it all, with a chalkboard reading "I will not shop at The Gap. I will not shop at the Gap. I will not . . ." ♦ M-Sa, 11AM-8PM; Su, 11AM-7PM. 215 Broadway E (between E Olive Way and E Thomas St). 328.7451. ⅃

14 CAFÉ SEPTIÈME

★★$$ Too hip for its own good, some complain, pointing to the dark red walls, black leather booths, and a waitstaff and management with attitude to spare. But the fact is, this international café tastes as good as it looks. Just try the polenta cakes with black-bean salsa at breakfast, the roasted eggplant sandwich at lunch, or the *schweines-schnitzel* (breaded pork loin) at dinner before you take sides. ♦ Daily, breakfast, lunch, and dinner. 214 Broadway E (between E John and E Thomas Sts). 860.8858. ⅃

15 HILL HOUSE BED AND BREAKFAST

$ A 1903 Victorian completely refurbished in 1990, this lovely bed-and-breakfast mixes contemporary and antique furnishings as comfortably as its gay and straight guests mingle at breakfast. Of the five rooms, three have private baths and two have telephones and TV sets. Make reservations about 6 weeks in advance for a summer stay. ♦ 1113 E John St (between 12th Ave E and 11th Ave E). 720.7161, 800/720.7161

16 THE CRYPT OFF BROADWAY

♂ Dildos, paddles, and pricey bondage gear ♀ will delight hard-core regulars and neophytes alike at Capitol Hill's premier leather boutique, part of the San Diego–based chain. There are plenty of other toys too, and the store's very own line of leather clothing. The magazine section is a veritable cruisefest, reaching its peak on Friday and Saturday nights. Most everything here is shrink-wrapped, including the magazines. ♦ M-Th, 10AM-midnight; F, Sa, 10AM-1AM; Su, noon-10PM. 113 10th Ave E (between E Denny Way and E John St). 325.3882. ⅃

17 BEST WESTERN LOYAL INN

$$ This perfectly decent hotel has 91 standard-issue rooms—its best selling point may be that it's not too far from the action downtown. There's no restaurant on the premises, which means no room service, but continental breakfast is served daily. A sauna and Jacuzzi open 'round the clock are nice pluses. ♦ 2301 Eighth Ave (off E Denny Way) 682.0200. ⅃

18 RE-BAR

♂ This funky club between Capitol Hill and ♀ downtown recently expanded its dance space to accommodate overflow crowds. The gayest night is on Thursday, when DJ Queen Lucky spins early 1980s dance hits, but there's an amalgam of club kids, buff boys, and hip young chicks any night of the week. On Wednesday, it's the sensational Big Wheel Bingo. In recent years, **Re-bar** has become extremely popular as an alternative theater space, producing and presenting irreverent and often bawdy revues (*Dirty Little Show Tunes*), lounge acts, takeoffs on classics such as *The Importance of Being Earnest* and *Saint Joan*, and the indescrib-able drag diva, Dina Martina. After the shows, the friendly staffers haul away the tables and chairs, strike the set, and turn the theater back into a nightclub. Arrive early to avoid the lines. ♦ Cover. M, W, F-Su, 9PM-2AM; Tu, 8PM-2AM; Th, 8:30PM-2AM. Shows: F-Su, 7PM. 1114 E Howell St (between Boren and Minor Aves). 233.9873. ⅃. www.rebarseattle.com

19 CRESCENT TAVERN

♂ Drunken sob stories are the order of the night here. If that's your bag, you'll have a grand old time on Sunday evenings with Julia ("The Poon that Croons") and Lady ("The Mouth") Lori onstage. If that doesn't ring your bell, be forewarned: Sunday is as good as it gets all week. ♦ Daily, 1PM-2AM. 1413 E Olive Way (between Bellevue Ave and E Howell St). 720.8188. ⅃

Phyllis Lyon and Del Martin, who in 1955 founded the Daughters of Bilitis, the nation's first lesbian rights organization, met in Seattle in the early 1950s.

The Seattle City Council voted to extend protection to lesbians and gays in employment in 1973 and in housing in 1975—pioneering steps for any city government in those days.

Restaurants/Clubs: Red | Hotels: Purple | Shops: Orange | Outdoors/Parks: Green | Sights/Culture: Blue

20 THE GASLIGHT INN

$$ Friendly and reasonably priced, this renovated 1906 mansion offers 15 comfy rooms and suites furnished in contemporary or period style. Most have private baths and telephones; a few have balconies and gas fireplaces. Mission-style antiques, lovely gardens, and a pool create an aura of luxury that keeps guests coming back again and again. The **No. 10** bus stops right out front, so getting downtown is a breeze. Continental breakfast is included in the room rate, but there's no restaurant. ♦ 1727 15th Ave (between E Olive and E Howell Sts). 325.3654. www.gaslightinn.com

21 CLUB SEATTLE

♂ This two-level, industrial-style playpen caters to younger, cleaner-cut guys than Seattle's other major bathhouse, **Club Z** (see page 205). There are Universal machines for that pre-prowl workout, a steam room for "introductions," and 50 cubicles for private discourse. The club music is loud, but it goes well with the porn vids and vintage films shown throughout. Things are hottest weeknights after 9PM and nonstop Friday through Sunday (especially after the bars close at 2AM). ♦ Daily, 24 hours. 1520 Summit Ave (between E Pike and E Pine Sts). 329.4813

22 R PLACE

♂ Most nights, this sports pub can give S&M ("stand and model," that is) an even worse name, especially on the third floor, where young guys pose around the horseshoe bar all night, cautiously eyeing each other and rarely making a move. If the **Mariners** or **Sonics** make the playoffs, the mood gets a little warmer; on the other hand, all eyes are focused on the game, so the poor boys still end up alone. The second floor, with its ice-breaking pool table, may prove more rewarding, whereas the first floor, where the guys are

The 1946 opening of a gay bar-cabaret called the Garden of Allah marked the first time Seattle gays had a place where they could openly be their flamboyant selves. And were they ever, with queens and divas seducing sailors in Pioneer Square, chugging bootlegged gin, and engaging in endless cat-and-mouse games with cops. Here, stars like Jackie Starr, Skippy LaRue, and Hotcha "Last of the Red Hot Mommas" Hinton helped create a vibrant Seattle drag culture, which continued even after the infamous Garden closed its doors in 1956.

a bit older, is friendliest of all. ♦ Daily, 2PM-2AM. 619 E Pine St (at Boylston Ave). 322.8828. &

23 THE CUFF

♂ After a major renovation and expansion, **The Cuff** reopened in late 1998 nearly double the size of its original cramped space. Don't be put off by the sign, with its scary-looking stud offering you an open handcuff—this Levi's-and-leather spot is, despite the logo, more of a friendly neighborhood bar these days. It may not be as sexually charged as the **Eagle**, but the cruise factor rises dramatically after sundown—especially on weekends, and particularly during the wild Sunday-night beer bust. Additions to the original bar space—with its pool table, shoe-shine corner, and massive bowls of peanuts and pretzels—include a small dining area featuring surprisingly good Cajun-themed meals (**The Cuff Kitchen**) enabling the bar to sell hard liquor), a dance floor (where the younger, thinner crowd tends to congregate), and an expanded "dog run," the alley out back that can get crowded to the point of claustrophobia on weekends. Special parties are held when the Seattle and Washington Mr. Leather contests take place, and the beer garden here is *the* place to party after the annual Gay Pride rally in June. ♦ Daily, 2PM-2AM. 1533 13th Ave (at E Pine St). 323.1525. &

24 CLUB Z

♂ A former hotel, this bathhouse caters to a hyperbutch, S&M-ish crowd big on fantasy attire, bondage, and discipline; lads too light in the loafers may get a not-so-subtle message to hit the road. Recent renovations have made the place more presentable, though one suspects the hard-core regulars don't much care. Mostly the guys meet in the sauna or the second-floor video room before retiring to one of 44 private cubicles (three with slings). One-month memberships are available. ♦ M-Th, 4PM-9AM; F-Su, 24 hours. 1117 Pike St (between Minor and Boren Aves). 622.9958. www.thezclub.com

25 SEATTLE EAGLE

♂ Smaller than its counterparts in L.A. and Portland, this is the cruisiest leather bar in town. Blasting the likes of Alice in Chains and Oasis along with Zeppelin and the Stones, Eagle packs in a big bunch of boys heavy on goatees and grunge—packs 'em in so tightly on weekends, in fact, that many escape to the open-air beer garden out back. The best spot in the house for scoping out potential dates, though, is the upstairs catwalk. ♦ Daily, 2PM-2AM.

THE BEST

John W. Marshall
Owner of Open Books

The **Hiram Chittenden Locks**—on a nice day, a parade of pleasure boats uses the locks to reach Puget Sound, but I like it best when a fishing season is about to open and the commercial fishing boats and tenders head out toward their difficult business.

The **Seattle Asian Art Museum**—one of my favorite buildings in Seattle, a stunningly grand Deco structure, which houses a wonderful permanent collection of Asian art and features traveling collections as well.

Bookstores—Seattle is a very literate city, so it is home to several good used-book, new-book, and specialty-book stores, far more per capita than most major cities. There's little better than spending time lost among and in literature.

Ferry boats—I remember riding the ferries as a child and still get that solitary joy from standing on a deck in any weather watching the water pass and the mountains, hills, and beaches that reach up from it.

The **Pike Place Public Market**—despite a dramatic increase in money and tourism in and around the market, it retains that fundamental honest seediness I remember being central to the Seattle I grew up in.

The **Japanese Garden** in the **Arboretum**—a lovely contemplative garden inside the rangier and also wonderful arboretum. I like the Japanese Garden best on misty, overcast days, of which there are so many.

Safeco Field—should it be Taxpayers' Field? Perhaps. Political wrangling aside, it's a truly lovely place to watch a ball game, and with Ichiro in right field and coming to the plate, now the ball games are fun to watch too.

Café Lago—said to be a neighborhood Italian restaurant, but people who've tried it come a distance back for more. The menu is limited, but that's no problem because everything there is quite good. Lago is well lit and has a family atmosphere, so kids are welcome, but with its style and great ambiance, a romantic dinner's certainly possible.

---

314 E Pike St (between Bellevue and Minor Aves). 621.7591. &. www.seattleeagle.com

26 NEIGHBOURS

♂ ♀ Very young pretty boys, gym queens, dykes, divas, and cool straights all get down together at Seattle's most cavernous and happening dance club. The high-tech trappings, massive (if a bit soggy-sounding) sound system, video screens, and hunky go-go dancers make for a souped-up scene that renders conversation all but impossible. A late-night buffet is thrown in on weekends, but veterans know to steer clear of the mystery meat. ♦ Cover F, Sa. M-Th, Su, 9PM-2AM; F, Sa, 9PM-4AM. 1509 Broadway (between E Pike and E Pine Sts). 324.5358. &. www.neighborsnightclub.com

27 1200 BISTRO & LOUNGE

★★★$$ This warmly lit restaurant presents an ever-changing bistro menu. The calamari with crème fraîche, roasted free-range chicken, and tangy, tender braised short ribs are customer favorites. In the heart of the Capitol Hill gay community, this place is hetero-friendly. ♦ Daily dinner. 1200 E Pike St (at 12th Ave E). 320.1200. www.1200bistro.com

28 C.C. ATTLE'S

♂ This grande dame of Seattle's gay bars sits up on the hill looking down into the Pike-Pine Corridor. Nicknamed "the wrinkle room," it is where many of the more senior members of the gay community congregate. The food is okay and so are the drinks. But happy hour is Monday through Friday, 8AM to midnight. So live it up, Mary! ♦ Daily, 6AM-2AM. 1501 E Madison St (at 15th Ave). 726.0565

At C.C. Attle's:

CADILLAC GRILL

♂ ★$ It's decidedly informal, with a "come as you are" attitude that stands out even in laid-back Seattle. The menu is not particularly Northwestern—or exciting—but the steaks, fresh burgers, and pot roast sandwich are perfectly edible. ♦ American ♦ Daily, 24 hours. 325.4017

29 SUMMERFIELD SUITES

$$$ Not exclusively gay, but homosexuals male and female love this modern hotel for

---

Restaurants/Clubs: Red | Hotels: Purple | Shops: Orange | Outdoors/Parks: Green | Sights/Culture: Blue

its great location and amenities: 193 comfy suites with kitchenettes, free daytime shuttles to downtown, a workout room, and Seattle's only year-round outdoor heated swimming pool. ♦ 1011 Pike Street (at Boren Ave). 682.8282, 800/426.0670. ♿

30 MANRAY

The post-modern décor here draws crowds in their 30s and 40s, as does the live dance-VJ and videos playing on dozens of monitors. Thers's karaoke on Mondays. Fantastic Bloody Marys! ♦ 514 E Pike St (at Belmont Ave). 568.0750. www.manrayvideo.com

31 ROSEBUD ESPRESSO & BISTRO

★★$$ Glam pix of classic movie stars grace this charming, pastel-colored country home split in two. On one side is a restaurant, where diners gobble up cheese-baked eggs (stuffed with a variety of meats and vegetables), chicken Dijon, and other such delights. On the other side is a living-room espresso bar, where antique couches invite reading or chatting over good mochaccino. ♦ American/coffeehouse ♦ M, lunch; Tu-F, lunch and dinner; Sa, breakfast and dinner; Su, breakfast. Espresso bar: M-F, 7:30AM-1AM; Sa, 9AM-3AM; Su, 10AM-11PM. 719 E Pike St (between Harvard and Boylston Aves). 323.6636. ♿

Sarah Yesler, founder of the Seattle Public Library system and wife of Seattle mayor and lumber magnate Henry Yesler, developed a passionate relationship with her friend Eliza Hurd. In 1860, Eliza wrote, "Oh Sarah I wish to say so much and I cannot say anything—I want to sleep with you again! hey!" Hey, indeed.

31 TOYS IN BABELAND

With a woman-friendly atmosphere and an award from the mayor's office, this classy boutique (which opened a second shop in New York City in 1998) is several cuts above most sex shops. The high-quality product line includes bizarre Japanese vibrators, silicone dildos, and fine handmade floggers, as well as a full range of toys, massage oils, S&M erotica, and lesbo porn. Although most of its customers are lesbians, there is a loyal gay and straight clientele as well. ♦ Daily, noon-8PM. 707 E Pike St (between Harvard and Boylston Aves). 328.2914, 800/658.9119. ♿

32 ARO.SPACE

♂ Despite the owners' somewhat lofty ambitions for the space (*ARO* stands for *ART & Revolution Organization*), it turned out a great club. A good-size dance floor with a balcony for watchers, quieter lounge spaces, and a striking, tall bar are the highlights of the nightclub area. Offerings vary weekly, so check the alternative newspapers to see who/what is performing. Some nights are more gay than others. On the other side of the wall from the dance floor, the **ARO cafeteria** offers affordable and exquisitely prepared vegetarian meals. Be sure to try the Baked Mac and Cheese, considered the best in the city. ♦ Cover. Club: daily, 8PM-2AM. Cafeteria: M-F, dinner; Sa, Su, brunch and dinner. 925 E Pike St (at 10th Ave). 320.0424; cafeteria, 860.7395. ♿

33 WILDROSE

♀ ★★$ Wild or not, women of all stripes have been jamming this lesbian institution and community forum since 1986. The pastas are good if unremarkable. The salads and sandwiches are a better bet; try the turkey. There's a pool table and a jukebox loaded with Melissa and Indigo Girls.

THE GREAT OUTDOORS

For years, gays who wanted to frolic with family in the great outdoors headed to **Triangle Recreational Camp (TRC)**, commonly known as **Index** for its proximity to the small town of the same name. A lost lease in 1995 sent TRC organizers looking for a new home, and they couldn't have done much better than **Bender Creek**, a serene, heavily forested setting on the banks of the **Stillaguamish River** about 60 miles northeast of Seattle. This campground, with hidden swimming holes and plenty of secluded forest areas, has become a big favorite with Seattle-area gays (and some lesbians), so prospective campers should book early for stays during the summer months, especially holiday weekends. Shower facilities and other amenities are planned, but at press time such comforts were still few, so bring everything you'll need.

To get to TRC, take **Interstate 5** north to exit 194, then **Highway 2** east to **Route 9**, then head north to **Route 92** east. Bender Creek is located about 22 miles east of **Granite Falls** on the **Mountain Loop Highway**. For more information, call 292.5118.

♦ American ♦ M-F, lunch and dinner; Sa, Su, brunch (with full bar), lunch, and dinner. Bar: M-Th; Su, 11AM-1AM; F-Sa, 11AM-2AM. 1021 E Pike St (at 11th Ave). 324.9210. ⅋

33 CAFFE VITA COFFEE CO.

The loud alternative music and the kind of art that doesn't hang in galleries continue to make this one of the hippest and most popular coffee hangouts on Capitol Hill. The young, fashion-conscious, and mixed straight/gay/lesbian crowd fill the place at all hours. ♦ Coffeehouse ♦ M-F, 6AM-midnight; Sa-Su, 7AM-midnight. No credit cards accepted. 1005 E Pike St (between 11th and 10th Aves). 709.4440. ⅋

33 HOTHOUSE SPA AND SAUNA

This spa, located behind the **Wildrose Tavern**, offers a hot tub, steam room, sauna, cold plunge, showers, and relaxation and massage therapy. Bathing suits are "allowed,

A lot of people in Seattle who don't have room in their yards, condos, or apartments are happily tilling the soil in one of 54 comunity gardens, ranging in size from 1,200 to 98,000 square feet. These are called P-Patches; they are managed by a community garden coordinator in the Department of Neighborhoods and manned by avid gardeners. The city proves a dedicated water tap and compost; the gardeners have to keep their areas clean and their practices organic. The name is said to derive from Picardo, after the family who owned a north-end farm, part of which became the original P-Patch.

but not encouraged." No reservations; first come, first served, shared space.
♦ Daily, noon-midnight. Admission $12. 1019 E Pike (enter around the corner on 11th Ave E). 568.3240. www.hothousespa.com

34 MADISON PUB

♂ Stay long enough, and everybody will know your name at this neighborhood pub, where pop and oldies rule on the jukebox. The regulars, most of a certain age, make their strongest showing weekdays after work and on Friday and Saturday nights. The group is close-knit but friendly to outsiders. ♦ Daily, noon-2AM. 1315 E Madison St (between 14th and 13th Aves). 325.6537. ⅋. www.madisonpub.com

35 HI SPOT

★★★$$ Gays and lesbians in Madrona, a forested section of Seattle near Lake Washington, frequent this bustling

Seattle is a moisturizing pad disguised as a city.
—Jerry Seinfeld

Restaurants/Clubs: Red | Hotels: Purple | Shops: Orange | Outdoors/Parks: Green | Sights/Culture: Blue

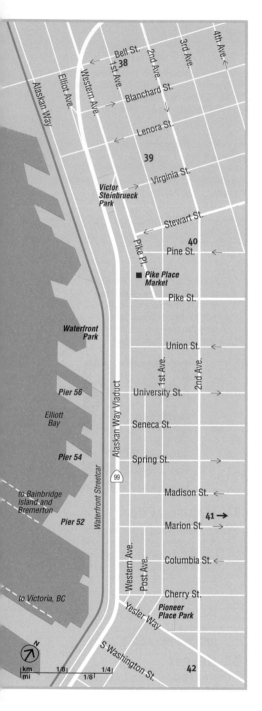

brunches when the girls and boys linger over celebrated omelettes like the Northwest Exposure (with wild mushrooms galore) and the Wake Up With Zorba (with feta, spinach, tomatoes, and onions). At night, the lights are low and diners feast on imaginative Asian, Mediterranean, or Moroccan dishes, depending on the month. ♦ International ♦ M, breakfast and lunch; Tu-F, breakfast, lunch, and dinner; Sa, brunch and dinner; Su, brunch. 1410 34th Ave (between E Union and E Pike Sts). 325.7905. ㅊ

36 World Gym

The former **Cascade Athletic Club** in the **Washington State Convention Center** is still the place to pump and be seen by young male gym bunnies, with 30,000 square feet on two levels and all the latest workout equipment. The men's locker room is not conducive to much beyond preliminary cruising, but (rumor has it) it's a good pickup spot. ♦ M-F, 6AM-10PM; Sa, Su, 8AM-6PM. 825 Pike St (at Convention Pl). 583.0640. ㅊ

37 The Garage

Swanky bowling and billiards plus a full bar. The menu features comfort food with a twist. ♦ Daily, 3PM-2AM; Happy hour, 3PM-7PM. 1130 Broadway (between E Madison and E Union Sts). 322.2296. www.garagebilliards.com

38 Flying Fish

★★★$$$ Opened in 1996, this lesbian-owned Belltown dining spot quickly earned a name as one of the best restaurants in town. Highlights of the globe-trotting menu include Thai crab cakes with lemongrass mayonnaise, salt-and-pepper Dungeness crab, and whole fried snapper in pineapple-anchovy sauce. The dress is casual and the décor festive—abstract art, lots of windows, and a zippy orange, yellow, black, and blue color scheme—but the prices are steep enough to keep the club kids out. ♦ International ♦ Daily, dinner. Reservations required (1-2 weeks in advance). 2234 First Ave (at Bell St). 728.8595. ㅊ

39 The Vogue

♂♀ The crowd at this Belltown club practically defines the word *bisexual* (not to mention the terms *pierced*, *tattooed*, and *terminally hip*), so the owner jokingly tried having Bisexual Night once a week. Nobody got it. Why would they? Labels mean nothing here, and anything goes—both sartorially and musically. Sunday's Fetish Night is a kinky treat. ♦ Cover. Daily, 9PM-2AM. 2018 First Ave (between Virginia and Lenora Sts). 443.0673. ㅊ

neighborhood bistro, but more than a few patrons drive from elsewhere in the city for its global menu, which changes monthly. It may feel like a small European country inn, but the morning atmosphere tends toward the raucous, especially during weekend

40 NORDSTROM RACK

With four floors of bargains on men's suits and shirts, womenswear, and enough shoes to make Imelda drool, this outlet of the main **Nordstrom** store (known to some simply as "the Rack") is a sprawling mess popular with gays and lesbians who don't mind the challenge of digging for a discount. Where else would you find Nikes and Italian imports for less than half price? ♦ M-Sa, 9:30AM-8PM; Su, 11AM-6PM. 1601 Second Ave (at Pine St). 448.8522. ⅄

41 DOWNTOWN YMCA

♂ Dubbed by some Club Seattle Downtown for its appeal to gay guys, this local institution offers the usual free weights, Nautilus equipment, and two rooms full of Life Circuit machines. It's the men's locker room, as well as the nearby whirlpool and steam room, however, that have brought the **Y** its notoriety. Cruising reaches its peak after work on weekdays, and Sunday afternoons aren't bad either. ♦ M-F, 5AM-9:30PM; Sa, 7AM-8:30PM; Su, noon-5:30PM. 909 Fourth Ave (between Marion and Madison Sts). 382.5010

42 DOUBLE HEADER

♂ This (rough) neighborhood bar near Pioneer Square is rumored to be the oldest continually operating homosexual watering hole in the country, and every group is represented here, except women. First opened in 1934, it evolved into a gay club soon afterward when patrons from **Madame Peabody's School of Dance** in the basement began heading upstairs for drinks. Alas, the Five Alive polka band, which played here for 17 years, is no more—patrons must make do with the occasional drag show, two pool tables, and what is probably the most antiquated dart board in Seattle. ♦ Daily, 10AM-2AM. 407 Second Ave (between S Washington St and Yesler Way). 464.9918. ⅄

Restaurants/Clubs: Red | Hotels: Purple | Shops: Orange | Outdoors/Parks: Green | Sights/Culture: Blue

DAY TRIPS

After four or five days in Seattle, travelers may start to feel somewhat edgy, a little trapped, worried that there isn't anything more to do than revisit **Pike Place Market, Pioneer Square,** or the **Space Needle.** But nearby are volcanoes, vineyards, and villages . . . and that's just the beginning.

Within three hours from the city are the rustic **San Juan Islands,** the majestic **Mount Rainier National Park,** ceremonial wine-grape crushings on the east side of **Lake Washington,** ski slopes, exotic summer gardens, and bird refuges. Architecture aficionados might want to head south for a look at Washington State's impressive capital complex at **Olympia,** whereas true urbanites who want a taste of international travel could venture north into two of Canada's most interesting cities: **Victoria** is the modest but growing island-bound capital of **British Columbia,** providing a wealth of history in a cozy, shop-laden English atmosphere, and **Vancouver,** just across the **Strait of Georgia** from Victoria, is Canada's third-largest metropolis (after Montreal and Toronto). Rudyard Kipling, seduced by the Vancouver area's beauty, proclaimed in his *Letters of Travel* that "such a land is good for an energetic man . . . it is also not bad for the loafer."

And then there's **Mount St. Helens,** to the south of Seattle, which caught the world's attention when it violently blew its stack back in 1980. Although the state of Oregon tries to claim St. Helens as its own (it is physically closer to the city of Portland than to Seattle), the now-decimated peak remains one of Washington's prime attractions.

EASTSIDE WINE COUNTRY

Washington State's oldest producer of premium wines is the **Columbia Winery** (14030 NE 145th St, between 148th Ave and Woodinville Redmond Rd, Woodinville; 425/488.2776, www.columbiawinery.com),

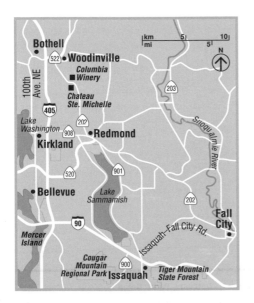

located northeast of Seattle, across Lake Washington. There are daily wine tastings and tours. Visitors can enjoy the patio, picnic grounds, and lawns and purchase cheese and crackers in a small gift shop. Phone ahead to check on occasional concerts held on the premises. Just across the street is the state's largest winery, **Chateau Ste. Michelle** (14111 NE 145th St, between Woodinville Redmond Rd and NE 140th Pl, Woodinville; 425/415.3632; www.ste-michelle.com).

The extensive grounds here are open to picnickers, and classical concerts are held in an amphitheater during the warm months. If you have time, take a tour of the two-acre garden behind the grounds' historic **Stimson Mansion.** Timber magnate Frederick S. Stimson arrived in Seattle in 1889, bought 206 acres of prime agricultural land on the **Sammamish River,** and built **Hollywood Farm,** a state-of-the-art dairy and poultry ranch, anchored by the manse. Around 1910, he hired the famed Olmsted brothers to plan a garden, bordered by trees and shrubs, that would be filled with exotic plants. The formal results are still maintained today.

For a guide to Washington's wine-touring opportunities, check out *Northwest Wines* (Sasquatch Press, 1994), coauthored by Paul Gregutt, wine columnist for the *Seattle*

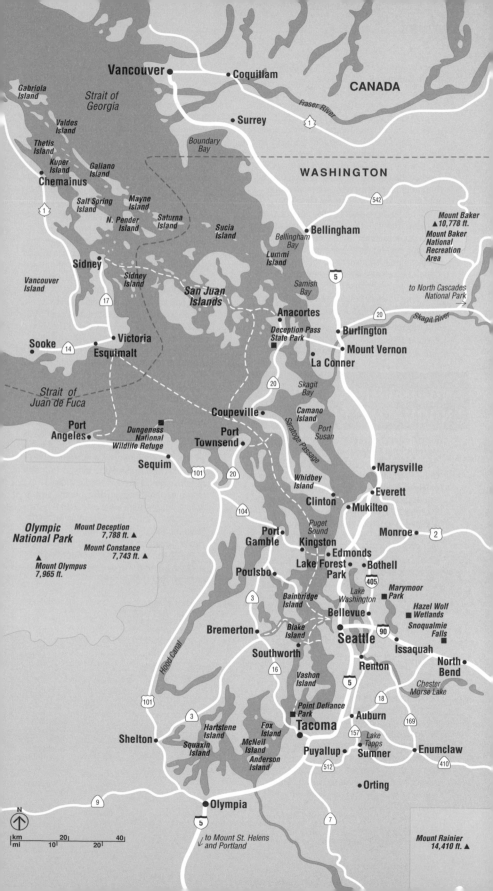

Weekly, and Jeff Prather, wine manager at **Ray's Boathouse** in Ballard.

An excellent eastside dining choice is the **Herb Farm** (Hedges Cellars, 195 NE Gilman Blvd, Issaquah; 425/485.5300; www.herbfarm.com), about 30 minutes east of Seattle. Chef Jerry Traunfeld oversees a restaurant that provides an exceptional experience as well as excellent food. Meals begin with a lively tour of the grounds, with Traunfeld nipping off leaves for you to rub and smell. After that sensual experience, you'll be far more aware of the flowers and herbs in what you taste; the legendary salads are a good example. All the produce (except for lemons) and herbs used in the food preparation are grown here. Prix-fixe meals (nine courses at dinner) are composed from fresh seasonal bounty and span the globe with their culinary influences—everything from Italian to Native American.

Unfortunately, getting a reservation here is no easy task. There is just one seating per day, and only Thursdays through Sundays.

SNOQUALMIE AND SNOQUALMIE FALLS

King County's eastern cantons won international fame when Washington native David Lynch chose to shoot his unsettlingly kinky TV series *Twin Peaks* in the small towns of **North Bend** and **Snoqualmie**, Begin your exploration of this area by taking **Interstate 90** to exit 27. Follow the signs to Snoqualmie, then through the north end of town to **Snoqualmie Falls**, or take **Routes 908** and **202** from Kirkland to reach the falls by a more scenic route. This 270-foot cascade is the place to bring out-of-town guests. City folks and other tourists have been coming here to gawk since the late 19th century. A lookout point on a bluff to one side of the falls was improved and expanded not long ago, but crowds mount quickly on weekends, everybody equipped with cameras; arrive early if you hope to beat the stampede.

The Snoqualmie Indians have traditionally viewed this as a sacred site, and they've been struggling in recent years to maintain its natural appearance. The tribe has not had a happy relationship with Puget Power, the hydroelectric company that owns the land surrounding the falls and regulates how much water passes over its lip. Information panels at the overlook outline these additions and renovations, which include consideration for fisheries, wetlands, and even flood prevention; the Snoqualmie are mentioned only in relation to the discovery of the falls by whites. Ironically, Puget Power's buildings at the falls are historic

landmarks, whereas the Snoqualmie have no legal means to protect the falls.

The world's first underground electric generator, built in 1898, lies 270 feet deep in a chamber excavated from solid basaltic rock behind the falls. From the lookout point, you can see the opening of the tailrace, a 450-foot-long tunnel where water diverted through the turbines rejoins the river at the base of the falls. A one-mile round-trip trail will take you down for a closer look and a faceful of spray.

Perched at the edge of the gorge is the **Salish Lodge** (6501 Railroad Ave; 425/888.2556; www.salishlodge.com). Formerly the **Snoqualmie Falls Lodge**, the landmark was remodeled in the late 1980s. Although a country feel was retained, the place has lost its authentic weathered look. The **Salish Lodge Dining Room** is famous for its front-row view of the falls and its six-course country breakfast: a platter of fruit accompanied by the Eye Opener (fresh-squeezed orange juice blended with lime juice, honey, and egg, and topped with grated nutmeg); an assortment of bran and fruit muffins baked every half hour and served with honey butter; old-fashioned rolled oats with cream and brown sugar; and the main course of apple-pork sausage, smoked bacon, and a grilled ham steak with your choice of egg preparations, plus hash browns and sourdough biscuits—buttressed by a stack of whole-wheat buttermilk flapjacks. (Be prepared to loosen your belt a notch—or two.) The wine list is also legendary. Sommelier Randy Austin says that at last count, there were over 700 labels available on the roster, including an 1882 Madeira Verdeljo ($250). Don't worry if you're not an expert oenophile; Austin has always been very helpful in educating the patrons about novel or arcane vintages to complement their meals.

The nearby town of North Bend is sprinkled with Swiss chalet-style shops and restaurants and loomed over by **Mount Si**. With a sweeping view of the **Snoqualmie Valley** and a trailhead that starts just outside of town, Si is a popular hike; on weekends, the 4.5-mile trail, though strenuous, is crowded with nature lovers. To get there, drive southeast on **North Bend Way**, turn left on **Mount Si Road**, and continue for about 2.5 miles, watching for the trail sign. Just one caution: Keep track of the time—many people have spent miserable nights lost in these woods because they didn't allow enough time to hike back before dark. And the Haystack, a knob of bare rock at Si's top, is officially off limits. Views from there may be panoramic, but sudden sidewinds and updrafts can pick off even the most macho sightseers like ripe fruit.

BAINBRIDGE ISLAND

Bainbridge has enjoyed some interesting history. In the late 19th century, the island's southern end sported a couple of saloons, a giant mill that could cut 500,000 board feet a day over two 10-hour shifts, and the 75-room **Bainbridge Hotel**. (All have since disappeared.) In the early 20th century, the island figured briefly in the well-publicized and often comic escape of Butch Cassidy cohort Harry Tracy from a maximum-security prison in Oregon. Most of that colorful heritage is gone, leaving a fairly peaceful, still heavily wooded retreat.

For years, Bainbridge—about 35 minutes west of Seattle by ferry—was a haven for hippies and others whose supreme desire was to drop out of the public eye. But things change. Although threats to build a bridge across **Puget Sound** have come to naught, as Seattle grew, well-to-do residents who didn't fancy moving to the Eastside suburbs looked west instead.

The Bainbridge-bound ferry (464.6400, 800/843.3779; www.wsdot.wa.gov/ferries) leaves from **Colman Dock** on Seattle's **Waterfront**. Ferries depart every 40 to 60 minutes, from just after 6AM until slightly after 2AM; the last return trip leaves Bainbridge at about 1:15AM. Ferries dock at **Winslow**, home to a small Saturday farmer's market (held midspring through fall at **Winslow Green**, Madison Ave and Winslow Way W), plus a couple of cafés and the small but interesting **Eagle Harbor Books** (157 Winslow Way E; 842.5332; www.eagleharborbooks.com).

Stop in at the **Streamliner Diner** (397 Winslow Way E; 842.8595; no credit cards accepted), an island institution, and get in line. Breakfasts are legendary (just ask any of the people waiting for a table), and they're

served all day. Try the omelettes, buttermilk waffles, or potatoes deluxe—a stir-fry of diced spuds, lots of onions, and fresh veggies, all beneath a generous layer of melted cheese.

Head north along **Route 305** and, in less than a mile, you'll come to the **Bainbridge Island Winery** (682 Hwy 305; 842.9463; www.bainbridgevineyards.com), the only estate winery in the Seattle area. Founded in 1981, it's only seven acres in size but has a growing reputation. Owners Gerard and Jo Ann Bentryn style the vintages in the German fashion—low in alcohol with some residual sweetness. The flagship wine is Müller-Thurgau, but Corbet Clark, in his book *American Wines of the Northwest*, also gives raves to the "surprising" Siegerrebe, "a cross of Gewürztraminer with Madeleine Angevine, itself an old French cross." The Bentryns also produce a popular strawberry wine. There's a picnic area, a wine-oriented antiques shop, and a wine museum on the premises.

The 150 acres of **Bloedel Reserve** (7521 NE Dolphin Dr, between Agate Point Rd and Agatewood Rd; 842.7631; www.bloedelreserve.org), about four miles farther north along Route 305, were once the estate of a Canadian lumbering family. But since the 1980s, these woodlands and

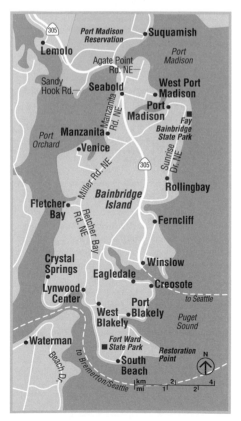

gardens have been open to the public Wednesdays through Sundays, with trails that give visitors a good look at exotic plant life imported from around the globe. Rhododendrons and azaleas are the most plentiful plantings, so spring is the prime viewing season. Bring binoculars; birds enjoy a refuge here. Only 150 guests are allowed in each day, so make reservations early. There is an admission charge.

Finally, cross the bridge onto the **Kitsap Peninsula** at **Agate Pass**, turn left onto **Sandy Hook Road**, and follow the signs to the **Suquamish Museum** (15838 Sandy Hook Rd; 360/598.3311 ext 422; www.suquamish.nsn.us/museum). This small museum recounts local history in a manner sensitive to the perspective of Puget Sound's Salish tribe. The life of Chief Sealth is illuminated through both displays and photographs. The museum is open daily; admission is charged.

Chief Sealth's burial site is nearby, next to **St. Peter's Catholic Mission Church** in the Kitsap village of **Suquamish**. It's hard to miss the leader's tomb, which is marked with a pair of long canoes mounted atop poles.

WHIDBEY ISLAND

Thanks to the US Supreme Court, **Whidbey Island**—a 50-mile snake of soil north of Seattle—is the longest island in the United States. (The court declared that challenger Long Island is a mere peninsula.) Unfortunately, the island's natural beauty and easygoing charm may soon be overrun in the rush to attract tourists. More and more amenities are being planned for Whidbey, causing a local backlash from Seattleites who liked the island before it became popular. The time to see this place is now, before it's too late.

No history of Seattle would be complete without a mention of Mercer's Maidens. In 1864, a young entrepreneur named Asa Mercer offered to travel across the country to New England to procure brides for a number of lonely local bachelors. After collecting a large sum of money from these men, he sailed away to Boston, returning that May with 11 young women. He repeated the feat two years later. Unfortunately, he overstepped himself a bit: He had promised to come up with 500 brides, but he could find only 100 or so. The firestorm created by all this caused Mercer (who had married one of the young women himself) to leave Seattle for the Rocky Mountains, where he lived the rest of his life as a rancher. This tale was the basis of the TV series *Here Come the Brides*.

Whidbey is reached via a 20-minute ferry ride from the town of **Mukilteo**, 27 miles north of Seattle. Call 464.6400 for schedules and information. The boat docks in the town of **Clinton**, where motorists can pick up **Route 525**.

Once on Whidbey, follow the highway for three miles, then take the marked turnoff north to **Langley**. This tiny town maintains a distinctly quaint air; it may be rivaled only by La Conner, Washington, in the number of new curio shops that sprout here annually. Yet Langley seems especially susceptible to the encroaching tourist industry: The town already has a glut in its number of high-priced but small-occupancy boutique hotels, which sell themselves on the basis of expansive views of **Saratoga Passage** and the **Cascade Mountains**.

Several fine restaurants draw day-trippers from the mainland. In downtown Langley, try the Middle Eastern **Cafe Langley** (113 First St; 360/221.3090; www.langley-wa.com),

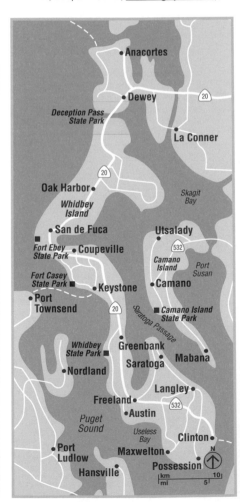

renowned for its crab cakes and hummus. Or sample innkeeper-chef Stephen Nogal's delectable five-course, prix-fixe weekend dinners at the **Inn at Langley** (400 First St; 360/221.3033; www.innatlangley.com), which concentrate on Northwest ingredients, from vegetables to seafood. There's one seating a night, three nights a week, expanding to four nights weekly in the summer; reservations are taken three months in advance.

A visit to the **Meerkeek Rhododendron Gardens** (Resort Rd, Greenbank; 360/678.1912) is a must for spring visitors. There are 53 acres covered with some 2,000 varieties of Washington's official state flower in peak bloom between mid-April and mid-May. The gardens also feature wildflowers and summer perennials. Energetic types might want to head up-island for a walk around the gorge at **Deception Pass**, with its 2,300 acres of forests and beaches. The gardens are open Wednesday through Sunday; there is an admission charge.

Midway between those two attractions, three miles south of **Coupeville** on **Admiralty Bay**, is **Fort Casey** (360.678.4519), decommissioned but still boasting its old gun mounts and some dramatic outlooks. It's open daily and is free.

Get a sense of history and stay a night or two at the **Fort Casey Inn** (1124 S Engle Rd; 360.678.8792; www.fortcaseyinn.com), 2.5 miles south of Coupeville. Children are welcome at this restored two-story, two-bedroom, Georgian Revival officers' quarters decorated with rag rugs, stenciling, and plenty of eagle motifs. Bikes are available free to guests. While in Coupeville, visit the free **Island County Historical Museum** (Alexander and Front Sts; 360/678.3310; www.islandhistory.org), which is full of old photographs and Native American artifacts. The museum is open daily May through October; it's closed Friday, and Saturday, Sunday the rest of the year.

As the sun finally fades from the sky, stop by the **Captain Whidbey Inn** (2072 W Captain Whidbey Inn Rd, just east of Madrona Way; 360/678.4097, 800/366.4097; www.captainwhidbey.com) west of Coupeville. This 1907 madrona-log lodge was once most reachable by steamship from Seattle. Now you can wheel up here in just a few hours for dinner or drinks on a terrific deck overlooking **Penn Cove**, where some of this region's finest mussels are harvested.

There is a plethora of bed-and-breakfast establishments on the island, as well as a number of cottages for rent; contact the **Langley Chamber of Commerce** (360/221.5676; www.whidbey.com) for more information.

SAN JUAN ISLANDS

There are 743 islands in the **San Juan** archipelago, but during high tide only about 170 of them are visible. Sixty of these are populated, most are privately owned (a few by hermits), and the vast majority are unreachable except by private craft.

Kenmore Air (425/486.1257, 866/435.9524; www.kenmoreair.com) offers scenic scheduled floatplane service from Seattle to the San Juans. But certainly the most relaxing means of travel to the four largest islands—**Lopez, Shaw, Orcas**, and **San Juan** (with an international spur on to **Sidney, British Columbia**)—is by ferry.

Washington State Ferries (464.6400, 800/843.3779; www.wsdot.wa.gov) bound for the islands leave from the town of **Anacortes**, 78 miles north of Seattle (take exit 230 from I-5 and head 15 miles west to the terminal). During summer months, there are 17 daily departures scheduled from Anacortes; there are fewer between Labor Day and Memorial Day. Return schedules vary for each island. The wait for space on ferry car decks can be long, so bring reading material; folks have spent 2 or more hours in line during the summer tourist crush. But if you begin early (the first sailing of the day varies slightly each quarter, but is sometime around 6AM), you'll improve your chances of getting on when you want.

While at sea, take advantage of the boats' huge picture windows for ample viewing of madrona-forested hills and narrow beaches. Eagles, gulls, and other able aviators are frequently seen, as are small fishing craft. Weather here tends to be milder than in Seattle, as the islands snuggle into the "rain shadow" of the **Olympic Mountains** to the southwest. It takes approximately 1.5 hours to sail from Anacortes directly to **Friday Harbor** on San Juan, the farthest you can go by ferry among these islands. But some visitors slow the journey's pace by getting off and on the boat periodically to tour the four principal isles.

The islands can be very crowded in the summer, so book accommodations early—preferably *weeks* before your planned excursion. **Visitor Information Service** (360/378.9551; www.visitsanjuans.com) provides accommodations listings, and the **Washington Bed and Breakfast Guild** (800/647.2918; www.wbbg.com) lists inns, farmhouses, and cottages run by charming and friendly innkeepers.

Flat, pastoral Lopez (about 45 minutes by ferry from Anacortes) provides the easiest bicycling on the islands, a 30-mile jaunt past sheep and cattle pastures that

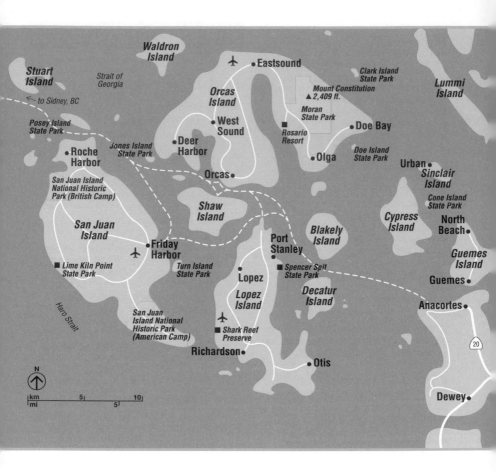

can be handled even by younger family members. One of the best ways to enjoy the island is to stay at the **Inn at Swifts Bay** (Port Stanley Rd, east of Ferry Rd; 360/468.3636, 800/903.9546; www.swiftsbay.com), which offers whatever amount of pampering or seclusion you might desire in their tasteful, comfortable mock Tudor home surrounded by perennial gardens. (They'll even pick you up at the ferry landing.) Five guest rooms are available in the inn. All guests have access to the hot tub down the garden path and are provided with robes, flashlights, and flip-flops.

Ride down to the island's west side and visit **Shark Reel Preserve** (Shark Reef Rd, south of Airport Rd) to observe seals barking and flopping about. Lopez village (known for its grapevine of information and liberal politics) barely makes it on the map. It boasts the small but interesting **Lopez Island Historical Museum** (360/468.2049; www.rockisland.com), which is open Wednesday through Sunday, May through September (donation requested), and a bakery, **Holly B's** (360/468.2133).

All four islands can claim parks, but underpopulated **Shaw Island**—dominated by three orders of Catholic nuns (one member of which always comes down to meet the ferry)—offers very little else in the way of traveler amenities.

At 57 square miles, horseshoe-shaped Orcas (1 hour and 20 minutes by ferry from Anacortes) is the largest of the islands. Generally hilly (okay for bike riding if you're in good shape), it's dominated by 2,409-foot **Mount Constitution**, on top of which is an old stone lookout that offers views of everything between **Mount Rainier** and Vancouver, British Columbia. Drive up this peak or get a better feel for the island by huffing to it on foot through 4,934-acre **Moran State Park**, overlooking the island's eastern end.

The town of **Eastsound**, about 10 miles north of the ferry landing, is slowly being transformed into a mini-Carmel, with bookstores, art galleries, and restaurants. On Saturday, April through October, local artisans and growers gather at a farmer's market on the grounds of the modest **Orcas**

Island Historical Museum (North Beach Rd; 360/376.4849), which is open Tuesday through Sunday. Also in Eastsound is **Bilbo's Festivo** (N Beach Rd and A St; 360/376.4728), a restaurant that serves food influenced by New Mexican, Mexican, and Spanish cooking styles in a setting of adobe walls and Navajo weavings. Mesquite-grilled dinners of either sirloin tips or local fish are excellent, but so are the burritos. The best seating is in the courtyard, where you can enjoy the quiet of early evening, and where it's not unheard of for patrons to begin sing-alongs. **Christina's** (Horseshoe Hwy and North Beach Rd; 360/376.4904; www.christinas.net) is a more romantic restaurant, a collection of small rooms with a dining porch that overlooks the water. Offerings consist mostly of satisfying preparations of local seafood (including halibut and oysters).

Take a little time to stroll the grounds of **Rosario Resort** (Horseshoe Hwy; 360/376.2222; 866/801.ROCK; www.rosarioresort.com), about 15 minutes from the ferry landing and 3 miles beyond Eastsound. A glistening white mansion on the waterfront, it was built in the early part of the 20th century by former Seattle mayor and zillionaire boat-builder Robert Moran, who left the city in 1904 after his doctor told him he had only 6 months to live. (As it turned out, Moran avoided the Grim Reaper for another 37 years.) With 179 charmingly decorated guest rooms, this resort is a wonderful place to hang out when the weather is good, drinking buckets of margaritas by the pool and finishing off lunch with a soothing afternoon massage. Meals in the dining room (including an almost-overwhelming Sunday brunch) are acceptable but not outstanding. Phone ahead for information on historical programs, including organ concerts and a history of the estate.

The most populated of the islands is San Juan. This was the site of a bizarre border dispute, the comic Pig War of 1859, at an uneasy time when the British and the Americans jointly occupied this island. The war was set off by an American farmer who shot and killed a pig that had been rooting in his garden. Turns out the porker belonged to the British Hudson's Bay Company. When the Brits sought to arrest the offending farmer, American infantry soldiers stepped in. Tempers and armaments escalated, until President James Buchanan dispatched General Winfield Scott to negotiate a temporary truce. Joint occupation of the island continued until 1871, when none other than Kaiser Wilhelm I of Germany was asked to settle the border dispute. He drew

the Canada–US border to the west of the island, through **Haro Strait**, thereby ceding San Juan to the Americans. You can visit the national historic sites of **American Camp** and **British Camp**. To reach the former, follow **Cattle Point Road** about 6 miles from the town of **Friday Harbor** toward the island's southern tip. The nattier British Camp is about 12 miles from the American Camp, located off **West Valley Road**.

Before or after taking in the old British installation, stop at **Lime Kiln Point State Park** (6158 Lighthouse Rd; 360/378.2044), which provides some of the best whale-watching opportunities in Washington State; posted signs will help you distinguish one species from another. (Premier viewing season is from late spring through early fall.) The **Friday Harbor Whale Museum** (62 First St; 360/378.4710, 800/946.7227; www.whalemuseum.org) in town is a warehouselike structure stuffed with gray whale baleen, cetacean skeletons, and information about orcas and dolphins. The museum can also provide information about whale watching excursions. It's open daily; there is an admission charge.

An unusual aspect of the San Juan Islands' beauty is that much of it is fairly new, reclaimed from previous devastation. As the 19th century became the 20th, the air here was muddied with noxious fumes from lime kilns operating on San Juan Island. **Roche Harbor**, at the north end of San Juan, once hosted some of the busiest kilns—not to mention a steam-belching railroad and lumberyards. Today the harbor's focal point is the **Hotel de Haro and Roche Harbor Resort** (4950 Tarte Memorial Dr; 360/378.2155, 800/451.8910) built in 1886 by John Stafford McMillin, a Tacoma lawyer and owner of the old Roche Harbor Lime and Cement Company here. McMillin built the hotel so his business clients (as well as a few other distinguished guests, including Teddy Roosevelt) might have a proper place to stay nearby. Accommodations include the 20-room hotel, 20 condos, and 9 cottages. Worth visiting—if only for its Stephen Kingish oddity—is a mausoleum, tucked amid a stand of Douglas firs about a half-mile from the inn. The seven-pillared monument contains a round table and six chairs in its middle, each representing a member of McMillin's family. After a roam in the woods, stop on the hotel's deck, overlooking the harbor, for a cold beer and to watch great blue herons coast forlornly over the evergreens.

Victoria, British Columbia

Author Rudyard Kipling may have gone a bit overboard when he described this city on the southern tip of **Vancouver Island** in the early 20th century. "To realize Victoria," he wrote, "you must take all that the eye admires in Bournemouth, Torquay, the Isle of Wight, the Happy Valley at Hong Kong, the Doon, Sorrento, and Camp's Bay—add reminiscences of the Thousand Islands and arrange the whole around the Bay of Naples with some Himalayas for the background." But things are changing here—rapidly. Finally shedding its reputation as a retirement camp to the world, Victoria has attracted some innovative shops and restaurants, and downtown sidewalks no longer roll up after 10PM.

To get there, you can extend your meandering journey through the San Juans via the Washington State Ferries (464.6400, 800/843.3779; www.wsdot.wa.gov) to the town of **Sidney** on Vancouver Island, and then drive 20 miles south to Victoria. Direct service to Victoria from Seattle is available via seaplane from **Kenmore Air** (425/486.1257, 866/435.9524; www.kenmoreair.com), which offers frequent scheduled flights daily, and by the **Victoria Clipper**'s (448.5000, 800/888.2535; www.clippervacations.com) passenger-only catamarans, which leave from **Pier 69**. There are one to three daily catamaran departures, with tour frequency highest between June and September. The trip lasts 2.5 hours. Board early for the best seats on the upper deck. Fares vary according to the time of year.

A good starting point for your explorations is the wonderfully innovative **Royal British Columbia Museum** (675 Belleville St, between Douglas and Government Sts; 250/387.3701, 888/447.7977; www.royalbcmuseum.bc.ca). Here dioramas record the extinction of woolly mammoths and the rise of Victorian storefronts; the area's Native American heritage is also well represented. The museum is open daily; there's an admission charge. Just across **Government Street** is the imposing neo-Gothic **Parliament Building**. Free 25- to 30-minute tours are offered daily May through Labor Day, and Monday through Friday the rest of the year; call 250/387.3046 (www.leg.bc.ca) for reservations.

One block north is the 487-room **Fairmont Empress Hotel** (721 Government St, between Belleville and Humboldt Sts; 250/384.8111, 800/441.1414; www.fairmont.com), opened in 1908 by the Canadian Pacific Railway and host to such luminaries as Winston Churchill, John Wayne, and Richard Nixon (he and Pat honeymooned here). Several luxury attic guest rooms offer magnificent perspectives over **Inner Harbour**. There was talk in the mid-1960s of razing this grand dowager; instead, **Canadian Pacific** spent $45 million on her restoration. The investment paid off, as the hotel is now an elegant center of Victoria life. While you're here, try to experience high tea; it's held in the lobby every afternoon (reservations required).

Continue still farther north on Government Street to downtown's central shopping district. Here you will find the Dickensian treasure box of **Roger's Chocolates and English Sweet Shop** (913 Government St, between Courtney and Broughton Sts; 250/384.7021, 800/663.2220; www.rogerschocolates.com), replete with chocolate creams and marzipan bars; **Munro's Books** (1108 Government St, between Fort and View Sts; 250/382.2464), the city's best and classiest bookstore; **Murchie's Tea and Coffee** (1110 Government St, between Fort and View Sts; 250/383.3112, 800/663.0400; www.murchies.com), redolent with the scents of buttery pastries and hot drinks; **Old Morris Tobacconist, Ltd.** (1116 Government St, between Fort and View Sts; 250/382.4811), with a floor-to-ceiling humidor, along with pipes and related products; and **Sasquatch Indian Sweater Shop** (1233 Government St, between View and Yates Sts; 250/386.9033; email: cowicham@pacificcoast.net), which offers handmade sweaters. **Bastion Square**, on **Wharf Street** between **Fort** and **Yates Streets**, is home to many sidewalk restaurants, a maritime museum, and what is reportedly the location of Victoria's old gallows.

East of downtown is **Craigdarroch Castle** (1050 Joan Crescent, just south of Fort St, between Pemberton Rd and Moss St; 250/592.5323; www.hatleycastle.com), a spooky climb of stone mounted above the city by coal tycoon Robert Dunsmuir, who built this estate in the late 19th century after the discovery of coal deposits made him the province's first millionaire. West of downtown, cross the **Johnson Street Bridge**, turn left on **Catherine Street**, and head down to the water and **Spinnaker's Brew Pub** (308 Catherine St; 250/386.2739; www.spinnakers.com) in the nearby **Esquimalt** community, for a giant burger, a cold beer, and a soothing view back toward Victoria.

For a relaxed, pampered stay along the ocean, drive out to **Sooke Harbour House** (1528 Whiffen Spit Rd, south of West Coast Rd;

250/642.3421; www.sookeharbourhouse.com), about 45 minutes west of Victoria in the town of **Sooke**. All 13 guest rooms overlook the ocean, and most have a balcony or terrace. The meals served in the restaurant are outstanding: Dinner may include fresh seafood caught by one of the owners, Sinclair Philip— an expert diver—and will definitely include vegetables, herbs, and edible flowers from the inn's extensive gardens.

When the weather is good, Victoria dresses up in nature's splendor with jewel-colored blossoms in its many gardens—from pocket-size to large estates—and in hanging baskets on nearly every street downtown. Contact the **Travel Infocentre** (812 Wharf St, just west of Government St; 250/953.2033; www.travelvictoria.com) for information on gardens at **Royal Roads**, the **Royal British Columbia Museum**, **Beacon Hill Park**,

Government House, **University of Victoria Finnerty Gardens**, and the **Gorge Waterway**.

The most famous spot is **Butchart Gardens**, 13 miles north of Victoria in **Brentwood** (800 Benvenuto Ave, west of Rte 17A; 250/652.5256; www.butchartgardens.com). The 50-acre manicured property is suffused with lavish displays of flowers and foliage, as well as fountains, gurgling brooks, a water-driven wooden chime, and deep rock bays. If you do nothing else, be sure to pay a visit to this beautiful and serene place. The scents are splendid and photo ops abound. Light meals, including a decadent high tea, are available at a restaurant with views of the garden, and concerts are held here during the summer months. There are special nighttime lighting displays around Christmas. The gardens are open daily; there's an admission charge.

VANCOUVER, BRITISH COLUMBIA

A little more than 200 years ago, Captain George Vancouver sailed into nearby **Burrard Inlet** in 1792 to proclaim the area's beauty and claim it for England. Today Vancouver is a big city, with all the civic, cultural, and mercantile amenities (as well as the traffic). It's a cosmopolitan city too. Former residents of Hong Kong, wanting to escape the city before the 1997 takeover by the Chinese, have migrated here in huge numbers. Meanwhile, Seattle has extended its tourist-oriented grasp 150 miles north to Vancouver, opening more than 50 **Starbucks** outlets in the area. There is daily **Amtrak** service between Seattle and Vancouver; call 382.4120 or 800/872.7245 (www.amtrak.com) for reservations. Make your plans well in advance, as the four-hour trip is very popular.

Begin your explorations at **Stanley Park**, a great peninsular greensward northwest of downtown (reached via Georgia Street), where there are swimming beaches, totem poles, and a zoo. Head downtown where all the establishments along **Robson Street** will attempt to drain away in an afternoon every dollar you've reserved for a week's worth of sightseeing. On a sunny summer afternoon, shoppers flock to the stretch between **Granville** and **Jervis Streets** to browse for linens and modernist lamps or to circle vulturelike around the shoe stores. The culturally inclined will want to visit the **Vancouver Art Gallery** (750 Hornby St, between Robson and Georgia Sts; 604/662.4706; www.vanartgallery.bc.ca), a former courthouse designed by Canadian architect **Francis Rattenbury**, who is also responsible for the **Empress Hotel** and **Parliament Building** in Victoria. Then it's on to big-ticket department stores, such as **Sears** and **Holt-Renfrew**, within the **Pacific Centre** mall (701 Granville St, at Georgia St; 604/685.7112; www.pacificcentre.ca), where the background music is of plastic slapping confidently against countertops.

Take a scenic drive along the water to the **University of British Columbia**, stopping at the **Museum of Anthropology** (6393 NW Marine Dr, at West Mall; 604/228.5087; www.moa.ubc.ca), an architectural marvel that contains an extensive collection of artifacts from native cultures of coastal B.C., including cedar war canoes, jewelry, sculpture, dishes, and a spectacular display of totem poles. It is open daily; there's an admission charge (free on Tuesdays, 5-9PM, June through August; free all day Tuesdays the rest of the year).

Granville Island Public Market (604/666.6477; www.granvilleisland.com), an island and former warehouse district on the south side of **False Creek**, is thick with shops selling fresh produce, Southwestern art, and the makings for beaded bracelets. Stop by the market area's **Granville Island Brewing Company** (604/687.2739; www.gib.ca) for excellent local craft beers, especially the Lord Granville Natural Pale Ale. If you visit on a Saturday or Sunday, arrive early or count on being engulfed by the masses who descend on this place at any hint of sunshine.

More endearing—for its eclecticism and richness of architectural fenestration—is **Gastown**, located on the north side of downtown. This area was once the center of Vancouver; then it was known as **Granville** (or "Luck-Lucky" to the local Indians) before an 1886 fire leveled much of it. Vancouver residents have preserved much of their heritage in this historic district.

The huge brick-and-terra-cotta **Canadian Pacific Railway Station** (601 W Cordova St, at Seymour St) has been refurbished as a terminus for the **Sky Train** system that links downtown Vancouver with the community of Surrey. Several turn-of-the-19th-century edifices have been connected with a skylight to become **Sinclair Centre** (757 W Hastings St, at Howe St; 604/666.4438; www.sinclaircentre.com), a vast hive of card shops and art outlets, leading some to say that Gastown has become too commercial.

Its opposite is **Chinatown**, just to the east, where gentrification has not shown its face. The area along **Pender** and **Hastings Streets** is thronged on weekend grocery shopping days. And, of course, there are plenty of restaurants to choose from. For a break, take a gentle, contemplative tour of the **Dr. Sun Yat-Sen Classical Chinese Garden** (578 Carrall St, at E Keefer St; 604/662.3207; www.virtualmuseum.ca/exhibitions/scholarsgarden).

Vancouver's restaurants (especially the Asian ones) offer a range of excellent dining choices that feature a wide variety of cuisines. One of the best in town is the **Imperial** (355 Burrard St, at W Hastings St; 604/688.8191; www.imperialrest.com), which serves wonderful Cantonese food in a beautiful, well-maintained Art Deco building with a fabulous harbor view. If continental food is more your style, try **Le Crocodile** (909 Burrard St, at Barclay St; 604/669.4298; www.lecrocodilerestaurant.com), where chef-owner Michel Jacob prepares such succulent dishes as salmon tartare, duck in a light orange sauce, and sautéed scallops; there's also an excellent wine list. For a taste

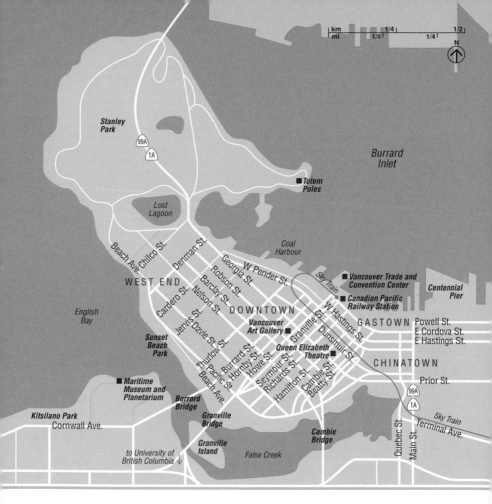

of fabulous seafood, try **C** restaurant (2-1600 Howe St; 604/681.1164; www.crestaurant.com), where, among many wonderful choices, you might try the pumpkin seed-crusted tai snapper (with braised endives, beets, roasted squash, walnut-Gorgonzola cream) or roasted turbot (lobster and crab stuffed, winter vegetable confit, hazelnut brown butter) for dinner.

OLYMPIA CAPITOL

In 1928, Governor Roland E. Hartley fumed over $7 million that had been spent to create a magnificent capitol complex for Washington State. Even on the day before state executives were to move into their new **Legislative Building** (14th Ave W, west of Capitol Way; 360/586.8687), Hartley couldn't resist launching a few last darts at Washington's profligate lawmakers. "Today is an epochal day," he told reporters, "but it brings no joy to the heart of the taxpayer." Hartley worked himself into a bluster as the newspaper reporters scribbled wildly. "May the new building be a deterrent, rather than an incentive, to future extravagance on the part of those in whose hands the business affairs of the state are entrusted." And he didn't stop there. After the complex's dedication, Hartley loaded some of the new capitol's "sumptuous furnishings"—including a few $47.50 spittoons—into an automobile and paraded them about the state to prove that his opponents in Olympia wouldn't hesitate to spend the taxpayers' hard-earned money. Of course, the governor neglected to mention that he had made sure his own office would be the most sumptuous in the building. Perched over **Budd Inlet**, at the southern tip of Puget Sound, Olympia shares the mediocrity of other small state capitols. But it is still worth visiting, if only to see the legislative campus and a couple of other sights.

Washingtonians first started talking about raising a permanent statehouse in 1892. The following year, a nationwide competition was launched to select an architect for the project. From 186 submissions, the commission chose **Ernest Flagg** of New York

City, a young relative of Cornelius Vanderbilt and a graduate of the Ecole des Beaux Arts in Paris. Flagg planned a compact, heavily ornamented structure with a short dome and Corinthian columns running the length of its entry façade. Unfortunately, income from government land grants fell short, and construction on the building had to be halted soon after its foundations were laid. In 1901, the state made do with downtown Olympia's lordly old **Thurston County Courthouse** (now the **Board of Education Building**) as the temporary residence for Washington state government.

Forces didn't gear up to launch another capitol design competition until 1911. More money was available this go-around, but the organizers of the competition insisted that Flagg's foundation should be integrated into any new conception, probably as the base for one of several buildings on a government campus. Flagg naturally assumed that his original commission was still in effect; in the ensuing years, he had enhanced his reputation by developing Manhattan's Singer Building and the Corcoran Art Gallery in Washington, DC. But the committee chose a couple of virtual unknowns: architects **Walter Wilder** and **Harry White**. Both had labored for a time with the famous New York firm of **McKim, Mead & White**, and in fact their plan for Washington's capitol owed an obvious debt to the work of that firm's late principal, **Stanford White**, who had created the Rhode Island capitol building in the early 1890s.

Wilder and White's initial Roman Classical Revival design called for a legislative building surrounded by five office structures (one of which would replace the 1908 brick Governor's Mansion), as well as an arrangement of stairs and landings descending to **Capitol Lake** and a grand promenade stretching into downtown, with a new railroad station at its terminus. Budget limitations doomed some embellishments, but results were still impressive. Of Olympia, architecture historians Henry-Russell Hitchcock and William Seale wrote in their seminal work *Temples of Democracy: The State Capitols of the U.S.A.*, "the American renaissance in state capitol building reached its climax." At the time of its raising, the building's dome was the fourth tallest in the world—287 feet from the base—sliding into order behind those of St. Peter's of Rome (408 feet), St. Paul's Cathedral in London (319 feet), and the US Capitol (307 feet). A massive Tiffany chandelier was hung inside its Alaskan marble rotunda. Other components are less ostentatious. Stairs leading to the north-side main entrance offer an imposing approach but pass beneath a largely unadorned pediment. The building presents colonnades on all four elevations, but most are fairly plain-looking.

Wilder and White concentrated much of their decoration along the roofline, giving it an anthemion cresting, and at the east and west ends of the building, where gables are fringed with dentiled cornices. A 1986 face-lift, directed by **Barnett Schorr Architects** of Seattle, scrubbed Mount St. Helens's ash from the dome's exterior. Polish and color—including 48 rosettes and false-gold flourishes on column capitals—now brighten the rotunda's interior. Architecture and history enthusiasts should not miss an opportunity to visit. Free guided tours are offered daily.

A number of other structures on the eight-acre campus are also worth seeing: the **State Library Building** (16th Ave W and Sylvester St; 360/753.5590), a more contemporary colonnaded edifice designed in 1959 by noted architect **Paul Thiry**, contains Northwest art by Mark Tobey and Kenneth Callahan, as well as a collection of published works by Northwest authors; the **Governor's Mansion** (14th Ave W, west of Capitol Way; 360/902.8800 for tours), a Georgian Revival–style relic, was designed in 1908 by **Ambrose J. Russell** and **Everett P. Babcock**, who created other manses and some churches around Puget Sound; and the Spanish-style **State Capitol Museum** (211 21st Ave W, between Columbia and Water Sts; 360/753.2580), formerly the home of banker Clarence J. Lord, which now houses old logging photos, Native American baskets, and more. The museum is open Tuesday through Sunday; a donation is requested.

Not far away is the **Board of Education Building** (Legion Way, between Franklin

---

The term *flying saucer* was first used after Civil Air Pilot Kenneth Arnold, who was searching on 24 June 1947 for a military plane that had gone down near Mount Rainier, spotted instead a formation of nine brilliant, boomerang-shaped objects flying from Rainier toward Mount Adams. Asked to describe his odd encounter, Arnold compared the flight of his bogeys to an undulating kite tail or a "saucer skipping across the water." Thus was born one of the most popular unsolved mysteries of the 20th century.

The deepest snowfall—a whopping 93 feet—ever recorded in the US was in Paradise, located at the 5,400-foot level on Mount Rainier, during the winter of 1972–1973.

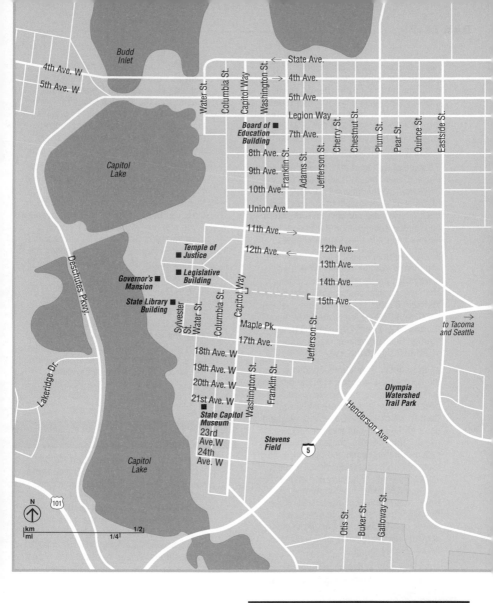

and Washington Sts), the former **Thurston County Courthouse** that was once home to Washington State's government. Architect **W.A. Ritchie**, armed with only a correspondent's education in architecture from the US Treasury Department, created this and other grand county courthouses in Spokane and Port Townsend. This imposing building blends massive stone archways nicely with rounded tower bases in a Romanesque Revival whole. There was originally a polygonal central tower on this structure, which added to its authoritative image, but that was destroyed by fire in 1928. A compatible west wing dates from 1905, when the courthouse began doubling as Olympia's city hall. Restoration has made this a most inviting structure.

MOUNT RAINIER NATIONAL PARK

About 90 miles southeast of Seattle, Mount Rainier soars to a commanding height of 14,410 feet above sea level. The towering mountain and the surrounding Cascades afford splendid views, including fascinating flora and fauna. Each year, more than two million visitors come to the 378-square-mile **Mount Rainier National Park** to picnic, climb, hike, cross-country ski, or just gaze in awe at the peak and its many glaciers. Mount Rainier is the largest volcano in the coastal range, and though it is dormant, steam emissions form caves in the summit's ice cap and often melt the snow around the rim of the twin cones. The mountain supports the largest glacier system in the continental US, with 27 different glaciers covering 35 square miles. **Carbon Glacier** is the longest, at 6 miles; **Emmons Glacier**, at almost 4.5 miles long and 1 mile wide, is the largest. The **Nisqually Glacier** may shift as much as 50 to 400 feet a year.

Because of its height and its proximity to the Pacific Ocean, Mount Rainier gets an average of 15 feet of snow each winter. Summer weather is warm and clear, and beginning in June, snowmelt fills the streams and creates thundering waterfalls, and flowers pop up in the alpine meadows.

You'll need to leave early in the morning if you plan to visit the park in a day trip; the drive from Seattle takes about 2.5 hours. The most popular destination is the **Paradise Visitors' Center**, 5,400 feet above sea level; get there by taking Interstate 5 south to **Routes 512, 7**, and **706**. You will pass through the Nisqually entrance on the southwest side of the park.

Another option is to approach Rainier from the northeast, via **Route 410**; the distance and driving time are about the same. The attraction here is the **Sunrise Visitors' Center**, which at 6,400 feet is the highest point of the mountain that can be reached by car. Other visitors' centers in the park include **Ohanapecosh** and **Longmire**. All of them feature spectacular views, modern visitor facilities, brochures and information, and miles of easy to moderate-level hiking trails. Guides conduct interpretive walks throughout the park in summer, and in winter, the **Paradise** section of the mountain is headquarters for snowshoe walks and cross-country skiing.

From Paradise, Longmire, or Sunrise, you can pick up the **Wonderland Hiking Trail**, a 90-mile route that runs along the base of the

mountain. The trail takes you past **Box Canyon**, waterfalls, fields of wildflowers, **Golden Lakes**, **Carbon River**, Carbon Glacier, and the **Mowich Glaciers**. The **Northern Loop Trail** extends 17.5 miles from Wonderland Trail through backcountry meadows to **Crescent Mountain**, at an elevation of 6,400 feet.

The park gets most of its visitors between June and October; the Nisqually entrance is open year-round, but in winter some of the other entrances, roads, and facilities close, and access to some areas is limited. If you plan to visit off-season, check current road and weather conditions and the status of park services by calling the 24-hour information line (360/569.2211; www.nps.gov/). If you decide to stay overnight, campsites are available on a first-come, first-served basis (get the required permits at a visitors' center), or you can lodge at the 25-room **National Park Inn** or the 125-room **Paradise Inn**, both on the park grounds. For accommodations information and reservations, contact the **Mount Rainier Guest Services** (P.O. Box 108, Ashford, WA 98304; 360/569.2275.

MOUNT ST. HELENS

Many mountains are taller than Mount St. Helens, with its summit 8,365 feet above sea level (it was 1,300 feet higher before its 1980 eruption), but the thrill of poking about what was recently an active volcano can hardly be beat. Over the more than two decades since the volcano last exploded, plants and wildlife have been returning to these slopes, and so have people—Mount St. Helens is now a national volcanic monument, attracting more than 600,000 people every year.

Begin your explorations with a stop at one or both of the two visitors' centers west of the mountain. Exit Interstate 5 at Castle Rock and head about 5 miles east on **Route 504** to the **Silverdale Visitors' Center**. This center focuses on the area's history and geology, Native American legends, and events leading up to the eruption; there's also an interesting 22-minute video of the blast. A few miles farther along Route 504 is the **Coldwater Visitors' Center**, which offers panoramic views of the crater and dome, as well as interactive exhibits that concentrate on the returning flora and fauna; there's also a bookstore, cafeteria, and gift shop.

For a good view of the blast's results (a crater 2 miles across and a half-mile deep), head to the northeast side of the mountain. You can pick up maps and get directions at

Ranger Station • ▲ Crescent Mountain · Sunrise Visitors' Center · Crystal Mountain · Golden Lakes · Wonderland Hiking Trail · White River Entrance · 410 · ▲ Mount Rainier 14,410 ft. · Ice Caves · Wonderland Trail · 123 · Box Canyon · Paradise Visitors' Center · Nisqually Entrance · 706 · Longmire Visitors' Center · Ohanapecosh Visitors' Center · N · 410

km 5 10
mi 5

the two visitors' centers (there are two additional information centers along the way) to guide you through the park. **Windy Ridge** (accessed via Forest Road 99) is about 4 miles north of Mount St. Helens and offers an unforgettable perspective. Park the car and climb a log-and-gravel path from there for still-better views of the mountain and what has become of **Spirit Lake**, once a popular vacation spot. It's so quiet up here, it's hard to imagine that in 1980 this place echoed with a sound equivalent to that made by 400 million tons of exploding TNT.

The mountain reopened to climbers in 1987; all must be registered, and steep fines are levied against hotdoggers. The peak season is mid-May through October, when 110 climbers per day are allowed up to the crater's lip. Permits may be obtained in advance from the **Forest Service** (Mount St. Helens National Volcanic Monument, 42218 NE Yale Bridge Rd, Amboy, WA 98601; 360/247.3900; www.fs.fed.us/gpnf). One hundred spaces per day are filled in advance, but 40 additional spaces are available on a first-come, first-served basis. Interested parties must put their names on a list at www.mshinstitute.org the day before they hope to scale the mountain. During the off-season (mid-November through mid-May), climbers must still register, but no advance permits are offered. Most climbers head up **Monitor Ridge** on the south face, a steep trek that may take 7 to 10 hours round-trip. (Other routes are also available; ask the Forest Service for maps.) It's a dusty climb during most of the summer, after the snow has melted, so wear high boots to keep the ash out of your socks. Also, don't wear

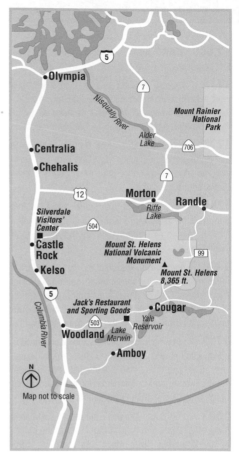

contact lenses, as the ash can get between them and your eyeballs, and do bring plenty of water and energy food.

12,000 YEARS AGO Evidence shows that Native Americans were living in western Washington.

1775 Spanish explorer Bruno Heceta sends a boat ashore south of today's **Cape Flattery**, a headland at the entrance to the **Strait of Juan de Fuca**. The crew is captured and killed by Native Americans.

1778 British captain James Cook, on his third round-the-globe tour, discovers Cape Flattery; however, he plies north rather than east, so he misses **Puget Sound** completely.

1786 Sealth, son of Schweabe, chief of the Suquamish and Scholitza Indians and a future chief himself, is born on **Blake Island**, on the west side of Puget Sound.

1790 The Spanish establish the first white settlement at **Neah Bay**, on the Strait of Juan de Fuca just east of Cape Flattery. Spanish explorer Manuel Quimper sails deep into the Strait of Juan de Fuca, encountering and naming some of the **San Juan Islands**.

1792 After circumnavigating **Vancouver Island** in southwestern British Columbia, English captain George Vancouver and his second lieutenant, Peter Puget, launch two separate explorations of the "inland sea," which Vancouver names Puget Sound.

1803 President Thomas Jefferson dispatches Meriwether Lewis and William Clark west to the mouth of the **Columbia River**, which they reach in 1805. Other Americans would follow.

1821 The Florida Treaty transfers all rights to territory north of the 42nd parallel to the United States. Britain's Hudson's Bay Company (HBC), however, still claims sole rights to the **Oregon Territory**, especially the property, north of the Columbia River, including present-day Washington State.

1845 In defiance of HBC hegemony, Yankees begin spilling north across the Columbia River.

1846 Finally yielding to US pressure, Great Britain agrees to cede lands south of the 49th parallel (today's US–Canada border) to the Yankees.

1850 The Donation Land Law encourages settlement of America's western territories by awarding 320 acres to every white or "half-breed" who will occupy and farm the land for at least 4 consecutive years. Another 320 acres are given to any couple married by 1 December 1851.

1851 On 13 November, 7 months after leaving Illinois, Seattle founder Arthur Denny and his party of 23 arrive at **Alki Point** aboard the ship *Exact*. Soon after, the families begin relocating to the east side of **Elliott Bay** for its thicker forests and deeper harbor.

1852 Pioneer Dr. David Swinton "Doc" Maynard from Ohio arrives at Elliott Bay and befriends Sealth, who is then the chief of the Suquamish and Duwamish. When he and other city founders decide that their settlement's informal moniker, **Duwamps**, is too inelegant, Maynard suggests *Seattle*, a spin on the good chief's name that's easier to pronounce than the guttural Salish original.

Henry Yesler builds Seattle's first steam sawmill. Yesler's initial location is in **West Seattle**, but other pioneers convince him to build instead on Elliott Bay. The strip of land over which he drags his felled trees becomes known as Skid Road.

1853 President Millard Fillmore signs the act creating the **Washington Territory**.

1855 Tensions between whites and Native Americans precipitate King County's so-called Indian War. The American sloop *Decatur*, sailing from Honolulu to protect Seattle settlers, rains cannonballs and grapeshot into forests beyond Third Avenue where invaders might be hiding. Natives retaliate by burning nearly every building in the county. After a final skirmish in March 1856, the first territorial governor, Isaac Stevens, encourages punishment of warring Indians and the banishment of others to reservations.

1861 Washington's **Territorial University** (later named the **University of Washington**) is built where downtown's **Four Seasons Olympic Hotel** now stands.

1863 Seattle's first newspaper, the *Gazette*, rolls off its homemade presses. It will publish irregularly for the next 3 years.

1866 Chief Sealth, who had persuaded his people to stay out of the Indian War, dies at the Port Madison Reservation in Kitsap County.

1867 Former San Franciscan Samuel Maxwell founds the *Weekly Intelligencer*, which becomes a daily in 1876 and merges with the failing *Post* 5 years later to form what is known today as the *Seattle Post-Intelligencer*.

1869 The territorial legislature grants Seattle a city charter. City population: 1,107.

1870 Seattle's first grade school is erected.

1872 Representatives of the **Northern Pacific Railroad** visit Puget Sound to discuss the location of the railway's western terminus. To the shock of Seattleites, Tacoma is selected.

1878 German immigrant Andrew Hemrich founds a small brewery in south Seattle. He calls his beer Rainier.

HISTORY

1879 The city's first big fire destroys a number of wooden structures bordering the **Waterfront**, including Yesler's Mill.

1885 Violence erupts when Seattleites hold an anti-Chinese congress and demand that local Asians leave western Washington. A similar declaration is made in Tacoma, which quickly puts its Chinese on trains headed for Portland. Seattle's Chinese don't depart so easily. After 197 of them are shipped to San Francisco, martial law is declared and US troops halt the forced exodus.

1889 In midsummer, the Great Seattle Fire destroys 30 city blocks in what is now the historical **Pioneer Square** area.

Washington becomes the 42nd state of the Union on 11 November.

1892 Reginald H. Thomson is appointed city engineer and begins a 20-year regrading program that will drastically change Seattle's topography.

1893 The first train traveling James J. Hill's new **Great Northern Railroad** line reaches Seattle from St. Paul, Minnesota. Hill goes on to create the first combined cargo and passenger services between Puget Sound and the Orient.

1896 Bombastic former Midwestern publisher Alden J. Blethen buys the ailing *Press-Times* newspaper and re-creates it as the *Seattle Daily Times*.

1897 The steamship *Portland* arrives in Seattle with a ton of gold from Alaska, beginning a well-publicized and profitable rush through this city of men bound for the Klondike.

1898 Hundreds of thousands of men are processed through a new 640-acre US Army base on **Magnolia Bluff**, bound for the Spanish-American War. The outpost is later named **Fort Lawton**, honoring a general killed in a Philippines skirmish.

1900 Illinois lumberman Frederick Weyerhaeuser, escaping diminishing timber reserves in the Midwest to land at Puget Sound, assembles a partnership to buy 900,000 forested acres in Washington and Oregon from the **Northern Pacific Railroad**. The Weyerhaeuser Company will dominate Northwest lumbering throughout the century.

The population of Seattle is 80,761—double what it had been just 10 years earlier.

1907 **Pike Place Market** opens.

1908 William Boeing, the son of a wealthy Michigan timber baron, moves to Seattle after several years of running an independent timber operation in Grays Harbor on the Pacific Coast.

1909 Seattle holds its first world's fair: the Alaska-Yukon-Pacific Exposition. After its close, the Olmsted

Brothers, famed landscapers from Massachusetts, re-plan the fairgrounds as today's University of Washington campus.

1910 Washington's constitution is amended to give women the vote, about 10 years before most other states do so.

The US Congress authorizes construction of a ship canal linking **Lake Washington** with Puget Sound, and ground is broken within a year for the first lock.

Bill Boeing attends an air meet in California, where he becomes fascinated with the art of flying.

1914 As Europe comes to a boil with World War I, a barge loaded with dynamite for shipping to Russia explodes in Elliott Bay. Sabotage is suspected but never confirmed.

1916 Bill Boeing, along with navy officer G. Conrad Westervelt, founds an airplane enterprise on the **Duwamish River**—the beginnings of the Boeing Company.

In **Everett**, just north of Seattle, labor conflicts between members of the Industrial Workers of the World ("Wobblies") and lumber companies lead to the so-called Everett Massacre, during which at least 7 men are killed and 31 others are wounded by rifle fire.

Washingtonians vote to make the sale and consumption of alcoholic beverages unlawful—4 years before national Prohibition begins.

1917 In April, President Woodrow Wilson engages the United States in World War I. A month later, the **Lake Washington Ship Canal** opens and US Navy training craft begin docking off the University of Washington campus.

1918 The nation's influenza epidemic hits Seattle hard, killing 252 people of every 100,000. Public assemblages are prohibited, and the local health department orders citizens to wear flu masks. The ban on congregation is lifted on 11 November, the day after the war's armistice is signed and a national holiday, so Seattleites can celebrate with each other.

1919 Three years after the Everett Massacre, Seattle hosts the nation's first general strike. A total of 60,000 organized workers walk off their jobs to protest the growing power of capitalists. The city lies tense and quite for several days, until strikers agree to return to work. Unlike the protest in Everett, no blood is shed here.

1926 Bertha Landes is elected mayor of Seattle. She is the first woman to hold such an exalted post in a major US city.

1929 New York stock markets crash in late October. As with so many other trends since, it takes several months for the Great Depression to affect Seattle.

1931 Huge shantytowns spring up near the Waterfront to house Seattle's many unemployed, mostly men. Officials try to burn out these "Hoovervilles," but they always sprout anew.

1934 Longshoremen in Seattle, San Francisco, and elsewhere are idled for 98 days by the Pacific Coast waterfront strike. Strikebreakers are tossed into Elliott Bay or killed. Mayor Charles Smith fires his police chief for being too lenient with protesters and orders a crowd of 2,000 strikers clubbed before the strike is settled.

1940 The **Lacey V. Murrow Floating Bridge** opens on what is now **Interstate 90**, connecting Seattle with its eastern suburbs.

1941 After the bombing of Hawaii's Pearl Harbor, the United States enters World War II. Boeing Company, the **Puget Sound Naval Shipyard** in nearby Bremerton, and other area manufacturers kick into high gear to feed the war machine. The US Navy assumes control of Puget Sound shipping, and Seattle becomes a major army transport center.

1942 Fearful of spies and saboteurs, the Western Defense Command orders that Japanese people living in Seattle and elsewhere on the coast be interned. Asians from **Bainbridge Island** are the first ones sent to detainment camps in Idaho.

1945 The atom-bombing of Hiroshima and Nagasaki ends the war with Japan. Victory celebrations are cooled, however, by news of peacetime economic declines, especially at Boeing, where annual sales drop from $600 million to $14 million.

1949 The worst earthquake recorded in Seattle history (measuring 7.2 on the Richter scale) strikes in mid-April.

1962 Seattle's second world's fair, the Century 21 Exposition, opens to 6 months of tremendous success.

1963 Proposals to level Pike Place Market in favor of high-rise rookeries prompt an aggressive preservation campaign.

1965 Efforts begin to revitalize Pioneer Square, the city's original—but deteriorating—downtown.

1967 National unrest reaches Seattle when the University of Washington's Black Student Union takes control of the university administration building.

Protests against the Vietnam War begin citywide.

Seattle advertising exec David Stern creates the now-ubiquitous happy face symbol.

1968 The city launches its Forward Thrust Program for improvements that include a new domed stadium, parks, and street repairs.

1970 Boeing, suffering after demand for its jet fails to measure up to estimates, lays off 65,000 workers over the next 2 years—two thirds of its workforce. Unemployment in the city leaps 12% as a result. Despair grows, and a billboard proclaims, "Will the Last Person in Seattle Please Turn Out the Lights?"

1971 The Starbucks coffee company is founded. Its name comes from the java-dependent first mate in Herman Melville's novel *Moby-Dick*.

1974 A 7-acre historic district is created to save Pike Place Market.

1975 *Harper's* magazine names Seattle the country's most livable city.

1980 **Mount St. Helens** explodes 100 miles south of Seattle, sprinkling King County with ash.

IBM execs meet with Bill Gates, a 25-year-old techie and co-inventor (with Paul Allen) of the computer language BASIC whom IBM hopes will create the software needed for a first generation of personal computers.

1983 Citing financial woes, the *Seattle Post-Intelligencer* wins a joint-operating agreement with its rival, the *Seattle Times*.

The Washington Public Power Supply System (not so fondly nicknamed Whoops) defaults on its $7 billion debt, ending hopes for cheap nuclear power in Washington and causing a tremendous ripple effect through Seattle financial circles.

1985 Aldus Corporation, an all-but-unknown Seattle computer software company, ships its first product, PageMaker, and creates a catchphrase to describe its operation: desktop publishing.

1986 Microsoft, Bill Gates's growing computer software company, offers its stock to the public. The value will go up 1,200% in just 6 years.

1989 Norm Rice, first African-American mayor of Seattle, is elected.

Seattle is named the most livable US city by *Money* magazine and the *Places Rated Almanac*.

1990 The Lacey V. Murrow Floating Bridge sinks into Lake Washington; it is later completely rebuilt.

1992 Race rioting in Los Angeles (a reaction to four Los Angeles Police Department officers' being acquitted of beating Rodney King) spills over into laid-back Seattle, where vandals and arsonists control city streets for most of a week.

1993 Boeing announces production cutbacks and massive layoffs, causing a tidal wave of doubt over Seattle's fiscal future.

1994 Nirvana rocker Kurt Cobain commits suicide by shooting himself at his home in Seattle.

1995   *Time* magazine puts Microsoft owner Bill Gates on its cover, proclaiming him "the world's richest man."

1996   Seattle is featured in a *Newsweek* magazine cover story that focuses on the city's growth as a cultural and business center.

Gary Locke becomes the first Asian-American governor of the state of Washington.

1997   The world's largest bookstore, Seattle-based Amazon.com, sells $81.7 million worth of books over the Internet in the first 9 months of the year.

1998   A 116-acre wetland near **Issaquah** is named for noted ecologist Hazel Wolf, former leader of the Audubon Society, on her 100th birthday in March.

1999   The National Marine Fisheries Service lists 14 species or stocks of West Coast salmon and steelhead as "threatened" under the Endangered Species Act.

Federal judge Thomas Penfield Jackson declares that Microsoft has monopoly power in the market, a key stage in the federal antitrust complaint urged by alternative operating systems and Internet browsers.

2000   According to the US census, Seattle's population exceeds 563,000, an increase of 47,000 since 1990; King County's population is over 1.7 million.

The first-ever commuter rail service in Seattle is launched in September, carrying 350 commuters from Tacoma to Seattle in about 50 minutes.

2001   The Nisqually earthquake, registering 6.8 on the Richter scale and centered 30 miles beneath

the Nisqually River delta some 50 miles south and west of Seattle, rolls through the city, causing damage to bridges, roadways, and to the older brick buildings in historic Pioneer Square. Damage estimates are well over $1 billion; some 200 people were injured in the 45-second quake.

After a bidding war in which several cities offered huge tax breaks, Boeing moves its corporate headquarters to Chicago.

2002   Seattle hosts a star-powered, sold-out international soccer match between Manchester United and Madrid. Local fans go wild.

2003   The City Council names the Great Blue Heron the official bird of Seattle.

Sound Transit begins construction on a 15.7-mile light rail to connect downtown with Sea-Tac airport. Ultimately the light rail system will connect downtown to University of Washington and the Northgate Mall to the north, Bellevue and Redmond to the east, and possibly extend as far south as Tacoma.

2004   Rem Koolhaas's $165.5 million marriage of glass and steel, the new **Seattle Central Public Library**, sees 9,000 visitors through its doors on opening day, first thing in the morning. By 6PM attendance climbs to over 26,000.

2005   **August Wilson** dies. Wilson was a Pulitzer Prize–winning Seattle resident and author of a 10-play cycle about the African-American experience spanning the 20th century.

2006   The **Seattle Seahawks** reach their first Super Bowl: Super Bowl XLI, Seahawks versus Pittsburgh Steelers. The score: Steelers 34, Seahawks 14.

INDEX

RESTAURANTS

Only restaurants with star ratings are
listed below. All restaurants are listed
alphabetically in the main (preceding)
index. Always call in advance to
ensure a restaurant has not closed,
changed its hours, or booked its
tables for a private party. The
restaurant price ratings are based on
the average cost of an entrée for one
person, excluding tax and tip.

**** An Extraordinary Experience
*** Excellent
** Very Good
* Good

$$$$ Big Bucks ($35 and up)
$$$ Expensive ($25-$35)
$$ Reasonable ($15-$25)
$ The Price is Right (less than
$10)

Hotels

The hotels listed below are grouped according to their price ratings; they are also listed in the main index. The hotel price ratings reflect the base price of a standard room for two people for one night during the peak season.

$$$$ Big Bucks ($225 and up)
$$$ Expensive ($175-$225)
$$ Reasonable ($100-$175)
$ The Price is Right (less than $100)

$$$$

$$$

$$

$

Features

Bests

Maps

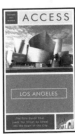